Teaching with The Norton Anthology of American Literature

FOURTH EDITION

A Guide for Instructors

THE EDITORS

Nina Baym
UNIVERSITY OF ILLINOIS

Wayne Franklin
UNIVERSITY OF IOWA

Ronald Gottesman
UNIVERSITY OF SOUTHERN CALIFORNIA

Laurence B. Holland
LATE OF THE JOHNS HOPKINS UNIVERSITY

David Kalstone
LATE OF RUTGERS, THE STATE UNIVERSITY OF NEW JERSEY

Arnold Krupat
SARAH LAWRENCE COLLEGE

Francis Murphy
SMITH COLLEGE

Hershel Parker
UNIVERSITY OF DELAWARE

William H. Pritchard
AMHERST COLLEGE

Patricia B. Wallace
VASSAR COLLEGE

Teaching with The Norton Anthology of American Literature

FOURTH EDITION

A Guide for Instructors

Marjorie Pryse
STATE UNIVERSITY OF NEW YORK
COLLEGE AT PLATTSBURGH

W · W · NORTON & COMPANY
New York · London

The text of this book is composed in Electra
with the display set in Bernhard Modern.
Composition by ComCom.
Manufacturing by Haddon Craftsmen.

Library of Congress Cataloging-in-Publication Data

Pryse, Marjorie, 1948–
Teaching with the Norton anthology of American literature, fourth edition : a guide for instructors / Marjorie Pryse.
p. cm.
1. American literature—Study and teaching (Higher) 2. Norton anthology of American literature. I. Title.
PS41.P79 1994
810′.07—dc20 93-48016

ISBN 0-393-96463-9

W. W. Norton & Company, Inc., 500 Fifth Avenue, New York, N.Y. 10110

W. W. Norton & Company Ltd., 10 Coptic Street, London WC1A 1PU

3 4 5 6 7 8 9 0

Contents

A Detailed Contents List for Volume 1

*For the convenience of teachers who wish to use *The Declaration of Sentiments* of the Seneca Falls Woman's Rights Convention in their classrooms, as occasionally suggested in this Guide, we have provided the text of that document—not readily available except in libraries—as an appendix. It may be photocopied and distributed to your students.

A Detailed Contents List for Volume 2

Teaching with The Norton Anthology of American Literature

FOURTH EDITION

A Guide for Instructors

CHAPTER 1

Author's Introduction

American Literature as an Encounter for Undergraduate Students

In previous editions of this Guide to *The Norton Anthology of American Literature* (NAAL), the model I used assumed that the instructor had already read the literature, knew the historical and critical "territory," and could serve as a knowledgeable guide for students entering that territory for the first time. In the mid-1990s, such a model of instruction in the American literature classroom no longer makes as much pedagogical sense as it did even five years ago, for two reasons.

First, the range and diversity of texts taught in American literature classrooms across the nation (and included in NAAL) have altered our understanding of the territory of American writing, and the boundaries and characteristics of this writing are subject to debate. What works should appear on any finite list or in the "canon" of "great American" texts? Does a fiction writer have to produce a long novel to merit inclusion on such a list, or does mastering the regional sketch earn an author canonization? What constitutes literary theory at any given historical moment, and is theory also a form of creative writing? Does early writing by Euro-American women and minority men and women merit inclusion on such a list when set against the novels of Nathaniel Hawthorne, Herman Melville, Samuel Clemens, and Henry James? In a critical climate that promotes reexamination of the very body of knowledge that constitutes the teaching field of American literature, we would do our students a disservice by solely presenting authors and texts standard to anthologies published a decade or longer ago (or when some of us were graduate students) as if these anthologies still represented what we have come to know as American literature.

Second, in light of the changing shape of this body of writing, a pedagogy that required the instructor to maintain a fiction of expertise would carry with it several hazards. On one hand, maintaining such a fiction would rule out introducing students to new or newly discovered works from the past or from writers who trace their literary and historical origins to non–Euro-American sources, because most of us in the American literature classroom in the 1990s have not become experts in this literature. Yet such a presentation of expertise contains within it an essential contradiction: one maintains the position of expert only by ruling out of consideration any work or writer he or she has not been "trained" to read. On the other hand, trying to teach writers and works with which the "expert" instructor is unfamiliar is equally untenable, because doing so creates a situation in which the instructor's ignorance may be easily unmasked. An American literature course built on the premise that the instructor serves as a guide remains useful only to the extent that we acknowledge our own limitations.

If we make it clear at the outset that the body of knowledge we know as American literature has changed and is in the process of further change and that we are willing to "get lost" with our students—to paraphrase Robert Frost's *Directive*—to "find ourselves" again, then the concept of instructor as guide is reinvented in a more vital and flexible way. Indeed, the exploration of American literature itself becomes an encounter in which students recognize both that the texts they read may alter their conception of *American* and that this altered sense may contribute to new configurations of what has been known as American literature. Like this set of teaching notes that purports to be a course guide, NAAL itself becomes provisional in such a configuration. This fourth edition represents less what Robinson Jeffers called in his poem *Shine, Perishing Republic* a "thickening to empire" and more what Adrienne Rich called, in *Diving into the Wreck*, "a book of myths / in which" more and more "our names [do] appear." Or it represents what Michael Harper has called *History as Apple Tree*, in which American myth becomes "my own myth: / my arm the historical branch, / my name the bruised fruit, / black human photograph: apple tree."

Indeed, the new section in Volume 1, "Literature to 1620," brings the concept of encounter directly into the pedagogy of the American literature course. In her essay *Arts of the Contact Zone* (*Profession* 1991) Mary

Louise Pratt uses the term *contact zone* "to refer to social spaces where cultures meet, clash, and grapple with each other, often in contexts of highly asymmetrical relations of power, such as colonialism, slavery, or their aftermaths as they are lived out in many parts of the world today." She observes that the Stanford University course Cultures, Ideas, and Values (CIV), which "centered on the Americas and the multiple cultural histories (including European ones) that have intersected here," itself became a contact zone in which students as well as texts brought "radically heterogeneous" reception to the intersection of these multiple histories and various "American" stories. In such a course, she writes, "we were struck . . . at how anomalous the formal lecture became," at how "impossible" and "unimaginable" became "the lecturer's traditional (imagined) task—unifying the world in the class's eyes by means of a monologue that rings equally coherent, revealing, and true for all." Pratt's description of her experience in the contact zone may characterize the experience of other classrooms in which the instructor takes seriously the concept of encounter. Ultimately, more is at stake than encounters on the page; what American literature reveals to students about their own lives, myths, and histories invites intellectual encounters in classroom discussion as well, and in the alchemical process of such discussion, NAAL becomes a catalyst, not a fixative.

And yet NAAL, indeed the very concept of the "anthology of American literature," itself represents both changes in literary taste and the politics of canon formation. Because of its structure—a two-volume book bound by limitations of space (even though some students may find the anthology practically infinite in length)—each new edition requires choice: what to add and what to delete to make room for new texts, new voices. In the process of revision, the editors of NAAL survey numerous instructors, who represent a wide range of institutions and who have experience teaching from the anthology, for suggestions: what do you currently include in your syllabus, what would you like to include, what might you recommend cutting? At one level, such a poll is simply market research, for NAAL is a publisher's commodity. At another, it represents the accretion of educated readers' responses to what ought to constitute the range of texts that make up the field of American literature. The responses are themselves subject to critical revision as a result of new scholarship, especially on women and minority men who have produced American texts; developments in literary and critical theory; the perceived relationship between cultural texts and social contexts of American diversity; and an increasing freedom to acknowledge the literary value of texts that traditionalists have not considered high culture—such as journals, oral literatures, political writing, and regional fiction. Indeed, the very contest concerning the inclusion of certain authors and texts in the literary canon may itself be characterized by a struggle between the high culture of American literature traditionally defined and an increasingly populist sense of the function and value of American literature.

And at yet another level, the questionnaire the editors ask instructors to complete also recognizes the role of NAAL in the undergraduate classroom; it gives the editors some means to measure the needs and expectations of the distinct audience of students who will be using the anthology. Thus NAAL becomes an ongoing collaboration among editors and teachers and, implicitly, students. The balancing act that the changes in NAAL reflect thus take into account the pragmatic need for instructors to hold to familiar texts and models while they learn, practice, and adapt to new ones—so that they can both orient and creatively *disorient* students at the same time, incorporating a sense of the process by which students learn.

Rather than overwhelming instructors with newly rediscovered texts and authors who may or may not, in the brevity of their inclusion, communicate their power to students, NAAL continues to offer as full a selection of familiar and uncommon writers as possible (and as many complete texts as possible for the writers it includes). At the same time, the editors recognize that the anthology must attempt to represent depth as well as breadth.

One of the particular strengths of NAAL is that its editors have taken their cuts as seriously as their additions and have treated each newly added author with the same care and respect granted to those previously included. As a result, the fourth edition of NAAL may itself be viewed as a site of encounter: between the newly and the previously included, between traditionalists and canon revisionists, between editors who have always collaborated with instructors and instructors who have been given continuing voice in determining the content of the anthology that becomes their fundamental teaching tool. Conveying the process of anthology formation and revision to students can increase their sense that as readers they can participate in this act, and art, of encounter, can alter the shape of American literature, and can themselves be altered as a result. The study of American literature demonstrates the series of radical inventions and interventions that produced government documents as well as creative texts, that constituted acts of autobiography as well as ethnography, that emerged as myths and countermyths reflective of their particular age and the aging of American culture. Why should the entity we know as the scholarly and teaching field of American literature be viewed differently? Like the society it in part reflects, it too is an invention (initially, by turn-of-the-century literary historians) and already the site of national, cultural, and political intervention. Teaching American literature as an encounter between the inventions of the past and the cultural interventions of the present becomes possible with the adoption of NAAL, which makes the pedagogy of encounter explicit from the earliest records of native peoples and Europeans (the explorers and the exploiters, the recorders and the critics), creating the context for understanding the United States and its literary expression more than five hundred years after the European "discovery" of the Americas.

Thinking about Planning a Course

Whether you are preparing to teach an American literature course for the first time or consider yourself well seasoned, perhaps you share my own experience that writing a syllabus is an art and that you can often find success—even before you have met your students—by making certain choices in the list, in the order of readings, and in the overall rationale for your course organization. How do you create a course outline that will guide, but not dictate, your students' approach to American literature; that will allow you a sense of mastery without precluding digression and idiosyncrasy; and that will make it possible to manifest for your students the pleasures you find in any given work? Such a task brings out in me an enormous sense of challenge and possibility as well as an awareness of my own limitations. Individual students, academic requirements, the size and quality of the physical classroom, the extent to which any of us has autonomy in creating a syllabus, and the scheduled hour of the day or the days of the week any given course meets will all affect any attempt to achieve coherence and clarity by design. Still, the moment of planning in the ideal becomes part of the process of making American literature realizable for students who will themselves, once the course begins, become inevitably—and delightfully—real.

Reading this Guide can help you clarify your objectives in teaching American literature before you enter the classroom. Beyond the concerns we all share—to introduce students to "great works" and help them read with appreciation, enjoyment, and understanding—what other goals are possible to achieve, particularly if you are teaching a required sophomore-level course? Students in certain majors may find studying literature of less apparent benefit to their projected careers than do liberal arts majors. Are there ways to teach American literature that can help all students perceive themselves as members of a larger society with a culture that includes them and see that their engagement in that culture and the literature records is, therefore, essential to their lives? Many students expect to be "taught" American literature as if it were a body of finite knowledge to be assimilated rationally. Is it possible to create a Guide that will help them see literature as a way of knowing the world as well as something worth knowing in and of itself? And, in the process, can this Guide lead students to rediscover or to find for the first time the capacity to develop their nonrational and nonlinear sensors—in effect, to make the very process of learning a significant part of what they learn?

In my own planning I begin with one goal: to encourage students to read, think, speak, and write from their own perspective as they simultaneously learn to place that perspective within a larger context. Pursuing this goal allows students to test their own responses and interpretations in a diverse group that can come to feel safe. This "safe space" can lessen the threatening feelings literature classrooms can evoke, in particular to students who have arrived in college without, in effect, having learned how to read. For the American literature course, especially at the sophomore level, for which I am most likely to draw students trying to satisfy general education requirements, I try to write an outline that will help undergraduates balance needs that appear to be in conflict. I'd like them to write about the loved and familiar author and to explore new and possibly more difficult works, to enjoy literature but still take it seriously, and to express their own response and yet not risk being "wrong" or "stupid."

Over the years, I have tried four different models of course organization and have become convinced of the value of choosing some model. Articulating my awareness of where I want to go in defining, conserving, and debating aspects of American literary history or cultural heritage has helped me read individual works through my students' eyes, knowing that the model of course organization will eventually demystify for them what initially appears to be the "boggy, soggy, squitchy picture" of American literature. They benefit from being able to see how and why I have selected the authors and readings that appear on their syllabus and from understanding that there may be no single best way to make that selection.

Choosing a model of course organization can give your students the coherence of an organizing principle—and the security that it represents—to risk moving beyond the known to writers they might otherwise find alien—because they write in a different century, out of an ethnic background other than the students' own, from the point of view of another gender, or by means of experimenting with language or genre. Younger students and students with previous difficulty in high school English courses need more assistance in recognizing their own response to or interpretation of a literary work and learning how to locate that response against a spectrum of cultural understanding. But students at any level can doubt their own reading and look to others—peers, the instructor, secondary materials in the library—to tell them how to think. The specific practical problem for us as we design our own course guides involves making choices from the array available in NAAL that will encourage developmental reading and thinking in our students. How do we get them to trust the authenticity of their own experience with the text and, at the same time, to want to know about history, about the aesthetic and linguistic choices writers make, and about what other readers in different times and places have thought about the same authors they are reading? In the chapters that follow, I describe the models of course organization that I have used to help students develop a conceptual framework for the study of American literature: the historical approach, the "major authors" approach, the literary traditions approach, and the inclusion approach: gender, race, and class. What are the reasons for choosing a model of course organization? Does one model work particularly well in a certain kind of classroom, given the class level and/or background your students have? How does a model allow detours as well as central focus? What are the advantages and special features of various rationales for course organization? How can you use each one to help students learn to think for themselves? Chapters 2 through 5 begin with general remarks that address these questions in light of each model. I encourage you to think through the general considerations before you decide how to present the material in NAAL. If you are a teaching assistant or if you are teaching in a department that prescribes a certain way to teach the course, you may have less autonomy in creating a syllabus. Chapter 6, which suggests ways to use genre and theme as organizing principles, may help you work toward coherence, even if you are using a departmental syllabus that appears to lack it. Following each discussion, I offer sample lists of readings from NAAL that illustrate the particular model of course organization or that categorize works by genre or theme. In each list I have tried to illustrate the range of choices available in NAAL; however, you will need to narrow each list further to write a manageable course guide.

Chapter 7 provides some readings of individual authors and works arranged to follow NAAL. In this chapter, I provide teaching notes, questions to stimulate discussion (or student writing), and commentary on historical periods. I intend that all of my commentary either will supplement the excellent period introductions and headnotes in the anthology or will adapt some of that material for specific use in the classroom.

Chapter 8 extends the teaching notes to include suggested exam questions and essay topics, arranged as general questions followed by questions about individual authors and texts. Implicit in these items are alternative approaches to the literary works that can both stimulate discussion in the classroom and provide students with out-of-class assignments. Following the chronological lists of questions, I include a second set designed to help anyone interested in teaching the course as a study of literary traditions developed by men and women from a variety of racial and cultural origins. This set complements my description of this model of course organization presented in Chapter 4.

The format and content of this Guide deviate considerably from what you might expect to find in the standard "instructor's manual."

Throughout, I have tried to keep in mind that we who use this anthology are teaching students, not established critics, although the patterns of feeling and analysis that students develop in our classrooms ought to lead them to greater critical sophistication. If this Guide helps you in any way or if you can offer suggestions for its future revision, please write to me c/o W. W. Norton & Company.

—Marjorie Pryse

CHAPTER 2

The Historical Approach

Planning the Course

NAAL is organized according to the chronology of the authors' birth dates, and most of us probably write schedules of required reading that are more or less chronological and thus basically follow the order presented in the anthology. But mere chronology does not produce a perspective on literary history, and many teachers would argue that it is impossible to understand literature without placing it in its historical context. The historical approach to teaching American literature makes room for students to ask questions that interest them about the writers' lives; about the ethnic, literary, geographical, and political environments within which they wrote; and about the ideologies or religious beliefs that influenced their readers. It also makes it possible for the instructor to combine the breadth of a survey with the coherence of a conceptual framework.

The specific framework that I adopt in teaching the historical approach examines the unfolding of ideas that dominate our literary history. In teaching from Volume 1, I choose works that have a connection to specific historical events; and the events themselves can generally inform the presentation of readings on the syllabus, can provide a focus for background discussion, and can give students the basis for asking questions in class or for selecting essay topics. One advantage to this approach for the Volume 1 readings is that it allows students to place literary works in the context of an American history course they may also be taking, or have taken, as part of their general education requirements. In Volume 2, in which American literature proliferates with such a variety of voices, themes, and degrees of connection to actual events, I focus on the development of an American literature itself and on both the individual writers and the aesthetic movements that produced it as events of historical significance.

Such an approach does not have to be proscriptive, although the catalog of "isms" in the list of suggested readings that follows may seem so to some teachers. The model offers the coherence of parallelism; many writers both before and after 1865 were influenced by prevailing assumptions, and although initially it may seem arbitrary to write a syllabus that eventually sets up Puritanism and modernism as equivalent terms (because they form parallel sections in the course organization), doing so can produce ongoing discussion in the classroom. What connections can students find, as they read specific works, between ideologies such as Puritanism and deism that suggest a worldview and others such as transcendentalism or realism that are more philosophical and aesthetic in their focus? At the same time, to what extent do particular writers enhance, subvert, or simply ignore the assumptions of their age? Class discussion and analysis of individual texts can usefully challenge the apparent subordination of writers and works to categories on a syllabus or course guide. The historical model helps students see each successive "ism" not as inevitable but rather as evolutionary change in the way people choose to express themselves as well as what that choice tells us about how they think. The framework of the course organization can provide a boundary or a container for the course as well as a series of abstract distinctions that students will probably be only too delighted to help you dismantle. Puritanism, for example, becomes a useful umbrella concept in discussing many of the writers in the 1620–1820 period in NAAL. However, the anthology includes in that period many writers who had no relation to Puritan thinking, and there are others—Hawthorne is the notable example—in later periods who continued to examine Puritan thinking in their works. How, then, can students learn to modify their understanding of Puritanism as a controlling idea in American literature? Similarly, coming to terms with the concept of modernism can help students understand many of the thematic and aesthetic choices writers make in the 1914–1945 period. But what happens to the concept if you ask students to consider the "modernism" of Whitman and Dickinson? Or to try to explain the persistence of interest in traditional themes and lyric forms in many poets from the modern period?

The historical approach certainly requires that the teacher be a course guide, and yet one of the fascinations in presenting American literature this way is that it gives each of us the opportunity to ask questions about the development of American writing that we may not have thought about when we were students. Why does *The Declaration of Independence* have the power it has? Is it just because we were taught to hold it sacred? And does it also *reflect* the power of particular groups as well as the disenfranchisement of others (see *The Declaration of Sentiments*, included as an appendix to this Guide as well as Frederick Douglass's *The Meaning of July Fourth for the Negro*)? How might certain works thought to influence the course of history—such as Thomas Paine's *Common Sense*, Harriet Beecher Stowe's *Uncle Tom's Cabin*, or W. E. B. Du Bois's *The Souls of Black Folk*—have influenced us had we been their contemporaries? And if, as the chronological development of American literature may seem to imply to students, we should all have been exposed to modernist thinking and writing, why do some of us still think, write, or read as Puritans or eighteenth-century people? To what extent does our national literature speak for all of us, and to what extent does it record the evolution in thinking of a very few? Do any students sense that they are in the process of evolutionary change in the present moment? Does critical thinking promote such change? How do individual readers give themselves over to the pleasure of reading American texts and still maintain the philosophical and political distance they need to develop their own ways of thinking? Conversely, does the goal of developing a conceptual view work against the experience of reading for pleasure? (Is the notion of a conceptual framework, which implies rational abstraction, the ultimate form of "escapist" reading?) The historical approach leads to these and many other questions and, in my own experience, helps students become deeply engaged in American texts. This model of course organization helps undergraduates explore the possibility that what they are reading may have significance for the development of their own identity—or cluster of identities—as Americans. It helps them find their own place, at any given point in time, in the history of American expression as our literature reflects that history.

Suggested Readings

Volume 1

LITERATURE TO 1620

Literature of Colonial Expansion

Columbus: *Letter to Luis de Santangel, Letter to Ferdinand and Isabella*
Cortés: *First Letter from Mexico to the Spanish Crown*

Harriot: A *Brief and True Report of the New Found Land of Virginia*
White: *The Fifth Voyage*
Percy: *Observations Gathered out of a Discourse of . . . Virginia*
Smith: *The General History of Virginia*

Literature of Witness and Encounter

Casas: *The Very Brief Relation of the Devastation of the Indies*
Díaz del Castillo: *The True History of the Conquest of New Spain*
Cabeza de Vaca: *The Relation*
Barlowe: *The First Voyage Made to the Coasts of America*
Champlain: *The Voyages*

Native American Literature

The Iroquois Creation Story
Pima Stories of the Beginning of the World

1620–1820

Puritan Writers

Bradford: *Of Plymouth Plantation* [The Mayflower Compact]
Winthrop: A *Model of Christian Charity*
Bradstreet: *The Prologue, Contemplations, The Flesh and the Spirit, The Author to Her Book, Here Follows Some Verses upon the Burning of Our House, As Weary Pilgrim, Meditations Divine and Moral*
Wigglesworth: *The Day of Doom*
Rowlandson: A *Narrative of the Captivity and Restoration*
Taylor: *Psalm Two*; the *Prologue* and *Preparatory Meditations* poems; *The Preface; The Joy of Church Fellowship Rightly Attended; Upon Wedlock, and Death of Children; Huswifery; A Fig for Thee, Oh! Death*
Sewall: *The Diary*
Mather: *The Wonders of the Invisible World, Galeacius Secundus: The Life of William Bradford, Nehemias Americanus: The Life of John Winthrop, Bonifacius*

"Other" Colonial Writers

Morton: *New English Canaan*
Byrd: *The Secret Diary*
Ashbridge: *Some Account of the Fore-Part of the Life*
Woolman: *The Journal* ("Some Considerations on the Keeping of Negroes")

The Puritan Vision under Siege

Edwards: *Personal Narrative, A Divine and Supernatural Light, Letter to Rev. Dr. Benjamin Colman, Sinners in the Hands of an Angry God*

Federalism and the Deist Vision

Franklin: *The Way to Wealth, An Edict by the King of Prussia, Information to Those Who Would Remove to America, Remarks Concerning the Savages of North America, The Autobiography*
Adams and Adams: letters
Paine: *Common Sense, The Crisis, No. 1, The Age of Reason*
Jefferson: *The Declaration of Independence, Notes on the State of Virginia, Letter to Peter Carr, Letter to Nathaniel Burwell*
Freneau: *On the Emigration to America and Peopling the Western Country, The Wild Honey Suckle, The Indian Burying Ground, On the Religion of Nature*
Tyler: *The Contrast*

The Issue of Slavery

Byrd: *The Secret Diary*
Woolman: *The Journal*
Crèvecoeur: *Letter IX*
Jefferson: *The Declaration of Independence*
Equiano: *The Interesting Narrative*
Freneau: *To Sir Toby*
Wheatley: *On Being Brought from Africa to America, To the University of Cambridge; in New England; Thoughts on the Works of Providence; To S.M., A Young African Painter, on Seeing His Works;* letters

The Treatment of Native Americans

Bradford: *Of Plymouth Plantation*
Williams: *A Key into the Language of America*
Rowlandson: *A Narrative of the Captivity and Restoration*
Franklin: *Remarks Concerning the Savages of North America*
Occom: *Sermon at the Execution of Moses Paul*
Freneau: *The Indian Burying Ground*

The Lives of Colonial American Women

Bradstreet: poems
Rowlandson: *A Narrative of the Captivity and Restoration*
Mather: *The Trial of Martha Carrier, Bonifacius*
Knight: *The Private Journal of a Journey from Boston to New York*

Byrd: *The Secret Diary*
Edwards: *Sarah Pierrepont*
Ashbridge: *Some Account of the Fore-Part of the Life*
Adams and Adams: letters
Jefferson: *Letter to Nathaniel Burwell*
Tyler: *The Contrast*

1820–1865

The New Americanness of American Literature

Irving: *Rip Van Winkle*
Cooper: *Notions of the Americans*
Bryant: *Thanatopsis, The Prairies, The Poet*
Emerson: *The American Scholar, The Divinity School Address, Self-Reliance, The Poet*
Hawthorne: *Young Goodman Brown, The May-Pole of Merry Mount, The Minister's Black Veil, The Scarlet Letter*
Poe: Poems, *The Raven, Annabel Lee, Ligeia, The Fall of the House of Usher, The Philosophy of Composition*
Melville: *Hawthorne and His Mosses; Moby-Dick* (Chapter 54); *Bartleby, the Scrivener; Billy Budd, Sailor*

American Transcendentalism

Emerson: *Nature*
Thoreau: *Walden*

Literature of the House Divided

Lincoln, *A House Divided, Address Delivered at the Dedication of the Cemetery at Gettysburg*
Fuller: *The Great Lawsuit*
Stowe: *Uncle Tom's Cabin* (Chapter VII)
Thoreau: *Resistance to Civil Government, Slavery in Massachusetts*
Douglass: *Narrative of the Life*
Whitman: *Drum-Taps* poems
Melville: *The Paradise of Bachelors and The Tartarus of Maids, Battle-Pieces* poems
Dickinson: 49, 185, 187, 199, 241, 258, 303, 305, 348, 435, 441, 510, 536, 547, 709, 732, 754, 824, 1099, 1129, 1138, 1545, 1575 (poems about being starved, silenced, constricted, and alienated)
Davis: *Life in the Iron-Mills*

Democratic Vistas

Lincoln: *Second Inaugural Address*

Whitman: *Preface to Leaves of Grass, Song of Myself, Letter to Ralph Waldo Emerson, From Pent-up Aching Rivers, Facing West from California's Shores, Scented Herbage of My Breast, Crossing Brooklyn Ferry, Out of the Cradle Endlessly Rocking, As I Ebb'd with the Ocean of Life, When Lilacs Last in the Dooryard Bloom'd, The Sleepers, A Noiseless Patient Spider, Democratic Vistas*

Dickinson: 67, 214, 249, 280, 303, 315, 322, 328, 341, 448, 465, 501, 505, 528, 632, 712, 822, 1540, 1593, 1651, 1732 (poems about struggle, triumph, and vision)

Volume 2

1865–1914

Regionalism and Local Color Writing

Harte: *The Outcasts of Poker Flat*

Harris: *The Wonderful Tar-Baby Story, Mr. Rabbit Grossly Deceives Mr. Fox, Free Joe and the Rest of the World*

Jewett: *A White Heron, The Foreigner*

Freeman: *A New England Nun, The Revolt of Mother*

Chesnutt: *The Goophered Grapevine*

Garland: *Under the Lion's Paw*

Austin: *The Walking Woman*

Bonnin: *Impressions of an Indian Childhood, The School Days of an Indian Girl, An Indian Teacher among Indians*

Realism

Clemens: *Adventures of Huckleberry Finn, Letter IV*

Howells: *Novel-Writing and Novel Reading, Editha*

Bierce: *Chickamauga*

James: *Daisy Miller, The Real Thing, The Turn of the Screw, The Beast in the Jungle, The Art of Fiction*

Wharton: *Ethan Frome*

Naturalism

Chopin: *The Awakening*

Washington: *Up from Slavery*

Gilman: *The Yellow Wallpaper*

Addams: *Twenty Years at Hull-House*

Du Bois: *The Souls of Black Folk*
Norris: *Suggestions, Frank Norris' Weekly Letter* [Truth and Accuracy], *Vandover and the Brute*
Crane: *An Experiment in Misery, The Open Boat, The Bride Comes to Yellow Sky, The Blue Hotel, An Episode of War*
Dreiser: *Old Rogaum and His Theresa*
London: *The Law of Life*
Adams: *The Education*

1914–1945

Thematic Modernism

I have found certain writers and works more teachable than others in presenting the 1914–45 period historically and choose these as focal points for our reading and discussion. At the sophomore level in particular, I emphasize thematic links between these writers to convey how it feels to write with a modernist sensibility.

Cather: *My Mortal Enemy, Neighbour Rosicky*
Stein: *The Good Anna*
Frost: *Mending Wall; The Death of the Hired Man; After Apple-Picking; An Old Man's Winter Night; The Oven Bird; Birches; "Out, Out—"; Nothing Gold Can Stay; Stopping by Woods on a Snowy Evening; Two Tramps in Mud Time; Desert Places; Design; Neither out far nor in Deep; The Gift Outright; Directive; The Figure a Poem Makes*
Anderson: *Winesburg, Ohio; The Egg*
Stevens: *The Snow Man, A High-Toned Old Christian Woman, The Emperor of Ice-Cream, Sunday Morning, Anecdote of the Jar, Thirteen Ways of Looking at a Blackbird, The Idea of Order at Key West, Of Modern Poetry*
Yezierska: *The Lost "Beautifulness"*
Williams: *Portrait of a Lady, The Widow's Lament in Springtime, Spring and All, To Elsie, The Red Wheelbarrow, The Dead Baby, The Wind Increases, Death, This Is Just to Say, Classic Scene, The Term, A Sort of a Song, The Dance, Lear, Landscape with the Fall of Icarus*
Jeffers: *Shine, Perishing Republic; Hurt Hawks; November Surf; Carmel Point*
Eliot: *The Love Song of J. Alfred Prufrock, Tradition and the Individual Talent, The Hollow Men*
O'Neill: *Long Day's Journey into Night*
Porter: *Old Mortality*
Cummings: *Buffalo Bill's; the Cambridge ladies who live in furnished souls; Poem, or Beauty Hurts Mr. Vinal; "next to of course america i";*

i sing of Olaf glad and big; anyone lived in a pretty how town; pity this busy monster,manunkind
Toomer: *Cane*
Fitzgerald: *Winter Dreams*
Faulkner: *As I Lay Dying, Barn Burning*
Hemingway: *The Snows of Kilimanjaro*
Hughes: *The Negro Speaks of Rivers, Mother to Son*

Formal and Technical Aspects of Modernism

In an upper-division class or with a particularly motivated group of sophomores, I also include selections from the following list of works that illustrate formal and technical aspects of modernism.

Stein: *The Making of Americans*
Lowell: *The Captured Goddess, Venus Transiens, Madonna of the Evening Flowers, The Weather-Cock Points South, Penumbra, Summer Night Piece, St. Louis*
Pound: *A Pact, In a Station of the Metro, Villanelle: The Psychological Hour, The Cantos*
H. D.: *Oread, Leda, At Baia, Fragment 113, Helen, The Walls Do Not Fall*
Moore: *Poetry, To a Snail, Bird-Witted, The Mind Is an Enchanting Thing*
Eliot: *The Waste Land, Burnt Norton*
Dos Passos: *The Big Money*
Crane: *Chaplinesque, At Melville's Tomb, The Bridge*

Social and Political Writing

Robinson: *Richard Cory, Miniver Cheevy*
Grimké: *The Black Finger, Tenebris, At April, Trees*
Yezierska: *The Lost "Beautifulness"*
Hurston: *The Eatonville Anthology, How It Feels to Be Colored Me*
Parker: *General Review of the Sex Situation*
Taggard: *Everyday Alchemy; With Child; A Middle-aged, Middle-class Woman at Midnight; At Last the Women Are Moving; O People Misshapen; Mill Town; To My Mother; Silence in Mallorca*
Brown: *Mister Samuel and Sam, He Was a Man, Master and Man, Break of Day, Bitter Fruit of the Tree*
Hughes: *I, too; Refugee in America; Madam and Her Madam; Madam's Calling Cards; Silhouette; Visitors to the Black Belt; Democracy*
Rukeyser: *Effort at Speech Between Two People, Movie, Alloy, For Fun, M-Day's Child Is Fair of Face, Suicide Blues, Who in One Lifetime, "Long Enough," The Poem as Mask, Poem, Endless, Myth, Painters*

Traditional Poetry, Other Perspectives, and Humor

At both the sophomore and the upper-division levels, I examine other writers who deal with more traditional themes and forms, whose work illustrates perspectives other than the modernist one, or who choose humor as a way of dealing with modern life. In any given course, I choose a few writers from the following lists:

Black Elk
Masters
Sandburg
Grimké
Ransom
Hurston
Millay
Parker
Thurber
Wolfe

The "New Negro" Movement
Grimké
Hurston
Toomer
Brown
Hughes
Cullen
Wright

AMERICAN PROSE SINCE 1945

Each of you will have your own reasons for making the choices you do in the post-1945 period. Rather than apply historical labels to contemporary writers, I choose a few who suggest the various traditions representative of twentieth-century literature. For a discussion of how to organize the entire course as a study of literary traditions, see Chapter 4. In any given course, I choose from among the following.

African-American Writers

Ellison: *Invisible Man*
Baldwin: *The Fire Next Time*
Walker: *Everyday Use*
Wilson: *Fences*

Southern Writers

Welty: *Petrified Man*
Taylor: *What You Hear from 'Em?*
O'Connor: *The Life You Save May Be Your Own, Good Country People*
Mason: *Drawing Names*
Walker: *Everyday Use*

Jewish Writers

Malamud: *The Magic Barrel*
Bellow: *Seize the Day*
Roth: *Defender of the Faith*

Dramatists

Williams: A *Streetcar Named Desire*
Miller: *Death of a Salesman*
Wilson: *Fences*
Mamet: *House of Games*

New Yorker *Writers*

Cheever: *The Country Husband*
Updike: *The Happiest I've Been, Separating, Dog's Death*
Stone: *Helping*
Mason: *Drawing Names*
Beattie: *Weekend*

Experimental or Postmodernist Writers

Nabokov: *Pnin*
Mailer: *The Armies of the Night*
Barth: *Life-Story*
Pynchon: *The Crying of Lot 49*

Native American Writers

Momaday: *The Way to Rainy Mountain*
Silko: *Lullaby*
Erdrich: *Lulu's Boys*

AMERICAN POETRY SINCE 1945

Grouping Individual Poets

In presenting the contemporary poetry included in NAAL, I have sometimes chosen a few poets who offer a variety of themes, techniques, and traditions and asked students to read all of the included selections. Two possible groupings follow:

(1) Warren
Bishop
Lowell
Rich
Baraka

(2) Roethke
Berryman
Brooks
Wright
Plath

Presenting Individual Poems

More often, I choose an array of individual poems. Some we analyze closely in class; others become the basis for student writing. I know that the following poems engage students in detailed discussion because I have taught them; no doubt you have successfully used others as the basis for extended analysis.

Roethke: *My Papa's Waltz*
Bishop: *In the Waiting Room, The Moose, One Art*
Hayden: *Middle Passage*
Jarrell: *The Death of the Ball Turret Gunner, Well Water*
Berryman: *Dream Songs* (esp. 1, 14, 40)
Lowell: *Memories of West Street and Lepke, Skunk Hour, For the Union Dead*
Brooks: *kitchenette building, the mother, A Song in the Front Yard*
Ginsberg: *Howl*
Wright: *Autumn Begins in Martin's Ferry, Ohio; A Blessing; A Finch Sitting out a Windstorm*
Sexton: *Sylvia's Death*
Rich: *A Valediction Forbidding Mourning, Diving into the Wreck, Twenty-One Love Poems* (esp. *The Floating Poem,* XIX)
Plath: *Lady Lazarus, Daddy*
Lorde: *The Woman Thing, Black Mother Woman*
Baraka: *An Agony. As Now.*
Dove: *Thomas and Beulah*

Poets Reflecting the Diversity of Contemporary American Life

Hayden
Brooks
Levertov
Merrill
Ginsberg
Rich
Lorde
Baraka
Harper
Dove
Ríos
Cervantes
Song
Lee

CHAPTER 3

The "Major Authors" Approach

Planning the Course

Presenting the American literature course as a study of single figures or "major authors" makes it possible to read more of each writer's work; to spend more class time discussing each writer; and to encourage in the students more sustained rumination, contemplation, and appreciation of each writer. This approach does not have to eliminate the historical context or the literary history within which any given writer wrote, although the course design does emphasize the development of each writer's individual career and relegates historical and cultural context to the background. NAAL provides excellent period introductions as well as headnotes for each writer in the anthology. If you require students to read these, they will be supplied with much of the contextual information they will need, so you do not have to schedule class time for it.

The major authors model of course organization works particularly well as the middle course in a three-tiered curriculum, for which first-year students may have already taken an "introduction to literature" course and upper-division students will be required to study several literary periods in detail. The major authors course can allow students to read more of writers they have become acquainted with, either in high school or in the first-year course and, at the same time, can increase their desire to read other writers who were contemporaries of major figures or who wrote in the same genre or literary tradition. If the American literature course is likely to be the last literature course many of your students will take, then your choice of the major authors model may be more complicated. Among my colleagues who have debated the question in a university where many of our students will probably not go on to take upper-division courses in literature, some advocate giving students more exposure to fewer writers in the hope that they will discover a love for reading. Others argue that students are more likely to develop this love if they read a wider variety of authors and understand the way literature is connected to history.

As part of writing an outline for a major authors course, you might find it useful to think through some of your own criteria for *major*. Some of the words we might casually use to explain our choices of certain writers over others—*great, universal, enduring,* and *major* itself—can actually obscure the process of literary evaluation. The major authors course highlights this process. How does an author become "major"? Who decides? Is the question open to debate? Is there a "dictionary" of major authors that establishes the criteria for inclusion or does the inclusion of any particular author reflect the opinions of readers over time? If so, which readers? Why do there appear to be so many major authors in one period (such as 1820–65), and so few in others (such as 1620–1820)? Where are the authors not included in the anthology? Can we be certain that we would not consider any of them "major"? One of the ways of opening up the question of literary evaluation implied in the design of the major authors model is to allow students to choose a favorite author not already on the syllabus—and perhaps not included in the anthology—and ask them to write an essay in which they struggle with the author's literary value. Does a student's literary taste reflect on his or her own value? And what is literary taste? Are some people born with it? Can it be learned? Asking questions like these throughout the course can help dispel one disadvantage to teaching by means of the major authors model: that the course design can have the effect of predetermining student taste and limiting students' ability to ask evaluative questions on their own.

In choosing selections for my own major authors course, I have tried to examine what the concept means. I have defined writers as "major" if they satisfy more than one of the following conditions:

1. Appeal to a variety of readers
2. Wrote works that influenced more than one other major author
3. Contributed an acknowledged "masterpiece" to American literature
4. Sustained a literary career beyond a single tour de force
5. Were pioneers or innovators in subject matter, literary tradition, technique, or genre
6. Have been recognized as major literary critics or historians

Applying these criteria to the writers in NAAL can help with a preliminary list of possible major authors to include in the American literature course; being selective in the number or length of works you assign by any given author will make room for more figures. The list that follows offers my own suggestions for a major authors syllabus. I have included a second list of authors who might be considered "major minor" writers, if we add at least the criterion that the writer has found literary expression for a particularly unique perception or experience.

The language of "major authors" and "major minor authors" itself contributes to confusion for students. We need to distinguish between *major* as it implies "significant" and as it is often used to mean "mainstream." If the space allotted to African-American male writers and African-American and Euro-American female writers in NAAL can be used as a yardstick here, those particular literary historians and critics who edited NAAL have identified several African-Americans and women as "major" authors. And the list of "major minor" writers includes several Euro-American men. Perhaps one of the ultimate challenges in teaching the major authors course is helping students break down any associations they may have that *major* always equals "Euro-American" or "male" and that women or Native American or African-American writers—because they appear as a numerical minority in NAAL—are always "minor" writers.

A related semantic problem is the hierarchy implied by the terms *major* and *minor*. While it might make sense to argue that certain writers "dominated" particular literary centers or circles, the language of dominance ceases to have meaning when we apply it to literary works themselves. Does *The Raven* dominate over *Uncle Tom's Cabin?* In teaching by means of the major authors model, I find myself continually working to correct the impression students have that literary evaluation resembles an athletic contest. Wherever possible, given the representation of works in the anthology, I try to design the course as a series of single authors, and I include some of my favorite noncanonical writers. Nothing tests the concept of major authors like the inclusion of a few good literary works that appear to satisfy none of the criteria for "greatness." In a third list, I suggest a few of these.

Suggested Readings

Volume 1

LITERATURE TO 1620

Díaz del Castillo
Cabeza de Vaca
Smith

1620–1820

Bradstreet
Taylor
Edwards
Franklin: including *The Autobiography*

1820–1865

Emerson: including *Nature*
Hawthorne: including *The Scarlet Letter*
Poe
Stowe
Thoreau: including *Walden*
Douglass: including *Narrative of the Life*
Whitman
Melville: including *Billy Budd, Sailor*
Dickinson

Volume 2

1865–1914

Clemens: including *Adventures of Huckleberry Finn*
James
Chopin
Wharton
Native American Chants and Songs

1914–1945

Cather
Frost
Stevens
Eliot
O'Neill
Faulkner
Hughes

AMERICAN PROSE SINCE 1945

Williams
Malamud
Ellison
Bellow
Miller
O'Connor

Momaday
Walker
Beattie

AMERICAN POETRY SINCE 1945

Roethke
Bishop
Lowell
Brooks
Wright
Rich
Dove

Some "Major Minor" Writers

Volume 1

LITERATURE TO 1620

Stories of the Beginning of the World
Champlain

1620–1820

Bradford
Crèvecoeur
Jefferson

1820–1865

Irving
Fuller

Volume 2

1865–1914

Howells
Jewett
Freeman
Chesnutt
Eastman
Crane
Dreiser
Adams

1914–1945

Stein
Anderson
Williams
Pound
H. D.
Moore
Porter
Hurston
Fitzgerald
Hemingway
Crane
Wright

AMERICAN PROSE SINCE 1945

Welty
Mailer

AMERICAN POETRY SINCE 1945

Olson
Hayden
Berryman
Levertov
Ammons
Merrill
Ashbery
Sexton
Plath
Lorde
Baraka

Works by Noncanonical Writers Worth Evaluating in a Major Authors Course

Volume 1

LITERATURE TO 1620

Barlowe: *The First Voyage Made to the Coasts of America*

1620–1820

Wigglesworth: *The Day of Doom*
Rowlandson: A *Narrative of the Captivity and Restoration*
Occom: *Sermon Preached at the Execution of Moses Paul*
Paine: *Common Sense* or *The Crisis, No. 1*
Wheatley: poems
Tyler: *The Contrast*

1820–1865

Bryant: *The Prairies*
Apess: *An Indian's Looking-Glass for the White Man*
Jacobs: *Incidents in the Life of a Slave Girl*
Davis: *Life in the Iron-Mills*

Volume 2

1865–1914

Harte: *The Outcasts of Poker Flat*
Bierce: *Chickamauga*
Harris: tales
Washington: *Up From Slavery*
Garland: *Under the Lion's Paw*
Gilman: *The Yellow Wallpaper*
Du Bois: *The Souls of Black Folk*
Norris: *Vandover and the Brute*

1914–1945

Black Elk: *Black Elk Speaks*
Masters: poems
Hurston: *The Eatonville Anthology*, *How It Feels to Be Colored Me*, *Their Eyes Were Watching God*
Parker: essays
Cummings: poems
Toomer: *Cane*
Wolfe: *The Lost Boy*

AMERICAN PROSE SINCE 1945

Cheever: *The Country Husband*
Baldwin: *The Fire Next Time*
Updike: *The Happiest I've Been* or *Separating*
Roth: *Defender of the Faith*

Pynchon: *The Crying of Lot 49*
Stone: *Helping*
Silko: *Lullaby*

AMERICAN POETRY SINCE 1945

Oppen
Jarrell
Wilbur
Hugo
Creeley
Snyder
Harper

CHAPTER 4

The Literary Traditions Approach

Planning the Course

Implicit in the framework of the literary traditions approach is a certain plurality: students will study more than one tradition, because American literature as we know it in the twentieth century combines several. The format of the course requires evaluative choice, but in a different way than either the historical or the major authors approach. Instead of initially dealing with writers either as part of a historical period or as single figures, you must decide instead which literary traditions you want to include and then which authors best represent those traditions. In doing so, each of us engages in the process of defining which literary traditions are more major than others, and at the same time, in presenting the development of various traditions, we will be locating that development historically.

NAAL offers the central figures and at least a representative selection from major works in each of the following literary traditions: Euro-American male and female, African-American male, Native American male, and southern writers. Also represented in NAAL are works that might be used to begin a discussion of African-American female and twentieth-century immigrant or Jewish traditions and a tradition that we might describe as labor, protest, or populist literature. In effect, the text is a statement that certain literary traditions are more major than others.

This approach raises the questions of literary tradition: How does any given tradition begin? What other writers influence the tradition? How do historical or social events contribute to or inhibit the formation and development of the tradition? Is the tradition imitative or self-defined? What are its distinctive genres? Who are its major figures? What are its central themes? What is its contribution to the concept of American literature itself? What is its relation to oral or folk traditions? What formal or cultural or thematic connections exist between any two literary traditions? And how do we define the boundaries of single traditions in American literature? To what extent does any given American writer express a self-conscious sense of inclusion within or exclusion from a particular literary tradition? Is the concept of literary tradition (and the concept of a plurality of literary traditions) invented by the writer or by the student- or teacher-critic? And to what extent is the concept of literary tradition useful as a way of providing the context for either writing or studying American literature? In my own brief listing of various literary traditions included in NAAL, I have implied that racial or ethnic origin and regional identity, gender, and class experience define boundaries or categories of authors and works. Are there some writers who defy categorization—either by their own disclaimers or by their thematic concerns? Are there some writers who belong to more than one literary tradition in such a way as to call into question the usefulness of the very concept of literary tradition? (African-American women writers, in particular, may belong to several literary traditions at once.) And after we have examined the disparate parts that form the whole of American literature, does it still make any sense at all to talk about an American literary tradition?

The pedagogical method I employ in teaching the course by means of the literary traditions approach expresses a general faith in the usefulness of analysis: that after dividing and examining the parts of American literature and spending class time discussing them, we will then be in a position to view American literature as a complex interweaving and unfolding of disparate threads and literary voices and that the result of the separate analysis will be an integrated vision for students. Including a discussion of contemporary literature—and the question of whether contemporary works also form a literary tradition is an interesting one—is crucial to helping students achieve this integrated vision. NAAL offers a wide variety of contemporary authors and works that demonstrate the influence of various literary traditions on each other. Here you can also ask students to think about how the contemporary writers and works they know from leisure reading (whether or not these are represented in NAAL) are also the products of an American literature that is increasingly pluralistic. Some students also write creatively. Do these students view themselves as part of a literary tradition? Are they conscious of writing, say, as southerners or as Euro-American women? And do other aspects of their lives so influence their writing as to seem categories that might define literary traditions? (Are they conscious, for example, of writing as students or as lesbians or as veterans?)

The approach raises the fundamental question of the universal. Without denying the existence of human commonalities that cross boundaries of ethnic, gender, or regional perspectives, the implied pluralism of the literary traditions approach may challenge the existence of any central point of view by which many of your students define their own value and identity. Without question, such an approach shifts the center of classroom discourse away from the Euro-American male tradition, challenges the concept of mainstream, and invites new questions. The experience of reading as integral to a literary tradition writers whom literary historians have referred to as "minor" or "minority" may initially disconcert students who identify themselves as members of a cultural mainstream; who value universals in literature; or who insist that humanism ought to erase boundaries of ethnic, gender, regional, or class identity. Perhaps it is particularly difficult for Euro-American students eighteen to twenty-two years old to participate in an intellectual process that will require them to take a "minority" perspective at a time in their lives when they are trying to achieve their own intellectual and emotional maturity (their "majority").

But even Euro-American male authors have written some of their best work from within the perspective of marginality. In *The Mark and the Knowledge: Social Stigma in Classic American Fiction* (1979), I examined works by Hawthorne, Melville, Faulkner, and Ellison to show how American writers often achieve their capacity for vision through the experience of feeling marked, alienated, or stigmatized. In the 1990s, when relatively few undergraduates will be preparing for a career as a creative writer, anyone who commits herself or himself to writing will already seem to your students, by that choice, to be marginal. In the Euro-American male tradition, writers such as Hawthorne, Thoreau, Whitman, Clemens, and many others suggest that beginning in the nineteenth century being a writer was itself enough to marginalize an American white man. (In the lists that follow, I include writers and works that develop themes of marginality among white male writers.)

You might want to discuss the differences between, for example, Thoreau's choice to write from the isolation of Walden Pond and to embrace eccentricity and Douglass's imposed position and perspective as slave and, later in his *Narrative,* as heroic fugitive. For Euro-American men, choosing marginality often helps them focus their individual vision. But they begin with a sense of their literary authority that minority writers do not share. Minority writers, on the other hand, must somehow transcend the apparent limitations of marginality—that they do not see themselves as possessing literary authority and, instead, feel silenced by

Euro-American male culture—to write at all. Who knows what individual writers within minority literary traditions might have accomplished in American literary history without the burden of social stigma? In the literary traditions of African-American male and female writers, Chesnutt and Hurston are extremely significant figures, for both of these writers were able to locate some other source than the Christian God for their own creativity. For both Chesnutt and Hurston, writing out of the perspective of black folk life allowed them to imagine a source for storytelling authority that was accessible to them—in particular, through the traditional figure of the story-telling conjure woman or man in the black community—and, thereby, to disengage the silencing function of Puritan and patriarchal typology. As the white writer Harris recorded in the Uncle Remus tales of the 1880s and 1890s (included in NAAL), black people on the Southern plantation well before emancipation were prolific oral storytellers and kept alive the traditions of African folklore.

Engaging your students in comparative discussions of the sources of literary authority available to Euro-American male writers and to writers from other traditions represented by American literature can help them break pervasive associations inherited from the Puritans that only white males have the authority to speak—for others as well as for themselves. It can also lead them to think in new ways about their own nascent authority—as thinkers, speakers, and writers in the classroom. When they see African-American and Euro-American female authors finding the power to speak, they find the models they may need to break down their own passivity. Instructors often find themselves perplexed by the lack of interest their students express toward the literature they are "forced" to read because the American literature course may be satisfying one of their graduation requirements. The classroom discussion that results when students consider the struggle for expression in others can ease the isolation and alienation white women and minority students often feel, and it can dissolve for all of your students their indifference to literary study. Students—whatever their gender or ethnic origin—learn to see cultural power as something they may not necessarily inherit, but may discover in themselves.

In the lists that follow, I have chosen writers and works that illustrate the development of several literary traditions. Within each tradition, I have evaluated writers only against each other. This process eliminates the necessity of weighing the relative significance of, say, Hurston and Hemingway. You may need to choose among Faulkner, Fitzgerald, and Hemingway because of the limitations of classroom time, but you can reserve the question of Hurston's influence for that part of your course set aside for studying the African-American female tradition. Within the tradition of literature by Euro-American males, you may want to discuss different choices of genre, perhaps even dividing the reading into subtraditions (I offer some notes on teaching genre in Chapter 5).

You may also need to decide how to order the traditions on the syllabus. If you begin with the white male tradition, will that once again set up white male experience as the norm, all others as marginal? White women and men and women from minority traditions have written in full awareness of the literary standards established by Euro-American men, and one way to organize the course is to remain roughly chronological but to discuss literary traditions as they emerge. This subsequently allows you to make specific connections between writers from different traditions who wrote at about the same time as well as to create a literary context within each tradition that will help students avoid setting minority writers against white male writers.

Another way to organize the syllabus is to group writers for periodic discussion. Early readings can introduce students to those writers who establish origins or are early figures in several literary traditions: William Bradford or Edward Taylor, Anne Bradstreet, Phillis Wheatley, and Frederick Douglass. Later, you may group polemical or political writers from several traditions: Jonathan Edwards and Thomas Jefferson, Margaret Fuller, Booker T. Washington, and W. E. B. Du Bois. At any point in the course, you may group writers from several traditions according to theme (see my lists in Chapter 5).

One specific grouping that I have used on the first day of class to set the tone of the course involves Frost's *The Gift Outright*, in which he writes ostensibly as an American poet but clearly, also, from the perspective of the Euro-American male writer (in the way he feminizes the land and makes it the task of the writer to "surrender" himself to her and to correct her "unstoried, artless, unenhanced" condition); and Brooks's *kitchenette building*, in which she suggests that being poor in Bronzeville—the fictional black neighborhood of the collection of poems in which *kitchenette building* first appeared—makes it difficult to "send up" a dream "through onion fumes" and "yesterday's garbage ripening in the hall." Such a pairing allows you to begin immediately to combine some analysis of specific poems with a general discussion of the goals of the literary traditions approach.

Supplementing NAAL with recent novels not included in the text can allow you to develop the pluralism of contemporary fiction. In the view of William Pritchard, the NAAL editor for "American Prose since 1945," "The major American novelists of the post–World War II decades are Saul Bellow, Norman Mailer, and John Updike," although he adds that there are easily "fifty or so American novelists and story writers . . . of real distinction." I have taught the following novels and story collections as part of the American literature course; each has engaged students in discussion and in out-of-class essays.

Rudolfo Anaya: *Bless Me Ultima*
James Baldwin: *Go Tell It on the Mountain*
Ann Beattie: *The Burning House*
Ralph Ellison: *The Invisible Man* (excerpted in NAAL)
John Gardner: *Grendel* or *The Sunlight Dialogues*
Lillian Hellman: *Pentimento* (autobiographical prose)
Norman Mailer: *An American Dream*
Bernard Malamud: *The Assistant* or *God's Grace*
Toni Morrison: *The Bluest Eye, Sula,* or *Beloved*
May Sarton: *Plant Dreaming Deep* (a journal) or *Mrs. Stevens Hears the Mermaids Singing*
Amy Tan: *The Joy Luck Club*
Alice Walker: *In Love and Trouble* or *The Color Purple*
Eudora Welty: *The Optimist's Daughter*
Richard Wright: *Uncle Tom's Children*

Charting the Traditions by Race and Gender

However you decide to present the literary traditions in your own course—chronologically or by means of groupings—it may help your students to visualize individual writers within their historical period. Included below, on pages 36–37, is a chart of major figures in Euro-American, African-American, Native American, Hispanic/Latino, and Asian-American literary traditions represented in NAAL, by tradition and according to chronology.

Suggested Readings: Organized by Race, Nationality, and Gender

Volume 1

Literature to 1620

Euro-American Male

Columbus: *Letter to Luis de Santangel, Letter to Ferdinand and Isabella*
Barlowe: *The First Voyage Made to the Coasts of America*
Champlain: *The Voyages*
Smith: *The General History of Virginia*

Native Americans

Stories of the Beginning of the World

VOLUME 1

Tradition	*To 1620*	*1620–1820*	*1820–1865*
Euro-American Male	Columbus Barlowe Champlain Smith	Bradford or Taylor Edwards Franklin de Crèvecoeur John Adams Jefferson	Irving Emerson Hawthorne Poe Thoreau Whitman Melville
Euro-American Female		Bradstreet Rowlandson Ashbridge Abigail Adams	Fuller Stowe Dickinson Davis
African-American Male		Equiano	Douglass
African-American Female		Wheatley	Jacobs
Native Americans	Stories of the Beginning of the World	Occom	Cherokee Memorials Apess
Hispanic Male	Casas Cortés Díaz del Castillo Cabeza de Vaca		

VOLUME 2

Tradition	*1865–1914*	*1914–1945*	*American Prose since 1945*	*American Poetry since 1945*
Euro-American Male	Clemens Howells or Dreiser or Adams James Crane	Frost Stevens Williams or Eliot O'Neill Fitzgerald Faulkner Crane	Williams Malamud Bellow Miller Mamet	Warren Berryman Lowell Merrill Ashbery or Wright

Tradition	*1865–1914*	*1914–1945*	*American Prose since 1945*	*American Poetry since 1945*
Euro-American Female	Jewett Chopin Freeman or Austin Gilman Wharton	Cather Stein Lowell Yezierska Moore Porter Taggard	Welty O'Connor Oates Beattie	Bishop Levertov Rich Plath
African-American Male	Washington Chesnutt Du Bois	Toomer Brown Hughes Wright	Ellison Baldwin A. Wilson	Hayden Baraka Harper
African-American Female		Grimké Hurston	Walker	Brooks Lorde Dove
Native American Male	Native American Oratory Eastman Oskison Chants and Songs	Black Elk	Momaday	Ortiz
Native American Female	Bonnin Chants and Songs		Silko Erdrich	
Latino				Ríos
Latina			Chávez	Cervantes
Asian-American Male				Lee
Asian-American Female				Song

Hispanic Male

Casas: *The Very Brief Relation Hispaniola, The Coast of Pearls*
Cortés: *First Letter from Mexico to the Spanish Crown*
Díaz del Castillo: *The True History of the Conquest of New Spain*
Cabeza de Vaca: *The Relation*

1620–1820

Euro-American Male

Bradford: *Of Plymouth Plantation*
or
Taylor: *Psalm Two; Prologue; Meditations* (8, 16, 38, 42); *The Preface Upon Wedlock, and Death of Children; Huswifery; A Fig for Thee, Oh! Death*
Edwards: *Personal Narrative,* [Sarah Pierrepont], A *Divine and Supernatural Light, Letter to Rev. Dr. Benjamin Colman, Sinners in the Hands of an Angry God*
Franklin: *The Way to Wealth, Information to Those Who Would Remove to America, Remarks Concerning the Savages of North America, The Autobiography*
Crèvecoeur: *Letters from an American Farmer*
John Adams: letters
Jefferson: *The Declaration of Independence, Notes on the State of Virginia* (Query VI, Query XVII), *Letter to Peter Carr, Letter to Nathaniel Burwell*

Euro-American Female

Bradstreet: *The Prologue; To the Memory of My Dear and Ever Honored Father, Thomas Dudley Esq.; To Her Father with Some Verses; Contemplations; The Author to Her Book; Before the Birth of One of Her Children; To My Dear and Loving Husband; A Letter to Her Husband, Absent upon Public Employment; In Memory of My Dear Grandchild Anne Bradstreet; Here Follows Some Verses upon the Burning of Our House*
Rowlandson: *Narrative of the Captivity and Restoration*
Ashbridge: *Some Account of the Fore-Part of the Life*
Abigail Adams: letters

African-American Male

Equiano: *The Interesting Narrative of the Life*

African-American Female

Wheatley: *On Being Brought from Africa to America; To the University of Cambridge, in New England; Thoughts on the Works of Providence; To S.M., A Young African Painter, on Seeing His Works*

Native-American Male

Occom: *Sermon at the Execution of Moses Paul*

1820–1865

Euro-American Male

Irving: *Rip Van Winkle*
Emerson: *The American Scholar, Self-Reliance, The Poet, Experience, Myself,* [Protest; Writing; America], [The Business of Education], [Dead Sentences Versus Man-Making Words], [The London Literati on Male Chastity], [Black Slavery Versus Quite Other Slaves to Free]
Hawthorne: *Young Goodman Brown, The Minister's Black Veil, Rappaccini's Daughter, The Scarlet Letter*
Poe: poems, tales
Thoreau: *Resistance to Civil Government, Slavery in Massachusetts, Walden* (Economy, Where I Lived and What I Lived For, Former Inhabitants; and Winter Visitors, Conclusion)
Whitman: *Preface to* Leaves of Grass, *Song of Myself, Calamus* poems, *The Sleepers*
Melville: *Bartleby, the Scrivener; Benito Cereno* or *Billy Budd, Sailor*

Euro-American Female

Fuller: *The Great Lawsuit*
Stowe: *Uncle Tom's Cabin, The Minister's Housekeeper*
Dickinson: 49, 67, 185, 187, 214, 241, 249, 258, 280, 303, 305, 322, 348, 435, 441, 448, 465, 501, 505, 510, 520, 528, 536, 709, 744, 754, 986, 1099, 1129, 1138, 1545, 1575, *Letters to Thomas Wentworth Higginson*
Davis: *Life in the Iron-Mills*

African-American Male

Douglass: *Narrative of the Life*

African-American Female

Jacobs: *Incidents in the Life of a Slave Girl*

Native-Americans

Cherokee Memorials
Apess: *An Indian's Looking-Glass for the White Man*

Volume 2

1865–1914

Euro-American Male

Clemens: *Letter to Will Bowen, Adventures of Huckleberry Finn*
Howells: *Novel-Writing and Novel-Reading*
or
Dreiser: *Old Rogaum and His Theresa*
or
Adams: *The Education*
James: *Daisy Miller, The Turn of the Screw, The Beast in the Jungle*
Crane: *The Open Boat, The Bride Comes to Yellow Sky*

Euro-American Female

Jewett: *A White Heron, The Foreigner*
Chopin: *The Awakening*
Freeman: *A New England Nun, The Revolt of "Mother"*
or
Gilman: *The Yellow Wallpaper*
Wharton: *Ethan Frome*
Austin: *The Walking Woman*

African-American Male

Washington: *Up from Slavery*
Chesnutt: *The Goophered Grapevine*
Du Bois: *The Souls of Black Folk*

Native American Male

Native American Oratory
Eastman: *From the Deep Woods to Civilization*
Oskison: *The Problem of Old Harjo*
Chants and Songs

Native American Female

Chants and Songs
Bonnin: *Impressions of an Indian Childhood, The School Days of an Indian Girl, An Indian Teacher among Indians*

1914–1945

Euro-American Male

Frost: *The Death of the Hired Man; Home Burial; A Servant to Servants; The Road Not Taken; An Old Man's Winter Night; The Oven Bird; Birches; "Out, Out—"; Stopping by Woods on a Snowy Evening; Two Tramps in Mud Time; Desert Places; Design; The Gift Outright; Directive*
Stevens: *Sunday Morning, A High-Toned Old Christian Woman, Thirteen Ways of Looking at a Blackbird, The Idea of Order at Key West, Of Modern Poetry*
Williams: *The Young Housewife, Portrait of a Lady, The Widow's Lament in Springtime, Spring and All, To Elsie, The Dead Baby, This Is Just to Say, A Sort of a Song*
or
Eliot: *The Love Song of J. Alfred Prufrock*
O'Neill: *Long Day's Journey into Night*
Fitzgerald: *Winter Dreams*
Faulkner: *As I Lay Dying*
Crane: *Chaplinesque, At Melville's Tomb*

Euro-American Female

Cather: *My Mortal Enemy, Neighbour Rosicky*
Stein: *The Good Anna*
or
Lowell: poems
Yezierska: *The Lost "Beautifulness"*
Moore: poems
Porter: *Old Mortality*
Taggard: poems

African-American Male

Toomer: *Cane*
Brown: poems
Hughes: *The Negro Speaks of Rivers, Mother to Son, Mulatto, Song for a Dark Girl*
Wright: *The Man Who Was Almost a Man*

African-American Female

Grimké: poems
Hurston: *The Eatonville Anthology, Their Eyes Were Watching God*

Native American Male

Black Elk: *Black Elk Speaks*

AMERICAN PROSE SINCE 1945

Euro-American Male

Williams: *A Streetcar Named Desire*
Malamud: *The Magic Barrel*
Bellow: *Seize the Day*
Miller: *Death of a Salesman*
Mamet: *House of Games*

Euro-American Female

Welty: *Petrified Man*
O'Connor: *The Life You Save May Be Your Own, Good Country People*
Oates: *Golden Gloves*
Beattie: *Weekend*

African-American Male

Ellison: *Invisible Man*
Baldwin: *The Fire Next Time*
Wilson: *Fences*

African-American Female

Walker: *Everyday Use*

Native American Male

Momaday: *The Way to Rainy Mountain*

Native American Female

Silko: *Lullaby*
Erdrich: *Lulu's Boys*

Latina

Chávez: *The Last of the Menu Girls*

American Poetry since 1945

Euro-American Male

Warren: *Audubon*
Berryman
Lowell: *My Last Afternoon with Uncle Devereux Winslow, Memories of West Street and Lepke, Skunk Hour, Night Sweat, For the Union Dead*
Merrill
Ashbery
or
Wright: *Autumn Begins in Martins Ferry, Ohio; A Blessing; A Finch Sitting out a Windstorm*

Euro-American Female

Bishop: *The Fish, The Bight, At the Fishhouses, Questions of Travel, The Armadillo, In the Waiting Room, One Art*
Levertov: *To the Snake, In Mind*
Rich: *Snapshots of a Daughter-in-Law, "I Am in Danger—Sir—," Orion, A Valediction Forbidding Mourning, Diving into the Wreck, Twenty-One Love Poems*
Plath: *Morning Song, Lady Lazarus, Daddy*

African-American Male

Hayden: *Middle Passage, Homage to the Empress of the Blues, Elegies for Paradise Valley*
Baraka
Harper: *American History, Martin's Blues, Tongue-Tied in Black and White, The Militance of a Photograph in the Passbook of a Bantu under Detention*

African-American Female

Brooks: *kitchenette building, A Song in the Front Yard*
Lorde: *Coal, The Woman Thing, Black Mother Woman, Chain*
Dove: *Thomas and Beulah*

Native American Male

Ortiz

Latino

Ríos

Latina

Cervantes: *For Virginia Chavez; Visions of Mexico While at a Writing Symposium in Port Townsend, Washington; Emplumada*

Asian-American Male

Lee: *The Gift, Persimmons, Eating Alone, Eating Together*

Asian-American Female

Song: *Beauty and Sadness, Lost Sister, Chinatown, Heaven*

The Southern Tradition

The Southern tradition is well represented in NAAL by the following authors.

Volume 1

LITERATURE TO 1620

Smith

1620–1820

Byrd
Jefferson

1820–1865

Longstreet
Harris
Thorpe
Douglass

Volume 2

1865–1914

Harris
Chopin

1914–1945

Porter
Hurston
Faulkner
Wolfe

AMERICAN PROSE AND POETRY SINCE 1945

Welty
Williams
Taylor
O'Connor
Mason
Walker
Warren
Dickey

The Protest Tradition

The tradition of protest literature begins early among the writers represented in NAAL and includes the following authors.

Volume 1

Casas
Cabeza de Vaca
Cherokee Memorials
Apess
Fuller
Stowe
Jacobs
Thoreau
Douglass
Davis

Volume 2

Native American Oratory
Gilman
Du Bois
Oskison
Bonnin
Black Elk
Yezierska
Taggard
Brown
Ginsberg

Marginality in the Euro-American Male Tradition

The following list presents a few works by white male writers that illustrate the relationship between marginality and vision, in effect suggesting that many white male American authors have been members of a self-defined minority.

Volume 1

1620–1820

Williams
Woolman

1820–1865

Irving: *Rip Van Winkle*
Hawthorne: *The Scarlet Letter*
Thoreau: *Walden*
Whitman: *Song of Myself*
Melville: *Bartleby, the Scrivener; Billy Budd, Sailor*

Volume 2

1865–1914

Clemens: *Adventures of Huckleberry Finn*
James: *The Beast in the Jungle*

1914–1945

Anderson: *Winesburg, Ohio; The Egg*
Jeffers: *Shine, Perishing Republic*
O'Neill: *Long Day's Journey into Night*
Fitzgerald: *Winter Dreams*
Faulkner: *As I Lay Dying, Barn Burning*

CHAPTER 5

The Inclusion Approach: Gender, Race, Class, and Region

Planning the Course

If you are new to the concept of inclusion, it may not occur to you to consider NAAL as a resource. You may find yourself in sympathy with the desire white women and women and men from U.S. minority groups have expressed to see themselves reflected in the curriculum, but you may not have believed that possible if your only experience with broadly designed American literature courses was the survey you yourself took as an undergraduate. One alternative is to consider the literary traditions approach (see Chapter 4), which in effect combines the major authors approach with an attempt to define major authors from various traditions. This approach asserts that major authors exist—perhaps in some unofficial canon—and that one way of reflecting white women and women and men from minority groups in the syllabus is to construct a series of alternative "canons." When I first created this Guide almost a decade ago, this seemed like a reasonable approach to inclusion.

By the mid-1990s, however, proponents of curriculum inclusion have begun to focus on the intersections of gender, race or ethnicity, class, region, and sexual orientation as they provide the social context within which writers create literature. The inclusion approach thus differs from the literary traditions approach by assuming that literary texts are written within social, historical, political, and economic contexts, indeed that social and material conditions affect the writing of the text as much as if not more than the individual character or personality of the author. Conversely, the inclusion approach also asserts that literary texts themselves affect the very social and cultural contexts from which they emerge. Therefore, much more is at stake than simply including a few white women writers or a few writers—men or women—from minority groups, if you are committed to presenting an inclusive American literature. In effect, the inclusion approach becomes a survey of the ways in which gender, race, class, and region intersect in the literary work as well as the way in which the literary text, in its representations of gender, race, class, and region, thereby constructs the reader's view.

NAAL allows you to begin with texts that introduce students to some preliminary concepts and still retain a chronological organization that may provide a degree of familiarity, since the course will otherwise challenge students' assumptions about literature and about the world in which they live. In particular, the "Literature to 1620" section (see Chapters 7 and 8) introduces students to the concept of encounter and displaces the term they are probably more familiar with—*discovery*—both as a reference to the early narratives that precede colonial American literature and as a description of the process of human and cultural interaction that Europeans and indigenous peoples experienced during exploration and colonization. To ask students to view colonization and conquest from the point of view of the colonized and conquered peoples—as some of the works included in the "Literature to 1620" section do—will likely produce resistance in some students, because it invites them to question the paradigm from within which they, and generations of American students before them, have been taught to view the earliest experiences of Europeans in the New World. Include especially the selections from Bartolomé de las Casas, Álvar Núñez Cabeza de Vaca, and Arthur Barlowe to provide evidence of the responses of the native peoples to their own encounter with the Europeans.

Each of the approaches to the teaching of the large body of material represented in NAAL offers in effect a conceptual framework for organizing that material, providing students with questions to ask as they read and the instructor with questions around which to shape discussion. The concept of encounter that emerges from the "Literature to 1620" section establishes a series of dialogical relationships that do indeed help the instructor "to organize" the teaching of NAAL: dialogue between reader and text; between text and social, historical, and cultural context; and between reading texts and "reading" culture. These dialogical relationships constitute the conceptual framework of the inclusion approach, because that approach asks students to take a complex view of the literature they read: How does a given work represent the material lives of the lyric voices or the characters it depicts? What cultural ideologies underpin this representation? Whose or what interests does the representation serve? How might the voices or characters in the literary work respond to their own representation? Such an attack moves considerably away from the formalism of the New Critics' close reading approach, but the inclusion perspective argues that students must still read closely and also promotes their ability to read their own culture critically.

In such an approach to the American literature course, gender, race, class, and region become categories by which society organizes hierarchies of status and value and by which literary texts either inscribe or critique. The approach assumes that literary texts contribute to constructing these cultural hierarchies, that this occurs even if the literary work (or author) appears to be unconcerned with politics or ideology, and that students read from within structures of value whether or not they are aware of doing so. The approach further assumes that any exploration of the question "What is American literature?" requires helping students bring into focus the particular strategies by which U.S. society has established its hierarchies. What is "American" about American literature thus becomes the extent to which these literary texts both reflect and construct—and more rarely, critique—social and cultural values that privilege Euro-Americans, the masculine gender, propertied persons of some wealth, and the perspective of the Northeast region over all others. The inclusion approach thus adds to the syllabus Native American writers and writers from other racial and ethnic U.S. minorities; women from all racial groups; and writers who bring issues of class, region, and sexual orientation into our scope. At the same time, it addresses questions about representations of gender, race, class, and region in the works of those Euro-American male writers whom anthologies like this one have helped canonize. In the American literature survey taught with the inclusion approach, students explore the ways cultural ideologies about gender, race, class, and region in the United States influence their interpretations of what they read (and what they believe constitutes "good" literature) and reflect on this influence both in oral and written work.

We've all heard that students retain only a small fraction of what they learn in any given course six months after the course is over. Such a fact, if true, makes organizing a survey course especially daunting. I have come to the conclusion, however, that what really happens is that when course material confirms the biases and paradigms students bring with them to class, they are even less likely to remember course content, because what they are really learning is that the content of this particular course confirms the map of the world they already have. There is little need for them to remember discussions that confirm what they already know. On the other hand, courses taught from an inclusion approach challenge those same biases and paradigms, and students respond in a variety of ways to the challenge. Because such a course teaches a new way of looking at the world (in this case, of American literature and, by extension, what it means to be an American citizen), some students become intellectually stimulated by the encounter and may retain more than they normally would have. And other students may resist learning at all, either grossly by working harder in class to reinforce the biases and paradigms, especially about gender and race, that they brought with them (I think it is no accident that students sometimes test the inclusion instructor by making comments and jokes that are sexist and racist or by claiming their right to continue to hold their own prejudices) or more subtly by raising questions about "good" literature and aesthetic value. If the combined effect of your choice of literary works for your syllabus and your decision to introduce gender, race, class, region, and sexual orientation as categories of analysis for the interpretation of those works produces resistance on your students' part, you may at least conclude that you have successfully adopted the inclusion approach.

Suggested Readings

Because this approach questions the idea that to be culturally literate, readers have to have read certain classic works that other readers will also have read, it becomes difficult to prescribe lists of authors and works (as I have done in other chapters in this Guide). Please consult Chapter 4 for lists that categorize works by race and gender for each period and volume of NAAL. Also consult particular thematic lists given in Chapter 6. The works cited in the lists titled "The Immigrant (and Migration) Experience"; "Family Relationships and Attitudes toward Children"; "Race, Segregation, and Slavery"; and "Gender Issues of Women's Lives, Work, and Vision" offer useful ideas for the construction of a syllabus that specifically addresses gender, race, or class. Many of the works cited in the lists "The Individual and the Community" and "The American Dream" allow you to explore the intersections of these categories of analysis.

Region as a category may include works from those in the thematic list "The American Landscape" and the series of what I have termed "indigenous genres" in Chapter 6. In fact, the lists of suggested readings in the "Genre" section may be read dialogically, as I have set them up for each period as major genres and indigenous genres. All of the indigenous genres are explicit in the way gender, race, class, or region inform the genres themselves. Most may be read at least in part as offering a critique, even as establishing a literature that resists hierarchies of dominance. The following list identifies those indigenous genres that offer a critique of American culture from the perspective of gender, race, class, region, and/or sexual orientation.

VOLUME I

Early regionalism
Slave narrative

VOLUME II

Folk literature
Feminist writing
Regionalism
Black fiction and poetry
Jewish fiction
Southern fiction
Regional fiction
Beat poetry
Feminist poetry
Protest and political poetry
Regional poetry

The "naturalist" writers of the 1865–1914 period also offer critique, especially of gender and class.

Some indigenous genres are more problematic in terms of critique and sometimes, but not always, work to reinforce cultural stereotypes. See, for example, Indian captivity narrative and humor of the old Southwest.

Sexual Orientation as a Category of Analysis

If you are interested in examining representations of lesbian and gay experience, you will need to make this category more visible for students. The following list includes writers believed to be lesbian or gay, writers whose work raises questions concerning what Adrienne Rich has called "compulsory heterosexuality," and writers who have produced works of interest in the study of cultural representations of lesbian and gay experience. Be prepared for much student resistance to discussing this category. Heterosexuality may not even be implicit in a work, and students will assume that any interaction between male and female characters is evidence of heterosexual attraction; conversely, unless a writer explicitly uses the term *lesbian* or *gay* (and few if any writers in NAAL do so), many students will resist interpretations of a literary work or a character that foreground the representation of lesbian or gay experience.

Volume I

LITERATURE TO 1620

(Representations of La Malinche in Cortés and Pocahontas in Smith suggest that colonization follows the paradigm of heterosexual conquest.)

1620–1820

Bradford: Book II, Chapter XXXII [A Horrible Case of Bestiality] (establishes Bradford's concept of sexual deviance)
Byrd: *The Secret Diary* (represents the politics of marriage as access to economic power for men)
Bradstreet: poems and Adams and Adams: letters (establish loving heterosexual relationships as the paradigm for the republic)
Tyler: *The Contrast* (mocks the "coquette" but constructs heterosexuality as a feature of Yankee life)

1820–1865

Irving: *The Legend of Sleepy Hollow* (represents the "masculine" Brom Bones and the "effeminate" Ichabod Crane; suggests that the real relationship in the story is not the putatively heterosexual attraction of Ichabod for Katrina Van Tassel, but rather the rivalry of dominance between the men, which ends in a variation on erotic conquest)
Longstreet: *A Sage Conversation* (male narrators mock the matrons for their lack of acquaintance with the fact of, and jokes about, male homosexuality)
Hawthorne: *The Scarlet Letter,* [Herman Melville] (contrasts relationship between Dimmesdale and Chillingworth with that between Dimmesdale and Prynne; notes evidence of his relationship with Melville from Hawthorne's perspective)
Poe: *The Sleeper, Annabel Lee* (represent the dead woman as the best partner for a male lover); *Ligeia* (constructs heterosexuality as death)
Fuller: *The Great Lawsuit* (critiques the reality of marriage and its effects on women)
Whitman: *Calamus* poems contrasted with *Children of Adam* poems
Melville: *Hawthorne and His Mosses, Letters to Hawthorne* (depicts the pervasive single-sex world of Melville's fiction)
Dickinson: 249, 520 (and other poems reflect homoerotic as well as heteroerotic themes)

Volume II

1865–1914

Clemens: *Adventures of Huckleberry Finn* (like the relationship between Dimmesdale and Chillingworth in Hawthorne's *The Scarlet Letter,* the relationships between Huck and Tom and Huck and Jim, as Leslie Fielder commented years ago, reflect the homoerotic bond that becomes possible to trace in much of American literature)

Jewett: A *White Heron* (Sylvy rejects the requirement of "compulsory heterosexuality" and refuses to tell the heron's secret to the attractive hunter)
Freeman: A *New England Nun* (Louisa Ellis rejects social pressures to marry)

1914–1945

Stein: *The Good Anna*
Lowell
Grimké
H. D.
Crane

AMERICAN PROSE SINCE 1945

Williams: *A Streetcar Named Desire* (see Chapter 7)
Baldwin: *The Fire Next Time*

AMERICAN POETRY SINCE 1945

Duncan
Merrill
Ginsberg
Rich: esp. *Twenty-One Love Poems*
Lorde

CHAPTER 6

Discussions of Genre and Theme

Genre

Genre raises one of the central questions in the study of American literature, namely the dialectic between imitative and indigenous voices and forms. Our own teachers taught us that those writers who imitated British poets and adapted English genres were thereby flawed, and we may find ourselves apologizing for the lack of originality throughout the entire body of American literature before the mid-nineteenth century, when we can finally point to Walt Whitman as the first "American" poet. Yet focusing on the awareness of form in our earliest writers can help students begin to consider American literature itself as a process rather than a product. And the continual metamorphosis of American literature often accompanies changes in the theological, political, or cultural "forms of being" that writers express and address. Unlike British literature, in which readers may compare ballads, sonnets, villanelles, and epic poems written in different centuries, American literature has produced a history of genre marked by idiosyncrasy and discontinuity between periods.

The perennial change in the forms of American literature from its colonial origins to the present day provides the instructor with a rich source of questions for consideration in the classroom: How do the major genres of a particular literary period reflect the thinking of the time? In what ways does experimentation with literary form produce change in social or political thinking? How does any given literary work both adhere to and work against its apparent form? What is the thematic or ideological "content" of certain genres in American literature? Do some genres (such as the Puritan sermon) actually contain elements of forms they appear to reject (such as drama)? In a literature marked by a proliferation of genres, what constitutes originality or experimentation?

In his general introduction to the 1820–1865 period in NAAL, Hershel Parker talks about what he calls "the new Americanness of American literature" and the difficulty critics have had then and ever since trying to define that "special quality" that makes a writer or a work American. What characterizes the special quality of American genres in that or any other period? Are some genres more "American" than others? Does indigenous vision per se help define the Americanness of American literature, and if so, does it produce indigenous genres? If not, what does explain the invention of the Indian captivity narrative or the slave narrative? How does a work written in a traditional genre, such as the picaresque *Adventures of Huckleberry Finn,* achieve its originality?

While autobiography itself was not an American invention, Benjamin Franklin invented his own *Autobiography;* what makes it unique? Are American writers such as William Cullen Bryant and Robert Frost less "American" when they choose traditional poetic forms?

The genres some writers choose are difficult to categorize. Is *The Scarlet Letter* a novel or a romance, and what is the distinction? Is *Moby-Dick* a novel at all? Is *The Education of Henry Adams* a work of fiction or history? Is Native American oratory literature at all (or what is the relationship between oral forms and their written transcriptions)? Should we worry that American literature has not yet produced an epic poet?

And what of those writers and works that really do create continuity of form that crosses literary periods? Despite the array of writers (especially in the nineteenth century) who appeared to invent their own forms and who produced texts that are "classic" partly because of their uniqueness, American writers also worked together in genres that would accumulate the force of tradition. Elements of Puritan literature continued to influence American forms long after the decline of Puritanism. The regionalism of late-nineteenth-century writers such as Sarah Orne Jewett and Mary E. Wilkins Freeman appears to undergo simultaneous metamorphosis and rebirth in the southern women writers of the twentieth century. Although modernists rejected tradition and Ezra Pound issued a call to "make it new," late-nineteenth-century literary realism provides the narrative design for our most experimental modernist fiction writer, William Faulkner. How does the presence of literary influence contribute to the development of an American literature?

Despite the individualism of American myth, each literary period has produced writers who worked closely together and commented on each others' work. How do the forms of, for example, *The Declaration of Independence* or *The Waste Land* reflect the collaborative process of their composition? The authors of slave narratives often quite literally worked in collaboration with Northern abolitionist presses and editors, as did the Native American writer Black Elk. Authors as different as Edward Taylor and Harriet Beecher Stowe claimed to owe their inspiration and even their works to God. How does a writer's understanding of his or her source of literary authority affect genre? How do related questions of audience and literary convention affect the American writer's choice of form?

In the lists that follow, I have summarized the multiplicity of American literary genres and identified writers by the forms in which they primarily worked. Whatever model you choose to guide your course organization, uncovering the peculiar facts about American genres that any attempt to categorize them reveals will enhance your ability to present the large picture of American literature for your students.

Suggested Readings

Volume 1

LITERATURE TO 1620

Major genre: Historical writing
Indigenous genre: Stories of the Beginning of the World

Writers Organized by Genre

Historical writing: Columbus, Casas, Cortés, Díaz del Castillo, Cabeza de Vaca, Barlowe, Harriot, White, Champlain, Percy, Smith
Stories of the Beginning of the World: Iroquois and Pima versions

1620–1820

Major genres: lyric (primarily religious poetry), nonfiction writing, sermon
Indigenous genre: Indian captivity narrative

Writers Organized by Genre

Historical writing: Bradford, Morton, Mather
Indian captivity narrative: Rowlandson
Journal: Winthrop, Sewall, Byrd, Woolman

Lyric poetry: Bradstreet, Taylor, Freneau, Wheatley (Wigglesworth and Edwards wrote theological poetry)
Mock epic: Barlow
Public/political writing: Bradford (Book II, Chapter XI [The Mayflower Compact]), Williams, Franklin, Crèvecoeur, Paine, Jefferson (*The Declaration of Independence* and letters), Hamilton and Madison (as *The Federalist* papers), Barlow (some of the poetry)
Sermon: Winthrop, Taylor *(Sermon VI)*, Mather *(Bonifacius)*, Edwards, Occom
Travel literature: Knight, Crèvecoeur
Conversion narrative: Ashbridge
Slave narrative: Equiano
Drama: Tyler

1820–1865

Major genres: fiction, journals and letters, literary statement, lyric poetry, philosophical essay
Indigenous genres: early regionalism, "Southwest humor," slave narrative

Writers Organized by Genre

Early regionalism: Stowe
Fiction: Irving, Cooper, Longstreet, Hawthorne, Poe, Stowe, Harris, Thorpe, Melville, Stoddard, Davis
Journals and letters: Emerson, Thoreau, Dickinson
Literary statement: Cooper, Emerson, Hawthorne, Poe, Whitman, Melville
Lyric poetry: Bryant, Emerson, Longfellow, Whittier, Poe, Holmes, Lowell, Whitman, Melville, Dickinson
Philosophical essay: Emerson, Thoreau
Political writing: Cherokee Memorials, Apess, Lincoln, Fuller, Thoreau, Douglass
Slave narrative: Jacob, Douglass
Southwest humor: Longstreet, Harris, Thorpe

Volume 2

1865–1914

Major genres: naturalism, realism, regionalism
Indigenous genres: folk literature, local color, regionalism, Native American oral literature

Writers Organized by Genre

Feminist writing: Gilman, Addams
Folk literature: Harris, Chesnutt
Historical writing: Addams, Adams
Humor: Clemens
Literary statement: Clemens, Howells, James
Local color writing: Clemens, Harte, Harris, Garland, Crane
Lyric poetry: Crane
Naturalism: Clemens, Chopin, Gilman, Norris, Crane, Dreiser, London
Public/political writing: Native American Oratory, Washington, Du Bois
Realism: Clemens, Howells, Bierce, James, Wharton
Regionalism: Jewett, Chopin, Freeman, Chesnutt, Austin, Oskison, Bonnin
Native American oral literature: Cochise, Charlot, Wovoka; The Navajo Night Chant, Chippewa songs, Ghost Dance songs
Autobiographical writing: Eastman, Gilman, Addams, Bonnin, Adams

1914–1945

Major genres: lyric poetry, realism in drama, fiction
Indigenous genres: African-American fiction and poetry, southern regionalism, Native American autobiography

Writers Organized by Genre

African-American fiction: Hurston, Toomer, Wright
Realistic drama: O'Neill
Experimental prose: Stein, Faulkner
Humor: Parker, Thurber
African-American lyric poetry: Grimké, Brown, Hughes, Cullen
Dramatic lyric: Masters
Folk lyric: Sandburg
Longer modernist poem: Williams, Pound, H. D., Eliot, Crane
Modernist lyric: Stein (represented in NAAL by prose), Lowell, Frost, Stevens, Williams, Pound, H. D., Jeffers, Moore, Eliot, Cummings, Crane
Political/feminist lyric: Taggard, Rukeyser
New critical lyric: Ransom
Traditional lyric: Robinson, Millay, Bogan
Realistic fiction: Cather, Anderson, Yezierska, Porter, Dos Passos, Fitzgerald, Faulkner, Hemingway, Steinbeck

Southern regionalism: Porter, Wolfe
Native American autobiography: Black Elk

AMERICAN PROSE SINCE 1945

Writers Organized by Genre

African-American fiction: Ellison, Walker
Drama: Williams, Miller, A. Wilson, Mamet
Fantasy fiction: Barth, Pynchon
Jewish fiction: Malamud, Bellow, Roth
New York fiction: Cheever, Malamud, Ellison, Bellow, Mailer, Updike, Stone, Beattie
Nonfiction: E. Wilson, Mailer, Baldwin
Southern fiction: Welty, Taylor, O'Connor, Mason, Walker
Regional fiction: Momaday (prose poem), Silko, Chávez, Erdrich

AMERICAN POETRY SINCE 1945

Writers Organized by Genre

Asian-American poetry: Song, Lee
Autobiographical poetry: Roethke, Bishop, Berryman, Lowell, Levertov, Merrill, Ginsberg, Sexton, Rich, Plath
Beat poetry: Ginsberg, Snyder
African-American poetry: Hayden, Brooks, Lorde, Baraka, Harper, Dove
Latino poetry: Ríos, Cervantes
Dramatic lyric: Jarrell, Berryman, Rich
Feminist poetry: Rich, Lorde
The long poem: Merrill, Dove
Love poetry: Roethke, Rich
Native American poetry: Ortiz
Nature and landscape poetry: Niedecker, Warren, Roethke, Bishop, Hugo, Ammons, Merrill, Wright, Snyder, Plath
New York School: O'Hara, Ashbery, Baraka
Poetry of private vision: Warren, Bishop, Berryman, Dickey, Ammons, Merrill, Ashbery, Wright, Merwin
"Projective verse": Olson, Levertov
Protest and political poetry: Lowell, Levertov, Ginsberg, Rich, Baraka
Regional poetry: Hugo
Short lyric meditation: Wilbur, Ammons, Merwin, Wright
War poetry: Jarrell
Experimental poetry: Oppen

Theme

Given the vast array of poems, essays, stories, plays, and literature in other genres included in NAAL, and considering that writers work out in each literary text themes that in a certain sense are individual and idiosyncratic, a listing of categories of themes and the American works in which they appear will necessarily be reductive. In the lists that follow, I have chosen some of the themes that recur throughout American literature and may, therefore, be integrated in classroom discussions however you choose to organize your syllabus. I also suggest some of the texts that directly address the themes. Instead of categorizing those themes that are often termed universal, I have limited myself to certain themes that are characteristic of, though not necessarily exclusive to, the American experience, including the problem of American identity; the individual and the community; the problem and expression of literary authority; the American dream; the American landscape; the immigrant (and migration) experience; family relationships and attitudes toward children; race, segregation, and slavery; gender issues of women's lives, work, and vision; and politics and war.

The Problem of American Identity

American literature becomes an epistemology, a way of knowing, for many American writers. This theme so pervades American literature that it might usefully serve as the basis for an entire course organization, one focused on an American studies approach that would work particularly well for students who are simultaneously enrolled in courses in American history and culture. Here are some of the works and the issues they raise in the texts included in NAAL.

Volume 1

LITERATURE TO 1620 AND 1620–1820

The New World and Its Nature

Casas: *The Coast of Pearls*
Harriot: *A Brief and True Report of the New Found Land of Virginia*
Smith: *A Description of New England*
Bradford: *Of Plymouth Plantation*
Williams: *A Key into the Language of America*
Rowlandson: *A Narrative of the Captivity and Restoration*
Crèvecoeur: *Letter X. On Snakes; and on the Humming Bird*
Equiano: *The Interesting Narrative of the Life*
Freneau: *On the Emigration to America and Peopling the Western Country, The Indian Burying Ground, On Mr. Paine's Rights of Man*
Wheatley: *On Being Brought from Africa to America*

How to Locate Personal Voice in a Theological Society

Bradstreet: *The Prologue, The Author to Her Book, Here Follows Some Verses upon the Burning of Our House, To My Dear Children,* poems addressed to or in memory of family members
Taylor: *Upon Wedlock, and Death of Children; Huswifery*
Ashbridge: *Some Account of the Fore-Part of the Life*
Occom: *Sermon Preached at the Execution of Moses Paul*

Private Papers as a Way of Knowing

Díaz del Castillo: *The True History of the Conquest of New Spain*
Sewall: *The Diary*
Knight: *The Private Journal of a Journey from Boston to New York*
Byrd: *The Secret Diary*
Adams and Adams: letters

Knowledge as Revealed by God

Bradstreet: *Contemplations, To My Dear Children*
Taylor: poems
Wigglesworth: *The Day of Doom*
Mather: *The Wonders of the Invisible World*
Edwards: *Personal Narrative, A Divine and Supernatural Light, Images or Shadows of Divine Things*
Ashbridge: *Some Account of the Fore-Part of the Life*
Woolman: *The Journal*
Wheatley: *Thoughts on the Works of Providence*

Inventing the Pre-Romantic Self

Franklin: *The Way to Wealth, The Autobiography*
Tyler: *The Contrast*

Public and Political Writing as Ways for a Nation to Know Itself

Crèvecoeur: *Letters from an American Farmer*
Paine: *Common Sense; The Crisis, No. 1; The Age of Reason*
Jefferson: *The Declaration of Independence, Notes on the State of Virginia,* letters
The Federalist
Barlow: *The Hasty Pudding*

1820–1865

Fictionalizing the Problem of American Identity

Irving: *Rip Van Winkle*

Defining American Intellectual Thought

Emerson: *The American Scholar, The Divinity School Address, Self-Reliance, The Poet, Fate*
Thoreau: *Thomas Carlyle and His Works*

Evading Self-Knowledge

Hawthorne: *Young Goodman Brown, The Minister's Black Veil, Wakefield, The Scarlet Letter*

The Literature of the Dream World

Poe

Personal Scripture as a Way of Knowing

Thoreau: *Walden*

Slave Narrative as Ontology

Douglass: *Narrative of the Life*
Jacobs: *Incidents in the Life of a Slave Girl*

Self-Invention in New Forms

Whitman: *Leaves of Grass* poems, esp. *Song of Myself; Live Oak, with Moss*

The Limitations of Vision

Melville: letter to Hawthorne [*The Whale*—"All My Books Are Botches"]; *Bartleby, the Scrivener; Billy Budd, Sailor*

Self-Revelation as Vision

Dickinson: 185, 214, 241, 258, 280, 303, 305, 341, 348, 435, 441, 448, 465, 505, 510, 520, 547, 632, 664, 754, 822, 986, 1099, 1129, 1581, 1651, 1732

Volume 2

In the works by writers included in the second volume of NAAL, the question of American identity becomes one among many that interest late-nineteenth-century and early-twentieth-century writers. Although citing the entire table of contents for Volume 2 makes sense here, a brief representative list of works that can organize a thematic syllabus on American identity includes the following.

1865–1914

Clemens: *Adventures of Huckleberry Finn*
James: *Daisy Miller*
Chopin: *The Awakening*
Washington: *Up from Slavery*
Eastman: *From the Deep Woods to Civilization*
Wharton: *Ethan Frome*
Du Bois: *The Souls of Black Folk*
Oskison: *The Problem of Old Harjo*
Bonnin: *Impressions of an Indian Childhood, The School Days of an Indian Girl, An Indian Teacher among Indians*
Adams: *The Education*

1914–1945

Black Elk: *Black Elk Speaks*
Masters: poems
Robinson: poems
Frost: poems, esp. *Once by the Pacific, The Gift Outright, Directive*
Sandburg: *Chicago*
Yezierska: *The Lost "Beautifulness"*
Jeffers: *Shine, Perishing Republic*
Hurston: *How It Feels to Be Colored Me*
Cummings: *Buffalo Bill's; Poem, or Beauty Hurts Mr. Vinal; "next to of course god america i; i sing of Olaf glad and big*
Thurber: *The Secret Life of Walter Mitty*
Toomer: *Cane*
Taggard: *O People Misshapen, Mill Town*
Dos Passos: *U.S.A.*
Fitzgerald: *Winter Dreams*
Crane: *The Bridge*
Brown: *Mister Samuel and Sam, Master and Man*
Hughes: *Refugee in America, Madam and Her Madam, Madam's Calling Cards, Visitors to the Black Belt, Democracy*
Steinbeck: *The Leader of the People*

AMERICAN PROSE SINCE 1945

Bellow: *Seize the Day*
Miller: *Death of a Salesman*
Mailer: *The Armies of the Night*
Momaday: *The Way to Rainy Mountain*
Pynchon: *The Crying of Lot 49*
Wilson: *Fences*

Mamet: *House of Games*
Chávez: *The Last of the Menu Girls*

AMERICAN POETRY SINCE 1945

Warren: *American Portrait: Old Style*
Lowell: *For the Union Dead*
Ginsberg: *Howl, A Supermarket in California, Sunflower Sutra*
Rich: *Diving into the Wreck*

The Individual and the Community

Volume 1

Bradford: *Of Plymouth Plantation*
Mather: *The Wonders of the Invisible World*
Ashbridge: *Some Account of the Fore-Part of the Life*
Jefferson: *The Declaration of Independence*
Hawthorne: *Young Goodman Brown, The May-Pole of Merry Mount, Wakefield, The Minister's Black Veil, The Scarlet Letter*
Thoreau: *Resistance to Civil Government; Walden*
Douglass: *Narrative of the Life*
Whitman: *Song of Myself*
Melville: *Bartleby, the Scrivener*

Volume 2

Clemens: *Adventures of Huckleberry Finn*
James: *Daisy Miller, The Turn of the Screw, The Beast in the Jungle*
Jewett: *A White Heron, The Foreigner*
Chopin: *The Awakening*
Freeman: *A New England Nun, The Revolt of "Mother"*
Wharton: *Ethan Frome*
Addams: *Twenty Years at Hull-House*
Crane: *The Bride Comes to Yellow Sky, The Blue Hotel*
Oskison: *The Problem of Old Harjo*
Adams: *The Education of Henry Adams* (Editor's Preface, Chapters I and XIX)
Bonnin
Masters
Robinson
Cather: *Neighbour Rosicky*
Frost: *The Tuft of Flowers, Mending Wall, The Death of the Hired Man, A Servant to Servants, Departmental, Neither out far nor in Deep*
Anderson: *Winesburg, Ohio*

Eliot: *The Love Song of J. Alfred Prufrock, Tradition and the Individual Talent*
Cummings: *the Cambridge ladies who live in furnished souls; anyone lived in a pretty how town; pity this busy monster,manunkind*
Faulkner
Ellison, *Invisible Man*

The Problem and Expression of Literary Authority

Volume 1

Bradstreet: *The Prologue, The Author to Her Book*
Taylor: *Prologue, Meditation 22, Upon a Wasp Chilled with Cold, Huswifery*
Edwards: *Personal Narrative, Sinners in the Hands of an Angry God*
Franklin: *The Way to Wealth*
Ashbridge
Wheatley: *To S.M., A Young African Painter, on Seeing His Works*
Emerson: *The American Scholar, The Poet, Merlin*
Hawthorne: *The Scarlet Letter* (The Custom-House)
Thoreau: *Thomas Carlyle and His Works; Walden, or Life in the Woods;* journal ([Writing "with Gusto"], [Minott, the Poetical Farmer], [Self-Injunctions on Writing], [The Purpose of a Journal], [Writers of Torpid Words], (Getting Distance before Rewriting], [Grammarians Versus Real Writers])
Douglass: *Narrative of the Life*
Whitman: *Preface to* Leaves of Grass, *Song of Myself, Letter to Ralph Waldo Emerson, Trickle Drops, Here the Frailest Leaves of Me, As I Ebb'd with the Ocean of Life, Good-bye My Fancy!*
Melville: *Hawthorne and His Mosses,* letters to Hawthorne (esp. [*The Whale*—"All My Books Are Botches"], *Moby-Dick*
Dickinson: 185, 441, 448, 505, 528, 754, 1129, 1545, 1575, 1651, letters to Thomas Wentworth Higginson

Volume 2

Clemens: [*The Art of Authorship*]
Howells: *Novel-Writing and Novel-Reading*
James: *The Turn of the Screw*
Chesnutt: *The Goophered Grapevine*
Gilman: *The Yellow Wallpaper*
Wharton: *Ethan Frome*
Adams: *The Education* (Editor's Preface, Chapter I)
Black Elk

Stein: *The Making of Americans*
Stevens: *A High-Toned Old Christian Woman, Thirteen Ways of Looking at a Blackbird, Of Modern Poetry*
Williams: *Portrait of a Lady, The Red Wheelbarrow, The Term, A Sort of a Song, The Dance ("In Brueghel's great picture, The Kermess")*
Moore: *Poetry*
Eliot: *The Love Song of J. Alfred Prufrock, Tradition and the Individual Talent*
Porter: *Old Mortality*
Ellison: *Prologue*
Mailer: *The Armies of the Night*
Barth: *Life-Story*

The American Dream

Volume 1

Columbus: letters
Barlowe: *The First Voyage Made to the Coasts of America*
Franklin: *The Way to Wealth*
Tyler: *The Contrast*
Irving: *Rip Van Winkle*
Hawthorne: *Young Goodman Brown*
Poe: poems and tales
Douglass: *Narrative of the Life*
Whitman: *The Sleepers*
Stoddard: *Lemorne* versus *Huell*

Volume 2

Clemens: *Adventures of Huckleberry Finn*
James: *The Turn of the Screw*
Jewett: *A White Heron*
Chopin: *The Awakening*
Garland: *Under the Lion's Paw*
Wharton: *Ethan Frome*
Adams: *The Education*
Masters: poems
Cather: *My Mortal Enemy, Neighbour Rosicky*
Anderson: *Winesburg, Ohio; The Egg*
Dos Passos: *U.S.A.*
Fitzgerald: *Winter Dreams*
Steinbeck: *The Leader of the* People
Ellison: *Invisible Man* (Chapter I)

Miller: *Death of a Salesman*
Pynchon: *The Crying of Lot 49*
Mamet: *House of Games*

The American Landscape

Volume 1

Barlowe: *The First Voyage Made to the Coasts of America*
Bradford: *Of Plymouth Plantation* (Book I, Chapter IX; Book I, Chapter X)
Morton: *New English Canaan* (Chapter I)
Knight: *The Private Journal of a Journey from Boston to New York*
Byrd: *History of the Dividing Line*
Crèvecoeur: *Letters from an American Farmer*
Jefferson: *Notes on the State of Virginia*
Freneau: *On the Emigration to America and Peopling the Western Country*
Irving: *The Legend of Sleepy Hollow*
Cooper: *The Pioneers*
Bryant: *The Prairies*
Thoreau: *Walden, or Life in the Woods*
Whitman: *Song of Myself* (section 33), *Crossing Brooklyn Ferry*

Volume 2

Clemens: *Adventures of Huckleberry Finn*
Jewett: *A White Heron*
Garland: *Under the Lion's Paw*
Wharton: *Ethan Frome*
Austin: *The Walking Woman*
Cather: *Neighbour Rosicky*
Frost: *The Wood-Pile; Birches; "Out, Out—"; Design; Directive*
Jeffers: *November Surf, Carmel Point*
Crane: *The Bridge*
Wilson: *The Old Stone House*
Momaday: *The Way to Rainy Mountain*
Wright: *A Blessing*
Snyder: *Milton by Firelight; August on Sourdough, A Visit from Dick Brewer; The Blue Sky*

The Immigrant (and Migration) Experience

Volume 1

White: *The Fifth Voyage*
Bradford: *Of Plymouth Plantation*
Franklin: *Information to Those Who Would Remove to America*
Ashbridge: *Some Account of the Fore-Part of the Life*
Crèvecoeur: *Letters from an American Farmer* (Letter III)
Equiano: *The Interesting Narrative of the Life*
Freneau: *On the Emigration to America and Peopling the Western Country*
Wheatley: *On Being Brought from Africa to America*
Cherokee Memorials (anticipating emigration from Georgia)
Whitman: *Song of Myself, Crossing Brooklyn Ferry*
Davis: *Life in the Iron-Mills*

Volume 2

Native American Oratory: esp. Cochise
Jewett: *The Foreigner*
Eastman: *From the Deep Woods to Civilization* (acculturation and assimilation as a form of immigration)
Garland: *Under the Lion's Paw*
Austin: *The Walking Woman*
Dreiser: *Old Rogaum and His Theresa*
Oskison: *The Problem of Old Harjo*
Cather: *Neighbour Rosicky*
Stein: *The Good Anna*
Yezierska: *The Lost "Beautifulness"*
Hughes: *Vagabonds, Refugee in America*
Nabokov: *Pnin*
Malamud: *The Magic Barrel*
Bellow: *Seize the Day*
Roth: *Defender of the Faith*
Levertov: *Illustrious Ancestors*
Plath: *Daddy*

Family Relationships and Attitudes toward Children

Volume 1

Cabeza de Vaca: *The Relation* (esp. [The Malhado Way of Life], [Our Life among the Avavares and Arbadaos], [Customs of That Region])

Bradstreet: *To the Memory of My Dear and Ever Honored Father Thomas Dudley Esq.; To Her Father with Some Verses; Before the Birth of One of Her Children; To My Dear and Loving Husband; A Letter to Her Husband, Absent upon Public Employment; Another* [Letter to Her Husband, Absent upon Public Employment]; *In Reference to Her Children, 23 June, 1659; In Memory of My Dear Grandchild Elizabeth Bradstreet; In Memory of My Dear Grandchild Anne Bradstreet; On My Dear Grandchild Simon Bradstreet; To My Dear Children*
Wigglesworth: *The Day of Doom*
Rowlandson: *Narrative of the Captivity and Restoration*
Taylor: *Upon Wedlock, and Death of Children*
Sewall: *The Diary*
Mather: *Bonifacius*
Byrd: *The Secret Diary*
Adams and Adams: letters
Irving: *Rip Van Winkle*
Longstreet: *The Horse Swap*
Hawthorne: *Young Goodman Brown, Wakefield, Rappaccini's Daughter, The Scarlet Letter*
Fuller: *The Great Lawsuit*
Stowe: *Uncle Tom's Cabin* (Chapter VII)
Jacobs: *Incidents in the Life of a Slave Girl*
Stoddard: *Lemorne* versus *Huell*

Volume 2

Clemens: *Adventures of Huckleberry Finn*
James: *Daisy Miller, The Turn of the Screw*
Jewett: *A White Heron, The Foreigner*
Chopin: *The Awakening*
Freeman: *The Revolt of "Mother"*
Gilman: *The Yellow Wallpaper*
Wharton: *Ethan Frome*
Austin: *The Walking Woman*
Dreiser: *Old Rogaum and His Theresa*
Bonnin: *Impressions of an Indian Childhood, The School Days of an Indian Girl*
Adams: *The Education* (Chapter I)
Masters: poems
Cather: *My Mortal Enemy, Neighbour Rosicky*
Frost: *The Death of the Hired Man; Home Burial; Birches; "Out, Out—"*
Anderson: *Winesburg, Ohio* (esp. *Mother*); *The Egg*

O'Neill: *Long Day's Journey into Night*
Porter: *Old Mortality*
Cummings: *if there are any heavens my mother will(all by herself)have, my father moved through dooms of love*
Thurber: *The Night the Bed Fell*
Taggard: *With Child, At Last the Women Are Moving, To My Mother*
Faulkner: *As I Lay Dying*
Wolfe: *The Lost Boy*
Hughes: *Mother to Son*
Steinbeck: *The Leader of the People*
Welty: *Petrified Man*
Cheever: *The Country Husband*
Malamud: *The Magic Barrel*
Bellow: *Seize the Day*
O'Connor: *The Life You Save May Be Your Own, Good Country People*
Updike: *Separating*
Stone: *Helping*
Mason: *Drawing Names*
Walker: *Everyday Use*
Beattie: *Weekend*
Silko: *Lullaby*
Erdrich: *Lulu's Boys*
Roethke: *My Papa's Waltz*
Lowell: *My Last Afternoon with Uncle Devereux Winslow*
Brooks: *A Song in the Front Yard*
Levertov: *Olga Poems*
Ginsberg: *To Aunt Rose*
Merwin: *To My Brother Hanson*
Rich: *Snapshots of a Daughter-in-Law*
Plath: *Daddy*
Ríos: *Madre Sofía*
Cervantes: *Uncle's First Rabbit*
Song: *Lost Sister*

Race, Segregation, and Slavery

Volume 1

Casas: *The Very Brief Relation*
Cabeza de Vaca: *The Relation*
Smith: *The General History of Virginia*
Bradford: *Of Plymouth Plantation* (Book I, Chapter IX, Book I, Chapter X, Book II, Chapter XIX)
Williams: *A Key into the Language of America*

Rowlandson: A *Narrative of the Captivity and Restoration*
Byrd: *The Secret Diary*
Franklin: *Remarks Concerning the Savages of North America*
Woolman: *The Journal*
Occom: *Sermon Preached at the Execution of Moses Paul*
Crèvecoeur: *Letters from an American Farmer* (Letter IX)
Jefferson: *The Declaration of Independence*
Equiano: *The Interesting Narrative of the Life*
Freneau: *The Indian Burying Ground, To Sir Toby*
Wheatley: *On Being Brought from Africa to America; To S.M., A Young African Painter, on Seeing His Works;* letters
Cherokee Memorials
Apess: *An Indian's Looking-Glass for the White Man*
Emerson: Journal ([Black Slavery versus Quite Other Slaves to Free])
Longfellow: *The Slave's Dream*
Lincoln: A *House Divided, Second Inaugural Address*
Fuller: *The Great Lawsuit* ([Two Kinds of Slavery: Miranda; No Man Is Willingly Ungenerous])
Stowe: *Uncle Tom's Cabin*
Jacobs: *Incidents in the Life of a Slave Girl*
Thoreau: *Resistance to Civil Government, Slavery in Massachusetts*
Douglass: *Narrative of the Life, The Meaning of July Fourth for the Negro*
Whitman: *Song of Myself, The Sleepers*
Melville: *Benito Cereno*

Volume 2

Clemens: *Adventures of Huckleberry Finn*
Native American Oratory
Harris: *The Wonderful Tar-Baby Story, Mr. Rabbit Grossly Deceives Mr. Fox, Free Joe and the Rest of the World*
Jewett: *The Foreigner*
Chopin: *The Awakening*
Washington: *Up from Slavery*
Chesnutt: *The Goophered Grapevine*
Eastman: *From the Deep Woods to Civilization*
Du Bois: *The Souls of Black Folk*
Oskison: *The Problem of Old Harjo*
Native American Chants and Songs
Bonnin: *Impressions of an Indian Childhood, The School Days of an Indian Girl, An Indian Teacher among Indians*
Black Elk: *Black Elk Speaks*
Grimké: *The Black Finger, Trees*

Hurston: *The Eatonville Anthology, How It Feels to Be Colored Me, Their Eyes Were Watching God*
Toomer: *Cane*
Brown
Hughes
Cullen
Wright: *The Man Who Was Almost a Man*
Ellison: *Invisible Man*
Baldwin: *The Fire Next Time*
Walker: *Everyday Use*
Wilson: *Fences*
Hayden
Lowell: *For the Union Dead*
Brooks
Lorde
Baraka
Harper
Dove: *Thomas and Beulah*

Gender Issues of Women's Lives, Work, and Vision

Volume 1

Winthrop: *The Journal*
Bradstreet: *The Prologue; The Flesh and the Spirit; The Author to Her Book; Before the Birth of One of Her Children; To My Dear and Loving Husband; A Letter to Her Husband, Absent upon Public Employment; Here Follows Some Verses upon the Burning of Our House*
Rowlandson: *A Narrative of the Captivity and Restoration*
Sewall: *The Diary*
Mather: *The Trial of Martha Carrier*
Knight: *The Private Journal of a Journey from Boston to New York*
Byrd: *The Secret Diary*
Ashbridge: *Some Account of the Fore-Part of the Life*
Adams and Adams: letters
Jefferson: *The Declaration of Independence; Letter to Nathaniel Burwell, Esq.*
Irving: *Rip Van Winkle*
Longstreet: *A Sage Conversation*
Emerson: Journal ([The Screaming of the Mad Neighborwoman])
Hawthorne: *Wakefield, Rappaccini's Daughter, The Scarlet Letter*
Poe: *The Sleeper; The Raven; To —— —— ——. Ulalume: A Ballad; Annabel Lee; Ligeia; Fall of the House of Usher; The Philosophy of Composition;* letters to Maria Clemm

Fuller: *The Great Lawsuit*
Stowe: *Uncle Tom's Cabin, The Minister's Housekeeper*
Jacobs: *Incidents in the Life of a Slave Girl*
Harris: *Mrs. Yardley's Quilting*
Whitman: *Preface to* Leaves of Grass, *Song of Myself, Letter to Ralph Waldo Emerson*
Melville: *The Paradise of Bachelors and The Tartarus of Maids*
Stoddard: *Lemorne* versus *Huell*
Dickinson: 67, 187, 214, 249, 303, 312, 322, 348, 435, 441, 505, 510, 520, 528, 732, 754, 952, 1099, 1129, 1545
Davis: *Life in the Iron-Mills*

Volume 2

Clemens: *Adventures of Huckleberry Finn*
Harte: *The Outcasts of Poker Flat*
Howells: *Novel-Writing and Novel-Reading, Editha*
James: *Daisy Miller, The Real Thing, The Turn of the Screw, The Beast in the Jungle*
Jewett: *A White Heron, The Foreigner*
Chopin: *At the 'Cadian Ball, The Storm, The Awakening*
Freeman: *A New England Nun, The Revolt of "Mother"*
Gilman: *The Yellow Wallpaper, Why I Wrote "The Yellow Wallpaper"*
Addams: *Twenty Years at Hull-House*
Wharton: *Ethan Frome*
Austin: *The Walking Woman*
Crane: *The Bride Comes to Yellow Sky*
Dreiser: *Old Rogaum and His Theresa*
Oskison: *The Problem of Old Harjo*
Native American Chants and Songs: *Chippewa Songs*
Bonnin
Adams: *The Education* (Chapter XXV)
Masters: *Serepta Mason, Margaret Fuller Slack, Lucinda Matlock*
Cather: *My Mortal Enemy, Neighbour Rosicky*
Stein: *The Good Anna*
Lowell: *The Captured Goddess, Venus Transiens, Madonna of the Evening Flowers*
Frost: *The Death of the Hired Man, Home Burial*
Anderson: *Winesburg, Ohio (Mother)*
Grimké: *The Eyes of My Regret, A Mona Lisa, To Clarissa Scott Delaney*
Yezierska: *The Lost "Beautifulness"*
Williams: *The Young Housewife, The Widow's Lament in Springtime, To Elsie, The Dead Baby*
Pound: *The River-Merchant's Wife: A Letter*
H. D.: *Leda, At Baia, Helen, The Walls Do Not Fall*

O'Neill: *Long Day's Journey into Night*
Porter: *Old Mortality*
Hurston: *Their Eyes Were Watching God*
Millay
Parker: *De Profundis, Résumé, General Review of the Sex Situation, The Waltz*
Cummings: *the Cambridge ladies who live in furnished souls*
Toomer: *Cane (Fern)*
Taggard: *With Child; To Mr. Maunder, Professional Poet; A Middle-aged, Middle-class Woman at Midnight; At Last the Women Are Moving; To My Mother*
Dos Passos: *U.S.A. (Mary French)*
Fitzgerald: *Winter Dreams*
Bogan: *Women, Cassandra*
Faulkner: *As I Lay Dying*
Hughes: *Mother to Son, Song for a Dark Girl, Madam and Her Madam, Madam's Calling Cards*
Rukeyser: *Effort at Speech Between Two People*
Welty: *Petrified Man*
Williams: *A Streetcar Named Desire*
Cheever: *The Country Husband*
Malamud: *The Magic Barrel*
Ellison: *Invisible Man* (Chapter I)
O'Connor: *The Life You Save May Be Your Own, Good Country People*
Mason: *Drawing Names*
Walker: *Everyday Use*
Wilson: *Fences*
Beattie: *Weekend*
Mamet: *House of Games*
Silko: *Lullaby*
Chávez: *The Last of the Menu Girls*
Erdrich: *Lulu's Boys*
Niedecker
Roethke: *Frau Bauman, Frau Schmidt, and Frau Schwartze*
Bishop: *In the Waiting Room, The Moose, One Art*
Hayden: *Homage to the Empress of the Blues*
Brooks
Levertov: esp. *Olga Poems*
Ginsberg: *To Aunt Rose*
Sexton
Rich
Plath
Lorde
Dove: *Thomas and Beulah*

Ríos: *Madre Sofía*
Cervantes
Song

Politics and War

Volume 1

Columbus: letters
Casas: *The Very Brief Relation*
Díaz del Castillo: *The True History of the Conquest of New Spain*
Cabeza de Vaca: *The Relation*
Stories of the Beginning of the World: *The Story of the Flood*
Bradford: *Of Plymouth Plantation*
Rowlandson: *A Narrative of the Captivity and Restoration*
Franklin: *An Edict by the King of Prussia, The Sale of the Hessians, The Autobiography* (esp. [Part Three])
Adams and Adams: letters
Paine
Jefferson: *The Declaration of Independence*
The Federalist
Freneau: *On Mr. Paine's Rights of Man*
Wheatley: *To His Excellency General Washington*
Barlow: *Advice to a Raven in Russia*
Irving: *Rip Van Winkle*
Cherokee Memorials
Bryant: *Abraham Lincoln*
Emerson: *Hymn Sung at the Completion of the Concord Monument, April 19, 1836*
Hawthorne: *My Kinsman, Major Molineux; [Abraham Lincoln]*
Lincoln
Holmes: *Old Ironsides, The Last Leaf*
Thoreau: *Resistance to Civil Government*
Douglass: *The Meaning of July Fourth for the Negro*
Whitman: *Drum-Taps, When Lilacs Last in the Dooryard Bloom'd, Specimen Days*, letters (to Thomas Jefferson Whitman, to Nathaniel Bloom and John F. S. Gray)
Melville: *Battle-Pieces; Billy Budd, Sailor*

Volume 2

Bierce
Native American Oratory
Eastman

Crane: *An Episode of War, War Is Kind*
Native American Chants and Oratory
Black Elk
Lowell: *September, 1918*
Taggard: *Definition of Song, Mill Town, Silence in Mallorca*
Mailer
Roth
Stone
Jarrell: *90 North, The Death of the Ball Turret Gunner, Second Air Force*
Lowell: *For the Union Dead*
Brooks: *The White Troops Had Their Orders But the Negroes Looked Like Men, The Blackstone Rangers*

CHAPTER 7

Teaching Notes for Individual Periods, Authors, and Works

NAAL contains excellent period introductions, headnotes on each author, and at the end of each volume, selected bibliographies. My intention in the discussions that follow is not to duplicate this material but to offer additional suggestions for teaching that emerge from my own readings of individual works. In some cases, I have chosen to write at length about works or concepts that students find difficult to read or understand at the sophomore or lower-division level. In others, I suggest connections that may stimulate students to compare authors and works, to think across periods or genres, or to assess the development of literary traditions at a given historical moment. I have included some general teaching notes for each historical period and have organized specific readings chronologically according to the placement of authors in NAAL; further suggestions on these and other writers and works in the anthology appear in Chapter 8, "Exam Questions and Essay Topics."

Volume 1

Literature to 1620

With the inclusion of this new section in NAAL, instructors as well as students confront a series of paradigm shifts in the way literary and cultural historians have begun to view the period. As recently as a decade ago, most historians would have referred to the literature before 1620 as the "literature of discovery," but with the realization that, as Wayne Franklin writes in his introduction to the section, "discovery was mutual rather than one-sided," it has seemed more accurate to view this literature as "narratives of encounter." Franklin observes that the different writers of these narratives used their work to serve different purposes: to disseminate information about the West Indies so as to stimulate exploration and colonization; to affect official policy in Europe; and on occasion to describe the behavior of Europeans with a critical eye, to serve as a literature of witness. Only the first two purposes may seem familiar to students from their previous study of the history of the period of colonialism. While reading those narratives that directly or implicitly stand in witness to European attitudes toward the native peoples they encountered, toward the land and its uses, or toward the Europeans' justifications for their behavior, students may begin to understand the devastating impact of colonialism on both the colonizers and the colonized. This collection of narratives comes alive in the classroom to the extent that you help students to encounter the paradigm shift—and in so doing, to recognize the limitations of their previous understanding of the significance of this literature.

Another paradigm that this section dispels for students is the idea that early writings from North America were solely an extension of English colonialism. While England eventually dominated Spain and France in North America, during the sixteenth century the English were followers, not leaders, in the age of European exploration. By beginning with some narratives of Spanish and French exploration and encounter, NAAL conveys the more accurate perspective that in the earliest century of European presence in the Americas, exploration involved several languages and cultures, what Franklin describes as a "great mixing of peoples from the whole Atlantic basin" and as "a many-sided process of influence and exchange that ultimately produced the hybrid cultural universe of the Atlantic world." Indeed, as the Native American creation myths indicate, the continent was already "peopled" upon the Europeans' arrival, and the languages of the native inhabitants of the Americas would also contribute to this hybrid cultural universe. One important result of including this section in your syllabus is that students who currently view their world as increasingly multicultural may understand that from a historical perspective, America has been multicultural from the moments of European discovery and encounter documented by these narratives. Thus the section also alters the paradigm of "American" literature for students.

As a corollary to this second paradigm shift, and as a preview for students of the shifting borders of American literature in our own time, you might assign Lorna Dee Cervantes's poem *Visions of Mexico While at a*

Writing Symposium in Port Townsend, Washington, from Volume 2. In one sense Latina writers like Cervantes have recently "emerged"; in another, they remind us that from its beginnings, American literature involved a multicultural response to land and its peoples and that this response has always created tension in the meaning of the concept American literature. With the inclusion of the "Literature to 1620" section, NAAL challenges the easy equation of American literature with the development of the political and national boundaries of the country that became the United States. The "Literature to 1620" section invites students to encounter the possibility that American literature is more fluid than these boundaries; it invites students to cross them.

CHRISTOPHER COLUMBUS

The selections from Columbus's letters demonstrate for students the contrast between European expectations and the reality of the early colonial experience and provide an exercise in European perspective. Ask students to look for the ways these letters confirm or challenge Columbus's initial assumptions, both about what he would find and about what he was capable of valuing. For example, although he encounters people who flee from him, he disregards the "small hamlets" and sends two men inland "to learn if there were a king or great cities." He reports that they "found an infinity of small hamlets and people without number, but nothing of importance." Apparently, if the people he finds do not have a king or great cities, he is unable to recognize them as important. In contrast, his catalog of the natural wonders of the West Indies—"Espanola is a marvel"—implies that the land itself offers riches of the kind Europeans can recognize—the trees are "as green and as lovely as they are in Spain in May."

Contrast his 1493 letter with his 1503 *Letter to Ferdinand and Isabella Regarding the Fourth Voyage,* in which he complains bitterly of his own abandonment and betrayal and reveals his disillusionment with the experience of colonization. What do students learn about the relative value of kings and great cities, the power of Spanish explorers, and the relative "importance" of the "people without number" who already inhabit the islands? Invite students to view Columbus's experience as as much an encounter with Spain's and his own assumptions as it is an encounter with what for him is a "new" world populated by people without importance.

BARTOLOMÉ DE LAS CASAS

The impact of the "Literature to 1620" section works cumulatively in the way it allows students to contrast perspectives. The excerpt from Casas's *The Very Brief Relation* will underscore the assumptions of the Spanish explorers in their treatment of the Native Americans and provide evidence that not all of the literature during the colonial period was written to justify colonialism. Ask students to comment on Casas's purposes for writing his text; discuss evidence that resistance and critique were powerful forms of writing even in the sixteenth century; locate and discuss passages in *The Very Brief Relation* about cultural genocide, the Spaniards' attitudes toward and treatment of Native American women, and slavery of the native peoples; and point out the early practices of treating American Indians as cargo (a foreshadowing of narratives of the African Middle Passage) and of exploiting them as pearl divers.

Casas witnesses the horrors of the Spaniards' treatment of native peoples. Ask students to detail the atrocities and to comment on Casas's indictment of the Spaniards' claims to be Christians.

HERNÁN CORTÉS

Many of the narratives of discovery include lists, catalogs, or inventories. For Cortés, the gifts of the Aztecs in his *First Letter from Mexico to the Spanish Crown* contrast in terms of both content and style with Casas's inventories of atrocities. Ask students to consider the various uses of the list in this and other narratives of encounter. Cortés's *First Letter* is striking in its suggestion that Mexico's value lies in its objects that can be given—or plundered. The rhetorical effect of such an inventory reduces the complexity of the colonial encounter. People matter so little that they are totally expendable, even in the prose relation of this letter "from Mexico." Spanish greed and Cortés's implementation of the agenda of Conquest define the occasion of the narrative, and the purpose of Cortés's mission is quite literally reduced, as in this narrative, to the desire for the possession of objects.

Ask students to extrapolate from Cortes's list: what skills in art and manufacture can we conclude that the Aztecs possessed?

BERNAL DÍAZ DEL CASTILLO

Like Bartolomé de las Casas, Bernal Díaz del Castillo writes a narrative of witness. Ask students to explore the differences between the imagined audiences for these narratives and those by Columbus and Cortés, who are writing official missives to the Spanish Crown. Does the difference in the implied reader make for differences in the kinds of observations Casas and Díaz del Castillo make and the images they choose? Does literature result in part from the choice to write for almost anyone other than the king and queen?

Díaz del Castillo's narrative "Gifts Presented to Cortés" provides more of the social context than Cortés's list does. Students can find evidence in this brief narrative that the meeting between Spaniards and Aztecs served as an encounter on both sides. The description of the physical resemblance between "our Cortés" and "the other Cortés," the Aztec chief Quintalbor, provides an emblem of the facing off between invaders and indigenous people. The first battle between Cortés and Montezuma is presented as a rhetorical one: whose insistence will allow the speaker to make the next move—Montezuma's that Cortés not try to travel to the Aztec capital to meet him, or Cortés's that he must account to his own king and, therefore, must see Montezuma in person?

The instructor's role in this text, as in the following segment, "The Approach to Tenochtitlán," is to help students locate the understated moments of tension between Cortés and his forces and Montezuma and the Aztecs. Otherwise, the descriptions of violence and the quick shifts from apparent negotiations to killing and Conquest, from gift giving to conflict, seem inexplicable. On Montezuma's side, Díaz del Castillo reports, the Aztecs call the Spaniards *teules*, or "gods," and this may explain why Montezuma does not simply crush Cortés, even though his own gods and priests *(papas)* urge him to do so. Yet such quick shifts perhaps convey the astonishment of Díaz del Castillo himself that such a marvelous place as Tenochtitlán should have been destroyed so quickly.

Another moment that also conveys both the understated tensions between Cortés and Montezuma and the volatility of their encounters occurs near the beginning of the "Cortés in Difficulties" segment. Díaz del Castillo writes, "On hearing Cortés say that he would have to come with us and visit the Emperor, Montezuma was even sadder than before." This "excited conversation" leads the soldiers to wonder "when the fighting would begin," but the shift from apparent diplomacy to anxiety continues to signal the understated conflict of the encounter between Cortés and Montezuma. The fact that Montezuma delays any attack and instead resorts to persuasion, expressing his annoyance that Cortés does not tell him about the arrival of Narvaez's ships and claiming to be "delighted" that "now you can all return to Spain without more discussion," suggests that Montezuma is simply not confident of victory over Cortés and Cortés's god.

Implicit in *The True History of the Conquest of New Spain* is the myth that has been perpetuated in Mexican history and culture that it was a native woman, Dona Marina—often called "La Malinche" to refer to the fact that she is believed to have served as Cortés's mistress (Cortés in this text is referred to as Malinche)—who betrayed the Mexican empire. She is visible in this text at the moment when Cortés first meets Montezuma and she serves as his translator ("Cortés, speaking through Dona Marina, answered him"). Later, she seems to be in Cortés's power or employ and continues to serve as a translator. Discuss with students the effect of introducing a woman as the cultural translator. In attempting to translate, or to mediate, between two such oppositional interests as those of Cortés and Montezuma, Dona Marina is said to have betrayed her country. By implication, without her treachery, the Aztec empire might not have fallen. Ask students to consider this rationally by focusing on the behavior of the Spaniards in this and in other narratives and to speculate on the reasons for the survival of the myth of La Malinche.

The narrator of *The True History of the Conquest* experiences the effects of colonial conquest in his own body. Ask students to locate the passages where this becomes clear and to speculate on his responses. Help students see the connection between the narrator's role in the Conquest of Mexico and his inability to sleep "even when I go to the villages of my *encomienda.*" Does Díaz del Castillo find himself unable to rest because he ever after expects the descendants of the Aztecs to rise up and avenge the Conquest?

Ask students to consider the Aztec practice of cutting out hearts from living persons. Viewed from the perspective of "encounter"—here between Aztec and Spanish forms of violence—discuss colonialism as one form of cutting out the heart from existing societies and invite students to extend the metaphor in specific ways.

ÁLVAR NÚÑEZ CABEZA DE VACA

Cabeza de Vaca's *Relation* contrasts markedly with the narratives of Cortés and Díaz del Castillo, and although this text is written from a European point of view, it attempts to present the native peoples' way of life as much as possible from the inside. Thus the *Relation* serves as evidence that the colonial encounter did indeed have two sides, and that the native peoples of the Americas did not view themselves as deficient before the arrival of the Europeans. Ask students to detail customs and manners of the various people Cabeza de Vaca describes. Notice that he is interested in aspects of their lives that bring women, children, and domestic life into view. Students could trace his references to women's lives in particular and thereby bring women into focus. Cabeza de Vaca's interest in and concern for women (he writes in "The Long Swing-Around" that "among this people, women are better treated than in any part of the Indies we had come through") helps compensate for the lack of attention most other narrators of texts in the "Literature to 1620" section give to women except as myths—such as the myth of Dona Marina in Díaz del Castillo's narrative or, later, the myth of Pocahontas in the writings of John Smith.

Cabeza de Vaca comes close to understanding and communicating with various American Indian groups. Locate with students those moments in his narrative when he seems to come closest to communicating—one may be his description of "Our Life among the Avavares and Arbadaos," in which he describes dressing, eating, and dwelling in the way of his hosts. Cabeza de Vaca resembles a missionary or an anthropologist in his approach to the native peoples he encountered, expressing his great respect for them: "They are a substantial people with a capacity for unlimited development." Perhaps the most significant test of how the Native Americans themselves received Cabeza de Vaca's respect and understanding for their way of life emerges in "The Falling-Out with Our Countrymen," when the American Indians refuse to believe that Cabeza de Vaca and his group were from the same race as the "Christian slavers." The passage near the end of the excerpt that begins "Conferring among themselves, they replied that the Christians lied," conveys the Indians' view of Cabeza de Vaca in imagery that comes close to giving them voice in this narrative.

In this beautiful work, students can deepen their understanding of "encounter" narratives. Cabeza de Vaca makes ample room in his work for readers to see the native people's view of their encounter with him as well as his encounter with them. In a further complication of the term, the *Relation* shows Europeans encountering their own internal contradictions. If resistance to the brutal practices of conquest and colonization was itself capable of transforming one group of Spaniards (Cabeza de Vaca and his group) into men the American Indians no longer recognized as "Christian slavers," then who are the true Europeans? Was it conquest and colonization that turned civilized men into monsters (so that Cabeza de Vaca may be viewed as someone who resists that transformation), or was it encounters with the native peoples themselves that turned Spaniards into potentially civilized men? In any event, the *Relation* offers an encounter between the elements of internal contradiction within European conquest itself.

STORIES OF THE BEGINNING OF THE WORLD

As Arnold Krupat writes in his introductory notes on these creation stories, both the Iroquois and the Pima narratives included here are in a Western chronological sense misplaced, since these versions date from the nineteenth and early twentieth centuries. However, including creation stories in the "Literature to 1620" section of NAAL is pedagogically appropriate. First, these written narratives are transcriptions or translations of oral stories whose origin long precedes such transcription. Second, the Iroquois and Pima narratives present a worldview that contrasts markedly with the worldview the colonizers brought with them. Although these mythological narratives do not address the relatively more recent historical period of contact with the European invaders, they serve as representations of early Native American culture. Teaching them side by side with European narratives of invasion and colonization allows students to view their own reading as encounters of cultures as well as of historical persons.

By far the greatest number of instructors who choose to assign these materials in an American literature course will have nontribal origins and will be trained in Western cultural perspectives—on mythological or cosmological origins as well as on narrative forms and elements. The inclusion of Native American materials in NAAL may occasion anxiety for those instructors who have not been trained to teach these materials or to recognize their distinctive features and who do not consider themselves experts or even knowledgeable in Native American culture, literature, or history. Most will acknowledge an uneasy sense that mainstream American history has contributed to stereotyping Native Americans. The question becomes one of whether there is a way to teach Native American materials in the American literature classroom without distortion and misrepresentation by the instructor who is seeking more knowledge about Native American literature but has not yet approached expertise.

Becoming grounded in the differently conceived and expressed worldview of the Native American creation stories should provide such an instructor with a base on which to build further knowledge. Thus it is worthwhile spending the time to become immersed in these texts and to examine some useful criticism about them. Clearly, this resembles the task students must also accomplish; therefore, I recommend reading an essay and having two introductory reference books on hand that will make the task of beginning to understand Native American literature finite and efficient for already overburdened instructors. The two books that will provide brief literary and historical background (and can serve as reference works) for most of the Native American texts included in NAAL are A. LaVonne Brown Ruoff's *American Indian Literatures: An Introduction, Bibliographic Review, and Selected Bibliography* (1990) and Andrew Wiget's *Native American Literature* (1985). The essay that teaches instructors how to recognize differences between elements of tribal narrative and superimposed elements of Western culture on transcriptions of tribal narrative is Paula Gunn Allen's "Kochinnenako in Academe" (in *Feminisms*, edited by Robyn Warhol and Diane Price Herndl, 1991). Allen's essay is also useful because she proposes a "feminist-tribal" approach to Native American narrative. This approach allows readers to understand the agency Native American narratives give women, and Allen distinguishes between feminist interpretations that fail to recognize elements of Western colonial content and a blending of feminist and tribal perspectives that may allow readers to read beyond the overlay of Western (and in the Yellow Woman story she is interpreting, patriarchal) perceptual modes. For Allen, these perceptual modes block the reader's ability to perceive Native American stories as about balance rather than conflict, agency rather than heroism, background rather than an overvalued foreground; indeed, these dualisms themselves become a Western overlay on an indigenous art better described, in Allen's terms, as a "living web of definition and depth" with an "importance of balance among all elements." Allen eloquently describes the implications of narrative structure: "tribal art functions something like a forest in which all elements coexist, where each is integral to the being of the others." For further discussion of the relationship between women and Native American texts and for alternative texts by and about women that can supplement your assignments in NAAL, see Paula Gunn Allen's *The Sacred Hoop: Recovering the Feminine in American Indian Traditions* (1986).

The Iroquois Creation Story

To begin to compensate for students' initial lack of familiarity, indeed, to increase their recognition that just because they can read written texts does not make them easy experts on written transcriptions of Native American oral texts, it is important to give class time over to a close reading of these creation stories. By *close reading* I do not mean to imply that attention to the texts themselves, and to the texts alone, will yield understanding for students who may become dispirited or impatient with the unfamiliarity of Native American materials. As you assign other Native American texts, these will create an intertextuality, and instructors will find much assistance from the headnotes and introductory materials in NAAL in providing the historical and oral/literary contexts for Native American stories and storytellers. However, readers trained in Western assumptions about literary texts will more readily discard these if the process of doing so emerges from their own response to the myths. Therefore, I encourage students to read closely in the sense of reading slowly, reading visually; and while beginning with the biblical creation story most of them already know, giving close scrutiny to the Native American creation myths and differences between these and the Bible's story. The instructor can do several exercises with students that will begin to demonstrate how these narratives are unfamiliar precisely because they originate from a worldview that is different from the Western, and certainly from the colonizers', view.

In one such exercise, construct with students (who may have been assigned this task before coming to class) a visual "map" or interpretive sketch of the events of the Iroquois Creation Story. You will end up with a diagram that has a vertical axis—the woman who conceived (note Krupat's reference to one version in which she conceives parthogenetically) begins in the "upper world" but falls to the "dark world," where "monsters" collect enough earth to make a seat for her, on which she gives birth to the twins, the good mind and the bad mind. (Wiget provides a diagram that connects events in origin stories with genres of

Native American oral narrative.) The twins transform the earthen seat, the Great Island that the monsters have created for the woman who fell, into a world that begins to resemble a world of humans rather than mythical people; indeed, the story ends with the twins retiring from the earth, as the creation has been accomplished. The visual diagram maps three "generations" of beings—the original parent (the woman who fell from the sky), the twins (one of whom, the good mind, creates the earth and, through deceiving the bad mind, sets in motion the "nature of the system" we know as the world), and the first people with souls (who come to inhabit the universe). Within these three levels, numerous narratives are possible; the Iroquois Creation Story students have before them is only one variant of a story whose main elements may be relatively fixed but that relies on communal and participatory retelling. Communal participation results from viewing creation as a process of descent rather than a consequence of a world constructed once, and for all time, in a single god's image.

Students may also read the account of the creation in the Book of Genesis and compare elements of the two myths: descent in the Iroquois story privileges a process of creation rather than the act of a single creator; the woman who fell from the sky may have become parthenogenically pregnant, thereby linking the origins of the world to women (or to an asexual being capable of parthenogenesis) rather than to a patriarchal god (note that the Iroquois were matrilineal); and the monsters in the "dark world" are benign compared with the devils that inhabit Western conceptions of hell, and these monsters actually help the falling woman give birth. Note that when the good twin begins the work of creation, it takes "the parent's head" (i.e., the mother's head) and sets it in the sky as the sun and takes the "remnant of the body" and sets it in the sky as the moon (thus associating the mother, instead of the father as in Judeo-Christian myth, with a life-giving, light-giving, and life-reflecting force). The good twin then creates "two images of the dust of the ground in his own likeness," unlike the single male image the Western god creates in Genesis; the second female image is later created from a rib of the male.

A third exercise that helps open up the Iroquois Creation Story for Western-oriented students involves making up a list of the characters in the myth and trying to determine each one's particular contribution, without which the creation would not be complete. While a Western-oriented, linear narrative might suggest that the woman who fell from the sky and the good twin are "central" characters, the Iroquois story highlights the importance of the other characters and the interdependence of all. The turtle, for example, who offers to endure the falling woman's weight and who enlarges to become an island of earth is essential to the origin of the world, as are the contrivances of the bad twin, without whom we would not have apes, mountains, waterfalls, reptiles, and the idea that even the good twin's powers are limited (as are those of humans). The points here seem to be that there is no human agency without emerging help from a variety of participants and there is no creative—or created—force that must not also recognize its limitations. How different is the worldview that such an origin narrative generates from a worldview in which a single creator elaborates a world in his own image and sets evil in the world to trap—rather than limit—humankind. If possible, read Wiget's beautiful interpretation of the story of the woman who fell. He says, in part,

> The Earth-Diver is the story of the Fortunate Fall played out against a landscape more vast than Eden and yet on a personal scale equally as intimate. It is a story of losses, the loss of celestial status, the loss of life in the depths of the sea. But it is also the story of gifts, especially the gift of power over life, the gift of agriculture to sustain life, and the gift of the vision to understand man's place as somewhere between the abyss and the stars.

Pima Stories of the Beginning of the World

As Wiget's diagram of Native American oral narrative genres makes clear, there are two main story lines within various Native American creation myths: the stories that center around the "woman who fell from the sky," and those that depict the "emergence" of the world. The Pima Story of Creation provides students with an example of the second kind, although students who wish to explore very different conceptions of emergence myths may want to read, or read about, Navaho or Pueblo myths. One of the images that distinguishes the emergence narrative, and here gives the Pima myth some elements of that genre, is the ability of Juhwertamahkai to poke a hole in the sky with his staff and to "emerge" through this hole into another dimension, where he begins his act of world creation anew. Some scholars have associated the emergence of a people through a hole in the ground or sky with the numerous migrations of Native American peoples and their myths that record those migrations.

In discussing this story, students can compare and contrast within Native American traditions—locating similarities and differences between Iroquois and Pima myths—as well as between Native American and Western versions of "genesis." The point to make here is that even though many Native American creation stories clustered around two main story lines, the very concept of creation, or origins, itself seems to have inspired the creation of many variations on creation itself. Unlike the Judeo-Christian story told in Genesis, which identifies one and only one story of origin (which was not seriously challenged until the work of Charles Darwin, another kind of storyteller), Native American traditions proliferate creation stories, as if the very fecundity of the creation process presupposed multiplicity not monotheism. And this particular Pima story does not include many elements of other emergence narratives (see Wiget for a description of these).

At first glance, the Pima Story of Creation resembles the story of Genesis more closely than the Iroquois story. In the Pima, as in Genesis, the world begins "in the beginning" with a person who floated in the darkness; in Genesis, the spirit of God hovers over the darkness. Understanding the perils of the transcription of Native American legends is crucial to "reading" the opening of this story, because the language of the transcription itself echoes the language of Genesis. This leads to the question of whether this language truly characterizes the original Pima oral narrative or if it represents that oral story as viewed through the eyes of a translator who, despite his intentions to transcribe the stories of Thin Leather, still views creation through the lens of the Western Bible.

As the story progresses, it ceases to resemble Genesis. Indeed, Juhwertamahkai makes several mistakes in the process of creating the world. Unlike the Western god, whose destruction of the world by flood is blamed on human behavior, Juhwertamahkai takes a trial-and-error approach to creation, starting over or letting the sky fall each time the creative act sets in motion a process that will not sustain life. As the notes point out, he makes the world four times before he is satisfied with his creation, establishing the number four (corresponding to north, south, east, and west) as significant in Native American cosmology.

The Pima Story of Creation includes the birth of Coyote, the trickster of many Native American legends, and the arrival of Seeurhuh, or the elder, who in this story seems to move the creation into a world of negotiation between powerful personages who "claimed to have been here first," perhaps suggesting the process of relating stories about the organization of the social world into native cultures. In the narrative that follows, the Pima Story of the Flood, Seeurhuh, or Ee-ee-toy, and Juhwertamahkai seem to engage in a struggle to determine, as the headnote points out, not creation but re-creation, "the reestablishment or rebirth of the divine, natural, and social orders." Ask students in reading the Story of the Flood to note images or details that indicate imbalance in this social order. For example, even though Juhwertamahkai has already created people, Ee-ee-toy makes a man of his own, arming him with bow and arrow. Then, when this man marries, word of him strikes fear in the marriagable daughter of the South Doctor (presumably a "doctor of the earth" or shaman with powers that resemble those of Juhwertamahkai and Ee-ee-toy). The arrival of the flood itself is an image of turmoil, as is the array of plans the doctors and other persons/animals make for escaping the flood. As the story unfolds, the arrival of the flood is linked to the birth of a child from the young man who turns into a pregnant woman;

the birth produces springs that "would gush forth from under every tree and on every mountain."

The struggle between Ee-ee-toy and Juhwertamahkai may also be an attempt to achieve balance. One way of showing this is to ask students to trace and try to account for Juhwertamahkai's behavior during and after the flood. The two doctors, Juhwertamahkai and Ee-ee-toy, and the person/animal Toehahvs (Coyote) face directions that may imply territories or tribal lands, and they make new dolls, or persons, to replace those who have drowned. Juhwertamahkai deliberately makes dolls that will not survive, "because he remembered some of his people had escaped the flood thru a hole in the earth, and he intended to visit them and he did not want to make anything better than they were to take the place of them." But the defective dolls break to pieces, Juhwertamahkai turns into waste and excretion, and the original creator of the world in the Pima Story of Creation brings sickness and death into that world. While the Story of the Flood may help listeners to understand death, and especially war, it may also associate such things with the work of the spirits; Juhwertamahkai's creation ultimately includes both birth and death, and this establishes order in the world.

ARTHUR BARLOWE AND THOMAS HARRIOT

As I noted in my comments on Álvar Núñez Cabeza de Vaca, the encounters between the Spaniards and the American Indians revealed an internal contradiction within the Conquest. This internal contradiction may seem more muted to students in the earliest English narratives, but there are enough similarities between Spanish and English encounters to suggest patterns. Arthur Barlowe's account of Wingina and his people resembles that of Cabeza de Vaca, and like the Spaniard, Barlowe also is interested in the customs of the American Indians, and in bringing women into focus; he describes their material lives in great detail. Barlowe's description of the people ranks with the respect Cabeza de Vaca showed; indeed, Barlowe's description creates a very different image of Native Americans from that of later English authors, especially when he writes, "We found the people most gentle, loving, and faithful, void of all guile and treason, and such as live after the manner of the golden age."

After reading Barlowe, students will find Harriot much less perceptive and more insensitive to the native peoples he meets. Ask students to locate evidence of Harriot's inability to move outside his own perspective: early in his *Brief and True Report,* he writes, "In respect of us, they are a poor people, and for want of skill and judgment in the knowledge and use of our things, do esteem our trifles before things of greater value." He also uses the American Indians' mythology to demonstrate their ignorance, thereby illustrating for students the limitations of his perspective.

One aspect of this mythology that contrasts markedly with Christianity concerns the Native American belief that "a woman was made first, who by the working of one of the gods, conceived and brought forth children." Harriot does not need to point out the absurdity of such a myth of origins, given the Bible's account of Adam; students in today's classroom will also notice the ideological link between religious belief and English attitudes toward women. Part of what Franklin terms Harriot's "propagandistic" purpose involves the conversion of the native peoples to "great doubts of their own [faith], and no small admiration of ours"; this reputed "conversion" lends credence to the English view of themselves as superior—in technology ("mathematical instruments" as well as "writing and reading"), in religion (God "so specially loved" the colonizers), and in ideology (any people who could make the error of believing they were descended from women must indeed be a "simple people"—they do conclude that the English are "not born of women").

SAMUEL DE CHAMPLAIN

Champlain's narrative demonstrates a different strategy for relationship with native peoples than some of the earlier Spanish and English explorers. For Champlain, as his *Voyages* suggests, is more aware of negotiating with people who are an established civilization and who possess their own power. Part of this, as editor Franklin points out, results from the fact that the region he explores is already "thickly settled" before his arrival; at least in part, his approach to negotiation recognizes both the agency of the native peoples he meets (which elevates their significance in his eyes) and his own and his compatriots' ability to make mistakes (which leads him to be more realistic about his own power in negotiation). At the end of Chapter VIII, for example, he writes that his own musket "exploded in my hands and nearly killed me"; at the end of Chapter XIV, some of the men in his group make a fatal miscalculation, disobeying orders to return to the ship and thereby setting themselves up as ready targets the next morning. Throughout Champlain's account, he makes it clear that there is strategy, power, and an agenda both for the French and for the American Indians. Direct your students' attention to one passage that clearly conveys Champlain's sense that while the French have encountered the Indians, they have equally, from their side, encountered the Europeans. The passage occurs near the middle of the excerpt from Chapter XIII, and it might serve as an emblem for the entire "Literature to 1620" section: "As I was walking along the causeway these Indians caught sight of me, and in order to put a good face upon the matter, since they saw clearly that I at the same time had discovered them, they began to shout and dance." Encounter involves both sides discovering that they are each, in turn, discovered. The passage (and Champlain's entire account) contrasts markedly with the narratives of Columbus, Cortés, and Harriot, all of whom seemed to believe that they might observe and judge the Native American without in turn being seen.

JOHN WHITE AND GEORGE PERCY

The brief excerpts from John White and George Percy are worth reading together as accounts of the early results of the English encounter with colonization. White writes about the disappearance of the colony at Roanoke, and Percy writes about "the starving time" in the Virginia colonies. Of the two, Percy's is the more interesting formally because it allows students to contrast his use of the catalog with earlier uses—the extensive lists of bounty in the early Spanish narratives, the inventories of features of landscape, the mappings of the Americas. The extensive list of deaths in Percy offers an ironic commentary on the early harvest of exploration and colonization. The experience of the English colonists proved them to be less godlike than Harriot claimed. The measure of English greatness becomes not victory on the battlefield but survival, made possible by Indians. In light of the genocide against the native peoples that Percy's descendants would practice over the next two centuries, the early equation of survival with victory makes an ironic statement. Ultimately, it was not the English but the native peoples themselves (who had made the survival of the English possible) whose ability to survive the colonial encounter would be in jeopardy.

JOHN SMITH

Although John Smith's *General History of Virginia* chronologically fits in the "Literature before 1620" section, ask students to explore ways in which this narrative has itself become more sophisticated than earlier accounts and in which the English attitudes toward Native Americans have become more set and their approach more determined. The moment of encounter has passed, for Smith, and the shift to systematic exploitation for economic ends—which he views in a heroic light that students at the turn of the twenty-first century may find ironic, if not sadistic—has begun. Indeed, Smith's series of accounts, culminating in his *Description of New England* (which may be read as an advertisement for himself as much as for New England), transforms the meaning of the word *colonize.* In his vision of the wealth that can be made in New England, he anticipates colonialism, the final disease the Europeans would bring to the native peoples who formerly held dominion over the waters and the woods of the Americas. As editor Franklin notes of the "First Charter" that established the southern part of Virginia as open to investment, Smith's accounts "marked a more corporate approach to colonization that was to become standard practice over the next hundred years." Indeed, Smith's job is to make the Americas safe for corporate colonial growth, and as his *General History of Virginia* demonstrates, when "trade and courtesy" fail, resort to military force. Smith, "though contrary to his commission, let fly his muskets." And "friendship" for Smith takes on a remarkably modern meaning: it simply means that if the native people give Smith what he wants, he'll give them back their idol and stop shooting at them.

In Smith's account of his captivity at the hands of Powhatan, friendship takes on a somewhat different meaning. In Smith's account, Powhatan's daughter, Pocahontas, intervenes, saves him from death, and falls in love with him. Most scholars suggest that Smith's account of Pocahontas may have been more fictional than historical and that he may have exaggerated her role and romanticized his own portrait. Yet Captain John Smith and Pocahontas survive in the popular imagination as an emblem of the early relationship between the English and American Indians of the eastern woodlands. Ask students to reread the references to Dona Marina in Cortés and to think about rhetorical connections between Dona Marina and Pocahontas. Both women, in surviving myths, cross cultural boundaries to embrace the conquering Europeans and, as a result, betray their people. Pocahontas does not survive as a cultural myth in the United States in the way La Malinche does in Mexico. Ask students to speculate on why this is the case. For Mexicans, the myth of the treacherous Dona Marina becomes an emblem of historical domination in a nation where native peoples and Europeans intermarried and the native strains remain strong but culturally subordinate. In the myth's endurance, La Malinche betrayed Mexico itself. In the United States, where Native Americans were subjected to genocide, Native American cultures did not become synonymous with American culture, and thus Pocahontas does not survive in myth as a betrayer of American interests.

Ask students whether they believe that the fact that both Dona Marina and Pocahontas are women is an important feature of the survival of each historical myth. At the very least, the fact that these are the only two women who are given significance throughout the narratives of encounter reflects European attitudes toward women and especially women European men perceived as being of another race. These attitudes were part of the European's earliest colonial presence, and like the "more corporate approach" to colonization students can see in Smith, Smith's approach to women—Native American women in particular—also anticipated attitudes about women and racial differences that would become features of colonialism, surviving to the present time. In this way, reading the "Literature before 1620" section also becomes an encounter for our students with their own attitudes—toward exploitation, toward racial differences, and toward the role of women in today's society.

1620–1820

I often begin by asking students to imagine what they would have felt, had they been citizens of the most civilized country in the seventeenth-century world, to leave England behind and to take one-way passage to the New World (no Holiday Inns at Plymouth, no jet service back home for those who survived the initial voyage, etc.). How did their view of hometown, family, or high-school friends change by the first Thanksgiving of their freshman year in college? Ask them to describe what happened to their consciousness of self or identity as a result of leaving home. The 1620–1820 segment of the course traces the general trajectory by which the colonials evolved from being British to possessing a consciousness of inhabiting a new world, to inventing themselves as Americans by means of the Revolution.

As English separatists, they were primarily, though not exclusively, Puritan in ideology, which meant that most believed in the literal authority of the Bible. They saw the Bible as a typological model for their own lives (Puritan writers use biblical metaphors to explain the Puritan condition; they often refer to themselves, for example, as Israelites, and the New World becomes Canaan). You will probably need to outline several basic tenets of Puritan thought: original depravity (we are all born sinners), limited atonement (there is little or nothing we can do to change that fact), irresistible grace (if God chooses us as members of his elect, there is nothing we can do about that either), and predestination (God has chosen his elect before we were born). Students are quick to see some of the contradictions in basic Puritan thinking. Why bother to live a good life, for example, if good works neither confer election nor alter damnation? But here you can point out that, by Cotton Mather's time, Puritan theologians devised a series of corollary ideas to resolve logical inconsistencies in their theology. Covenant theology was one of these. Puritans viewed the Bible as God's covenant to them, and in reading the Bible they discovered that God, though arbitrary in his power, was not malicious or capricious. The evildoers in the Old Testament die in the Flood; when God chooses someone to survive, he picks Noah, a good man. So covenant theology taught that although individual Puritans could never know for certain whether or not they were saved, the chances were excellent that members of the elect were the good people, those who would behave accordingly.

Still, students can see that not even covenant theology could definitively ease the anxieties of individual Puritans. If no one can know his or her fate for certain (although outward actions might give one a clue), the question of individual salvation remains of major significance throughout life, and Puritans engaged in personal meditation—a process of lengthy closeted soul-searching—to discover whether they might have on their souls any black spots or marks. Students can understand the combination of self-confrontation and self-evasion that such a process might entail—and that Hawthorne, later, explores in his fiction. Ask them to consider what might happen if a Puritan minister engaged in meditation should discover that he had such a black mark. The possibility must have made the act of self-confrontation extremely difficult.

WILLIAM BRADFORD

Of Plymouth Plantation is an excellent foundation text for the study of colonial American literature. Writing more than a century before the colonists would begin to imagine independence, William Bradford seems to have envisioned what a new country would need and to have supplied it, both in his public service and in his written legacy. I begin by asking students what Bradford's text created that would provide the foundation both for a new country and a nascent New World identity. Like John Smith, earlier, and the journal writers of the period, Bradford records details of early obstacles and colonial life; even more than other historians, however, Bradford develops in *Of Plymouth Plantation* a larger sense of the meaning and importance of colonial history. Creating an awareness of history while the colonists were yet engaged in the process of establishing their society gave colonial America a cultural foundation. In addition, he offers the colonists a written document ([The Mayflower Compact]) as a cornerstone of government, and he associates their origins with sacred rebirth, typologically interprets events as signs of connection with a higher authority, and in the later chapters of Book II, conveys a sense of prophecy that serves to link his own historical text with the colonists' future.

The early selections from *Of Plymouth Plantation* help students visualize the combined practical and spiritual concerns of the earliest colonials. In trying to find a harbor (Book I, Chapter X), the "lusty seaman" on board the shallop reminds the pilot to row, "or else they were all cast away." Bradford's account reveals the necessity for self-reliance among the first Puritan settlers; only after they reach "the lee of a small island" can they afford to give thanks to God "for His mercies in their manifold deliverances." Students are surprised to discover how secular and pragmatic the Puritans had to be in the process of creating their spiritual New World. In Book I, Chapter IV, Bradford cites physical hardships, premature aging, lack of control over their children, and only last (if not least), their hope of "propagating and advancing the gospel of the kingdom of Christ" as the Puritans' reasons for "removing" to the "vast and unpeopled countries of America." How does Bradford's text challenge undergraduate students' preconceptions of the Puritans and their literature?

Among the excerpts from *Of Plymouth Plantation*, [The Mayflower

Compact] (Book II, Chapter XI) deserves close analysis for classroom discussion. Bradford writes that the document was "occasioned partly by the discontented and mutinous speeches that some of the strangers [non-Puritans aboard the *Mayflower*] amongst them had let fall from them in the ship." How does what Bradford calls "the first foundation of their government in this place" establish a Puritan community from the beginning as one that excludes "strangers"? Locate evidence in the [Compact] that even before landing the Puritans defined themselves as an elect group in the secular as well as the spiritual sphere. And what implicit effect does writing and signing the Mayflower Compact have? Putting their first agreement into written form was an act of major significance for the Puritans—who believed in the Bible's literal truth and authority. Written words, from the beginning of American culture, carry the associative power of God's word. What does the writing of the Mayflower Compact indicate about the Puritans' need for divine authority? From the point of landing in the New World, the Puritans were already setting into motion the necessity of inventing for themselves solutions to material concerns that the Bible does not address. In [The Mayflower Compact] we see them trying to create other documents that would, like the Bible of their covenant theology, possess the power to compel respect and obedience.

I ask students to read later segments as if Bradford's own text were a prefiguring: in what ways do the anthologized excerpts from *Of Plymouth Plantation* recall for students later moments or patterns of thought in American history, even in our own time? Compare Book I, Chapter IV, with Book II, Chapter XXXII ([A Horrible Case of Bestiality]): both demonstrate early attempts to rationalize colonial life, but in Book II, Chapter XXXII, Bradford's own logic breaks down. In his "endeavour to give some answer hereunto," he ends by raising an unanswerable and prophetic question: "And thus, by one means or other, in 20 years' time it is a question whether the greater part be not grown the worser?" As Bradford records successive years in his history, he continues to convey a pattern of rise and fall, of end prefigured in the beginning. In Book II, Chapter XXXIV ([Proposal to Remove to Nauset]), he describes the split in the church that resulted from the removal to Nauset and characterizes the "poor church" as "an ancient mother grown old and forsaken of her children." Do the selections from Book II in particular suggest a less-than-optimistic view of our colonial origins? Social problems existed from the beginning—corruption, dissent, falling away from the "ancient mother," abandonment, lack of fidelity.

JOHN WINTHROP

A *Model of Christian Charity* (1630) gives students the earliest example of a Puritan sermon delivered in the New World (or en route to the New World, because Winthrop delivered it on board the *Arbella*). Ask students to trace the image patterns by which Winthrop characterizes the community he envisions; find allusions to biblical passages and persons and consider the application to the Puritans; discuss the discursive form of the sermon, pointing out to them that the sermon was one of the literary genres in Puritan culture.

The Journal of John Winthrop offers examples of typology and evidence of the principle of exclusion by which the Puritans founded their New World government. Ask students to assess Winthrop's comments on Roger Williams (possibly asking them to read the selections from Williams) and Anne Hutchinson. What were the Puritans' attitudes toward women, as reflected in Winthrop? Who could speak with divine authority in Puritan society? What might the "devout women" who attended services with Williams and Hutchinson have found in their teachings that severely distressed Puritan theologians?

ANNE BRADSTREET

Bradstreet's poetry further illustrates the conflict the Puritans experienced between secular and spiritual life. She tries to humanize her religion—an attempt that the learned ministry of Puritan fathers would have opposed on the grounds that Puritan election could not be earned or "felt." Poems that students respond to in line-by-line analysis in class include *The Prologue, The Author to Her Book, To My Dear and Loving Husband,* and *Here Follows Some Verses upon the Burning of Our House.* Students respond to the personal voice and the element of self-disclosure in Bradstreet that make for moving lyrics and can lead into a discussion of the constraints on individual expression in Puritan society. Ask students to find explicit evidence of Puritanism in Anne Bradstreet's poems of domestic life. Does her typological way of thinking affect her choice of metaphor in *The Author to Her Book* or increase her distress in *Some Verses upon the Burning of Our House?* Although some poems (*Contemplations* and *As Weary Pilgrim*) reveal Bradstreet as a Puritan of strong faith, others demonstrate her doubts and the limitations she feels in trying to write poetry as a woman in her culture. What does *The Prologue* reveal about Bradstreet's struggle to locate literary authority within herself? Is she really as self-deprecating as a quick first reading of the poem might suggest? How does she assert her own achievement despite the poem's apparent apologetic tone? What are the several meanings of the line "It is but vain unjustly to wage war" in the context of Bradstreet's self-assertion?

Other selections in NAAL underscore Bradstreet's self-disclosure and search for personal voice in her work. The contrast between form and feeling in *Another* [Letter to Her Husband Absent upon Public Employment] emphasizes the radical nature of Bradstreet's writing. Although she builds her verse on a series of closely connected conceits and the conventional forms of iambic pentameter and end rhymes, she writes a deeply personal, rather than conventional, love poem. And in *To My Dear Children,* she further explores her own doubts and perplexities "that I have not found that constant joy in my pilgrimage . . . which I supposed most of the servants of God have."

Even more striking and apparent in *In Reference to Her Children, 23 June, 1659* and in *To My Dear Children,* Bradstreet conveys her sense of God as a mother. She writes in *To My Dear Children* that when she has been troubled "concerning the verity of the Scriptures," she has found comfort in the order of things, "the daily providing for this great household upon the earth, the preserving and directing of all to its proper end." How does the language of "providing" help her view herself in God's image? She, too, has preserved and directed a household and speaks a language of provisions. Here, too, Bradstreet's vision expresses a departure from conventional Puritan thinking. In Puritan typology, it was the father, not the mother, who figured divine authority and power, and the literature of the colonial period noticeably omits references to mothers. Bradstreet clearly had a close relationship with her father (see *To the Memory of My Dear and Ever Honored Father Thomas Dudley Esq.* and *To Her Father with Some Verses*), but she must also have learned her pattern of devoted and nurturing motherhood from her relationship with her own mother. In *In Reference to Her Children,* she writes lovingly of her children and gives central importance, at the end of the poem, to the relationship between mother and children: "You had a dam that loved you well, / That did what could be done for young." What students may initially pass over as commonplace in this imagery (as a result of nineteenth- and twentieth-century institutionalization of motherhood) in effect was Bradstreet's attempt to repair the invisibility of mothers in Puritan society and Puritan theology. Bradstreet knows she will survive her death in the memory of her own children: "Thus gone, amongst you I may live, / And dead, yet speak, and counsel give."

MICHAEL WIGGLESWORTH

The Day of Doom presents difficulties for students unless you tell them what to look for as they read. Point out that the poem became a best-seller, and ask if they can figure out why. Ask them to find specific evidence of the tenets of Puritan theology, to characterize the contrast between Wigglesworth's sheep and goats, to summarize the portrait of hell in the poem, and to locate passages that suggest the nature of family relationships in Puritan society. In discussion, ask them to contrast Wigglesworth's descriptions of place (heaven and hell) with Bradford's in *Of Plymouth Plantation* and to reread Bradstreet's *Here Follows Some Verses upon the Burning of Our House* (1666) in light of Wigglesworth's 1662 poem.

MARY ROWLANDSON

A *Narrative of the Captivity and Restoration of Mrs. Mary Rowlandson* will fascinate students at the same time as it helps them make thematic connections between several Puritan writers. Ask students to describe the plot or design of the Indian captivity narrative. Does Rowlandson have a literary or a didactic purpose? How does the narrative compare with other Puritan works that show triumph or redemption after suffering? Suggest that they think specifically about Bradford's portraits of American Indians in *Of Plymouth Plantation* or the form of salvation for the elect at the end of *The Day of Doom*. What do the poems of Bradstreet and the *Narrative* of Rowlandson together reveal about the fears, anxieties, and accommodations that comprised ordinary life for women in Puritan society?

EDWARD TAYLOR

The success by which Taylor works through his extended metaphors to imagery of salvation demonstrates the energy that must have been required for the Puritan to engage in spiritual introspection. Help students focus their attention on Taylor's use of poetic form. Ask them to describe the stanzaic pattern of any of the *Preparatory Meditations*, to locate and examine his use of the extended metaphor, and to discuss the imagery of the poem. *Prologue* works well to analyze with them line by line and, especially by way of contrast with Bradstreet's poem of the same title, shows Taylor's awareness that his spiritual salvation and his poetic imagination depend on each other. Taylor's problem as a Puritan is to demonstrate to himself over and over again that he is one of the elect, and he does this by using the metaphysical conceit as a focus for literal as well as poetic meditation. If he can turn the mark or spot—the poem's central metaphor—into an image of salvation, then he will have proven his election both spiritually and aesthetically. How does Taylor resolve the problem of literary authority? Does he have difficulty seeing himself as God's pen? What does his struggle for poetic inspiration suggest about those who wrote poetry in Puritan society? Examine *The Preface* from *God's Determinations* to elicit Taylor's Puritan vision. What is the relationship between "nothing man" and "Might Almighty"? Ask students to trace the formal as well as thematic cohesion Taylor achieves through repetition of "nothing" and "might," "all might," and "almighty" throughout the poem. Trace Taylor's references to children in some of his poems; analyze his use of erotic and scatalogical imagery; or trace the triumph over death in *A Fig for Thee, Oh! Death,* possibly asking students to compare the poem with John Donne's *Death Be Not Proud.*

Discussing Bradstreet's *To My Dear and Loving Husband* side by side with Taylor's *Huswifery* can demonstrate the contrast between the two poets. Bradstreet is interested in physical life, is aware of love as a physical tie, views heaven as a consequence of human faithfulness, and chooses imagery from daily life and classical mythology; Taylor depicts spiritual rebirth, his dependence on God, and love as a spiritual tie and depends on the poetic conceit and biblical imagery to carry the power of his poems. Bradstreet gives us the sense of the individual; Taylor's poetry stifles or subordinates the individual to the spiritual type. Bradstreet's poetry allows her to express her doubts; Taylor tires to contain his within the tight form of the extended metaphor.

SAMUEL SEWALL

Discuss *The Diary* as Puritan introspection in practice. Contrast the form of the diary with Taylor's poetic forms in *Preparatory Meditations.* Weigh Sewall's expressed commitment to "great exercise of mind" in approaching his "Spiritual Estate" with his interest in daily life, "outward causes" of conflict, and public events. Summarize what Sewall's *Diary* reveals about personal life and human relationships in Puritan society.

COTTON MATHER

The headnote to Mather points out that the *Magnalia Christi Americana* "remains Mather's most impressive work" for its portraits of Bradford and Winthrop. Students will find the excerpts from *The Wonders of the Invisible World,* Mather's history of the Salem witch trials, and *Bonifacius,* his discussion of family and community life and child rearing, equally interesting. *Bonifacius* can serve as the thematic culmination for a discussion of what it was like to have been a Puritan child. Ask students to reread Bradford, Bradstreet, and Taylor for references to children and child rearing. It's clear that (1) God's will is more important than the love between parents and children; (2) children are born sinners and must be taught obedience, submission, and fear; and (3) children have the capacity to destroy Puritanism by becoming degenerate and following false teachers. Emory Elliott has written an account of the life of the young Puritan and how life was different for second- and third-generation children (like Mather himself) in *Power and the Pulpit in Puritan New England.*

WILLIAM BYRD

Students need continual reminding that by no means all who settled the New World were Puritans and that we emphasize them as founders by choice, not historical necessity. Ask them to compare Sewall's *The Diary* with Byrd's *The Secret Diary*. How does the Virginian Byrd's view of life differ from his New England Puritan counterpart? In form and apparent intention, Byrd's regular writing in his "secret diary" resembles the Puritan practice of introspection and meditation. But students will find it a refreshing contrast. Is Byrd's repetition of his prayers for "good health, good thoughts, and good humor" a cynical response to religion or an expression of well-being that we should take at face value? And what *does* he mean by doing his "dance"?

JONATHAN EDWARDS

A reading of *Personal Narrative* will set up a contrast between the Puritan Edwards and the Quaker John Woolman; it also shows Edwards's interest in science—linking him with Enlightenment thinking—despite the fact that we read him for his sermons and his narrative of his religious conversion. Students ought to read all of the Edwards selections, but I have found it most useful to them to analyze closely *Sinners in the Hands of an Angry God*. In my own classroom, I discuss the earlier sermon *A Divine and Supernatural Light* after we have analyzed *Sinners*, and we focus on the contrast between the two.

In analyzing *Sinners* in the classroom, it's useful to trace the evolution of semantic meaning in the sermon. Edwards takes a verse from Deuteronomy as his apparent text—"Their foot shall slide in due time"—but as a result of applying what I call a process of "literary interpretation" to the verse, he manages to convince his audience that he is justified in replacing God's words with his own: "There is nothing that keeps wicked men at any one moment out of hell, but the mere pleasure of God." He then dissects every word, idea, and element of syntax from his own statement and performs that same process of "logical" interpretation and extrapolation on it as he did on the verse from Deuteronomy. The following ten numbered points in the sermon may be shown to correlate with each of these. For example, in point 4 ("They are now the objects"), students can see Edwards focusing on the present tense of his own restatement of Deuteronomy (clearly a revision, since the verse uses future tense); and point 6 expands on the implications of the word *wicked*, and so on. The significance of tracing through this process, which culminates in the famous passage at the end of the first part of the sermon, "So that, thus it is that natural men are held in the hand of God," is that Edwards has managed to reconstruct a kind of scripture, but the language he interprets is his own. In the "Application" section of the sermon, he then chooses imagery that allows his audience to visualize their plight—here using biblical language to reinforce his own—and comes close to equating death of the individual with the day of judgment. If you take students through the sermon slowly enough, you can expect them to discover for themselves what is required for a Great Awakening that is also a reawakening, a revitalization of a theology. Edwards's sermon uses visual imagery as a means of spiritual revival; it provides the possibility of seeing damnation clearly and as if for the first time. *Sinners* is also a performance; Edwards's audience is clearly in the hands of an angry minister as well as an angry God.

A Divine and Supernatural Light defines religious conversion; *Sinners in the Hands of an Angry God* instills fear in the unconverted—a subject that students may feel has more varied and interesting literary possibilities than the subject of the earlier sermon. In *A Divine and Supernatural Light,* Edwards tried to find words for his feeling of the infusion of the Holy Spirit, to express an ineffable experience; *Sinners* creates an experience for its listeners, as if Edwards believed that sinners wouldn't have the equivalent sense of being damned that the elect have of being filled with grace. It's also interesting to note that Edwards, like Taylor, seems to equate complying with form (whether of religious poetry or of the sermon) with adhering to theology; that is, it allows him to contain his experience within a prescribed form. However, students can see that *Divine Light* is tighter in form than *Sinners;* it is also more straightforward and requires fewer turns in logic. Does this possibly suggest that the experience of feeling damned is more difficult to contain and even somehow more human? And is the chaos of human life relatively more simple and comprehensible than the complexity and abstractness of "divine and supernatural" life?

Undergraduates may find the excerpt from Chapter I of *The Nature of True Virtue* daunting for Edwards's abstraction and his ability to discourse on virtue, benevolence, beings, love, and beauty without conveying that these qualities belong to living, flesh-and-blood persons. Suggest that—as in the contrast between *Sinners* and *A Divine and Supernatural Light,* where students may find Edwards's portrait of the damned more interesting than his description of salvation—Chapter III will, by contrast, redeem the value of *The Nature of True Virtue* and make Chapter I worth considering. For in Chapter III, Edwards takes up the question of the relation between spiritual beauty and "another, inferior, secondary beauty," which he views as a fixed "law of nature" and which will elicit challenges from students. The very simplicity and harmony of Edwards's values—"uniformity and mutual correspondence," "agreement and union," "consent or concord," all parts "sweetly united in a benevolent agreement of heart"—reduce society to a "beauty of order," in which all persons keep their "appointed office, place and station" and leave no room for dissent. From the retrospective view of our own mid-century's history, does Edwards's sense of order as a "law of nature" exclude social progress that may result from challenging the "natural" order of things? In preparation for their reading of Emerson later in the study of American literature, allow students to challenge Edwards's eighteenth-century conception of nature.

BENJAMIN FRANKLIN

From William Bradford on, the requirements of the actual wilderness and the Puritans' expectations for their spiritual Promised Land decidedly contradict each other—so much so that for a Great Awakening audience to be able to visualize themselves in hell, Edwards must write as if his listeners were not in Enfield, Massachusetts, at all. The radical split between actual place and spiritual "place" creates an anxiety that Benjamin Franklin and his "theology" of economic "salvation" can address. By contrast with Edwards, Franklin, the paradigmatic eighteenth-century man—scientist, inventor, deist—yet pontificates in various modes (humor, in *The Way to Wealth;* fatherly piety, in *The Autobiography*) as if he, too, were a minister. For Franklin—despite his move to Quaker Philadelphia at the age of seventeen—retains many of the forms of Puritan thinking and simply alters its content in addressing his readers.

The transition to Franklin is an easy one after Edwards, partly because students find him more pleasurable to read and partly because, if you begin with *The Way to Wealth,* almost all of them will have the feeling that they have read him before. I like to ask students how many have heard some of Poor Richard's maxims. Almost all of them will, even those who don't remember ever reading Franklin in high school. How, then, did they hear these maxims, and what does that say about the transmission, by means of an oral tradition, of American values and language? We choose a few of the maxims to analyze closely, focusing in particular on the way Franklin exploits the religious metaphors his audience, like Edwards's, would have already been familiar with—for example, "God helps them that help themselves," or "Those have a short Lent who owe money to be paid at Easter." Here students can see Franklin keeping the language of Puritan theology but changing its meaning—reversing Edwards's transformation of Deuteronomy in *Sinners in the Hands of an Angry God* (see previous discussion). For *The Way to Wealth* is an antisermon—ironically in the tradition of Jonathan Edwards, even though Franklin's "salvation" is financial prosperity. His language crosses religious metaphors and images from home industry, and his advice becomes the religious "practice" by which common people may increase their worldly (not spiritual) effects and position. He even associates his "old Gentleman" in the piece with a minister, concluding that Poor Richard's advice has as little effect "as if it had been a common Sermon."

The Autobiography introduces students to their first long work of significance, and no brief discussion can do more than suggest a few general ways to organize class analysis. One point I try to make is that in *The Autobiography*, as in *Poor Richard's Almanack*, Franklin offers practical solutions for the material concerns of the common people, in effect exchanging the spiritual goal of their religious practice for one of secular and economic salvation. *The Autobiography* gives us our earliest example of "business literature." In detail after detail that Franklin chooses to relate (and the book is a highly selective account of his life—ask students to compare it with Sewall's *Diary* or Byrd's *Secret Diary*), it's possible to show students that the development of the embryonic individual for Franklin takes precedence over any interest a person of his time might have had in received theology. Still, it's fascinating to see how Franklin takes the forms of that theology and turns them to his own use. Ask students how Franklin's "Project of arriving at moral Perfection" is similar in form to Puritan introspection and meditation. (He writes that "daily Examination would be necessary," and he uses a "little Book" duly lined, "on which Line and in its proper Column I might mark by a little black Spot every Fault I found upon Examination to have been committed respecting that Virtue upon that Day." Yet Franklin is attempting to alter his own moral character, not to find evidence of his soul's salvation. Franklin's life and his "instruction" through his *Autobiography* transform the daily routine into a religious practice. Practical life itself becomes a "religion," governed by more precepts, self-discipline, introspection, and, above all, the desire for self-improvement, so that Franklin's work both derives from Puritan religious method and is a reaction against it.

How does *The Autobiography* reveal Franklin as an eighteenth-century man? Discuss Franklin's fascination with invention, scientific discoveries, and social institutions. In what ways does he adapt what he calls the "Age of Experiments" to political as well as personal life? Describe his plan for the "union of all the colonies," and suggest that it is as much a practical solution to a problem—another "invention"—as any of the more tangible projects he writes about. Final discussion of *The Autobiography* can prepare the way for *The Declaration of Independence*, for which Franklin offered some revisions and directly influenced Jefferson's conceptual thinking. The title of Garry Wills's book on the Constitution, *Inventing America*, can help students think about what both Franklin and Jefferson are trying to do in their political writings. Franklin is motivated by the advice he receives to "invite all wise men to become like yourself," and students can get a clear picture of Franklin as both a self-made man and a "self-invented" one. Franklin offers his life as a blueprint, a repeatable experiment, evidence that an American can resolve the confusion involved in being a colonial by "inventing" himself or herself as a new kind of person.

Franklin's other prose both confirms and enlarges on his self-portrait as a rational man. Discuss Franklin's use of satire, especially in *Rules by Which a Great Empire May Be Reduced to a Small One,* as an eighteenth-century rhetorical device. Compare the form of *Rules* with the numbered, discursive, rational forms that William Bradford attempts (see *Of Plymouth Plantation,* Book I, Chapter IV) and Jonathan Edwards perfects (see especially *Sinners in the Hands of an Angry God*) and evaluate the power of Franklin's work. Recast each satirical point into a direct statement and examine the quality of Franklin's logic. See also his letter to Joseph Priestley, in which Franklin describes his method of thinking through difficult cases. Contrast Franklin's self-presentation in *The Autobiography* with moments in the letters in which he reveals more of himself. See in particular his letter to his father, Josiah, written when Franklin was in his early thirties, in which he gives us a rare glimpse of family dynamics; his letter to his sister, Jane Mecom, in which he assumes a didactic stance but also expresses filial concern; and his letters to Georgiana Shipley and Madame Brillon, which suggest Franklin's fondness for relationships with women other than his wife (a well-known fact of his biography that he does not mention in his autobiography).

ELIZABETH ASHBRIDGE

After the absence of self-disclosure in Edwards and Franklin's guarded self-presentation, students may welcome Ashbridge's *Some Account of the Fore-Part of the Life.* Although Ashbridge expresses her intent to write a spiritual autobiography and although her conversion to the Quaker faith substantially enhances John Woolman's self-portrait in his *Journal* (note that although both Quakers published their narratives in England in the same year, 1774, Ashbridge wrote hers much earlier), Ashbridge's account portrays much more than spiritual conversion. More than any other selection in the 1620–1820 period, Ashbridge conveys in detail the quality of her relationship with her mother, patterns of early-eighteenth-century family life and the inflexibility of the father's role, and her own particular form of what twentieth-century readers may call adolescent rebellion. Here, it may be interesting to take another look at Franklin's 1738 letter to his father. Franklin expresses a certain amount of rebellious independence in that letter, at an age well past what we would consider adolescence, and Ashbridge was about the same age as Franklin was in 1738 when she wrote her 1744 *Account* and gave us the portrait of her life's "fore-part." Might we speculate, with students, that our early identity as colonials replicated stages in human growth and development—the mid-eighteenth century, culminating in our collective *Declaration of*

Independence, epitomizing cultural adolescence and the transition to adulthood? In Ashbridge's development, adolescent rebellion seems all the more striking because she was a girl, and our students may delight when she reports that she "sometimes grieved at . . . not being a boy."

Her youthful independence may reflect the antics of the tomboy, but in the context within which she makes her statement—that she had a high regard for ministers and grieved that she could not be one because she was not a boy—she is also identifying the compelling theme that unites the secular and spiritual aspects of her conversion narrative. In effect, she describes the process by which she began her New World life in servitude (she uses the word *sold* to describe her indenturing) and silence and, through a long process containing much forward and backward movement, achieved freedom and speech as well as sufficient literary authority to write her *Account.* In class discussion, trace the various stages of Ashbridge's development, focusing on those moments in which she keeps or breaks silence (see, for example, the incident with the whipper, the scene in the tavern when her husband tries to make her dance, and her determination to attend Quaker meeting) and in which she discovers, to her surprise, that Quaker women become preachers.

Ashbridge uses silence as a defense against her husband's abuse; her silence may lead students to ask for whom Ashbridge wrote her story. The headnote describes *Some Account* as resembling an eighteenth-century popular novel; furthermore, Ashbridge's language is colloquial, and she explicitly states her concerns for her reader. Did she see herself writing for women? In a useful digression, you might, in conjunction with Ashbridge, assign Thomas Jefferson's 1818 letter to Nathaniel Burwell on the subject of women's education in which he complains that women have an "inordinate passion" for novels, which poisons their minds. Although Ashbridge does not explicitly state that she writes her *Account* for a female audience, in stating that "it was required of me in a more public manner to confess to the world what I was," she is clearly referring to her social position as woman as well as Quaker. Does she decide to write her story of life as a woman who becomes a Quaker in part to demonstrate that such a story is not "poison" at all, but moral edification? A related aspect of *Some Account* is Ashbridge's description of interaction between husband and wife. She is particularly likely to report her husband's actual words when he criticizes her speech. It appears that for her husband, her "clack"—her speaking—is itself sufficient poison.

Ashbridge's description of her indenturing and passage to the colonies invites comparison with Olaudah Equiano's *Narrative,* in which he portrays life aboard the slave ships. While Ashbridge describes herself as "pretty well" treated, she also states that her master forced her to go barefoot in snowy weather "and to be employed in the meanest drudgery, wherein I suffered the utmost hardships that my body was able to bear."

JOHN WOOLMAN

The Journal of John Woolman is well taught in conjunction with Jonathan Edwards, for it allows students to see that Puritanism didn't simply disappear when deism walked in the door but, rather, that the writings by colonial writers (both Puritans and non-Puritans, such as Woolman) reveal stresses on Puritanism from the beginning that foreshadow its own eventual decline as the dominant theology. The Puritan practice of inner scrutiny, the use of the poetic conceit in Edward Taylor's poetry, and the social ritual of executing witches all serve an analogous function: to allow the Puritans to externalize their own inner doubts and confusion and to create a false sense of security concerning their own salvation or election. In reading Woolman's *Journal*, students may wonder what was so terrible about the Quakers that the Puritans felt such a need to pass laws against them and to persecute them. The excerpt will also give students a different view of religion than the one they find in the selections from Puritan writers. Ask them to think about what Woolman means when he writes that "true religion consisted in an inward life." His consciousness of that inward life or the "inner light" of the Quakers may seem more closely akin to the development of individual voice in the poetry of Anne Bradstreet than the didactic poetry of Taylor or Wigglesworth. Woolman's *Journal* suggests that one of the schisms within Puritanism resulted from the discovery, by some colonials, of religious faith that was connected more to feeling than to the purely intellectual "delight" Edwards's work reveals. Are there other ways in which the *Journal* illustrates an increasingly deep split within colonial consciousness? Ask students to think about connections between expressions of self-reliance as early as Bradford's *Of Plymouth Plantation*, Woolman's "inward life," and the popular climate that led to Franklin's great popularity in Quaker Pennsylvania.

In the selection included from "Some Considerations on the Keeping of Negroes," students can see an excellent example of the logical extension of Quaker values and their application to the question of slavery. Even before the American Revolution and the writing of a Constitution that did nothing to end slavery, Woolman reveals the great sadness concerning the "general disadvantage which these poor Africans lie under in an enlightened Christian country." Ask students to locate the fundamental assumptions of Woolman's argument—an argument addressed to empathy, based on what students will know as the Golden Rule, and derived from the attempt to "make their case ours." In the Age of Enlightenment, Quaker thinkers like Woolman demonstrated that rational thinking must also involve "life guided by wisdom from above," that both individual and social policy decisions must derive from moving beyond "self-love" to considering what is "truly beneficial to society."

Rational thinking without moral reasoning, Woolman implies, leads to a "darkness in the understanding." Clearly Woolman's position did not prevail, and yet the terms of his plea as well as his conscious awareness of the politics involved in arguing against slavery remain of interest to twentieth-century readers. He portrays a society more interested in "gain" than in right action, which some students may believe continues to characterize our own society, and he early argues that it becomes necessary to advocate "the cause of some" to promote "the good of all," a principle that implies the interconnectedness of prejudice, oppression, and discrimination. Close readers may find a moment of inconsistency in Woolman's text; he mentions but fails to examine how "the natives are gone from before us," despite his implication that it is as a result of the "disappearance" of the American Indians that he and his contemporaries enjoy "our civil and religious liberties."

SAMSON OCCOM

Students may read Occom's *Sermon Preached at the Execution of Moses Paul* in the context of other sermons or didactic religious literature also included in NAAL: John Winthrop's *A Model of Christian Charity,* Cotton Mather's *Bonifacius,* and Jonathan Edwards's *Sinners in the Hands of an Angry God.* Rather than arguing a point of theology, as does Edwards, Occom reminds his listeners of the relationship between sin and death and of the relationship between temporal behavior—here, the drunkenness of some American Indians—and sin.

Unlike other sermons, however, Occom's raises the question of representation; he is speaking as an Indian to a mixed audience of Euro-Americans and Native Americans at the execution of an Indian who was drunk when he killed a white man. Ask students to consider whether this occasion may dictate Occom's rhetorical strategies as much as his "text"—the relationship of sin and death. Notice that Occom does not ask who introduced Indians to alcohol and procured it for them—or even how they have come to be wandering naked through the streets, in poverty in the midst of civilization. For further preparation and discussion, see David Murray's insightful comments in *Forked Speeches: Speech, Writing & Representation in North American Indian Texts* (1991). Murray calls the sermon's occasion "a pre-arranged conversation between Indians" and suggests that Occom's exhortations to the Native Americans in his audience may have as much to do with encouraging them to prove false their representation by Euro-Americans as it does with encouraging them to follow Christian precepts and avoid drunkenness.

J. HECTOR ST. JEAN DE CRÈVECOEUR

Letters from an American Farmer asks the famous question, "What is an American?"—a question that takes on heightened resonance for this generation of students, as it has for many others. Letter III may in part romanticize the "perfect society" about which Crèvecoeur writes, but in providing a series of answers to the question "What is an American?" it leads to a great deal of discussion in the classroom. For example, Crèvecoeur asserts that "the rich and the poor are not so far removed from each other as they are in Europe," and implies that the United States is founded as a classless society. At the same time, he seems unaware of the contradiction that results from a society built on individual enterprise, where "labor is founded on the basis of nature, self-interest." Furthermore, he also makes it clear that the Native Americans (and the Africans he writes about in Letter IX) do not figure in his definition of an American. For Crèvecoeur, the American "is either a European, or the descendant of a European," and his list of eligible Europeans only includes Western Europeans: "English, Scotch, Irish, French, Dutch, Germans and Swedes." Students may wish to comment on the origins of Eurocentrism in American society as part of this discussion. At the same time, Crèvecoeur also confronts the barbarousness of the pioneers, locating the ill manners of the Native Americans as well as the "European medley" in the observation that when "either tawny or white" men become hunters, they give up civilized values and cease to be the "disciples" of religion. Indeed, as his narrative reveals in Letter XII, he prefers to accommodate to life with the Indians than with some of the Europeans who have become settlers in the American woods.

Throughout a discussion of Crèvecoeur, asking students to locate both his assumptions and his contradictions will help them read his letters within their own historical context as well as identify their significance for present-day readers. Letter IX offers an implicit contradiction to his statement, in Letter III, that "we know, properly speaking, no strangers," when he describes coming on the caged African who has been left to die. The letter ends with his report that when he asked why the slave had been punished in this manner, "they told me that the laws of self-preservation rendered such executions necessary." Focusing on this phrase *the laws of self-preservation* reveals the cynical contrast with his own language in Letter III (and with Woolman's argument in *Some Considerations*) and reflects Crèvecoeur's increasingly ambiguous relation to this invention he calls "an American." Letter X, in which he writes about the mortal conflict between a black snake and a water snake, seems a parable of a growing pessimism concerning the ability of good and evil to resolve themselves as well as an ironic comment on the concept of the "laws of self-preservation" used by the slaveholders to justify their treatment of the slaves. If we read this parable as a statement about the relationship between power and corruption, then even within the brief period of time that elapsed between the composition of Crèvecoeur's earliest letters (about 1769), the *Declaration of Independence* and American Revolution (1776), and the composition of his later letters and their publication (1780–82) his altered perception of American life may more accurately reflect the contradictions inherent in the creation of the United States than the utopian vision reflected in Letter III, particularly when Crèvecoeur writes, "we have no princes, for whom we toil, starve, and bleed; we are the most perfect society now existing in the world." In response to Crèvecoeur's question "What is an American?" some students may want to ask, What does he mean by *we?*

JOHN ADAMS AND ABIGAIL ADAMS

In the letters of John and Abigail Adams, students can see the rare intersection of public and personal life in colonial America, as well as evidence of intimate human relationship between two people. Organize class discussion of the letters by asking students to list the various conflicts that each of these writers reveals in his or her letters: Abigail is concerned with smallpox, lack of pins and other domestic equipment; encroachments of war with England; fear that others might read her letters; and pride in her connection with John's work. John is concerned about keeping his private identity alive, affairs of the Continental Congress, shaping the new country's independence, and fear that others will intercept his letters. Both are capable of praising and chiding in the same letter and of complaining about the other's lack of attention or expression of feeling. John's letter of July 20, 1776 (less than three weeks after the signing of *The Declaration of Independence*) opens, "This has been a dull day to me," because a letter he had expected to receive from Abigail did not arrive. John is writing from the absolute center of political action, yet he worries that his friends at home may think he has forgotten his wife and children.

Ask students to compare the letters of John and Abigail Adams with those of Ashbridge, Franklin, and Jefferson. Like Ashbridge, John and Abigail Adams use language to communicate with a reader whom they know to be a real person; in contrast, Franklin and Jefferson produce letters that seem written for a general audience. John and Abigail transcend the formal requirements of eighteenth-century letter writing and allow feeling to interrupt form. John can write, in his letter of October 9, 1774, that "the Business of the Congress is tedious, beyond Expression," a sentiment that he clearly reserves for the private sphere of his relationship with Abigail, and the following year, in his letter of October 29, 1775, he can recite the virtues of New England as if he were delivering a public speech. Abigail prefers those letters in which John transgresses conventional form, writing about one of his letters, in hers of July 21, 1776, that "I think it a choise one in the Litterary Way, . . . yet it Lacked some essential engrediants to make it compleat." She wants from John more personal discourse and more words "respecting yourself, your Health or your present Situation." These letters exist within the dual contexts of personal relationship and political change, and the rapid shifts in the discourse reflect the way attention to audience changes the use of language, even in the late eighteenth century.

THOMAS PAINE, THOMAS JEFFERSON, *THE FEDERALIST*, *THE DECLARATION OF INDEPENDENCE*

Throughout the 1620–1820 period, I trace the way each subsequent shift in thinking retains old forms. The need the *Mayflower* Puritans felt for a document that would put their authority into writing is the earliest example of the pattern; the way Edwards uses biblical language and Franklin retains the forms—but alters the content—of Puritan thinking are eighteenth-century examples. In the writings of the Federalist period, the pattern continues to hold. James Madison, in Federalist Paper No. 10, argues that one of the advantages of union is "its tendency to break and control the violence of faction." By 1787, when Madison wrote his paper, Puritanism had long disappeared as an apparent force, and yet Madison's concern that factions be controlled by means of a union that possesses a written document—the Constitution—establishes him as a distant cousin to his Puritan predecessors in the way that he views the power of the written text.

Many instructors find the Federal period difficult to teach in a literature course. Thomas Paine and Thomas Jefferson can seem more like figures from the historical record than recorders of individual aesthetic vision. Yet if we focus on the ways the American Revolution and *The Declaration of Independence* address—like Franklin's work—the wide gap the Puritans experienced between the dictates of their theology and the pressing material concerns of their daily lives, the significant documents of the American Revolution can appear as a collective fiction. For *The Declaration of Independence*, in particular, manages to create the illusion of identity that seems to have been required before early-nineteenth-century writers could begin to give us an imaginative literature.

The Declaration of Independence

Like Franklin's *Autobiography*, *The Declaration of Independence* is a blueprint, an experiment that the French would repeat, and another invention. Yet many students won't do more than skim it out of class—believing that they don't need to, either because they read it in high school or because they are somehow "living" it. It has the aura of sacred text, and I've found it necessary to break down their assumption that *The Declaration* is like the Bible, another divinely authored text, to show them that it has motive, intention, character, and plot—as if it were a work of fiction. Ask your students to consider the way it "makes" history the same way Franklin "invents" his own life in *The Autobiography*. Do they see any resemblance between *The Declaration* and the sermon form, especially in *Sinners in the Hands of an Angry God?* And what level of diction does Jefferson use? Compare the language with Franklin's in *The Way to Wealth;* compare it with Edwards's as well. Show Jefferson trying to imbue secular and political concerns with the semantic aura of spiritual salvation. I suggest that the "art of virtue" that Franklin recalls in *The Autobiography*" but never actually wrote finds its "text" in *The Declaration,* democracy's "bible." Whatever else you choose to teach from Jefferson and the Federalist era, *The Declaration of Independence* becomes the central work to read closely with students. I have often moved outside of chronology at this point and circulated copies of the brief *Declaration of Sentiments,* modeled on *The Declaration,* that Elizabeth Cady Stanton wrote and women at the Woman's Rights Convention in Seneca Falls in 1848 signed (see Appendix). Examining the two documents together stimulates as much discussion as you want to allow time for.

EXPLORING THE ISSUE OF SLAVERY

An approach to teaching American literature that neglects the evidence of dissenting voices within apparent union makes it difficult for the classroom teacher to explain why anything ever changed—why writers in any historical period began to think differently, and why they experimented with different genres. Given the principle of exclusion that is our heritage from the Puritans (however far back and from whatever origin we are able to trace our personal lineage) and looking ahead to the Civil War of the 1860s, how our founders saw fit to deal with factions, with social difference, and in particular, with the issue of slavery can help us describe the tensions that have always been, and still remain, a part of American life (and that become part of our teaching whenever we make decisions based on the "major" or "minor" significance of particular texts or authors). In the literature of the Federal period, then, in addition to discussing major figures and ideas of the Enlightenment, I also focus on the ways various writers and works address the issue of slavery.

Long before the early nineteenth century, slavery was a national issue, and in failing to resolve it, Jefferson, James Madison, and the Continental Congress created another "new world" with its own stresses—like those on Puritan government—that involve students of American literature in a discussion of the relationship between liberty and literary authority. The language of liberty that makes Thomas Paine's writing and *The Declaration of Independence* particularly effective suggests that it is the very articulation of the "United States of America" that makes revolution possible and thereby brings the country into being. The documents of American Revolution achieve their power in the same way that William Bradford does in [The Mayflower Compact]: they focus the nebulous thinking of a larger group, and they offer the familiar form of written covenant. The writers of the Federal period put language in the service of human liberty—for some but not all. And it seems important to point out to students that the unspoken omissions from the language of "all men are created equal" will require other internal revolutions—for the abolition of slavery and the fight for women's suffrage—before the liberty that makes possible the literary achievements of the 1820–65 period will also support the literary authority of black men, white women, and black women.

Students can find discussions of slavery in several writers whose works may otherwise seem difficult to connect. John Woolman, in his *Journal*, records being reluctant to write a bill of sale for a black woman as early as the 1740s, and in "Some Considerations on the Keeping of Negroes" he argues that his listeners must empathize with the plight of the slaves and apply moral reasoning to their "considerations." William Byrd of Virginia writes casually of whipping black houseservants in his *Secret Diary*. Crèvecoeur, in Letter IX, describes the miserable condition of the slaves in Charles-Town. Jefferson, in *Notes on the State of Virginia*, objects to slavery as much for what it does to the masters as for what it does to the slaves, fears "supernatural interference" and even the "extirpation" of the masters—yet makes no concrete proposal for ending slavery (and he himself owned many slaves). *The Declaration of Independence*, in its original version (NAAL includes the original document Jefferson submitted to the Continental Congress, with the changes as adopted noted in the margins), clearly shows Jefferson's abhorrence of the institution of slavery. The passage in *The Declaration* that begins "He has waged cruel war against human nature itself," which was completely excised from the document based on objections from representatives from South Carolina, Georgia, and some northern colonies engaged in profit from the slave trade, helps students understand the inherent contradiction in the document's reference to "all men." The textual revisions show them that the Continental Congress addressed the issue of slavery, then decided to eliminate it from consideration in *The Declaration*. One essay that I have found extremely useful in preparing to teach *The Declaration* is Edwin Gittleman's article "Jefferson's 'Slave Narrative': *The Declaration of Independence* as a Literary Text" (*Early American Literature* 8 [1974]: 239–56).

OLAUDAH EQUIANO

Equiano was born in Africa and, after buying his freedom in 1766, chose to settle in England. One of the first questions you might raise with students concerns the inclusion of Equiano's *Narrative* in NAAL. What makes it "American" literature? Does Equiano qualify as an "American" writer because he was bought and owned by a Philadelphia merchant, even though he did not choose to emigrate to the New World and left the colonies as soon as he was able? The circumstances of its author's citizenship (or lack of it) give reality to the term *colonial literature* as a category that includes Equiano's *Narrative.* For, as a slave, Equiano was indeed "colonized" in body, and his writing is, therefore, colonial.

Like Elizabeth Ashbridge's *Account,* Equiano's *Narrative* gives students a new perspective on life in the American colonies. Servitude and slavery did not begin with the southern plantation economy, but much earlier, soon after the first colonial settlements. Literature as early as William Byrd's *The Secret Diary,* written between 1709 and 1712, reflects the presence and ill treatment of slaves. Ashbridge was indentured in 1732, and Equiano was stolen by African traders in 1756. Although the original version of *The Declaration of Independence* includes a reference to the slave trade (see the changes Jefferson notes in the text included in his *Autobiography*) and although during the writing of the Constitution the prohibition of the slave trade was discussed, stipulations concerning slavery were omitted from the Constitution, and Congress was prohibited from abolishing the slave trade for 20 years. Although Britain outlawed the slave trade in 1807, it was not abolished in the United States until the Emancipation Proclamation of January 1, 1863. Equiano's narrative exists within the context of that history and provides a great deal of information about life in Africa, the internal African slave trade (Equiano's own father owned slaves), and conditions on the slave ships themselves.

One of the most fascinating aspects of Equiano's narrative is the way he creates an African perspective on European life; to cite a term Equiano, in effect, defines for us, even though he would not have used the term, his text embodies the concept of *Afrocentric.* His fear of "water larger than a pond or a rivulet" begins when he nears the coast of Africa and encounters a people "who did not circumcise, and ate without washing their hands." The fact that he never learns to swim suggests that the fear of water was early associated, for the eleven-year-old boy, with his own enslavement. Much that he sees when he becomes acquainted with Europeans makes him afraid and astonished; he fears being eaten by white men, and he believes that sails, anchors, clocks, and pictures are magic.

The world Equiano depicts enshrines the merchant. King, the Philadelphia merchant, eventually keeps his promise and allows Equiano to buy his freedom. Equiano does so by becoming a merchant himself. Cargo thus becomes central to Equiano's freedom; he begins as "live cargo," becomes a trader in various goods, and literally reverses his fortunes. Unlike the authors of later slave narratives, such as the *Narrative of the Life of Frederick Douglass*, and unlike Elizabeth Ashbridge, Equiano does not achieve freedom by finding his voice. Neither does he feel compelled to keep silent. By including his manumission papers in his *Narrative*, he seems to suggest that, indeed, it is only a reversal of fortune, not his own power, that has produced his freedom, for the "absolute power and domination one man claims over his fellow" that allowed Robert King to emancipate Equiano equally allowed other white men to enslave the freeman Joseph Clipson, whose story Equiano relates. The reversal of fortune that produced Equiano's *Narrative* remains valuable "cargo" in our attempts to instruct students in the literature of New World colonials.

PHILIP FRENEAU

Freneau's poetry directly addresses the social and historical events of his day and anticipates the influence of the Romantic poets on American writers in poems such as *The House of Night* and *On Observing a Large Red-streak Apple. On the Emigration to America and Peopling the Western Country* and *On Mr. Paine's Rights of Man* derive their force from their historical situation. The poems suggest that the American Revolution made the development of American poetry possible, and yet, as Francis Murphy notes in the NAAL headnote, Freneau was not "the father of American poetry." Ask students to think about what limits Freneau. Freneau's brand of eloquence as it survives in his poetry (he also wrote political pamphlets) has not appeared to be as lasting in its significance as our country's founding documents; the political covenant and the autobiography absorb almost all of the literary energy available during the Revolutionary and Federal periods and serve as the major literary genres of the late eighteenth century. Still, Freneau's choice to respond to political and social conditions in *To Sir Toby*, written about slavery (although he addresses a sugar planter in Jamaica rather than a southern slaveholder), demonstrates his faith in the power of language used in the service of political and social change. This faith has its roots in the Puritan belief in the literary authority of the Bible, but it also anticipates the First Amendment to the Constitution, and the idea that freedom of speech is the most important freedom, because it is speech that leads to freedom itself.

PHILLIS WHEATLEY

Wheatley is a fascinating poet for anyone interested in literary history, for she reflects Puritan influence, wrote poetry that imitates Alexander Pope, and was the first African-American to publish a book. Wheatley writes about abstract liberty rather than about freedom from slavery. In *On Being Brought from Africa to America,* the kind of enslavement she seems most concerned with is that of her former ignorance of "redemption." Her letters provide a valuable addition to students' understanding of Wheatley's life, documenting her correspondence with abolitionist groups in England and America and with other Africans in servitude in America. Her letters continue to suggest that she views spiritual salvation as "the way to true felicity," as she expresses this in her letter to Arbour Tanner but also that she is aware of the needs of both Africans and American Indians for help in this world. Her letter to Samson Occom comes closest to revealing the development of Wheatley's voice as an advocate for the natural rights of blacks.

Wheatley was freed after the death of the Wheatleys, and her circumstances would have been radically different from those of the southern slaves. Yet the very existence of her poetry provides evidence to students that there is a direct correlation between liberty and literary authority. Ask students to compare Wheatley with Bradstreet. What explains the absence of personal voice in Wheatley? Is she writing in imitation of eighteenth-century British poets or has she chosen a poetic style that calls the least possible attention to the speaking voice? Wheatley does make a connection between achieving exalted language in poetry (or in art, as in *To S. M., A Young African Painter, on Seeing His Works*) and rising on "seraphic pinions." Placing Wheatley in her historical context, a reader can see the appeal for southern slaves of spiritual "rising" and the "liberty" of religious salvation—an appeal that white slaveowners ironically exploited as an effective panacea to silence the slaves' dissatisfactions. In offering the language of "wings enraptured" and "celestial choir," Wheatley resembles the earlier colonial writers (such as Wigglesworth and Taylor) for whom personal concerns and personal voice are largely absent. And yet the imagery of "rising" and racial uplift would reappear in black prose and poetry from Booker T. Washington to Countee Cullen.

ROYALL TYLER

In his exit lines, Dimple summarizes the play's "main chance" when he contrasts himself, "a gentleman, who has read Chesterfield and received the polish of Europe," with Manly, "an unpolished, untravelled American." But long before the closing scenes Tyler establishes contrast as the play's dramatic principle. In opening a discussion of the play, ask students to comment on Tyler's use of contrast. Letitia and Charlotte begin the play by disagreeing on the merits of the pocket hoop and the bell hoop; they discuss the contrast Maria finds "betwixt the good sense of her books, and the flimsiness of her love-letters" so that she spoke of Mr. Dimple "with respect abroad, and with contempt in her closet"; and, in Act 2, Charlotte describes her brother as "the very counterpart and reverse of me." The servants Jonathan and Jeremy contrast with each other and mirror the contrast between Manly and Dimple, and the contrast between country and city reinforces the contrast between American style and European influence. Low-life scenes between the servants extend the humor among the protagonists, and the apparent triviality of the play's subject matter—style—contrasts with the seriousness of an American's attempt to write "a piece, which we may fairly call our own."

Some of the play's humor derives, as the headnote points out, from its Americanization of the basic story line of Sheridan's *The School for Scandal.* Tyler also overloads the play with conventions of eighteenth-century comedy, especially at the end, when we discover two eavesdroppers, one of whom hides in a closet, and when the play's *denouement* rests on Van Rough's disclosure that he, too, had eavesdropped from within a closet. The play that begins in disagreement ends in harmony, with the promise of weddings between Jonathan and his Tabitha, and between Maria and Manly.

A literary period that essentially begins with the deaths of half the original settlers of Plymouth, and which predicts a day of doom for sinners in the hands of an angry God, ends, perhaps surprisingly, in comedy. Such is the true contrast in Royall Tyler's play, the reversal of literary fortune from the sermon to the drama. Instead of telling late-eighteenth-century Americans how to live, Tyler is more interested in portraying the way they live. Much of the play's value will demonstrate itself if you allow students to experience the comic relief of Tyler and the drama, after what may have seemed to them to be a long struggle with Puritans and historians. If there is time, forgo discussion long enough to assign parts, and allow students to walk through Act 5, Scene 2, up to Dimple's exit. The scene includes everyone but Jonathan and Jenny, and walking through it will bring to life the eavesdroppers and the "heroism" of Manly's defense of his sister's honor.

1820–1865

One way of creating a context for discussing early-nineteenth-century authors is to analyze closely with students several works related in theme before proceeding to a more chronological examination. I sometimes ask students to read *Rip Van Winkle* (see discussion of Rip's dream below) in conjunction with *Young Goodman Brown* (another story that shows the male protagonist waking from a dream), *Bartleby, the Scrivener* (where

Bartleby's "dead wall revery" becomes a variation on the dream motif), and Thoreau's *Resistance to Civil Government* (in which he describes his night in jail as "a change [that] had to my eyes come over the scene." Students have heard the phrase "American dream" used as a cliché; beginning the nineteenth century with works in which American dreams actually figure in the plot helps them look for new meanings in the theme. In these four works the dreamers share confusion concerning the nature of reality. I ask students to keep in mind the larger historical context—the abolitionist movement, early manifestations of the women's rights struggle in the temperance society, the emerging American economic system, the near-extinction of the American Indians, and the imperialism of the war with Mexico—as they study a literature that explores the power of the imagination at the same time that it often denies or ignores the unresolved conflict at the center of early-nineteenth-century American social and political life.

Yet, despite that frequent denial, the literature of the 1820–1865 period gives us evidence of an awakening. As Hershel Parker notes in his period introduction in NAAL, by the 1850s "there was some elusive quality about [the country's] new literature that was *American*." Even though many of our early-nineteenth-century writers may have turned inward—to the world of romance, Gothic fantasy, dreams, idealized portraits of the West and the American Indians, or the microcosm of individual perception, or the single-sex universe of Melville's sea fiction—even the transcendentalist Thoreau, in separating himself from society at Walden Pond, tries to give imagery of waking literal—and literary—body. Is an American identity the creation of a few early-nineteenth-century dreamers or does it result from the rhythms of dreaming and waking, of separation and engagement, of evasion and confrontation?

As the literature of the 1820–1865 period particularly shows, writing helps Emerson, Hawthorne, Dickinson, and others to discover who they are in what they see and the language they find to express that vision. At this point, I suggest to my students that what we are exploring, in part, as we read American literature is the development of ways of thinking and seeing the world as well as ways of imagining and creating the self. In rejecting the rationality of the Enlightenment, early-nineteenth-century writers yet were evolving their own vision. Thoreau, in *Walden*, explicitly exchanges Enlightenment thinking for Eastern mystical enlightenment. Can students see the early-nineteenth-century writers' rejection of rationality as part of a larger pattern in American literary history? The Puritans were typological, the eighteenth-century writers exalted reason and logic, but the early-nineteenth-century writers were analogical in their way of seeing. Perhaps the emergence of an "American" imaginative literature in the early nineteenth century may itself be seen as evidence of evolution in epistemology. Once writers became capable of inventing metaphors for their own imagination or for telling stories about either private or public life, they became equally capable of exploring the meaning of their experience and for defining it as "American."

Transcendentalism took the separatism of early-nineteenth-century writers to its extreme limit. Yet, as I try to show in our class discussion of *Nature* and *Walden*, the transcendentalists' theory of language becomes the basis for yet another American spiritual movement, and in retrospect, every prior moment of separation in colonial and American literary history may be seen as a variation on that pattern. When the Puritan reliance on God's word seems in need of strengthening, Jonathan Edwards rewrites the Bible; when theology fails to solve material problems, Benjamin Franklin invents a language with which to address the common people and to create himself as a blueprint; when Britain no longer speaks for the colonists, Jefferson writes a document that enacts the very independence it declares; and in the early nineteenth century, Emerson calls for a literary separation ("We have listened too long to the courtly muses of Europe," from *The American Scholar*) and for an American poet capable of finding the language for the "as yet unsung" American experience ("Yet America is a poem in our eyes," from *The Poet*). The evolution from typology to logic to analogy is progressive, even though the early-nineteenth-century writers were the first to see the pattern. The "forms of being" change, and the theories of language change, but American writers become increasingly aware of their powers to name themselves and thus to write themselves into being. From Rip Van Winkle's dream to Adrienne Rich's "dream of a common language," the meaning of both American identity and American literary history are intimately tied to the evolution of an American language.

By the end of their study of the first volume of NAAL, students can see that while American writers may continue after the Civil War to struggle with language and literary forms that will make it possible for them to write an American literature, from the Revolution on they learn to look to themselves for their literary authority and to their own experience for the emotional and aesthetic power of their work. Despite Stowe's comment about taking dictation from God, American writers after the Federal period no longer have even the illusion, as Edward Taylor had written, "that Thou wilt guide my pen to write aright." Nineteenth-century authors make creative literature out of the economic and spiritual self-reliance of which Franklin and Emerson wrote. Nevertheless, the prohibitions against writing and speaking that American white women and black and Native American men and women suffered throughout the 1620–1865 period in American history would mean that many Americans, then and now, continue to be silenced and that the act of writing for white women and for black writers would reflect acts of heroic rebellion.

WASHINGTON IRVING

Rip Van Winkle is the work I choose to open the 1820–1865 segment, and we analyze it closely. Many of my students entirely pass over Irving's references to the American Revolution until we discuss them in class. I call the story the first "American dream" in American literature, and we talk about the implications of that dream. Students make connections between the confused state of mind the earliest colonists must have experienced and Rip's confusion on "waking" to discover that he is a citizen of a new country, an event that must have seemed to many to have taken place overnight. In one central passage in the story that recurs almost as a template in later American literature, Rip asks, "Does nobody here know Rip Van Winkle?" Irving writes, "The poor fellow was now completely confounded. He doubted his own identity, and whether he was himself or another man. In the midst of his bewilderment, the man in the cocked hat demanded who he was, and what was his name?" Rip's reply echoes with contemporary resonance to undergraduate students: " 'God knows,' exclaimed he, at his wit's end; 'I'm not myself—I'm somebody else—that's me yonder—no—that's somebody else, got into my shoes—I was myself last night, but I fell asleep on the mountain, and they've changed my gun and every thing's changed, and I'm changed, and I can't tell what's my name, or who I am!' " The story suggests as one meaning of the American dream that, like Rip, we are confused and about twenty years behind accepting or understanding our own national history. The new country begins in uncertainty and confusion; the new American's sense of identity falters, then gains in confidence, much as the tale itself shows Rip, by the end, invested with new authority.

But what is the nature of that authority? For Rip, who becomes "reverenced" as a storyteller, a "chronicle of the old times 'before the war,' " is the same person who, twenty years earlier, owned the "worst conditioned farm in the neighbourhood" and was "ready to attend to any body's business but his own." Here Irving shows Rip as a type of the artist before his time; it is only *after* history catches up with him, in a sense, and he manages to wake up after the Revolution that he finds his vocation (the resonance with American literary history seems almost allegorical in this reading of the story). Is the story Irving's comment on the absence of imaginative literature before the American Revolution? What happens to Rip's cultural identity that makes it possible for the townspeople to produce their first storyteller? I suggest that the story documents the transition between the moment in which the new country had a potential chronicler (Rip Van Winkle) but no history, to the moment just a "dream" later when its new identity gave it both a storyteller and a story to tell. Like the moment of the decline of Puritanism and the emergence of enlightenment thinking that we see in Franklin's *Autobiography* (where Franklin keeps the form of Puritan introspection and changes its content), there is a similar moment of transition between pre- and postrevolutionary thinking for the new American Rip Van Winkle. In changing only the red coat of King George to the blue coat of George Washington on the sign that used to stand over the village inn (and now advertises the Union Hotel), Irving suggests that the "singularly metamorphosed" country may have undergone radical change, but retains a similar form. What, then, happens to political analysis in the story? Irving writes that "Rip, in fact, was no politician; the changes of states and empires made but little impression on him."

At the end of the story Irving evades exploring the ironies implicit in the American dream by turning all of Rip's confusion into a joke at Dame Van Winkle's expense: "But there was one species of despotism under which he had long groaned, and that was—petticoat government." Here Irving establishes a theme that would become characteristic of much nineteenth-century fiction, in which the male character represents simple good nature, artistic sensibility, and free spirit and the female character, all of the forces that inhibit that sensibility and spirit and make Rip miserable. The spirit of American Revolution, in which the colonists threw off the fetters of "mother England," becomes the rationale for nineteenth-century American man, who would rather kill American Indians and explore the wilderness than stay home minding his own farm. The American woman becomes the new villain. Dame's "curtain lectures" vie only with Puritan sermons in their severity, and it is her "dinning" voice, her tongue that was "incessantly going," that Irving blames for silencing the budding artist in Rip. ("Rip had but one way of replying to all lectures of the kind. . . . He shrugged his shoulders, shook his head, cast up his eyes, but said nothing.") American fiction begins in triumph over the silencing of Dame Van Winkle—for Rip's real victory is not the one he wins over the British, but as a result of Dame's death. One might conclude that for Irving—as for Cooper, Poe, Hawthorne, and Melville—the real American dream is of a world in which women are either silent, dead, or in some other way entirely excluded from the sphere of action. (See Judith Fetterley's *The Resisting Reader* [1978] for a fuller examination of this story from a feminist perspective.)

Whether you present these readings of *Rip Van Winkle* directly or try to elicit them through questions, I guarantee that the material this single story generates will wake up your students and keep them awake through many later discussions.

THE CHEROKEE MEMORIALS

Students can derive most of the relevant historical information they need to understand these documents from the Memorials themselves: they were written in response to the Indian Removal Act of 1830, which authorized the removal of Indian groups to lands west of the Mississippi. Although these Memorials were not written until 1829 and 1830, they may be read as a response to the invasion and colonization by European settlers two centuries earlier. The Memorials reveal inconsistencies in the U.S. government's treatment of the Cherokee—on the one hand viewing them as subjects and on the other negotiating with them as independent people of a separate nation. "The answer must be plain—they were not subjects, but a distinct nation." Furthermore, the Memorials point out that treaties enacted between the Cherokee and the U.S. governments were "always written by the Commissioners, on the part of the United States, for obvious reasons: as the Cherokees were unacquainted with letters." In each of these arguments, students can see evidence of awareness on the part of the Cherokee themselves; indeed, reading the Memorials may help students become aware that *even at the time of their own removal,* the Cherokee were articulate analysts of their own situation and of U.S. policies and accurately predicted the disastrous outcome of the Indian Removal Act. In the document dated November 5, 1829, the authors note that the doctrine will be "fatal in its consequences to us," and urge the House and the Senate to take action so that "our national existence may not be extinguished."

What seems particularly compelling about these Cherokee Memorials is that, according to historical accounts, and noted in the text as well, the Cherokee in Georgia had endeavored to improve themselves on the model for civilization encouraged by their white neighbors: they had built roads and houses, become Christianized, published books in an alphabet invented by Sequoyah, and adopted a national constitution. In light of these efforts, students may see in the hope that "our national existence may not be extinguished" a double meaning: the Cherokee do not wish to lose either their cultural identity or their new attainments as "civilized" or "national" persons. They doubly express their feelings of betrayal, because they not only are asked to leave their ancestral lands but also understand that their efforts to "improve" their society have not merited what they had expected—"the voice of encouragement by an approving world."

The Cherokee would lose a fourth of their population in their journey out of Georgia. And Georgia would mine and extract the gold that had been discovered on Cherokee lands. Meanwhile, these Cherokee Memorials remain as an opportunity for late-twentieth-century students to trace the historical consciousness and protest of Native American peoples.

AUGUSTUS BALDWIN LONGSTREET AND "OLD SOUTHWEST HUMOR"

Among the three "Southwest humorists" included in NAAL (Longstreet, Thorpe, and Harris), Longstreet was the only one who did not publish in *The Spirit of the Times*, a sporting magazine of the 1830s and 1840s that avoided political commentary and references to slavery and provided gentlemen interested in the leisure pursuits of horse-racing, hunting, and listening to tall tales with a way of gratifying fantasies of upper-class superiority; of ratifying their belief in masculine values and male dominance; and of relegating women to the source, butt, and object of sexual humor. Considering Longstreet's tales along with the works of the other two "humorists" of the 1820–1865 period can raise ideological and literary controversy in the classroom, for Longstreet confirms what the *Spirit of the Times* writers assumed—that storytelling is a masculine activity. Furthermore, the Southwest writers exclude the moralistic position of their women contemporaries from their fiction (remind students that the 1830s was also the decade of the beginnings of the temperance and abolitionist movements, in which women began to participate as public figures for the first time in American history). Among this group, only Longstreet suggests a lingering fluidity in the relationship between gender and genre in early American fiction, before literature became the self-designated province of men for writers such as Hawthorne and Melville as much as for the Southwest humorists.

As a way of examining Longstreet's interest in gender, contrast Lyman Hall, Longstreet's narrator of *The Horse-Swap* with Baldwin, the narrator he chooses to relate *A Sage Conversation.* Baldwin is an ineffectual moralist, reduced to reporting the cleverness of his friend Ned Brace in fooling the three aged matrons of *A Sage Conversation;* Hall, on the other hand, represents successful masculinity, competence, and the ability to influence others through his storytelling. (In the larger collection in which these tales appeared, *Georgia Scenes,* Longstreet continues to oppose Hall and Baldwin as narrators, and he continues to set up Baldwin as a foil for the masculine Hall's exploits.) In examining *A Sage Conversation,* consider how Longstreet links Baldwin to the world of women that he simultaneously mocks. The matrons in the tale do not manage to figure out the mysteries of gender-crossing, much less engage in the actively masculine pursuit of contriving and telling a story; even though they light their pipes and sit around the fire until late in the night, their talking never rises above the level of "old woman's chat." Unlike Longstreet himself, the women miss the narrative potential of their material, and the final message of *A Sage Conversation* offers its own moral: women are "harmless," by which Longstreet means that they are incapable of storytelling and, therefore, pose no threat, even to the effeminate Baldwin.

WILLIAM CULLEN BRYANT

More than Freneau, Bryant exemplifies the new "Americanness" of nineteenth-century literature; yet Bryant will not serve as Emerson's American poet. Ask your students why; ask them, as well, to compare

Thanatopsis with Freneau's *The House of Night.* Which of Bryant's poems look to eighteenth-century values, both in philosophy and aesthetics? I often closely analyze *The Prairies* in class, for this poem is the most clearly "American" of the selections in NAAL. What aspects of the poem are either neoclassical or derivative of British forms? What marks the poem as American? We discuss the way Bryant draws his imagery from the great plains, takes as his subject the "dilated sight" of the romantic perceiver, and associates the source of perception with change in the "forms of being." The mixture of styles, philosophies, and attitudes toward poetry that students find in *The Prairies* helps them see that evolution in thinking and writing takes place slowly. Some might justifiably argue that the "British" elements in Bryant's poetry contribute greatly to its beauty and power and that the evidence of continued influence is one valid response to the confusion the new Americans must have felt post-Revolution, as well as a tribute to the enduring cultural and emotional content of the new country's relationship to things British, despite the radical change in our form of government.

WILLIAM APESS

Apess's *An Indian's Looking-Glass for the White Man* merits comparison with Samuel Occom's *Sermon Preached at the Execution of Moses Paul,* for both Occom and Apess were Christian preachers and both worked as missionaries of and reformers to American Indian peoples. Furthermore, in both of these texts, Occom and Apess are addressing a white audience; Apess, however, is much more direct in criticizing the audience he is addressing.

Ask students to comment on the image of the looking-glass. In one sense Apess's essay holds a mirror up to his Euro-American audience, but that mirroring also creates a rhetorical form of encounter, thus linking Apess's text with the "Literature to 1620" section of NAAL and hinting at several new ways to interpret this trope in light of the history of Native Americans in the nineteenth-century United States. Encounter means war and genocide against the native peoples of North America in the nineteenth century just as it did for the earliest European explorers and colonizers. But in Apess's text, such encounters ought to tell whites more about themselves.

For the looking-glass also holds up to his audience the reality of the lives of Indians, particularly of women and children in poverty—"Let me for a few moments turn your attention to the reservations in the different states of New England"—thus asking his audience to encounter in a literal sense the lives he describes for them and in a spiritual sense the racism they have condoned and that Apess deems responsible for the material condition of the Indians' lives. The looking-glass thus becomes both self-reflexive and reflective of the racialized "others" in American history—a history that, for Apess, includes the treatment of African-Americans as well as American Indians.

In some ways the rhetoric of Apess's text may seem uncomplicated, perhaps partly because the arguments he raises to counter racism may be familiar to students in your class. He argues that Euro-Americans use skin color to racialize the difference and hence the inferiority of both Native Americans and African-Americans; he reminds his audience that there are by far more skins of color in the world than white skins (he cites the ratio of fifteen to one), he makes his audience aware of the theory that Jesus Christ and the Apostles were themselves persons of color, and he protests the double-standard that has allowed white men to marry native women but has not allowed native men "to choose their partners among the whites if they wish." Many of these and other points of his argument actually seem quite forward-looking for 1833, anticipating analyses of racial formation in our own time. And Apess cites Scripture to underscore his reasoning.

In another way, his rhetorical strategy is complex and provocative. After all, as a Christian Indian, he is himself the product of a particular aspect of white culture, the aspect he now invokes to affirm his perspective. Thus, as he addresses his white audience, he himself becomes a looking-glass; in Apess, his Christian audience can see their own creation and their own best selves taken as gospel and then held back up to them. Point out to students that Apess does not base his essay on the Scripture and in fact does not even quote from the Bible early in his text. It is only later, when he is looking for support for his own argument, that he quotes. Examine the particular passages he includes; these passages become the ultimate moments of encounter with the self for his Euro-American audience, for they have ostensibly served as models for New England character. When he examines them, he states his purpose, namely "to penetrate more fully into the conduct of those who profess to have pure principles and who tell us to follow Jesus Christ. . . . Let us see if they come anywhere near him and his ancient disciples." The act of examining the principles of Christ—including especially "Thou shalt love thy neighbor as thyself" and "Let us not love in word but in deed"—becomes the rhetorical act of holding up the looking-glass, but in effect, the Indians themselves are what Apess wants his audience to see when they look in a mirror. "Thou shalt love thy neighbor as thyself" becomes, in Apess's text, "Thou shalt see thy neighbor as—and in—thyself."

Apess's text thus becomes an emblem of American literature viewed as encounter: without the meeting of Native American and Christian cultures in Apess himself, he would not be speaking texts in a language that can be transcribed (but rather, perhaps, be an orator of native myths or songs). What he has to say, as a product of that encounter, is conveyed by the word *looking-glass.* Thus the history of relations between Indians and whites explains the emergence of Apess's text: *encounter* serves as a figure for another creation myth, this one for a Native American's creation of American literature and his implied white reader.

RALPH WALDO EMERSON

The Emerson selections in NAAL give us more than any of us can teach in any one course, and therefore, you can vary your choices, depending on your model of course organization or what themes or concepts you are emphasizing. I asked my colleague William Shurr, a lover of Emerson and a specialist in the early nineteenth century, how he makes his own choices for the American literature course. He teaches excerpts from *Nature* (Chapters I, III, IV, and VIII outline one possibility), then chooses essays and poems that will allow students to understand Emerson's basic philosophy. He reported to me that he has found *The Rhodora* to be the single Emerson poem that consistently produces the best student response. In this poem, Emerson addresses the poem as "dear," and Shurr said that he always asks students if they have ever addressed a poem this way and what it does to the poem. He also suggested an article on *Uriel* by Kevin P. Van Anglen, titled "Emerson, Milton, and the Fall of Uriel" (*Emerson Society Quarterly* 30, no. 3 [1984]), as an essay that "unlocks" this poem and might give instructors help in defining transcendentalism for students.

If you are focusing on the New Americanness of American literature in the early nineteenth century, one or more of the following essays will help you develop the theme: *The American Scholar, The Divinity School Address, Self-Reliance,* and *The Poet.* If you are interested in discussing Emerson's philosophy and contrasting it with his commentary on social issues of the day, choose from the list I suggest in Chapter 4. The journal entry of August 1, 1852, in which Emerson rationalizes one of the rare twinges of social conscience in his writing—"I have quite other slaves to free than those negroes, to wit, imprisoned spirits, imprisoned thoughts, far back in the brain of man"—is essential reading for students, however you set up your course. In my own classroom, whatever model of course organization I choose, I ask students to read all of *Nature,* and we then spend several class meetings analyzing it. The key to understanding Emerson for students rests, I have found, in my own success in helping them understand this essay, so I will offer some detailed suggestions from what has worked for me. Following the discussion of *Nature,* I will also comment on two additional essays, *The Poet* and *Fate,* which will help span the chronology of Emerson's career and provide works of particular interest to students.

Nature

Emerson loses many students in the opening paragraphs of *Nature*, and it might be useful to read the "Introduction" with them during the class period before you turn them loose on the entire essay. Certain sentences contain kernel ideas that I work with at length in discussion. One of the earliest—"Every man's condition is a solution in hieroglyphic to those inquiries he would put. He acts it as life, before he apprehends it as truth"—initially gives students difficulty, but as we talk about it, always trying to find something in their own experience that will give them some "felt" affinity for what Emerson is saying, they begin to see that, for Emerson, nature includes our own "condition." He breaks down boundaries between self and body, between our own feeling and the natural world, with the result that he achieves a spiritual vision of unity with nature—"I become a transparent eye-ball. I am nothing. I see all. The currents of the Universal Being circulate through me; I am part or particle of God."

I have found that, pedagogically, the most important single concept in the essay is contained in the following sentence: "Each particle is a microcosm, and faithfully renders the likeness of the world." Students can see this visually by turning to an example Emerson uses earlier in the essay, at the beginning of "Language," in which he writes, "Who looks upon a river in a meditative hour, and is not reminded of the flux of all things? Throw a stone into the stream, and the circles that propagate themselves are the beautiful type of all influence." Almost everyone in the class, at some point in childhood, will have done just that—and all will remember the series of concentric circles that radiate out from the point at which the stone enters the water. I ask them to reconstruct what happens as we look further from that central point; they all remember that the circles grow larger but fainter, and some of them will recall from a high-school math class that, theoretically, the circles continue infinitely, even though they might not be visible to the eye. We talk about this example as an analogy for Emerson's entire philosophy, for it contains several essential ideas: (1) that our observation of the finite ripples on the water leads us to "see" the ripples that ease out into infinity, (2) that the concentric circles made by the ripples themselves form a series of analogies, and (3) that in the act of throwing one stone we can manage to contact an infinitely enlarging sphere. This discussion helps with the related ideas that "man is an analogist, and studies relations in all objects" and that "the world is emblematic. Parts of speech are metaphors because the whole of nature is a metaphor of the human mind." Each of these points takes time, but the rewards are great. Students begin to see that, through analogies, we can understand the world and our own relation to it. Chapter IV, "Language," is important to this discussion, because Emerson sees the very process of creating analogies or metaphors as essential to human understanding. Therefore, he can quote Plato—"poetry comes nearer to vital truth than history"—and can state, "Empirical science is apt to cloud the sight . . . a dream may let us deeper into the secret of nature than a hundred concerted experiments." Here you can ask students to compare Emerson with Franklin and Jefferson; Emerson's philosophy is deeply antithetical to the Age of Experiment.

Why do students find *Nature* so difficult? Most of them describe having trouble with Emerson's syntax. Ask them to think about what constitutes the unit of thought for Emerson. Is it the sentence, the paragraph, the section? He uses a linear form, prose, but does not write discursively. I suggest to them that the *analogy* is Emerson's basic unit of thought. His ideas move out from an analogical center like the ripples on the pond, even though he is forced to write about them as if he is thinking linearly and logically.

Another central concept that students need help with is what Emerson means by transcendence. How does an understanding of analogies, or of the microcosm that is nature, help us to transcend the limitations of our material existence and our own finite abilities to "see"? Here, viewing his use of the analogy as the unit of thought is crucial to our understanding, for he seems to be saying that if we focus on the analogy and on the single part, we will be able to understand the whole. To this end, he states, "Whilst we behold unveiled the nature of Justice and Truth, we learn the difference between the absolute and the conditional or relative. We apprehend the absolute. As it were, for the first time, *we exist*." If you have any students in your class who have studied transcendental meditation, or any other Eastern meditative technique, you can ask them to talk about how they have understood and experienced the difference between the "absolute" and the "relative." Sometimes these students can explain what it feels like to begin with a mantra in meditation and then "transcend" into an oceanic feeling of oneness with the universe. (This is also an ideal moment to ask students whether they find any lingering Puritanism in Emerson. Are there similarities in form between Emerson's focus on the analogy as the vehicle for transcendence and the Puritan's search for the black mark or spot?)

I try to describe a series of American themes that Emerson gets at in the essay: reliance on the self; the idea that the possibility of redemption lies within the individual; a belief in the perception of the individual and the intimate connection of human beings with nature (if students have studied the British Romantic poets it will help here); the ability, the imperative, of Americans to "build their own world"; and essential to his philosophy, the conflict between empirical knowledge and intuition, between logic and analogy. We talk about the way that conflict is apparent in students' own lives, even in their own choice of major fields of study at the university: Do they become technologists or humanists? Do they choose applied or theoretical science? Do they elect courses in computer science or poetry? Emerson is certain to challenge their conception of thinking as linear, for he shows that analogy possesses its own logic, and that poetry and imaginative literature can help us to live in the world, perhaps better than science and technology—for, if analogy is the means of transcending, then analogy holds ascendancy over logic and helps us reunite body and spirit, thought and feeling. "What we are, that only can we see" brings the essay back to the beginning, to the idea of "solution in hieroglyphic."

The Poet

With the humanities under increasing attack in our society, students who choose to study literature need some support for their choice. Emerson's essay *The Poet* makes an argument for the value of poetry and the significance of language that remains compelling in the late twentieth century.

As the NAAL headnote observes, Emerson considered himself a poet, and I often teach an Emerson essay as if I were teaching the work of a poet; we respond to individual sentences and to Emerson's specific expression of particular ideas, much as if we were trying to close-read a lyric poem. In this essay, we begin with his central idea that all of us "stand in need of expression . . . we study to utter our painful secret. The man is only half himself, the other half is his expression." Asking students to respond to this idea can lead into a discussion of voice, one of their own specific tasks as undergraduates, as well as the ongoing task of American writers throughout our literary history. Emerson suggests that the poet possesses both a complete vision as well as the tool—language—for expressing what we would all understand if we were just given the analogies for doing so. The poet finds those particular analogies (metaphors, similes, images) that allow us to understand what we might have been just on the verge of seeing, but were never able to fully see without the analogies themselves.

Therefore, Emerson writes, "Words are also actions, and actions are a kind of words." Someone who is able to express the inchoate understandings of other human beings allows us to integrate our being and our experience in the world. (You might digress here to look back to the role expression played in the American Revolution. Would we have been able to articulate *The Declaration of Independence* without Adams, Franklin, and Jefferson?) This idea may generate some controversy for students, unaccustomed to viewing language as action. Ask them to talk about related ideas they find in their reading of the essay, perhaps Emerson's statement that "language is fossil poetry," or that the world is "thus put under the mind for verb and noun." Asking students to explain what it might mean to see the world as "put under the mind for verb and noun" may help them to become more conscious about the relationship between words and actions.

Emerson's poet does more than help us create a bridge between what we see and what we can express; the poet also enables us to recreate ourselves. Thus, Emerson writes, "All that we call sacred history attests that the birth of a poet is the principal event in chronology." In direct challenge to particular theologies, Emerson asserts that, as young Americans (whether we interpret him to refer specifically to the young culture of the new Republic, or more loosely to the process of forming American identity in each of us as one of the tasks of undergraduate intellectual development), we look for a poet who will be able to tell us who and what we are. "Poets are thus liberating gods," he writes, "They are free, and they make free," and they keep us from miserably dying "on the brink of the waters of life and truth."

At the end of *The Poet*, Emerson writes the famous lines, "I look in vain for the poet whom I describe. . . . We have yet had no genius in America. . . . Yet America is a poem in our eyes." If you are looking ahead to reading Whitman, *The Poet* helps students create a context of continuity between writers of the 1820–1865 period. Emerson would not have to wait long for the particular American poet he longed for; he would be able, after the 1855 publication of Walt Whitman's *Leaves of Grass*, to greet Whitman "at the beginning of a great career" and to see some of his own prophetic hope for the unsung poem of America realized in Whitman's verse.

Whatever your own personal attitudes toward feminism, if you wish to include fully women students in the discussion of Emerson, it will be useful to bring out into the open Emerson's repeated use of masculine imagery to extol the qualities of the poet. How do your students respond to the following statements? "The man is only half himself, the other half is his expression." "The religions of the world are the ejaculations of a few imaginative men." "Hence the necessity of speech and song; . . . that thought may be ejaculated as Logos, or Word." In this context, refer students to Emerson's journal entry of November-December 1841, [Dead Sentences Versus Man-Making Words], in which he writes, "Give me initiative, spermatic, prophesying, man-making words." Does Emerson's language of action, initiative, and ejaculation include or exclude women from the realm of poetic genius?

Fate

The late essay, *Fate*, is practically guaranteed to elicit controversy among your students and, at the same time, to give them a rare glimpse of Emerson responding to the current events and spirit of his own times. Throughout the essay, Emerson variously defines fate as the laws of the world, as what limits us, as unpenetrated causes, and he writes that "once we thought, positive power was all. Now, we learn, that negative power, or circumstance, is half. Nature is the tyrannous circumstance." Contrast what he says here about nature with the essay *Nature* itself. How do your students respond to Emerson's position that the "fate" of our limitations cannot be transcended, except by accepting it and building "altars" to the "Beautiful Necessity"? Is there no hope for reform in the world if "the riddle of the age has for each a private solution"? Is Emerson asking us to accept what he himself terms the "complicity" of "race living at the expense of race" because "Providence has a wild, rough, incalculable road to its end," and therefore it is futile to "whitewash its huge mixed instrumentalities"? Had Emerson been able to imagine a Hitler, would he have included Nazi Germany in his "Beautiful Necessity"? Is there no hope for environment or the "nurture" side of Emerson's portrait of nature? He writes of the ditch-digger that "he has but one future, and that is already predetermined in his lobes, and described in that little fatty face, pig-eye, and squat form. All the privilege and all the legislation of the world cannot meddle or help to make a poet or a prince of him." Is Emerson's own essay itself an ironic example of "organization tyrannizing over character"? If we accept the "Beautiful Necessity" of things, are we enshrining elitism, the New England Brahminism of ideological caste and class? Allowing your students to challenge Emerson is one way of teaching them to take his ideas seriously, to be critical as well as appreciative; it is a way of allowing them to participate in the shaping of ideological debate that characterizes American cultural history.

NATHANIEL HAWTHORNE

Hawthorne presents a special problem for a teacher because students often look for "morals" in his work. They confuse his use of Puritan subjects and themes with his own values and conclude that Hawthorne is himself a Puritan. They also need help in understanding the concept of allegory and how it works in Hawthorne. *Young Goodman Brown, The Minister's Black Veil,* and *Rappaccini's Daughter* all invite students to find allegorical "equations"—and all deliberately frustrate the attempt. In each of these stories, I challenge students to identify the "good" character, and in every case, they end by qualifying their initial response. For Hawthorne's moral universe is ultimately ambiguous.

Rappaccini's Daughter works particularly well in classroom study of Hawthorne's use of allegory, for students have fun trying to work out the parallels between the Garden of Eden and Rappaccini's garden. The role of the serpent (after the lizard is poisoned by the flower) remains open by the end of the story: who *is* responsible for Beatrice's death? Rappaccini? Baglioni? Giovanni? Hawthorne himself? How does the story, in creating an antigarden, actually affirm the moral universe of the Garden of Eden, despite its attempt to invert those values? Is the story a variation of *Rip Van Winkle,* in which Irving triumphs over Dame Van Winkle's power by silencing her at the end?

Asking students to read Melville's *Hawthorne and His Mosses* can lead into a discussion of the "blackness" Melville saw in Hawthorne's fiction. Is that "blackness" a reference to Hawthorne's moral universe or a reflection of his use of dream imagery (explicitly in *Young Goodman Brown* and implicitly in the atmosphere of his other work)? I suggest to students that the ambivalence they find in Hawthorne actually expresses the mingled self-confrontation and self-evasion that characterize his protagonists. Rather than try to "solve" the ambiguities one finds in Hawthorne, I try to show students, instead, that his choice to be ambivalent is deliberate and conscious. We talk about the way Young Goodman Brown, Reverend Hooper, Rappaccini, and the speaker in "The Custom-House" (from *The Scarlet Letter*) are all, in part, Hawthorne's self-portraits, or at least portraits of the artist. Unlike Thoreau, who values facing life "deliberately" in *Walden,* Hawthorne goes only so far in trying to see what is *there*—in his characters and ultimately in himself. Hershel Parker, in the period introduction in NAAL, describes the "crucial aesthetic problems" early nineteenth-century writers face, and suggests that Hawthorne's involved his attempt to "strike a balance between the allegorical and the realistic." What might this mean, if we consider the actual moment of confrontation between the writer and the blank page? "The Custom-House" provides a rich opportunity for students to consider the struggles of the writer and to see that these struggles take place within the depths of the psyche, perhaps at the source of the individual writer's (or the culture's) dream life.

Wakefield

Wakefield provides an opportunity to study, in detail, Hawthorne's mingled self-confrontation and self-evasion, and the tale is brief enough for close analysis, either in class discussion or as an essay assignment. In trying to determine what motivates Wakefield, Hawthorne is also exploring what motivates his own story, and if we view Wakefield as a projection of the artist himself, we learn a great deal about Hawthorne. Hawthorne gives us explicit permission to mingle his own projections with his creation of character when he writes, "We are free to shape out our own idea, and call it by [Wakefield's] name."

The point of inception of the tale, as Hawthorne writes in the opening sentence, is a man "—let us call him Wakefield—who absented himself for a long time, from his wife." Although Hawthorne does not explicitly link Wakefield with Rip Van Winkle, the resemblance of Wakefield's twenty-year absence to Rip's twenty-year sleep is unmistakable. In studying Irving, we could view Dame Van Winkle as Irving's allegorical representation of "mother England" and explain away some of the misogyny in Irving's characterization of this character. But *Wakefield* does not have the American Revolution as allegorical underpinning. Wakefield's own twenty-year absence seems unmotivated, and Hawthorne's perception that such an absence is "not very uncommon" leads him to "meditate" on Wakefield.

Hawthorne does not excuse Wakefield's action, using terms like *cold, quiet selfishness,* and *vanity* to describe his character. Nevertheless, neither does he empathize with Wakefield's wife, despite his portrait of the woman as close to death in the aftermath of her husband's mysterious abandonment. Hawthorne approaches self-revelation when he turns away from exploring the effects of Wakefield's behavior on his wife (much as Wakefield himself does) and writes, "But, our business is with the husband." In that single statement, Hawthorne summarizes much of American literature among our classic writers during the 1820–1865 period, and he creates the condition for recognizing his own complicity with Wakefield. He might as well be saying that, in the early years of the American republic, male American writers turned inexplicably away from exploring women's lives and experience, for more than twenty years. Is Wakefield's twenty-year absence from domestic life the true American dream for our earliest classic writers? Hawthorne chooses to analyze Wakefield's "chasm in human affections," but in omitting any meditation on Mrs. Wakefield's motivations, he veers off from the possibility of self-confrontation. At the tale's end, Hawthorne avoids even considering the possibility that Mrs. Wakefield might not take her husband back. She remains, to the end, a "grotesque shadow," an "admirable caricature," and all Wakefield has to do to regain what Hawthorne terms his "place" in the system, is to open the door, stop playing his "little joke" on his wife, and take a "good night's rest."

The moral, "done up neatly, and condensed into the final sentence," allows Hawthorne to side-step the very question he began by exploring: "What sort of a man was Wakefield?" He evades a fuller exploration of the complexity of Wakefield's character by suggesting that it was Wakefield's action, not his failure of empathy, that led him to the brink of becoming the "Outcast of the Universe." In effect, then, Wakefield becomes the self-portrait of Hawthorne the artist. By refusing to explore Mrs. Wakefield as character rather than caricature, Hawthorne repeats Wakefield's act of evasion, and by averting his gaze from Wakefield's empathic failure, Hawthorne subordinates his portrait of Wakefield to his own projected fears of isolation from the "reciprocal influence" of human sympathies.

The Scarlet Letter

The Scarlet Letter has been interpreted in many different ways, and most of you have probably written about the book at some point, whether as students or as publishing critics. (My own discussion of the novel appears in *The Mark and the Knowledge: Social Stigma in Classic American Fiction.*) Yet, teaching the book is always, for me, a challenge and a delight. In my classroom, I try to remember what it was like to read the book for the first or second time and to give students a chance to appropriate its meaning on their own before I turn them loose on a writing assignment that may send them to the library. One of the ways of doing this is to ask questions of the book that link it to discussions of previous authors and to the focal concepts and themes of the course.

I begin with "The Custom-House": the atmosphere of dream or hallucination that accompanies the speaker's discovery of the scarlet letter and his entire memory of the custom-house itself; the differences between this essay and Hawthorne's more conventional use of the preface (in *Preface to* The House of the Seven Gables); the sense of delay the essay gives the reader—and the blame the narrator places on others for his own "torpor" and his inability to write; and the imagery of the essay—the memorable meals Hawthorne describes, the portrait of the inspector, and his vision of reconciling "the Actual and the Imaginary." I ask them to consider the statement Hawthorne makes early in the essay: "To this extent and within these limits, an author, methinks, may be autobiographical, without violating either the reader's rights or his own." Is "The Custom-House" a revelation of its author or a veil like the one Reverend Hooper wears?

The novel itself (or the romance—ask students to talk about what they think Hawthorne means by the difference in *Preface to* The House of the Seven Gables) raises a lot of related questions. Hawthorne bares Hester; does he reveal or conceal Dimmesdale? Examine the imagery of revelation in the book: Hester's first appearance in the prison door, the scarlet letter itself, the scenes on the scaffold, Chapter XXIII, itself titled "The Revelation of the Scarlet Letter." Does Hawthorne's symbol, literally fastened to Hester's breast, allow him to bridge "the Actual and the Imaginary"? Compare Hawthorne's use of tangible symbol with Emerson's use of analogies. Is the scarlet letter also a way of seeing and of knowing, for Hawthorne's characters and for himself? What is the relationship between symbol and stigma? And why does Chillingworth, twice in *The Scarlet Letter*, have the privilege of seeing what is on Dimmesdale's breast, while Hawthorne averts his own eyes—and ours? Who are the "good" or "evil" characters in this book? What limits Hawthorne's sympathy for Chillingworth? What limits his portrait of Hester? In Chapter II he writes, "The women, who were now standing about the prison-door, stood within less than half a century of the period when the man-like Elizabeth had been the not altogether unsuitable representative of the sex." Yet, Hawthorne implies that, by the early nineteenth century, American women have changed. "There was, moreover, a boldness and rotundity of speech among these matrons, as most of them seemed to be, that would startle us at the present day." Is Hester herself a variation on Dame Van Winkle?—silenced by her author, as much as by her society? And to what extent is *The Scarlet Letter* not "about" Hester Prynne at all? To what extent does she merely catalyze the "real" drama of the dynamic and developing association between the minister and the physician? And how does Hawthorne use Pearl, particularly at the end of the book, to affirm a certain view of femininity and to reject others? He writes that her tears "were the pledge that she would grow up amid human joy and sorrow, nor for ever do battle with the world, but be a woman in it." Is *The Scarlet Letter* itself an indictment of Hester? And a vindication of Dimmesdale? And how do we interpret the "moral" Hawthorne "presses" upon his readers at the end: "Be true! Be true! Be true! Show freely to the world, if not your worst, yet some trait whereby the worst may be inferred!"

EDGAR ALLAN POE

The dream world characterizes Poe's work as well, and students may study his dream imagery in the poems *Introduction*, *The Sleeper*, *Dreamland*, and *The Raven*. Is there any connection between Poe's dream worlds and those of *Rip Van Winkle* or Hawthorne's fiction? Many writers in American literary history serve as spokespeople for others; does Poe? What effects does his poetry create in the reader, and how? His poetry lacks specific references to American places or American life; is it, like Freneau's or Bryant's, derivative of British poetry? I read *The Philosophy of Composition* closely with students, and we compare it with "The Custom-House." How is the act of writing different for Poe and Hawthorne? Ask them to evaluate Poe's description of the composition of *The Raven* against their experience of reading the poem.

We analyze *Annabel Lee* line by line in the context of Poe's statement in *The Philosophy of Composition* that beauty moves the soul best when the subject is sad and that, therefore, the death of a beautiful woman becomes the "soul" of poetry. Why does Poe need to kill Annabel Lee to achieve the male speaker's maturity and poetic inspiration? By dying young, she doesn't live to become another Dame Van Winkle for the male speaker, and her death allows him to retain complete control over the way he uses her as material for his poetry, even for the necrophilia the last stanza implies. What reason does the poem give for her death? Poe suggests that the angels—with their associations of being female or possessing "feminine" values—have "coveted" her beauty (as if angels, or women, could never be supportive of each other). And her love has given the narrator status, for she has "highborn kinsmen," and although they take away her dead body, they cannot take away the class status he has achieved by his conquest. Like those in Irving and Hawthorne, Poe's protagonist/narrators empower themselves by the silencing or death of their heroines.

Among the tales included in NAAL, *The Fall of the House of Usher* and *Ligeia* further demonstrate the effects Poe creates by idealizing women and therefore earns at the expense of his female characters. *Ligeia,* in particular, shows Ligeia becoming the male narrator's muse in the process of developing anorexia, in effect conspiring to her own death. How does Poe's use of doubling in *The Fall of the House of Usher* reinforce the effect of the torture and death of Madeline? Ask students to think about the "organic" relationship between human beings and nature, or the supernatural, in Poe, especially *The Fall of the House of Usher,* as another form of doubling. In what other tales does Poe use doubling between characters and events? Does he alter the effects of the dream world by portraying events as nightmares (in *The Black Cat,* for example)? From the point of view of twentieth-century psychology, do Montresor and Fortunato in *The Cask of Amontillado* represent shadow elements of the same personality?

As Hershel Parker points out in the headnote, Poe created the detective story "with all its major conventions complete." Ask students to analyze *The Purloined Letter,* deducing from it some of the conventional elements of the detective story. Compare it with Poe's tales of the supernatural; what are the different effects he achieves in *The Purloined Letter?* How do Dupin's cleverness and rationality go together with his idea that "the material world abounds with very strict analogies to the immaterial"? Consider the statement in light of Emerson's use of the analogy in *Nature.* Compare Dupin's language with Poe's in *The Philosophy of Composition:* is the character a double of his author? Compare their relationship with Hawthorne's relationship to Dimmesdale in *The Scarlet Letter.* What is Poe trying to reveal and conceal in his own fiction? Does the genre of the romance, for both Hawthorne and Poe, predetermine the nature of meaning?

MARGARET FULLER

Unlike Emerson, Hawthorne, and Poe, Margaret Fuller wrote in direct response to her social and historical context, expressing her concern in particular for women's rights. In *The Great Lawsuit,* Fuller is explicit in her condemnation of constitutional policy. Ask students to find language of servility in *The Great Lawsuit* and to compare it with the language of slave narrative in *The Declaration of Independence.* Locate Fuller's commentary on the fight for the abolition of slavery, and ask students to reflect on her perception of "a natural following out of principles" by which the "champions of the enslaved African," "partly because many women have been prominent in that cause, [make], just now, the warmest appeal in behalf of women." Both Fuller and Harriet Beecher Stowe (in the anthologized excerpt from *Uncle Tom's Cabin*) depict women as engaged in heroic struggle; ask students to find parallels among colonial writers. In the early nineteenth century, while white American men were producing the first great imaginative literature, white women and black slaves were just beginning to find spokespersons, writers able to articulate the contradiction between constitutional liberty and their own lack of rights. (Students interested in Fuller may also want to read Elizabeth Cady Stanton's *Declaration of Sentiments* [included in the Appendix to this Guide] or Sojourner Truth's *Ain't I a Woman?* [not anthologized in NAAL but included in NALW].)

HARRIET BEECHER STOWE

"The Mother's Struggle" may initially appear melodramatic to students, but the very fact that Stowe wrote *Uncle Tom's Cabin* in the first place displays the fierceness with which some northern white women fought for the abolition of slavery. And although Eliza's character is not created by a black writer, she possesses several characteristics that would later appear in the earliest fiction by black writers—Charles Chesnutt and Zora Neale Hurston (included in NAAL)—and many others of the late nineteenth century and the Harlem Renaissance period. For Eliza is "so white as not to be known as of colored lineage, without a critical survey, and her child was white also," making it "much easier for her to pass on unsuspected." This detail makes it possible for an instructor to ask some interesting questions: for whom is Stowe writing? Clearly, white Northerners and, in particular, white women who supported the abolitionist movement. How does Stowe elicit the sympathy of that audience? In large part, by presenting Eliza as a *mother* as well as nearly white. Some students may want to do background research on the nineteenth-century view of motherhood. Clearly, even in this brief excerpt from Stowe's novel, motherhood parallels Christianity in spiritual significance, and when the white Kentuckian Mr. Symmes helps Eliza and her child up the riverbank on the Ohio side, Stowe writes ironically that "this poor, heathenish Kentuckian, . . . had not been enlightened on his constitutional relations, and consequently was betrayed into acting in a sort of Christianized manner, which, if he had been better situated and more enlightened, he would not have been left to do." Stowe directly criticizes the Fugitive Slave Law here, by which Mr. Symmes ought to have returned Eliza to the hands of the slave catcher Haley instead of pointing her in the direction of a safe house. She is also describing a kind of Christianity that is activist and contextual in its care for the fleeing slave. The nineteenth century gave over the spiritual and moral development of children to women, in their place within "women's sphere"; here Stowe links nineteenth-century Christianity with warrior mothers, for Eliza possesses "strength such as God gives only to the desperate." It is significant for the development of both white and black American literature that Stowe depicts Eliza as a heroic fugitive—a character with the stature of myth. As late as Ralph Ellison's *Invisible Man* (1952), black writers would depict the road North and the fleeing slave as archetypal in American black experience. Like the earliest Puritan settlers, slaves adopted Old Testament typology as a way of understanding their condition—the Ohio River, for Eliza, becomes the biblical Jordan, and the other side, a type of Canaan.

The Minister's Housekeeper locates Stowe's stylistic realism and her contributions to the beginnings of literary regionalism. Thematically, you might ask students to compare Huldy with earlier female characters in American fiction, particularly Dame Van Winkle and Hester Prynne. How does the realistic portrait of an American woman differ from her portrait in the romance? You might also raise the question of literary authority and examine one of Stowe's solutions to the dilemma of trying to write professionally as a woman in mid-nineteenth-century America. In one of her letters, she claimed that she didn't write *Uncle Tom's Cabin*, but was merely taking dictation from God. (Recall Edward Taylor's plea for God to guide his pen in *Prologue*.) In *The Minister's Housekeeper*, she creates a male narrator (Sam Lawson) to tell Huldy's story. Might we consider Sam Lawson a variation on Rip Van Winkle, once he becomes a storyteller after the war? Would the story have had a different effect had Stowe been able to allow Huldy to tell it herself? Compare Irving's creation of Diedrich Knickerbocker with Stowe's need to write in the voice of Sam Lawson.

HARRIET JACOBS

Although some instructors may regret that NAAL offers excerpts from *Incidents in the Life of a Slave Girl* rather than the complete text, the six chapters included represent a coherent and integrated unit that conveys the power of Jacobs's narrative and, at the same time, shows her raising questions about slavery and particularly the experience of women in slavery. Chapters I and VII focus on family connections. Jacobs contrasts the powerful emotional bonds enslaved families felt for each other and the horrors of a legal system that did not recognize slave marriages or the primary bonds between parents and children. Chapters X and XIV explore what students might term Dr. Flint's sexual harassment of Linda and Jacobs's presentation of Linda's moral right to choose a lover. Throughout Jacobs's description of Linda's relationship with Mr. Sands, she addresses herself to white women readers and is concerned that they will both identify with Linda as a woman and, later, a mother and yet not judge her behavior by their own codes, which prescribed chastity. Jacobs implies that Linda felt she could achieve some measure of protection for children she might have with Sands, and so this proved to be in the short term; later, in part of the text not excerpted in NAAL, Sands marries and, under the guise of taking Linda's daughter Ellen to educate her, turns her into a house servant for his family. Yet she knows that she cannot shelter her child when it is born a girl: "slavery is terrible for men; but it is far more terrible for women." Explore with students differences between Frederick Douglass's *Narrative* and Harriet Jacobs's *Incidents*. Without *Incidents*, would we know much from Douglass's account concerning the sexual harassment and abuse of enslaved women?

After an abortive attempt to run away, Linda hides in the garret of her grandmother's shed, and Chapter XXI will raise many questions for students. In this chapter Jacob uses the intriguing metaphor "loophole"; what does this mean? The image "loophole" seems accurate to describe the garret in which she hides; she lives in a space that would not be visible to anyone who looked. It is as if she had "escaped" slavery by finding a "loophole" within the institution; has she "all but" escaped Dr. Flint by hiding for seven years in her grandmother's shed? If so, her "freedom" does her little good, and her children might have been better served had she escaped to the North. Why does she stay? She implies that she wants to remain near her children, even though for a long time they do not know she is there; does she remain a mother, except for the "loophole" that her children do not know where she is? She compares herself to Robinson Crusoe; ask students to explore the accuracy of this comparison. Chapter XLI, "Free at Last," serves as an ending for Jacobs's narrative, and, as she writes, her story "ends with freedom; not in the usual way, with marriage." Ask students to explore what *freedom* means for Linda and her children. "Free at Last" shows Linda still with no home of her own, and her daughter has not received the education she has wanted for her. The chapter hints at the lingering ravages of slavery and the deficits the newly freed persons experienced by virtue of being propertyless, uneducated, and separated from family members.

HENRY DAVID THOREAU

In Thoreau's *Resistance to Civil Government* and *Slavery in Massachusetts* we see him as the prominent exception among his white male contemporaries to the pattern of evading confrontation with social and political issues of his day. And *Walden*, despite the premise of separation from society on which it opens, emphasizes the practical aspects of transcendentalism. Ask students to locate Thoreau in a tradition of American writers from Bradstreet through Franklin who speak in a personal voice and address the common reader. How do the effects Thoreau achieves in *Resistance to Civil Government* or *Walden* differ from those Emerson creates in *Self-Reliance* or *Nature?* Ask students to compare and contrast *Nature* and *Walden* as literary works: how are they conceptually similar but technically different? Many who found it difficult to find logical discourse in *Nature* will perceive a narrative design in *Walden*. How does Thoreau manage a happy balance between logical and analogical thinking?

Walden

I organize my own class periods on *Walden* around the following series of points:

1. Focusing on "Economy," ask students to address Thoreau's practical concerns. What, for Thoreau, is wrong with the daily life of his contemporaries? What were his motives for going to Walden? What led him to write the book? How does his version of writing in the first person compare with Hawthorne's in "The Custom-House"? Find evidence that he is making a pun on *I* and *eye*; recall Emerson's "transparent eye-ball" in *Nature*. Are Thoreau's criticisms of his own society applicable to ours? How seriously are we to take his suggestion that students ought, quite literally, to build their own colleges? Compare Thoreau's list of materials for his house at Walden with Franklin's list of virtues in *The Autobiography*. Is there evidence in "Economy" that Thoreau is constructing an analogy, or is he writing a "how-to" book in the tradition of *The Way to Wealth?*
2. In "Where I Lived and What I Lived For," I ask students to consider again the creation of analogies in *Walden*, suggesting here that analogy becomes a method of introspection and religious meditation for Thoreau. Stanley Cavell in *The Senses of "Walden"* suggests that *Walden* is a scripture. We review the ways various American writers before Thoreau achieved literary authority and what different relationships writers have to scripture, especially the Bible. Does Thoreau achieve literary authority by going back to what he sees as the very source of creation, in nature at Walden? Ask students to comment on the following quotation from Hershel Parker's headnote: "The prose of *Walden*, in short, is designed as a practical course in the liberation of the reader." Thoreau's experience at Walden becomes a record of his way of seeing the world; as it is for Emerson, the process of learning, for Thoreau, involves making the

analogies he discovers as a result of going to the woods. In Thoreau's very ability to create the analogy he has the experience; transcendentalism can thus be seen as the first American spiritual movement based on a theory of language. That theory is Emerson's as well as Thoreau's, but Thoreau is able to find the analogies he wants in the life he is living on an hourly, daily, and seasonal basis at the pond.

Crucial to considering *Walden* as scripture are the frequent references Thoreau makes to Eastern religious experience. He writes that every morning "I got up early and bathed in the pond; that was a religious exercise, and one of the best things I did." How can bathing in the pond be a religious exercise? (He seems to mean that it is a spiritual experience, not just part of his routine that he follows religiously.) Following his own inclination toward analogy, bathing in the pond metaphorically suggests his daily immersion in the meaning of the experience of the pond. To jump into it suggests, by means of analogy, his daily attempt to understand it—at the same time as he is *literally* (like Emerson's stone) entering the pond. It cleanses, renews, wakes him up—provides a rippling effect by which he can reach Eastern enlightenment, "to reawaken and keep [himself] awake, not by mechanical aids, but by an infinite expectation of the dawn." Bathing in Walden becomes an interim "mechanical aid"; when he becomes able to keep himself awake without the pond, he won't need it any more. You can ask students, at this point, how Thoreau's meditation differs from Puritan meditation. Thoreau (like Franklin) is also focusing on a single mark or spot—but instead of looking for his theological or economic salvation, he is attempting to transcend the world of literal limits, what Emerson calls the relative world. Yet, there is so much of the literal world in *Walden*. There is a sense in which the very rhythm of working in the physical world, finding an analogy in that work to spiritual life and feeling, temporarily, at least, at one with the universe, becomes cumulative for Thoreau. The process enables him to make successive leaps between relative and absolute worlds, to transcend the limits of material existence, truly to become eccentric (a word that he cites as particularly important at the end of *Walden*). Walden Pond becomes his eye (see the chapter "The Ponds").

3. Beginning with "Brute Neighbors," I trace Thoreau's deep submergence into the character of Walden Pond as nature's "face." Then the last three chapters, "The Pond in Winter," "Spring," and "Conclusion," all build to Thoreau's description of the transcendent moment in which he has the experience of confronting absolute truths. In "The Pond in Winter," Thoreau makes the analogy between sounding the depths of a pond and "sounding" the depths of the human mind, as one might theoretically do by pursuing Eastern meditation techniques. Thoreau has no

mantra but his pond; his "depth" of knowledge of the pond prepares him for an even deeper dive into his own imagination, his own consciousness.

"Spring" heralds new life at the pond and new light in the writer. Here he discovers that "the day is an epitome of the year"; the small scale of Walden Pond (and ultimately of *Walden* as book or scripture) is what makes it useful as an analogy. He concludes, at the end of "Spring," that "we need to witness our own limits transgressed, and some life pasturing freely where we never wander." Becoming eccentric, getting outside our own limits, trying to transcend the narrowness of our own experience, can give us the vision of larger life, of some life "pasturing freely where we never wander." The exploration of life by means of analogy possesses a spiritual dimension that logic does not.

But he leaves the pond because he has learned its lessons. When the person becomes enlightened, the vehicle of enlightenment is no longer necessary. The religious technique, or the poetic analogy, is viewed not as an end in itself, but as means to an end. The basic idea in *Walden,* then, is that of self-expression, Thoreau's attempt to find a way to make visible and concrete his sense of who he is. His greatest fear, as he expresses it in "Conclusion," is that his "expression may not be *extra-vagant* enough." It's hard to get students to be extravagant themselves, because it means encouraging them to "wander outside" the limits of everything they have learned as received knowledge, prescribed feelings, and "right" and "wrong" ways to think.

FREDERICK DOUGLASS

Douglass wrote his 1845 autobiographical *Narrative* the year before Thoreau began to write *Walden*. Ask students to consider the following quotation from *Walden* in connection with *Narrative:*

> I sometimes wonder that we can be so frivolous, I may almost say, as to attend to the gross but somewhat foreign form of servitude called Negro Slavery, there are so many keen and subtle masters that enslave both north and south. It is hard to have a southern overseer; it is worse to have a northern one; but worst of all when you are the slave-driver of yourself.

Would Douglass agree? Are there conceptual and thematic similarities between *Walden* and *Narrative of the Life of Frederick Douglass, an American Slave?* Do Douglass's escape to freedom and Thoreau's transcendence at Walden Pond suggest connections between abolitionism and transcendentalism? Both narratives imply that the experiences that are their subjects also confer literary authority on their narrators. Evaluate the *Narrative* as autobiography; what are its formal and thematic similarities to Franklin's *Autobiography?* Is the slave narrative a variation on autobiography or a distinct genre? The central feature to focus on in Douglass's *Narrative* is the way he, like many white writers before him, articulates himself into being, creates an ontological model for black male identity: "You have seen how a man was made a slave; you shall see how a slave was made a man," he writes. And he makes himself a man by refusing to submit to Mr. Covey. Therefore, Douglass achieves ontological freedom before he escapes to actual freedom, and in portraying his own courage in fighting Mr. Covey, he sets himself up as a model for other slaves much as Franklin did in his *Autobiography*. Ask students to compare Douglass's *Narrative* with Jacobs's *Incidents*. Does Douglass's assertion about the ontological freedom of manhood apply to the experiences of women slaves? Would the quotation work for Linda Brent ("You have seen how a woman was made a slave; you shall see how a slave was made a woman)? Douglass portrays himself as a "heroic fugitive" for others to imitate. Contrast Douglass and Stowe. Might we consider "The Mother's Struggle" a form of the slave narrative? Can the warrior mother be a heroic fugitive? Douglass and other escaped slaves wrote their stories with the encouragement and support of the northern abolitionist press, and there is clear didactic intent in Douglass's *Narrative* (as there is in *Uncle Tom's Cabin*). Does didacticism weaken the narrative as a work of literature? Students may find it interesting to discuss the contrasting effect didacticism has in works produced under the umbrella of a reigning theology (such as Puritan literature) and works that are clearly trying to change people's ideas. From the literary perspective, the year 1845 is as important as 1776 because it shows a former slave writing in his own voice and naming and claiming his own liberty. Douglass's *Narrative* and Fuller's *The Great Lawsuit* suggest that, while going to Walden may be an effective technique for some Americans to achieve transcendence, black Americans and white women must first adopt defiance.

The Meaning of July Fourth for the Negro demonstrates Douglass's rhetorical skills. Students will be powerfully affected by his arguments, both in their historical context (he delivered the speech two years after the enactment of the Fugitive Slave Law of 1850) and in their continuing significance for our own time. Identify with students his rhetorical strategy: first he lauds the founders, the principles of liberty they espoused, and the language of the *Declaration of Independence* (while subtly maintaining his distance by referring to the United States as "your country," the country of his white audience, rather than his own); then he raises the case of slavery, which totally contradicted the language of liberty and freedom on which this country was founded; and he ends by demonstrating that Americans and their politics are "flagrantly inconsistent," calling for an end to this inconsistency and a return to the principles of freedom: "interpreted, as it ought to be interpreted, the Constitution is a glorious liberty document." Much of Douglass's argument remains relevant to late-twentieth-century American society; and Douglass offers students a model for the way his own words can be applied to ongoing discrimination in American society—against poor people, against African-Americans, against white women, and against lesbians and gay men. He writes, "We have to do with the past only as we can make it useful to the present and to the future . . . now is the time, the important time." Ask students to discuss this statement and to find others that might have been written in the 1990s as well as in 1852. Some of the most powerful might include, for many disenfranchised groups, "I am not included within the pale of the glorious anniversary!" and "There is not a nation on the earth guilty of practices more shocking and bloody than are the people of the United States, at this very hour" and "Americans! your republican politics, not less than your republican religion, are flagrantly inconsistent."

WALT WHITMAN

In teaching both Whitman and Dickinson, I try to show students how these two poets are pivotal figures, summarizing in their work many of the themes and concerns of earlier writers, yet looking ahead to the twentieth century in their poetic technique and the high level of self-consciousness that each brings to the act of writing. How, in particular, does Whitman express a culmination of American impulses in poetry? Ask students to reread Emerson's *The Poet* and to evaluate Whitman; is Emerson prophesying the kind of poetry Whitman would write, especially in *Song of Myself*? Or are both writers responding to the same cultural need? I ask students to discuss the detailed catalogs of American people, places, and human feelings that Whitman creates in *Song of Myself*. How does Whitman's portrait of human life differ from those of earlier writers? I introduce the concept of realism and suggest elements of realism in Whitman's language, looking ahead to the "local color" impulse of some of the post–Civil War writers that students will read in the second course or second half of the course in American literature. We consider aspects of dream in Whitman, particularly in *The Sleepers*, which illustrates the process by which Whitman works through the "night" of his analogy to "awaken" into a diffused and enlarged sense of self; students can then trace the same pattern through the much longer *Song of Myself*, at the end of which the poet transcends even his physical body, becoming effused flesh that drifts "in lacy jags." How does Whitman's use of analogy compare with Emerson's or Thoreau's? And how does reading Whitman compare with reading earlier writers? What is the conceptual unit of a Whitman poem?—possibly the catalog? What is the effect of the repetitions? What evidence can students find of discursive reasoning in Whitman? I suggest that Whitman requires immersion ("religiously," the way Thoreau bathes in the pond). Is *Song of Myself*, like Walden, a kind of scripture?

Students understand Whitman better when they locate the same image in several different poems; the imagery I ask them to focus on shows Whitman's vision of physical life. Harold Aspiz's *Walt Whitman and the Body Beautiful* (1980) is extremely useful reading as you prepare to teach Whitman. Aspiz suggests that "Whitman's physical self is the authentic vital center of *Leaves of Grass*. By idealizing his body, Whitman created a model that his fellow Americans could emulate." Such a reading of the poems makes it possible to suggest pedagogical connections between Walt Whitman and Benjamin Franklin, for Whitman clearly "invents" himself as the American poet in the same way that Franklin invents himself as American man. And it may lead students to see that *Leaves of Grass* is as much a poetry of evasion (Aspiz makes the point that for all of Whitman's pretense to health in his poems, from childhood on he had physical problems, was fascinated by physical illness, and spent many years as a sick man) as it is of self-disclosure (as in "I celebrate myself, and sing myself"), in its own way another *Minister's Black Veil*. I ask students to examine *Trickle Drops* and other *Calamus* poems included in NAAL for evidence that Whitman's analogue for vision is male sexuality. In *Trickle Drops*, they can see most clearly and succinctly the way Whitman views poetry as spermatic fluid; the image is pervasive in his work, including his discussion in *Preface to "Leaves of Grass."* Male physical health and robustness, in general, becomes a metaphor for vision. Does that make male sexuality, for Whitman, as much a product of the creative imagination as Walden is for Thoreau? Is the version of sexuality Whitman proposes (and suggests, throughout his work, that women share) another variation on the early-nineteenth-century American dream?

The newly anthologized sequence of poems, *Live Oak, With Moss*, demonstrates more specifically Whitman's interest in male sexuality and in personal as well as public poetry. The headnote and footnote discussions provide the essential literary context for reading the poems in *Live Oak, With Moss* in their own sequence, as they exist in unpublished manuscript, rather than as Whitman collected some of them in his *Calamus* poems. And, as editor Hershel Parker suggests, had it been published, "the sequence would have constituted a new and highly public sexual program, nothing short of an open homosexual manifesto." Trace with students the various "narratives" embedded in this poem sequence: (1) a love affair begun, then ended, with the speaker abandoned; (2) the speaker's growing wonder, as in VIII, whether there are other men like him; and (3) the narrator's emerging awareness of the relationship between poetry and "manly love" and how this relationship comes to matter more to him (in V) than being the "singer of songs." In a sense, *Live Oak, With Moss* serves as a revision of what Parker calls Whitman's "tributes to the American people" and, as such, invites comparison with Douglass's question, "What to the slave is the Fourth of July?" in *The Meaning of July Fourth to the Negro.* Consider with students the irony that the "good grey poet" who created himself and has been constructed by critics as our first truly *American* poet should also be our first gay poet struggling for freedom of expression both as a poet and as a lover. In Whitman's time, as in our own, *Live Oak, With Moss* suggests the contradictions between free speech and the expression of sexual orientation; as Whitman writes in XI, "I dare not tell it in words—not even in these songs."

Recognizing that some instructors teach Whitman, along with Dickinson, in the second half of the American literature course (when students will be using volume 2 of NAAL), Norton makes available a separate volume, free of charge, *Walt Whitman/Emily Dickinson: Selections from* The Norton Anthology of American Literature, Fourth Edition.

HERMAN MELVILLE

The Melville selections in NAAL give students a sense of Melville's range, and the set of letters to Hawthorne will help create obvious connections between the two writers. Students respond particularly well to *Bartleby, the Scrivener* and can see Melville, in contrast to Hawthorne, being more courageous in confronting and exploring "dead-wall" reflections of the self. In the narrator's discovery of a "fraternal melancholy" with Bartleby, and in his depiction of the scrivener as "absolutely alone in the universe. A bit of wreck in the mid-Atlantic," a teacher can suggest connections with *Moby-Dick.* "The Town-Ho's Story" is an interesting choice for an excerpt from that novel, partly because it takes place *after* the events in the novel have passed but *before* Ishmael begins to write *Moby-Dick.* So the chapter uniquely shows Ishmael "rehearsing" the larger story he wants to write before the audience of sailors in Lima. The chapter is anomalous in *Moby-Dick*—but usefully suggests the way a major author's works are often rehearsals, preface (like *The Piazza*), or sketches (*The Encantadas, or Enchanted Isles*). Students may speculate on nineteenth-century gender roles in *The Paradise of Bachelors and The Tartarus of Maids.* Is Melville writing social commentary here? Point out to students that most of his fiction depicts a single-sex universe. What happens to values associated with "women's sphere" in *Moby-Dick,* or in *Benito Cereno,* or *Billy Budd, Sailor?* Is Melville, too, engaging in the silencing of women? Or does his single-sex universe actually allow him to break down gender boundaries in the ways that different (male) characters reflect attributes often culturally assigned to male *and* female behavior? Is *Benito Cereno* social commentary? What cultural assumptions does Captain Delano bring into the fiction? How does Babo compare with the autobiographical narrator in *Narrative of the Life of Frederick Douglass?* Are Melville's portraits of black characters realistic?

Billy Budd, Sailor

Billy Budd, Sailor may be the most difficult for students of the long works by Melville included in NAAL. In addition to discussing central characters; trying, with my students, to figure out whether the novel is an allegory, and, if so, of what; and tracing Melville's elegiac tone in his last work, I also focus on some specific points somewhat off the main track that, yet, lead into interesting discussion. The digression on Nelson—Chapters 3 and 4—is one of the most interesting. Is Melville associating Nelson with Captain Vere? or with himself? At his report of Vere's death, he alludes again to Nelson, stating about Vere that "unhappily he was cut off too early for the Nile and Trafalgar." Is Melville undercutting the value of Vere as heroic commander here, and, if so, what fascinates him so much about Nelson's type of heroism? He suggests at the end of Chapter 4 that "the poet but embodies in verse those exaltations of sentiment that a nature like Nelson, the opportunity being given, vitalizes into acts," and perhaps Melville sees Vere as triumphant in part because he makes an absolute judgment and proceeds to enact it. But there are dramatic contrasts in style between Nelson and Vere that might inspire a bit of student research. Melville, digressing on Nelson and confessing to having committed a "literary sin" in doing so, suggests a compulsion to model himself on Nelson rather than Vere. Vere lacks above all Nelson's passion; but Melville shares it.

Yet Vere's judgment concerning Billy, despite its apparent rationality, seems spontaneous, if not altogether passionate. What might Melville have been trying to understand, in weaving a fiction based on the arbitrary, even vengeful, judgment of an otherwise intelligent and human man? Students recalling Jonathan Edwards might find the atmosphere of the drumhead court familiar; when Vere states that " 'We must do; and one of two things must we do—condemn or let go,' " he expresses the absolute Calvinist separation between damned and elect, guilty and innocent. The sailors listen to the results of the deliberations of the drumhead court "like that of a seated congregation of believers in hell listening to the clergyman's announcement of his Calvinistic text." In giving us his portrait of Captain Vere's rigidity, Melville explores the effect of a continuing and pervasive Calvinism—fictionally transposing its visible effect on the nineteenth-century American mind to the deck of a British warship in 1797, a year belonging to a period of transition from one conceptual view—neoclassicism—to another, romanticism.

The question of Billy Budd's guilt can lead into lively classroom discussion, particularly if students are guided to see the terms of the debate as absolute versus conditional or contextual justice. Carol Gilligan's *In a Different Voice* assigns gender categories to moral development that can lead to these mutually exclusive perceptions of justice; interestingly, Melville characterizes Billy as a type of the Handsome Sailor, a beardless, "feminine" martyr—possibly Christlike, possibly "female." Students might find it interesting to apply Poe's statements on beauty and sadness to *Billy Budd, Sailor*. For, in some ways, Melville, too, achieves his tragedy by the silencing and death of a beautiful sailor (students can list the many ways in which Melville gives Billy female characteristics, and can consider the effects on their tragic feeling had Billy and Claggart retained their own characters, but exchanged physical types). And what of the evasion in the final interview between Vere and Billy?—we are told only that they are "briefly closeted." Does this resemble the way Hawthorne averts his eyes at crucial moments in his fiction? *Billy Budd, Sailor* remained unfinished at Melville's death; does this affect our ability to interpret its meaning? Does the work itself—like Billy—retain a stammer and a hesitancy in its "speech"? It's difficult to teach Melville without including *Moby-Dick*, and if you have somehow found class time to include this novel, then students will more easily be able to understand the problem of Billy's death within Melville's larger work. For, in the earlier novel, Melville suggests that tragedy for Ishmael is not death but a return to the necessity for vision. Unlike Thoreau, who leaves Walden after he no longer needs the pond as a vehicle of transcendence, Ishmael, after his brief moments of oceanic vision in the vortex in the "Epilogue" to *Moby-Dick*, gets picked up by the *Rachel* and returned to the landed world of what he calls, in the opening chapter, his "hypos," his nebulous depression of spirit. Melville himself, as his biographers have made clear, fell into deep depression after finishing *Moby-Dick*, as if the tragedy of his own life resembled Ishmael's: the vehicle he chose to achieve his vision, writing, served only temporarily to ward off his creditors in the physical world and his own metaphysical despair. No wonder he wrote, in the letter of June 1(?), 1851 to Hawthorne included in NAAL, "all my books are botches." A teacher doesn't need to be an expert in Melville biography to engage students in biographical speculation: why does Melville portray, as his final tragic vision in *Billy Budd, Sailor*, a world in which only absolute justice prevails? Might he be making an attempt to justify or explain the fate he received as a writer—that of obscurity during most of his life?

EMILY DICKINSON

There is much in the Hershel Parker headnote to guide a discussion of Emily Dickinson and her poetry. NAAL 4 includes two of the specific poems Parker mentions in his discussion of Dickinson's "rebellion against the theology of her town" (Nos. 324 and 1068); poems that reflect her deep regard for British writers Elizabeth Barrett Browning (Nos. 312 and 593), the Brontë sisters (No. 148), and James Thomson (No. 131); and numerous poems that reflect T. W. Higginson's groupings for the first (1890) edition of her work, his response to Mabel Loomis Todd's efforts to secure posthumous publication for Dickinson. Although each individual poem reflects larger formal and thematic interest than grouping it under one heading indicates, the process of creating the thematic groups (according to the categories Higginson created: life, love, nature, time, and eternity) gives students one way of looking for intertextual connections and, indeed, of beginning to create interpretive patterns within which to analyze and appreciate Dickinson's work. Thus one homework exercise you might assign students would ask them to group the poems under Higginson's headings, then, in class, to discuss the difficulties involved in doing so.

My own preliminary attempt to do so produced the following lists:

Life: Nos. 67, 187, 241, 258, 341, 536, 650
Love: Nos. 249, 303, 322, 1078
Nature: Nos. 130, 285, 314, 328, 520, 978, 986, 1068, 1138, 1397, 1463
Time: No. 305
Eternity: Nos. 214, 216, 280, 287, 315, 322, 324, 449, 465, 501, 510, 528, 547, 664, 712, 822, 824, 829, 978, 1099, 1125, 1126, 1540

What becomes interesting about this exercise is less the extent to which individual readers agree concerning which poems to include in each group and more their reasons for inclusion as well as their interpretations of the categories themselves. For it struck me in creating these lists that the very categories express more about the themes and worldview Higginson reflected a century ago than the themes and interests of our own time.

A follow-up exercise, then, would involve asking students to identify the themes by which they would group Dickinson's poetry if they were creating their own edition for contemporary readers. As readers still trained to revere modernist and postmodernist aesthetics, some of them may want to include a category that reflects Dickinson's self-consciousness concerning poetic form and practice; the poems they may group together for such a list may include Nos. 185, 285, 303, 326, 441, 448, 488, 505, 709, 952, 1129, and 1138. Discussion of this list may also follow from

Parker's observation that in a poem like No. 326, Dickinson reveals her awareness of her own originality, her own "genius."

The exercise also leads into questions of editorial selection. Thomas Johnson's *The Poems of Emily Dickinson* (1955) includes 1,775 poems. NAAL 4 includes 86 poems, many of which have frequently been anthologized. One question that emerges from the process of editorial selection concerns the role a particular editor's interests or tastes play in such a process. Put one of the Johnson editions on reserve and assign individual students clusters of 75 or 100 poems so that all 1,775 are covered. Then ask the students to make a case (either in a class presentation or in a paper) for the inclusion of one or two additional poems. On what grounds would the students argue for inclusion? What different portrait of the poet, or of the body of poetry, would emerge if the poem or poems (and others like them) were included?

Such an approach makes it possible for students to evaluate the representativeness of certain poems that appear to reflect Dickinson's perspective or to follow through on suggestions in Parker's headnote. For example, NAAL 4 includes several poems that appear to address women's lives as wives: Nos. 199 ("I'm 'wife'—I've finished that—"), 732 ("She rose to his Requirement—dropt"), and 1072 ("Title divine—is mine!"). For a different perspective on the life of a wife, students may discover in one of the Johnson volumes Nos. 154 ("Except to Heaven, she is nought") and 219 ("She sweeps with many-colored Brooms—").

Parker's headnote characterizes Dickinson as "undaunted by her powerful father's domestic tyrannies." While many of the poems—indeed the very existence of the poems—provide evidence that Dickinson remained "undaunted" either by her mortal father or her immortal one, students attuned to the way Dickinson claims to, as she expresses it in No. 1129, "Tell all the Truth but tell it slant—" will find in other poems, not anthologized here, further complexities concerning Dickinson's view of her relationship to her particular father (Parker describes No. 61, "Papa above!" as an example of her religious rebellion, but it also conveys overtones of rebellion from paternal authority) and of her portrait of white upper-class women's constricted lives in the patriarchal world of nineteenth-century Amherst, Massachusetts. The first lines of most of the following poems, not included here but worth analysis by students for their challenge to the more mainstream Dickinson often presented in anthologies, hint at Dickinson's critique of the lives her society sanctioned for women: Nos. 77 ("I never hear the word 'escape' "), 146 ("On such a night, or such a night"), 178 ("I cautious, scanned my little life—"), 182 ("If I shouldn't be alive"), 248 ("Why—do they shut Me out of Heaven?"), 439 ("Undue Significance a starving man attaches / To Food—"), 476 ("I meant to have but modest needs—"), 540 ("I took my Power in my Hand—"), 579 ("I had been hungry, all the Years—"), 612

("It would have starved a Gnat—"), 613 ("They shut me up in Prose—"), 773 ("Deprived of other Banquet"), and 791 ("God Gave a Loaf to every Bird—"). In creating this list, I have only surveyed the poems Dickinson wrote between 1858 and 1863; if students read later poems, they will find others that critique the social position accorded to white upper-class women in nineteenth-century America.

Parker's selections include a number of love poems, and he provides students with background information about the major contenders for what he terms Dickinson's "passionate relationships." He observes that one of these relationships "may have been with the friend who became her sister-in-law," Susan Gilbert. Students may be interested in reading the selection of poems (not anthologized here) that provide grounds for such an observation. This list includes, from the poems written between 1858 and 1863, the following: Nos. 14 ("One Sister have I in our house"), which ends "Sue—forevermore!"; 27 ("Morns like these—we parted—"); 44 ("If she had been the Mistletoe"); 84 ("Her breast is fit for pearls"); 91 ("So bashful when I spied her!"); 156 ("You love me—you are sure—"); 208 ("The Rose did caper on her cheek—"); 218 ("Is it true, dear Sue?"); 251 ("Over the fence—"); 427 ("I'll clutch—and clutch—"); 446 ("I showed her Heights she never saw—"); 474 ("They put Us far apart—"); and 704 ("No matter—now—Sweet—"), a poem that may reflect Sue's rejection of her sister-in-law. Bring in some or all of these poems (it doesn't violate the copyright to put them on the board, and they are all short enough to do so) and discuss how Dickinson's perspective on same-sex love compares with Whitman's in the *Live Oak, with Moss* and *Calamus* poems included in NAAL 4.

For a more traditional discussion of Dickinson, note that many of her poems are transcendental in method and ask students to select a favorite and discuss affinities with Emerson and Thoreau. At the same time, Dickinson is often considered an early modernist, because of the way her poetic technique calls attention to itself and reflects a high level of self-consciousness (see the specific list of anthologized poems I discuss above in connection with poetic form and practice). I often begin discussion of Dickinson by asking students to contrast her with Whitman—and not just in the poets' perspectives on same-sex love. Both poets reverse students' expectations concerning traditional poetic form, and comparing and contrasting the ways they do this leads to an extensive discussion of what each poet might have been trying to do in poetry. Sheer size is one of the most striking points of contrast; see No. 185, in which Dickinson writes, " 'Faith' is a fine invention / When Gentlemen can *see*— / But *Microscopes* are prudent / In an Emergency." Compared with Whitman's "Walt Whitman, a kosmos" and the "magnifying and applying" of *Song of Myself*, Dickinson's small poems seem microscopic. Exploring the freedom with which Whitman creates the vast catalogs in *Song of Myself* and allows himself endless repetition and then contrasting that freedom with No. 185 or with No. 1099 ("My Cocoon tightens—Colors teaze—") can move the discussion from formal differences to thematic ones, and to the question of literary authority. Where does Whitman find his? How does it appear as an assumption in his poetry, although Dickinson, as in No. 505 ("I would not paint—a picture—"), must struggle to achieve it? How does the smallness of her poetry suggest her own assumptions about the nature of literary authority?

Unlike Whitman, Dickinson appears uninterested in the physical body, grounding many poems in a specific image from nature that she then proceeds either to transcend, as in No. 328 ("A Bird came down the Walk—") or 348 ("I dreaded that first Robin, so"), or to despair in finding her own inability to transcend human limitations and the limits of poetry, as in No. 465 ("I heard a Fly buzz—when I died—"). Like Whitman, Dickinson also writes analogically, following Emerson's technique for transcendental vision. Many poems illustrate her use of analogies to express and contain her vision, particularly the poems that appear to be about death but actually show the poet trying to see beyond the limits of human vision that death, as life's limit, symbolizes for her. Nos. 465 ("I heard a Fly buzz—when I died—), 510 ("It was not Death, for I stood up"), and 754 ("My Life had stood—a Loaded Gun—") are just three of the many poems that illustrate this pattern, and many others write thematically about the process, as No. 67 ("Success is counted sweetest") or No. 528 ("Mine—by the Right of the White Election!"). Many of the Dickinson poems that initially appear so elusive to students can become deeply revealing of the consciousness of the woman who wrote them—and of the fact that they were written by a woman, as my list above (beginning with No. 77) indicates. No. 1129 ("Tell all the Truth but tell it slant—") also becomes another Dickinson variation on Emerson's use of the poetic analogy to achieve transcendental vision. But her reasons for choosing analogies that move in "slant" fashion rather than in concentric circles (like the ripples that result when Emerson throws a stone) suggest that Dickinson, unlike Whitman, may have seen herself as self-conceived, self-born—not because she has invented a new kind of poetry but because she has dared, as an American woman, to write at all (especially in light of the fact that her models were British women). In inventing herself as woman and poet, how does she differ from other self-inventors: Franklin and Douglass? Does she imagine setting her life up as model for others? And does the biographical fact that she published only seven poems in her lifetime imply self-censorship or feminine reticence? Ask students to reread Bradstreet's *Prologue* and *The Author to Her Book*. To what extent does Dickinson's use of smallness in her imagery reflect her sense of inadequacy at the same time that it gives her the analogical vehicle for transcending that sense?

Finally, for some intriguing contradictory readings of Dickinson that are certain to provoke discussion in the classroom, and which may provide students with some support for their own readings, see, in particular, William Shurr's *The Marriage of Emily Dickinson* and essays by Adelaide Morris and Joanne Dobson in *Feminist Critics Read Emily Dickinson,* edited by Suzanne Juhasz.

Recognizing that some instructors teach Dickinson, along with Whitman, in the second half of the American literature course (when students will be using volume 2 of NAAL), Norton makes available a separate volume, free of charge, *Walt Whitman/Emily Dickinson: Selections from* The Norton Anthology of American Literature, Fourth Edition.

REBECCA HARDING DAVIS

Davis's rediscovered story *Life in the Iron-Mills* allows you to end your course by making a lot of thematic connections with earlier writers and introducing your students to an early work of literary realism. Ask students to compare the atmosphere in Davis's mill with Melville's *The Tartarus of Maids;* to evaluate the nightmarish realism of Davis's description against Poe's tales of the supernatural; to contrast Hugh Wolfe's creation of the korl woman with women characters created by Irving, Poe, and Hawthorne; to think about the korl woman's special hunger in light of Dickinson's own poems about hunger and deprivation; to see *Life in the Iron-Mills* as a story about what happens when a man like Wolfe or a woman like Deborah are denied liberty and equality by others; to analyze similarities between the bondage of Davis's mill workers and Douglass's portrait of actual slavery; to recall Thoreau's view from inside his prison cell in *Resistance to Civil Government* with Hugh Wolfe's view—which is more powerful?; to compare Wolfe's last moments in his cell with Billy Budd's "God rest Captain Vere!"; and to compare the last lines of *Walden* ("Only that day dawns to which we are awake. There is more day to dawn. The sun is but a morning star."), and of *Life in the Iron-Mills*" ("its groping arm points through the broken cloud to the far East, where, in the flickering, nebulous crimson, God has set the promise of the Dawn"). Discuss in particular Davis's appeal to her readers to accept the realism of her description of Hugh Wolfe ("Be just: when I tell you about this night, see him as he is") and of his korl woman ("A working-woman,—the very type of her class"). What might have led Davis to write realism in a literary era still influenced by the British Romantic poets and the work of the American authors Hawthorne and Poe in the Romance form? What gave Davis another view of American life than that of the New England transcendentalist writers? What differentiates Davis's realism from Stowe's indictment of slavery in the earlier *Uncle Tom's Cabin?* And where did Davis find her own literary authority?

How did she manage to write realistically about what it means to be working class, female, and hungry in a country still dominated, in its literature, by the attempt to define white American male identity?

Volume 2

1865–1914

REALISM AND ITS VARIANTS: REGIONALISM, LOCAL COLOR, AND NATURALISM

The question of realism and the genre of narrative fiction dominate the concerns of post–Civil War writers. The meaning of the term *realism* is complicated by the fact that, as the general introduction to the period in NAAL suggests, there were "other realists" and there were critical categories that seem somehow both related and different: regionalism, local color writing, and naturalism (which at the turn of the century was often termed "new realism"). Furthermore, this is the period for which we have the richest array of surviving Native American texts; how do these texts intersect with critical categories such as realism or regionalism?

The traditional approach to teaching the period is to begin with the triumvirate of Clemens, Howells, and James and then touch on the "others." One of the difficulties with this approach is that American authors (as a reading of *Life in the Iron-Mills* at the end of Volume I suggests) began writing in a realistic mode decades before Clemens, Howells, and James published their major works. If we begin teaching the period not with Clemens, but with the realistic literary works that were published in the 1860s and 1870s, we can give students a better sense of the evolution of American literary realism, which began as a mode of perception and a way of thinking about American life. It only achieved the stature of "theory" when Howells (and James) wrote so many editorial columns (and prefaces) in an attempt to define the American "art of fiction." In the notes on specific authors that follow this general discussion, I have kept to my practice of following the chronology in NAAL. However, in my own classroom I teach the authors who represent the various genres in the order in which the genre developed, even though this often means teaching writers out of strict chronological order. I begin with regionalism and local color writers, then teach Clemens as part of a group of realists, and end with naturalism and turn-of-the-century nonfiction.

The earliest writing in a realistic mode begins with Harriet Beecher Stowe (illustrated by *The Minister's Housekeeper* in Volume 1) and some of her contemporaries, Alice Cary and Rose Terry Cooke (not anthologized) as well as Rebecca Harding Davis. Literary historians also trace strains of early realism in the Old Southwest humor writers (anthologized in Volume 1): Augustus Baldwin Longstreet, George Washington Harris, and T. B. Thorpe. To understand the evolution of American realism, students need to see what happens to these early strains, and what happens is that a group of writers—mostly women, beginning with Cary, Stowe, and Cooke—develop the genre of regionalism, represented in Volume 2 by Sarah Orne Jewett, Kate Chopin (in her anthologized stories), Mary E. Wilkins Freeman, Charles W. Chesnutt, Mary Austin, possibly John M. Oskison, and Gertrude Simmons Bonnin (Zitkala Śa). In my attempt to convey the features of the earlier literary tradition, I teach Jewett and Chesnutt before Clemens, even though all of the particular regionalist texts anthologized in NAAL were published after *Adventures of Huckleberry Finn*.

The chronological point I try to make is that regionalism preceded realism as a literary genre and serves as a bridge between early- and late-nineteenth-century American writers. Then, regional elements of Clemens's work (and its strain of anecdotal humor) can be placed in their context, and students can also understand the differences between the realism of Henry James and that of writers like Jewett, Freeman, and Austin. But even within writing that contains regional elements, students will find the local color fiction of Bret Harte and Hamlin Garland to contrast with the regionalism of Jewett and Freeman. In my own discussions of these writers I make one major distinction between regionalism and local color writing based on where the author locates the center of perception in the story. Regionalist writers tell the story empathically, from within the protagonist's perspective; local color writers often stand back from their characters and look at, not with, them. This distinction prepares students well to think about point of view in Henry James.

What all of the writers in realistic modes share is a commitment to referential narrative. Despite the evidence of invention, the reader expects to meet characters in the fiction who resemble ordinary people in ordinary circumstances, and who often meet unhappy ends. (The pattern of the unhappy ending is much less prevalent in regionalism, however.) The realists develop these characters by the use of ordinary speech in dialogue, and plot and character development become intertwined. Some writers make use of orthographical changes to convey particular speech rhythms and other elements of dialect peculiar to regional life. They all set their fictions in places that actually exist, or might easily have actual prototypes, and they are interested in recent or contemporary life, not in history or legend. Setting can become conspicuous as an element of theme in local color and regionalist fiction. And the realists rely on first- or third-person-limited point of view to convey the sensibility of a central character or, in the case of the local color writers, the altered perception of the outside observer as he or she witnesses the scene.

Realism and Native American Literature

I have written above that realism began as a mode of perception and a way of thinking about American life, that as genre it takes the form of referential narrative, and that in the hands of most realist writers (with the exception of the regionalists), stories do not have happy endings. I have also noted that realism has recent or contemporary settings, that setting matters particularly in regionalism and local color writing, and that such literature often implies or records the presence of a contrasting or "outside" observer or narrator. If we read all of the anthologized selections from Native American oratory, songs, legends, fictions, and autobiographical memoirs, even though these materials in one sense belong to a variety of different genres, they also comment in interesting ways on the phenomenon of literary realism. As the headnote materials indicate, each of the summary statements I make at the beginning of this paragraph also applies, if not to a specific Native American text, then to the larger phenomenon of the move from "orature" to literature.

As the headnote material points out, Native American literature during this period represents an "encounter" between traditional Native American oratory and the new and contemporary demands of the practices of Euro-American culture, namely the occasions at which Indians used both oratory and writing to try to make beneficial treaties, to achieve their land claims, or to adapt their own practices to meet the demands of the whites. Thus the body of Native American literature represented in this period indeed records a particular and quite evidently referential perception of white American life. The larger history of the encounter between Euro-Americans and Indians during the post–Civil War period, or more accurately between 1830 and 1890, does not have a happy ending. Setting is everything in some of these narratives; land becomes the fundamental source of conflict as well as the source of metaphor, spirituality, and identity for large groups of native peoples. Furthermore, read together as well as interwoven with Euro-American texts, the Native American materials all imply the existence of and looming threat by an outside observer (sometimes equipped with Hotchkiss guns) who, alas, is also the narrator of a conflicting story of events and the narrator who controls not only the guns but also the language of legal discourse.

Although some readers may object to discussing Native American "realism" because this concept clearly emerges from a Euro-American perspective and literary tradition, it may make pedagogical sense to expand the meaning of realism to accommodate those historical events that do become referential in Native American texts. Once students explore the suitability of terms like *realism* and *regionalism* (as I discuss further on) for Native American texts, they may then discard them—but the terms may have served the function of pedagogical bridge to an enlarged appreciation for Native American literature taught, inevitably in a survey course, as part of literature in the United States.

To help students make connections between the anthologized Native American texts and the much more familiar concept of realism—as well as to understand crucial distinctions between the two—encourage them to view realism as a literary effect as much as, if not more than, a genre. Then even the Ghost Dance narrative—which incidentally is told by a variety of narrators in a variety of genres, including Wovoka and his transcribers, Charles Alexander Eastman, tribal songmakers, and Black Elk (at the beginning of the 1914–1945 section of NAAL)—may be viewed as a collectively told "text" of Native American realism, despite its origins in a vision, its survival in songs and legends, and its reemergence once again in Black Elk's revisionary history of the events at Wounded Knee. This collectively told narrative also serves as a useful corrective to the theory of realism as articulated by Henry James, which focuses on a single stationary observer and his particular perspective from "the house of fiction" (or what he calls "the posted presence of the watcher, . . . the consciousness of the artist" in his preface to the New York edition of *The Portrait of a Lady*). The collectively told narrative of the Ghost Dance and its aftermath, Wounded Knee, can only be viewed from several perspectives at once in Native American literature. The realist observer becomes apparent to the reader, "appears" to the reader (as if reader response to Native American texts involved forming a Wovoka-like vision of his or her own), as a collective, even "tribal," grouping of observations that confirm each other. These observations share a common theme and referentiality (the focus is on the gulch in which the women and children were massacred and buried in snow), emerge from more than one "watcher," and are confirmed by more than one pair of eyes, and above all provide a counternarrative to the absence of this story in Euro-American "realism" of the period.

The particular mode of realism that seems to assume the closest kinship to the perspective from which the body of Native American literature is spoken or written is that of regionalism. While it is certainly true that traditional Native American literature must be viewed as central to itself and not even part of "American literature," American literary history (and canon-revision politics) have led to the revision of anthologies of "American literature" in the late twentieth century to "include" Native American materials and literary scholarship about these materials. From the perspective of such anthologies (as NAAL), both regionalism and Native American literature are noncanonical, marginal representations of American life; both cannot separate setting from the development of character; and both foreground the contrasting perception of persons on the margins of American life in the nineteenth century with those who own the land and the property, who make (and break with impunity) the laws, and who consign certain persons to separate lands (or "separate spheres" or regions). In the specific commentary that follows, I have highlighted some of the connections between regionalism and Native American literature. It is no coincidence that the headnote refers to the efforts of Mary Austin to make a critical and aesthetic connection between what she called "the landscape line" of Native American poetry and early modernism. She also wrote an essay titled *Regionalism in American Fiction* (that to my knowledge has never been reprinted; it appeared in the *English Journal* [February 1932]), in which she asks, "what is a race but a pattern of response common to a group of people who have lived together under a given environment long enough to take a recognizable pattern?" Austin's sense of the "pattern of response common to a group of people" more accurately describes the collective point of view on the "text" of Wounded Knee than James's theory of the single "watcher," and it is clear that for Austin, living together in a "given environment" is a precondition for the pattern of response that we know—differently yet with some similarities in late-nineteenth-century American fiction—as regionalism and as Native American literature.

SAMUEL CLEMENS

Adventures of Huckleberry Finn

Clemens defies classification as humorist, local color writer, or realist; *Adventures of Huckleberry Finn* is all of these. I usually spend several class periods on the novel and focus more on close analysis than on trying to definitively identify the book's genre. I urge students to slow down in their reading and to pay attention to the development of the text. In this novel, where one of the significant questions concerns the extent to which Huck Finn develops or doesn't develop in his moral character and depth of self by the novel's end, the process of focusing on the way Clemens unfolds his fiction can highlight, at any given moment, whether Huck himself has developed or whether he has just moved on to another adventure. As part of a "warmup" discussion, I ask my students to consider why so many critics have called the book particularly American and to make a running list (if they have studied the 1820–1865 period with me, they are used to thinking about this question): the contrast, from the beginning, between Huck's love of wildness and the Widow Douglas's attempt to "sivilize" him; the central problem of the book once Huck and Jim start down the river on the raft, namely that Jim is trying to escape to the free states; Samuel Clemens's use of various dialects and of vernacular language, both in Huck's own narrative and in the book's dialogue; the "back woods" humorous presentation of characters and events; and the importance of the longest North American river to the plot. In close analysis we discuss the novel according to the following general outline:

CHAPTERS I–VII

• Read closely the opening passages and evaluate the language: Huck is an ordinary boy, uneducated, a plain speaker; he feels the need to introduce himself and doesn't claim either reputation or literary authority; his idea of story simply concerns the actual events; moves from one report to the next, using very few subordinate clauses.

• Discuss the way Huck's language resembles the novel's plot—events, like clauses, are strung together in linear fashion rather than woven together; discuss Tom's allusion to Cervantes's *Don Quixote* (the first novel) as his own model and Clemens's choice of the picaresque form (from the Spanish *picaro,* wanderer).

• Contrast the adventures Huck has as a member of Tom's "boys' gang" and the real escape he makes from pap's cabin; compare Huck's search for adventure and his quest for his own identity (one of his "American" characteristics); ask why Tom's gang doesn't work very well for Huck: even if the boys did manage to have some real adventures, Tom would offer no real alternative to the life the Widow Douglas wants for Huck; Tom still tries to regiment Huck—whether the rules are based on boys' books or on the Bible (cite Huck's conclusion after the adventure with the "A-rabs" and elephants—"as for me I think different. It had all the marks of a Sunday-school").

• Evaluate the attraction Tom holds for Huck: what does Huck want from Tom that he can't find in Miss Watson's world? Consider Tom's values as companion, his cleverness (he manages to live in both the world of the boys and the world of the grown-ups); discuss Tom's limitations: while Huck may tell a few "stretchers," Tom Sawyer actually lies and won't admit even to himself that he is pretending; Tom doesn't face the raw necessity that governs Huck Finn's life (Tom has a family; Huck, despite the existence of pap, is for all practical purposes an orphan).

• Talk about Clemens's class analysis here. In Miss Watson's world, where Tom manages to feel comfortable, Huck will always be an outsider. The son of a bum, Huck will always be lower class in the widow's world; it's only when he manages to slip away to sleep in the woods or to imagine himself escaping for good that he can free himself both from the constraints of "sivilization" and from its class system, which places him at the bottom. Note Huck's commonality with Jim here; when Huck finds himself in real trouble with pap, he goes not to Tom but to Jim for some of his "magic." (A related discussion of the Uncle Remus tales and Chesnutt's use of folklore can lead into a consideration of the extent to which Jim "teaches" Huck.)

• Discuss the sequence of events with pap: how does the previously humorous tone change? Huck here becomes homeless and friendless. Analyze the social commentary in these chapters, in which Huck is beaten and abused, enslaved and imprisoned by the drunken pap. Focus on Huck's increasing need for separateness. Escaping the widow seemed necessary if Huck were to be free to live without having his spirit stifled; escaping his father is necessary if he is to avoid imitating him.

• Analyze Huck's symbolic death: how does he forge a new identity for himself? how does it separate him from Tom Sawyer as well as from pap?

• Discuss the final metaphor of Chapter VII, in which Huck floats down the river lying in the canoe, then writes: "I run the canoe into a deep dent in the bank that I knowed about; I had to part the willow branches to get in; and when I made fast nobody could a seen the canoe from the outside." Connect the image to the tale the Widow Douglas tells Huck in the novel's opening pages, the story of Moses in the bulrushes that Huck cared so little about because "he had been dead a considerable long time." Suggest Huck Finn as an American Moses: newly born, an orphan, and if not a prophet, at least prophetic in his attempt to express the nature of experience.

CHAPTERS VIII–XV

• Allusions to *Robinson Crusoe*; shipwreck as a motif to characterize human loneliness and isolation, and discussion of Jim as Huck's Friday.

• The relationship between Huck and Jim; ways in which Jim's flight from slavery comments on Huck's own need for freedom.

• The quality of experience Huck and Jim have, at first on the island and then on the raft; connections with New World settlements and (ironically) with the Middle Passage for American slaves; Leslie Fiedler's argument from "Come Back to the Raft Agin', Huck Honey"; discussion of single-sex relationships in other American works (Dimmesdale and Chillingworth in *The Scarlet Letter*, Ishmael and Queequeg in *Moby-Dick*) and the extent to which the single-sex world in the nineteenth century frees the protagonist to develop gender characteristics of both sexes; thematic connections to *Rip Van Winkle* or the stories of Harte and Garland that show a male writer portraying women characters as limiting human freedom.

• Close analysis of Chapter XV, in which Clemens gives us what becomes yet another American dream. The "dream"—more precisely, Huck's successful attempt to convince Jim that he was asleep and only "dreamed" his separation from Huck in the fog—opens a complex discussion of the possibility of friendship between Huck and Jim. Some students will not have noticed the age difference between the two until you point it out to them. But they will see Huck wavering on the subject of slavery. Here, and later, whenever Huck views Jim as a slave, or as a "nigger," Jim loses his individuality. So what is at stake as the two make their way down the river is not only Huck's identity, but Jim's as well, and because Jim's individuality depends on Huck's willingness to recognize his humanity, Huck comes closest to being human and in full possession of his own identity in the moments when he recognizes Jim as a person. In the dream scene at the end of Chapter XV, students can see the complex irony Clemens is portraying here. For, as they will find out in Chapter XVI, Huck and Jim miss Cairo in the fog, and therefore, Jim's "American dream" of becoming a free man has evaporated. Jim's loss of his hopes and his loss of individuality (as Huck turns him into the butt of his own joke) is nothing more than a game for Huck. The contrast here between Jim, the slave, and Jim, the person, is never again too clear: when Jim realizes he has been duped, he tells Huck, " 'trash is what people is dat puts dirt on de head er day fren's en makes 'em ashamed.' "

CHAPTERS XVI–XXX

In this section, Clemens concentrates on social commentary. The Shepherdson-Grangerford feud (itself a comment on the Civil War) divides the novel roughly in half, and also marks a shift in the novel's focus that neatly parallels historical contrasts between antebellum romanticism (which can be linked to the idyllic scenes of freedom on the raft) and the Reconstruction period (marked by the carpetbagger morality of the king and the duke). The analysis of the king and the duke that is possible in the classroom is far too comprehensive to do more than sketch in some of the central points here:

- The historical commentary, in which, although the American Revolution appeared to throw off monarchy, the new government doesn't really protect the common man.
- The social commentary, in which the king and the duke seem just as "American" as Huck and Jim, and so the new country seems to have replaced a hierarchical system (in which everyone might know who is privileged and who is colonized) with a more insidious system of human oppression, made even more so because the "innocents," Huck and Jim, can't tell the difference between what is real and what is not. The Royal Nonesuch is just one incident that illustrates the chameleonlike qualities of some new Americans, in which their apparent sincerity proves to be a sham and a worse form of humanity than Huck tried to escape. Here the book sets up a hierarchy of its own, in which Huck encounters worse forms of degradation than he had ever suspected (previously viewing his own father as the lowest form).
- The epistemological commentary, in which Huck learns the use of disguises as a means of self-preservation and in which the raft itself (invaded by the king and the duke) becomes only an illusion of freedom. Here the book (like the river) has also shifted shape, possibly like the shape shifting of African-American folktales (see Joel Chandler Harris), and Huck's identity becomes mercurial, indeterminate.
- The literary commentary, in which the Shakespearean parodies (the king and the duke are themselves parodies of the traveling Shakespearean

actors of the late nineteenth century) suggest the inability of American art to "render" experience in the same forms that the greatest British writers chose. Just as there is no certainty for Huck Finn once he moves outside a world that has rules, there is none for Samuel Clemens except the shape-shifting form of creating for the first time a fictional character with an American voice. The literary commentary can lead into a discussion of the way Clemens refers to fate's wheel and the dramatic sense in which tragedy and comedy are inversions of each other. America seems to be a place, the novel suggests, where one day a crook can become a king, a slave can become free, a person within sight of freedom can become a slave again. The security and freedom of life aboard a raft can be transformed into their very opposites and the raft a kind of prison—a literal prison for Jim, who is tied up as if he were a runaway slave. The irony, of course, is that he actually is a runaway slave, and in any world but the novel (where the boards of the raft become the "boards" of the stage) Jim's ropes would be appropriate and would signify that the author was adhering to the conventions of realism.

• The central theme of "pretending," in which the absence of any reality that doesn't shift shape begins to unify the entire novel. Students here can go back to the "pretending" of the boys' gang, can discuss the king's and the duke's scams, can see "pretending" as one of the ways Huck eases his conscience when he tries to "pray a lie," and can think about the way "pretending" can lead to self-invention (making connections back to Benjamin Franklin's "real," as opposed to Huck Finn's "fictional" autobiography).

The king and the duke sequence finds its end in the scene at the Wilkses, where Huck's conscience finally starts working and he sympathizes with the plight of the Wilks "orphans." It's as if he is able to put himself inside another's clothes for the first time—literally, when he hides among Mary Jane's dresses. But wearing women's clothes, for Huck, makes it possible for him to perform a kind of literary transvestism, a costume change that alters his moral sense—and all of Miss Watson's teachings come back to guide him when he decides to turn in the frauds.

CHAPTER XXXIII–CHAPTER THE LAST

The final section of the novel always generates discussion in the classroom, and I ask students to take sides on the problem of the novel's ending. Many readers of *Huck Finn* consider the ending flawed—Hemingway, for example, said that Clemens "cheated"—while other readers have praised it, and I ask students to defend or to criticize the ending.

At issue for the defense: The ending completes the novel, provides unity, since it returns the reader to Tom Sawyer's world, and actually shows Tom in a successful adventure; the ending completes the novel's form as well, starting roughly in the same place where it began, with another woman, Aunt Sally, wanting to adopt Huck Finn and ending with Huck's reaffirmation of his own need for freedom in the novel's famous closing lines, "I reckon I got to light out for the Territory"; and for readers who view the novel as picaresque, the ending appropriately sets the hero out on another adventure.

At issue for the critique: The novel moves back from Huck's initial quest for separation, shows him once again under the influence of Tom Sawyer and, therefore, prevents him from developing further. In fact, the entire sequence of events at the Phelps farm seems to portray him as having regressed. He doesn't think twice about imprisoning Jim, treating him like property again; and either his character is presented inconsistently—since as late as Chapter XXXI he was ready to go to hell for Jim's sake—or Clemens has backed off from confronting the moral dilemma of slavery within his novel's social commentary. The novel finally treats Jim's freedom unrealistically, since Clemens achieves his "happy ending" by revealing that Tom has known since his arrival at the farm that Miss Watson set Jim free in her will. Students may see the ending as Clemens's own evasion and may make connections in particular with Hawthorne (the boys and Jim persist in describing the escape as an "evasion"). When Aunt Sally asks Tom why he wanted to set Jim free when he was already free, he replies that it is "*just* like women" to ask such a question. Earlier, when Huck, Jim, and Tom are running from the armed men and Jim volunteers to stay with the injured Tom even though he knows he is risking his own freedom again, Huck writes, "I knowed he was white inside."

At the end, the novel can seem to confront none of the serious issues of inequity in American society. But, as one student pointed out to me, perhaps that makes *Adventures of Huckleberry Finn* most realistic. Although the novel has a happy ending, Clemens doesn't manage to achieve what he seemed to be setting out to do: to create Huck as a developing individual, capable of managing reality, able to shift for himself in a new country. The novel's realism here becomes Samuel Clemens's problem, not Huck Finn's; the novel's form becomes as elusive as the "real" identity of the king and the duke, and what the novel demonstrates historically is that realism itself proves too confining a form within which to contain the changing shape of American reality.

BRET HARTE

In *The Outcasts of Poker Flat,* Harte creates central characters who become the object of perception by someone outside the setting or region. Oakhurst is the outsider, and the reader's views of Madam Shipton, Piney

Woods, and the others are all filtered through Oakhurst. When Oakhurst kills himself at the end of the story, Harte presents this scene also as a tableau for other outsiders—his readers—to see. Ask students to consider the humor of the story: does Harte achieve it at the expense of any particular characters more than others? Had he tried to depict the experience of western life from Mother Shipton's point of view, would *Outcasts* have been a different story? How much does Harte assume that his readers will find women, in general, and western prostitutes, in particular, laughable? Is he laughing at or with his characters?

W. D. HOWELLS

Novel-Writing and Novel-Reading gives students a chance to read some of Howells's literary theory, and then to test the application of that theory in *Editha*. Howells's definition of realism requires that fiction be "like life," and the central statement in his essay is the following: "The truth which I mean, the truth which is the only beauty, is truth to human experience. . . . It is a well ascertained fact concerning the imagination that it can work only with the stuff of experience. It can absolutely create nothing; it can only compose." For students who come to Howells after studying *Adventures of Huckleberry Finn*, notions of "like life" and "truth to experience" will seem justifiably naive. For all of the complexities of the world in which he lived, Howells's own view of reality remains a simplistic one—that somehow reality may be verified and agreed on. However, Howells's theory makes more sense if we focus on the word *compose*. He seems to be saying here that the novelist must "place together" elements from real life that he is unable to create, that the novelist's art reveals itself in the relative placement of real things. Later in the essay he draws the analogy of a cyclorama to explain what he attempts in his fiction. He describes beginning "with life itself" and then going on to "imitate what we have known of life." The good writer will "*hide the joint*. But the joint is always there, and on one side of it are real ground and real grass, and on the other are the painted images of ground and grass." The realism of Howells describes the way existing elements are placed together. But composing implies assertion. To pose a question is to assert it, to propound it, to put it forth for examination. Therefore, in the very process of "composition," Howells and his hypothetical realistic writers are trying to set forth reality itself for examination, as if it were the proposition of an argument. *Editha*, for all of the realism of its portrayal of sexist stereotypes in late-nineteenth-century American society, is superficial in its attempt to find and define motivation in Editha's character. Is Editha a real person or a "painted image"? And if she is a "painted image," does she project social reality or her author's distorted view of women? Compare her with Dame Van Winkle, Ligeia, Freeman's Louisa Ellis in *A New England Nun,* and James's May Bartram in *The Beast in the Jungle.*

NATIVE AMERICAN ORATORY

In his discussion of Native American oratory, Andrew Wiget (*Native American Literature,* 1985) observes that "from the first centuries of white settlement in America, the oratorical ability of Native Americans, their artful talent for persuasion, was noted by Europeans," and he cites Thomas Jefferson's *Notes on the State of Virginia* (1784) as offering the "moment of highest praise." In preparation for a discussion of Native American oratory, ask students to read the excerpt from Jefferson's *Notes,* "Query VI. Productions Mineral, Vegetable, and Animal," anthologized in Volume 1, which includes Jefferson's comments.

Cochise

Cochise's speech makes a plea for the Apaches, though much reduced in number by the wars with the Euro-Americans, to retain "a part of my own country, where I and my little band can live." As the headnote material observes, this is an example of oratory addressed to white listeners, and its theme is land. You can make the speech live for readers in a couple of ways.

First, ask students to recall (and reread) the Pima Stories of the Beginning of the World (NAAL, Volume 1), for the opening sentence of Cochise's speech makes an indirect reference to the emergence myth of creation of some Southwest Indians, a myth in which humans crawl out from a hole in the ground: "This for a very long time has been the home of my people; they came from the darkness, few in numbers and feeble." It's important that students catch this reference, what Euro-Americans would call a literary allusion, but what for Cochise links the spiritual origins of his people with their present predicament (and the occasion for his oratory). It also provides evidence for the headnote's observation that for Native Americans, there were no fixed distinctions between the spiritual and the secular.

In light of Cochise's allusion to the emergence myth of the Pimas and the Apaches (locate for students the reference at the end of the Pima Story of the Flood to the origins of the Apaches as "the first ones that talked"), you might want to make the ironic point that Native American literature itself "emerges" with such power during the years 1830–90 when the Indians themselves were losing their battles with the whites. And yet the emergence myth implies the cyclical destruction and reemergence of native peoples as well as their migrations. Perhaps (I would say to my own students) the new "emergence" of Native American literature into the larger canon of American literature through the contest for space or literary "territory" in anthologies represents the triumph, or at least the persistence, of Native American cultures despite several acts of destruction by the world maker (and its modern-day literary equivalent, the anthology editor).

Second, trace with students the numerous and pervasive references to land in the speech, and all of the different ways in which Cochise configures the meaning of land to his people. Variously, land becomes imaged as "these mountains about us," "home," and "our country," and the Apaches are portrayed as integral to that landscape, as, early in the speech, Cochise compares the way his people "covered the whole country" to the way "clouds cover the mountains." The rhetorical occasion for the speech, namely to arrive at a treaty that would yield "a part of my own country," establishes its form, in the sense that Cochise defines himself and his people as quite "part" of the country. In formal terms, the speech becomes synedoche: he speaks for all, and the terms in which he speaks establish an identity between people and their land. To take away the land kills the people who are "part" of that land; if the people have been reduced in numbers, then they can survive on "part" of that land, but they must be on that land. Like the deer that flee the hunter in a later image from the speech, the Apaches only exist on the land that has been their home.

Charlot

This speech addressed to Charlot's fellow Flathead Indians lives up to its description in the headnote as "a powerful critique of the white people's ways." Contrast with students the tone and language of Charlot's speech with Cochise's; focus on the evocation of shame in the speech and discuss the way racism attempts to obliterate emotions of shame; compare and contrast with William Apess's *An Indian's Looking-Glass for the White Man*, another powerful indictment of white treatment of native peoples. Ask students if the rhetorical stance of the speaker reminds them of any historical works in Euro-American literature; I would suggest Franklin's *An Edict by the King of Prussia*, Thomas Paine's "Thoughts on the Present State of American Affairs" from *Common Sense*, or especially Thomas Jefferson's *Declaration of Independence*. Without suggesting that the *Declaration of Independence* serves as a literary model (which nevertheless it may, even though the headnote does not indicate this, since Charlot delivered the speech "in the year of the centennial celebration of American independence"), compare the rhetorical construction of King George III in Jefferson's *Declaration* with Charlot's rhetorical construction of "the white man" whom he personifies as an individual power throughout his speech, as in "is his prayer his promise" and "he wants us to pay him besides his enslaving our country." Another interesting text to examine in such a discussion is Elizabeth Cady Stanton's 1848 *Declaration of Sentiments* (included as an Appendix to this Guide), which similarly personifies not "white man" but "man," protests not "shame" but "tyranny," and lists moral and political grievances. In the documents by both Charlot and Stanton, the speaker/writer addresses oppressed people with the sense of being overheard. The press, at least, was present to transcribe Charlot's speech, and after its signing by a hundred men and women supporters of women's rights in 1848, presumably the *Declaration of Sentiments* also became a public document (although its inclusion as part of this Guide instead of NAAL itself suggests that it has not yet approached even the neocanonical status of Charlot's speech). Examining the rhetorical strategy of constructing the oppressor in each of these three political statements designed simultaneously to arouse enmity against "King George," "man," and "the white man," and support for the cause of the oppressed, also increases students' perspective on the use of rhetorical devices as part of the process by which writing becomes a form of political action that Native American speakers, perhaps because of their tradition of oral practice, as well as of the extent of their own grievances, were quite skillful in employing.

Wovoka

For Wovoka's vision, offered here in two versions as "Messiah letters," the headnote is as important as the text to the classroom reception of the entire range of Ghost Dance/Wounded Knee narratives included in NAAL. Spend time going over the details of the Ghost Dance religion and the subsequent massacre at Wounded Knee. Explore with students the statement from the "Native American History and Literature" segment of the period introduction that "armed action against the settlers and U.S. troops had failed. . . . Many American Indians turned to spiritual action as a means of bringing about desired ends. From this impulse arose what has been called the Ghost Dance religion." The implication here is that some northern Plains Indians knew that they could no longer defend themselves in battle and, therefore, turned to spirituality to save themselves and give themselves hope. Read the two "Messiah letters" carefully with students and identify specific aspects of the letters that link them both with Native American traditions and with Christianity. Ask students why Euro-Americans seem to have had such difficulty imagining the concept of religious freedom for Indians. Recall Apess's *An Indian's Looking-Glass for the White Man,* and apply his strategy of eliciting shame in his white Christian readers to the white settlers' resistance to the practice of a Christian-inspired religion by a few defeated bands of Indians. Speculate about the ironic possibility that the Ghost Dance religion might have been less threatening to white settlers if it had not contained so many elements of Christianity.

HENRY JAMES

The Art of Fiction shows that James shares Howells's theory of fiction, in part. He writes, "The only reason for the existence of a novel is that it does attempt to represent life." However, what James means by "life" and what Howells means by it are two different things. Unlike Howells, who asserts a reality that is referential and shared, James suggests that creation resides in the author's perception. Without the perceiving eye there is no art. James implicitly links realism with point of view and with the "quality of the mind of the producer." He writes, "A novel is in its broadest definition a personal, a direct impression of life: that, to begin with, constitutes its value, which is greater or less according to the intensity of the impression." Thus reality is subjective for Henry James, and he suggests that, far from being referential, realism reveals aspects of life that cannot be seen. He insists on "the power to guess the unseen from the seen, to trace the implication of things, to judge the whole piece by the pattern," and he writes, "Experience is never limited, and it is never complete; it is an immense sensibility, a kind of huge spiderweb of the finest silken threads suspended in the chamber of consciousness, and catching every airborne particle in its tissue."

If, as Howells writes, the reader is the arbiter of a fiction's realism, and if "the only test of a novel's truth is his own knowledge of life," then many of our students will have difficulty seeing realism in Henry James. The challenge in teaching James is to try to get students to follow the psychological complexity of the relationships James creates—between Daisy and Winterbourne in *Daisy Miller*, and between John Marcher and May Bartram in *The Beast in the Jungle*—as well as to see his interest in relationships per se as an aspect of realism that makes James stand out among many of his contemporaries. Compare James's analysis of the complexity of emotional and psychological development with Clemens's in *Adventures of Huckleberry Finn* and with Howells's in *Editha*. The regionalists link emotional development to the development of community—here portrayed by Mrs. Todd's empathy with the French woman in Jewett's *The Foreigner*. And Freeman and Chopin show that the individual develops emotionally within the context of human relationships, but their focus remains the quality and development of individual or shared vision. Only James, among his contemporaries, focuses on human relationships themselves as the source of experience. The single context within the meaning of human experience may be explored. In the shorter works anthologized here, we see relationships that are primarily dyadic. In the novels, James interweaves pairs of intense personal relationships with each other to form the "huge spiderweb" of his psychological fiction. Although instructors will probably want students to read *Daisy Miller*—it establishes James's themes of the innocence of Americans in Europe and the way individuals are bound by convention, and it focuses on a female protagonist in a way that is representative of many of the novels—the works anthologized in NAAL that I find more successful as a way of demonstrating James's power as a storyteller are *The Turn of the Screw* and *The Beast in the Jungle.*

The Turn of the Screw

As students conclude from studying Clemens and Howells, the 1865–1914 period may be viewed, in part, as a series of experiments in how to tell a story. In *The Turn of the Screw,* James offers his own theory of fiction, demonstrated in the telling. As much as any work by James, *The Turn of the Screw* illustrates the idea, from *The Art of Fiction,* that the perceiving eye creates the artistic impression.

Many critics have attempted to unravel the meaning of this short novel, and students may find their own ingenious ways of interpreting the governess, Mrs. Grose, the children, or the apparitions, but in my own teaching I present the work as a *tour de force* of narration rather than a work with explicit thematic content. We begin by reading closely the opening prefatory chapter, in which the first-person narrator describes the way Douglas prepares his audience to be receptive to his tale. We talk about the way James's own narrator is also preparing his reader, and I suggest that eliciting reader response is James's primary objective in the tale. We trace the stages of offering up and withholding that Douglas engages in, and I comment that the prefatory chapter "trains" James's own reader in the act and art of reading the work that will follow.

Critics have made much of the concept of the "unreliable narrator" in Henry James, but rather than dismiss any of James's narrators in this tale as unreliable—the first-person narrator, Douglas, or the governess herself—I read the novel as a series of stages in the development of an engaged reader: the governess establishes her own literary authority; engages the trust of Mrs. Grose, who becomes a type of the innocent and unsuspecting hearer or reader; begins to "read" or to interpret the events of the narrative for herself, for Mrs. Grose, and for James's own readers; formulates a "theory" based on that reading; comes up against ambiguity or difficulty in fitting both her own perceptions and the perceptions of others (Mrs. Grose, Flora) into the theory that evolves from her progressive acts of interpretation; and finally becomes unable to tolerate ambiguity and acts in such a way as to "kill" both little Miles and the illusion of being "at the helm" in her own fictional creation.

James's prose style masters the art of building a believable fiction based on empirical inference—both the governess's inferences or "reading" from the events she experiences, and our own reader response to the inferences we draw from her own incomplete disclosures to Mrs. Grose. In the process, James suggests a depth and quality to human interaction that is representative of his "major phase" fiction, for he documents how much human relationship is based on the art of "reading" and interpreting from the inferences we make about other people. The governess makes this explicit when, at the end of Chapter XII, she tries to interpret Mrs. Grose's response to her latest revelation about the children's danger and thus concludes from the expression on Mrs. Grose's face "as a woman reads another" that "she could see what I myself saw." James draws a fine line, at the end of the novel, between a well-articulated interpretation and a delusion. Ultimately he throws his own reader back on the difficulty of interpretation and leaves us with two choices: either we accuse James himself of betraying us with an "unreliable" narrator (and if we do this, we become as "mad" as the governess herself seems to be at the end of the novel), or we are forced to accept the potential unreliability of a theory based on empirical interpretation, no matter how persuasive or internally consistent the theory itself may be, and no matter how worthwhile are our motives for formulating the theory—the governess herself believes that she wants to "save" the children.

Among the numerous approaches that critics have taken to *The Turn of the Screw*, several may intrigue your students, or they may offer them as their own interpretations of the novel. Various approaches focus on the governess herself: (1) the novel explicates the governess's sexual repression (the Freudian approach); (2) the governess's social isolation has made her insane (a social systems approach); (3) the governess is searching for her own identity: who *is* the "governess," that is, the "person who cares for children"?; and (4) the governess has frightened the children to death in a display of the undercurrent of distrust, and even hatred, that characterized the Victorian attitude toward children. Other approaches focus on the text itself. I have explicated one approach to reader-response criticism of the novel. In addition, you may identify the novel as working out problems in realism for Henry James: the use of narrative point of view characterizes the development of realism as a genre. A psychological approach suggests that James blurs the boundaries between inner and outer, anticipates the concept of projective identification defined by twentieth-century psychoanalytic theorists, and questions our ability to distinguish between perception and reality. Finally, James also anticipates the birth of modernism in the twentieth century by asking us to consider what happens when we can't believe a story that has been so convincing. In essence, James rejects both Clemens's despair and Howells's optimism; *The Turn of the Screw* confronts his readers with the idea that realism itself is a comforting fiction—no more than a fiction—

in a world in which we may ultimately be unable not only to control or save others from the powers of evil, but even to recognize or to substantiate the existence of good and evil except as we project out of ourselves images of our own inner psychic structures.

The Beast in the Jungle

In this story, James fully develops his theory of the novel as "a personal, direct impression of life," for it is actually such an "impression" that Marcher expects to have, and by which he figures his "beast." James's use of third-person limited point of view to define the unfolding of Marcher's perception serves as a laboratory of the use of technique. Marcher's point of view gives the reader a sense of reality as being bounded by the limits of perception and consciousness; yet James so skillfully creates May Bartram that, without ever entering her consciousness, we know what she is thinking and feeling—even more than John Marcher, despite the fact that he sees and hears everything the reader does.

I like to ask students "what happens" in this story. The wide range of responses creates a spectrum of the kinds of experience that constitute "reality" for James. Some will reply that nothing happens—which, in a sense, is true enough. Others will wonder whether Marcher dies at the end of the story—a valid speculation. Some will reply that he discovers he has been in love with May Bartram all along—an assertion that seems both true and false in light of the story. A few will focus on the developing portrayal of character as "what happens" for James. You can help them see what interests James in the relationship between his two characters by asking them which character they, as readers, most resemble. They will certainly align themselves with May—for, in a sense, Marcher and May are acting out the ideal relationship between author and reader. He is his own author, like many American male protagonists before him; she is his ideal reader—she grants him his *donnée*—as, James states in *The Art of Fiction*, the reader must do for the novelist. So that when the two meet again after ten years' time and May Bartram remembers Marcher's old impression, he asks, " 'You mean you feel how my obsession—poor old thing!—may correspond to some possible reality?' " "Corresponding to some possible reality" is the precise problem of the story, of James's other work and of realism itself. If reality is only "possible" and if two different characters within the same story, in which nothing else happens but their relationship, have such different perceptions of what is real, then what happens to realism itself?

James's interest in convention and social forms in *Daisy Miller* is apparent in *The Beast in the Jungle* as well. Marcher's very "unsettled" feeling about the nature of reality makes it difficult for him to go along with social forms. And so he lives with his "figure" of the beast as the hypothesis by which he understands his life. When the beast springs, in a sense, he will be able to live; until then he can't consider marriage. The beast becomes his disfiguring quality—he calls it "a hump on one's back"—and it is necessary for May to "dispose the concealing veil in the right folds." James, here, continues Hawthorne's fascination with the contradictions between apparent self-confrontation (Marcher tries to think of himself as courageous) and actual self-evasion (even when the beast finally springs, he turns "instinctively . . . to avoid it" as he flings himself, face down, on May Bartram's tomb). Ironically, his relationship with May contributes to that process of self-evasion. For she helps him "to pass for a man like another"; with her, Marcher appears to be conventional and to be living an ordinary life. He says to her: "What saves us, you know, is that we answer so completely to so usual an appearance: that of the man and woman whose friendship has become such a daily habit—or almost—as to be at last indispensable." Although they aren't married, Marcher believes that he has the "appearance" of it. He uses May to "cover" his apparent deficiencies. But certain kinds of experience and certain kinds of psychological development cannot be acquired by what "passes for" living, and neither can they be taught; they must be lived. Therefore, although the reader perceives that May Bartram understands much more of Marcher than he does of himself, she restrains herself, as James restrains himself, from telling him what it all means. He has to figure it out for himself—or not know it at all.

The story ends "happily" in a sense, because, although Marcher discovers the limitations of his fate, James manages to achieve his own goal—namely, that of portraying a character having a "personal, direct impression"—a literal *impress* of "letters of quick flame." The question becomes, How does Marcher finally achieve that impression? What is responsible, what is the catalyzing moment? Students will remember the scene in the cemetery, when Marcher sees the ravaged mourner, who is apparently a widower, and whose manifestation of grief makes Marcher ask, "What had the man *had*, to make him by the loss of it so bleed and yet live?" The apparent answer, and perhaps the only "right" answer, is that the other man has been touched by passion, has loved, whereas Marcher "had seen *outside* of his life, not learned it within." And he concludes, "The escape would have been to love her; then, *then* he would have lived."

But it seems curious that the other man at the cemetery seems—possibly, to Marcher—aware of an "overt discord" between his feelings and Marcher's. The significant thing, to Marcher, is that the other man showed his feelings, "*showed* them—that was the point." And he is aware of his own presence as "something that profaned the air." In my own reading of this scene, I see James as more interested in Marcher's inability to find the appropriate *form* for his feeling than in his inability to feel at all. He describes Marcher at May's funeral as being "treated as scarce more nearly concerned with it than if there had been a thousand others." As the author of his own fate, Marcher has failed in its execution. He has failed to find any manifest form for his own "personal, direct impression" that would have allowed him to "learn from within." And James links that failure with Marcher's refusal to make "real" what is only "appearance"—his "daily habit" of relationship with May Bartram. For James, consciousness requires a social context. Therefore, "it was as if in the view of society he had not *been* markedly bereaved, as if there still failed some sign or proof of it." James's characters may defy convention, as Daisy Miller does, but they don't escape having to confront it. The intrusion of convention in James's fiction establishes its social realism, the limitations within which his characters may establish themselves as conscious.

JOEL CHANDLER HARRIS

The "Uncle Remus" tales depend for their narrative success on the contrast between black storyteller and white audience. Harris includes in his work "instructions" to his readers, writes for a white audience, and yet manages to avoid caricaturing his black characters or turning them into mere entertainment. In his extensive use of southern black dialect and African-American folktales as the source of his subject matter, Harris might easily have been perceived in his time, and in ours, as a local color writer. I explain my own distinction between regionalism and local color—that the regionalist narrator looks *with* the regional protagonist, while the local color writer looks *at* regional experience—and ask students to consider the location of Harris's own perspective on his characters.

SARAH ORNE JEWETT

In the traditional presentation of late-nineteenth-century American fiction, Sarah Orne Jewett and Mary Wilkins Freeman are often grouped with the local color writers, and *regionalism* becomes a descriptive term for the entire group. A closer look at American literary history reveals that regionalism and local color writing developed as distinct but parallel genres and that if we look at chronology, regionalism was the first of the late-nineteenth-century fictional genres to emerge. Harriet Beecher Stowe published *The Pearl of Orr's Island,* the work that influenced Jewett's own development, five years before Clemens's *The Notorious Jumping Frog of Calaveras County,* and during the same decade that Hawthorne and Melville were publishing their most significant work (the 1850s), Alice Cary, Rose Terry Cooke (not anthologized here), and Stowe herself were establishing regionalism as a genre. By the time Jewett published *Deephaven,* in 1877, she already had a regionalist tradition to write within, and although by the chronology of birth order she and her work appear to follow Clemens, Howells, and James, *Deephaven* precedes publication of *Adventures of Huckleberry Finn, The Rise of Silas Lapham,* and *The Portrait of a Lady.* A brief discussion of the early appearance of regionalism and Jewett's significant contributions to the genre opens my own discussion of Jewett's work in the classroom. The two Jewett stories included in NAAL, *A White Heron* and *The Foreigner,* represent her work at its best.

A White Heron

In *A White Heron,* Jewett chooses as her center of perception a character who lives within the region she is writing about. In *A White Heron,* Sylvy (whose name means "woods") is indigenous to the setting (even though she has moved there from the city) because she speaks the language of nature; it is the ornithologist who is the outsider, implicitly resembling the local color writer in his quest to come into the rural scene, shoot and stuff a bird, and bring it back for urban people to see. In refusing to reveal the secrets of the white heron's nest, Sylvy protects the regional perception from exploitation. The contrast between Sylvy's desire to allow the bird its freedom and the ornithologist's desire to kill and stuff the bird provides a focal point for a discussion of the contrasts among regionalism, realism, and local color writing. Consider Bret Harte's story, *The Outcasts of Poker Flat,* and James's *The Beast in the Jungle* in conjunction with *A White Heron,* and ask students to describe differences in point of view, the extent to which the story includes the perspective of other characters, and the text's depiction of female characters. Ask them to imagine that *The Outcasts of Poker Flat* included the perspective of the Duchess, Mother Shipton, or Piney Woods, instead of turning them into caricatures, or to imagine that *The Beast in the Jungle* included May Bartram's perspective and gave her a voice, and you will begin to convey some of the particular features of regionalism as a genre. In *A White Heron,* Jewett shifts the center of perception not only to a poor, rural, female character but also to a nine-year-old child and makes it possible for her reader to understand the disenfranchised perspective.

The Foreigner

The Foreigner depicts the relationship between the female narrator of *The Country of the Pointed Firs* and her guide in that novel, Mrs. Todd, but Jewett wrote *The Foreigner* after publishing the novel and the story stands alone. In this text, students can experience the power of the earlier, longer work. Like Clemens, Howells, and James, Jewett as regionalist also experimented with storytelling, but *The Foreigner* adds empathy to the requirements of relationship between storyteller and reader/listener/audience. In characterizing the tale Mrs. Todd relates in *The Foreigner* as a "ghost story," Jewett's narrator invites us to contrast her approach with James's narrators in *The Turn of the Screw.* For James, the "impression" the teller makes on the listener becomes the standard of the tale's success. For Jewett, the tale becomes a medium for relationship between teller and listener, and although the narrator of *The Foreigner* says very little while Mrs. Todd tells her story, her choice to remain silent at crucial points in the narrative establishes her as a partner in the telling. The listener/reader has a role to play, in Jewett that goes beyond the reader response James's narrator tries to teach in *The Turn of the Screw.* Without relationship between teller and listener, there is no text. The power of Jewett's narrator is that she does not attempt to "read" the meaning of Mrs. Todd's narrative but allows the other woman to tell the story as its meaning deepens and dawns on her. Ask students to contrast the tone of *The Foreigner* with *The Turn of the Screw.* In James, the suspense builds; in *The Foreigner,* students may find at several points that they think the story is over. The appearance of the "ghost" at the end is not Mrs. Todd's attempt to frighten her listener, or to create a narrative effect, but to move beyond her storm fear for her aged mother, who, with Mrs. Todd's brother William, lives on one of the "outlying islands." The story begins with Mrs. Todd, separated from her mother by the raging gale, and dramatizes her use of storytelling to ease her anxiety and to regain inner peace. By the end of *The Foreigner,* Jewett has taught her readers how to feel a different kind of suspense than they might have expected in a "ghost story." The story's climax occurs not with the appearance of the ghost, but in Mrs. Todd's recognition that Mrs. Tolland has been reunited with her mother. In the larger story, the narrator also feels the strengthening of her ties to Mrs. Todd, and fiction, for the regionalist Jewett, becomes reparative and inclusive. Neither Mrs. Tolland nor Mrs. Todd is a caricature set up for readers to laugh at; the comedy of *The Foreigner* makes possible the continued "harmony of fellowship" that eases separation anxiety and social isolation.

KATE CHOPIN

At the 'Cadian Ball

This story was Kate Chopin's first significant regional publication, and it establishes an interest in hierarchies of southern society according to categories of race, class, and gender that would characterize much of her regionalist fiction. In the southern Louisiana locale of her work, her characters establish superiority for the Creoles, descendants of the original French settlers of Louisiana, and lower-class status for the Cajuns, descendants of the French Acadians exiled by the British from Nova Scotia in the late eighteenth century. Black characters occupy the lowest social position in this society, and within the rank of Cajuns (" 'Cadians"), status is granted according to racial characteristics that are viewed as European rather than African. Helping students sort out the social codes among the characters will help them understand the way class power and sexual desire are constructed and become interconnected. For example, Calixta, a Cajun woman with a Spanish Cuban mother, has more "status" than other women because she has blue eyes and flaxen hair—even though it "kinked worse than a mulatto's"; but she has no power at all against Clarisse, the upper-class Creole woman, "dainty as a lily." The racial codes in this society are complex. Bruce, the black servant, does not go to the 'Cadian ball, but the 'Cadians are not apparently considered white, for Chopin writes, when Alcee Laballiere arrives, that "anyone who is white may go to a 'Cadian ball, but he must pay for his lemonade. . . . And he must behave himself like a 'Cadian." Once students sort out the intricacies of power and hierarchy in this story, it becomes easier for them to understand Calixta's attraction for Laballiere and yet her decision to marry the "brown" Bobinot. The story leads to a more general discussion concerning the way racial and class status construct sexual desire and even sexual attractiveness in American society.

The Awakening

In seeing Edna Pontellier as yet another American on a quest to become self-reliant and to establish her identity within a hostile society, students might consider whether *The Awakening* could be titled "Adventures of Edna Pontellier." This can lead into a brief discussion of Huck Finn, and students can see essential differences in design between the two novels. Briefly, Edna Pontellier is not a "picaro"—and Chopin does not present her awakening as a linear series of adventures but rather as an interwoven account of the relationships Edna has with other characters and the way in which her awakening becomes her own "education." Conversely, you may ask students whether Clemens might have subtitled his book "The Awakening of Huckleberry Finn"—and the incongruity of the two portraits of nineteenth-century life becomes even clearer. (If you have taught Volume 1 to the same group of students, you can also make connections between Chopin's novel and earlier American dream fictions, especially *Rip Van Winkle, Young Goodman Brown,* Thoreau's *Resistance to Civil Government,* and certainly to Jim's dream in Chapter XV of *Huckleberry Finn.*) In Chopin's successful attempt to present Edna's life from her own point of view—so that students can see that even physical sex is not an end in itself for Edna, but rather only one aspect of her artistic and spiritual awakening and her struggle to achieve autonomy—she uses the technique of shifting the center that characterizes the best of regionalist writing. (One essay that will help students place Edna's attempts to reach toward limits that seem radical for women in her time is Elizabeth Cady Stanton's 1896 *The Solitude of Self,* which is brief enough to circulate as background reading.)

But Edna's attempt to achieve her own limits is thwarted—by her husband, by the attitudes of men, like Robert, whom she respects, and by the society in which she lives. In describing the limitations Edna constantly comes up against, Chopin writes literary realism, because in *The Awakening,* Edna's identity is finally so contingent on her social context that it becomes impossible for her to reconcile her sense of her own individual identity with society's expectations. But does she commit suicide? Some students may want to argue that her death is not actually suicide, but rather the consequences of Edna's choice to immerse herself quite literally in a context (the sea) that is the only place she can transcend her own limits (with connections here to Thoreau's "immersion" in Walden Pond). To put it another way, if Edna's death is suicide, then Huck Finn's choice to evade the conflicts of civilization is suicide by other means.

I find it profitable to close read one scene in the novel (the closing scene of Chapter XXIII, in which Edna and Leonce have dinner with Edna's father and Dr. Mandelet) as a way of demonstrating Edna's inability to transform the world she lives in into one that will seem real to her. In this scene, each of the four characters tells a story that reveals a great deal about the teller's character. Leonce tells an antebellum tale of "some amusing plantation experiences" and casts himself as a paternalistic Huck Finn, Edna's father depicts himself as a "central figure" in the Civil War, Dr. Mandelet tells a tale of a woman who moves away from her husband but whose love returns "to its legitimate source," and Edna tells a romantic story of two lovers who paddle away one night and never come back. What is interesting about the scene is that only Edna's story engages the imaginations of her audience. Despite its romanticism, the story possesses some compelling truth. Ironically, the anecdotes the other three relate are equally romantic projections of themselves or, in the doctor's case, of his ability to "cure" Edna, but in each case, the society has provided mirrors that appear to confirm the self-portraits. Leonce can depict himself as Huck Finn without seeming ridiculous, the colonel can aspire to having a war-hero's reputation without attracting scorn, and the doctor can presume to understand the nature of women without losing patients. But Edna cannot find in her culture—except in the invention of her own imagination—any ratification of her self-concept.

Edna's confusion can be viewed as a variation on Du Boisean "double consciousness," for throughout the book she constantly lives in a state of tension between her emerging sense of self and the limitations her society imposes on her. You might ask your students if Chopin is portraying Edna as the victim of social forces over which she has no control and if the novel can, therefore, be viewed as naturalistic. But I always feel the need to point out here that sexism (a view of human beings that divides consciousness into "masculine" and "feminine" and prescribes that certain individuals manifest only certain sets of attributes) does not evolve from scientific thinking of the day (in the way that both Stephen Crane and Theodore Dreiser are influenced by Darwin) but rather from conceptions of men's and women's "spheres" that become crystallized in nineteenth-century society. To call it a social force in the same way that Darwinism might be seen as a social force obscures the fact that theories of separate spheres were viewed as the underpinnings of American culture, rather than as new "discoveries." The force over which Edna has no control leads her to look for some other form within which to make manifest her "double consciousness." In the "real" world of Edna's family and society, the only person capable of understanding her death on its own terms might be Mlle. Reisz—another woman who has engaged in a similar struggle and taken the life of the artist as her own form within which to express the tensions of the solitude (also the title of the piece of music she plays) of self. From a realist's view, Edna's last act appears to be meaningless suicide. From a regionalist's view, however, it becomes the only form of expression available to her.

Yet, perhaps the novel's limitations partly reside in Chopin's limited vision of what an American woman might achieve. Edna isn't strong enough or talented enough to live like Mlle. Reisz, and Chopin doesn't even present this as a serious possibility for her. Neither does she perceive the possibility of extending her own desire for awakening to the countless, and generally nameless, women of color in the novel. (I have often suggested to students looking for a paper topic on *The Awakening* that they count and study the great variety of servant women who pervade the novel's background, but no one has ever done this.) Neither Edna nor Chopin herself seems to perceive Edna's concerns as applicable to women of color or different social class. Perhaps Edna's limitations are Chopin's own: for Chopin, implicitly viewing sexism with the naturalist's eye, cannot achieve the full shift of the center of perception that would be necessary to produce works of regionalism in the nineteenth century or modernism in the twentieth, a shift that in Chopin would have to focus on Edna's perception as normal and the perceptions of other characters as skewed. The only nineteenth-century work by a woman writer that really accomplishes this is Sarah Orne Jewett's 1896 *The Country of the Pointed Firs*—not anthologized but available in paperback in a Norton edition (with my introduction).

MARY E. WILKINS FREEMAN

Like Jewett, Mary Wilkins Freeman wrote in the genre of regionalism, and also like Jewett, Freeman places women's lives as well as regional vision at the center of her stories. Freeman's *A New England Nun* makes a useful companion story to Jewett's *A White Heron*. Ask your students to evaluate the motivations and final choices of Louisa Ellis and Jewett's Sylvy. Compare and contrast *A New England Nun* with Bret Harte's *The Outcasts of Poker Flat*. Although Freeman focuses on Louisa Ellis's experience, she portrays her male character, Joe Dagget, more sympathetically than Harte or Hamlin Garland do their female characters. *A New England Nun* presents Louisa Ellis's vision and decision not to marry as valid and normal, but Freeman doesn't earn the reader's sympathy for her female character at Joe Dagget's expense. She portrays Joe as well meaning and honorable, if typical of his time and place (many young men left New England to make their fortunes elsewhere in the years following the Civil War). Some critics have called Louisa sexually repressed. A lively discussion will follow if you ask your students whether they agree.

The Revolt of "Mother" earns Freeman a place in the humorist tradition, with a difference. Once again, she includes "Father's" perspective in her story of "Mother's" revolt, and suggests "Father's" ability to enlarge his own capacity for empathy. Unlike writers of the Southwest humorist school, for whom local color implied acceptance of "off-color" jokes about women, Freeman does not elevate Sarah Penn by caricaturing Adoniram and making him the object of ridicule. Like Jewett's *A White Heron, The Revolt of "Mother"* may be read as Freeman's response to local color writing. From the opening line of the story, what Sarah Penn seems to want most of all is to engage her husband as her audience and to find acceptance for her own voice. *Revolt* may be too strong a word to describe Sarah Penn's attempt to make herself heard; she remains within the family structure, even if she has managed to redefine its terms; Nanny's impending marriage, not Sarah's own frustration, moves her to act.

Freeman contributes to the development of regionalism by collapsing narrator and female protagonist. Ask students to consider the absence of narrators in Freeman's stories and to contrast this with the reliance on narrators by her contemporaries, most notably Jewett and James. Where Jewett makes it possible for a reader to empathize with a regional character, and to imagine that character speaking in his or her own voice, Freeman actually stands back from her own regional canvas, allowing her characters' voices, not a narrator's perspective, to create their own stories. Unlike Jewett, Freeman does not dramatize a shift in the center of perception, from, say, the ornithologist of *A White Heron* to the nine-year-old rural child; instead, Freeman writes from a position where such a shift has already occurred. She frames her stories carefully—Louisa Ellis's window and the Penns' barn door carefully limit the world she depicts—but within that frame, she creates a fictional territory in which characters can articulate the perspective of marginal women as central. The tight form of her fiction both fences out and fences in; she writes as if regionalism both opens up and protects that small space within which late-nineteenth-century women were free to express their vision.

BOOKER T. WASHINGTON

Washington, like his contemporary W. E. B. Du Bois, is searching in *Up from Slavery* for a theory of human identity that would both explain the forces on which black identities are contingent and offer programs for future action. He tries to explain the forces ranged against black people and to evolve a plan to counteract these forces. In the Washington-Du Bois controversy, Washington's position of "Atlanta Compromise" presents the powerlessness of black people as *donnée* and proposes to accept "severe and constant struggle" rather than "artificial forcing" in the question of social equality. Contrast his position with that of Du Bois's. Consider whether the black polemical writers of the late nineteenth century, in their attempts to explain social forces, share the perception of naturalists Stephen Crane or Theodore Dreiser, who also turned to theories to try to explain our human position in the universe.

CHARLES W. CHESNUTT

The problem of aesthetic distance is more complex for Chesnutt, a black man, than for Joel Chandler Harris, a white. Like Harris's tales, Chesnutt's *The Goophered Grapevine* and other stories from *The Conjure Woman* might have been perceived as local color writing. However, Chesnutt, in particular, deliberately works in opposition to the expectations of local color writing as his way of realistically portraying the experiences of African-Americans in slavery and Reconstruction. Students can see Chesnutt inventing his own form. For Chesnutt must write as if his white readers might be as obtusely condescending as the Yankee who buys the plantation in *The Goophered Grapevine.* How does Chesnutt avoid the anxiety of writing in the first person as a black man? (Students may need to consider his historical situation to perceive that anxiety before responding to the question.) He embeds Uncle Julius's narrative within the larger story, in which the white man officially narrates *The Goophered Grapevine,* thereby allowing the white narrator to reveal his own limitations. Still, the story manages to portray Uncle Julius's reality—one dominated by the need to use folklore and the cunning of the powerless as a way to get what he wants—which, in this story, is a job that will continue to give him free access to the grapevine, despite the fact that, as Theodore R. Hovet points out in an interesting essay ("Chesnutt's 'The Goophered Grapevine' as Social Criticism," *Negro American Literature Forum,* Fall 1973), Julius is also aware of the "cycle of exploitation" that will "begin again with the appearance of the Yankee." Hovet sees the story as the continuation of slavery by the means of wage-slavery—an interpretation that he also admits may be buried "a little too deeply within the folk tale," but perhaps not too deeply for students taking a historical perspective on Chesnutt.

CHARLES ALEXANDER EASTMAN (OHIYESA)

In light of the headnote's assessment of Eastman's assimilationist tendencies, read the chapters from *From the Deep Woods to Civilization* with particular awareness of Eastman's references to whites; to other Sioux, such as Blue Horse, who claim to be "friends" with white men; and to Sioux who are intolerant of relationships with whites. Then recall Charlot's speech, in which "the white man" is portrayed as a monolithic villain. Does Eastman's narrative confirm or refute Charlot's speech? To what extent would students argue that Eastman's assimilationist perspective is the product of his white education in the Indian boarding schools of the period? Is it possible for Eastman to be both an assimilationist and a spokesman for Native Americans? He summarizes the ambivalence of his position at one point early in the excerpt when he writes about the difficulty parents had separating from their children who were attending government boarding schools and would ask him to write letters excusing their children on account of illness: "I was of course wholly in sympathy with the policy of education for the Indian children, yet by no means hardened to the exhibition of natural feeling." Yet later (in Chapter VII) he seems to give meaning to the phrase he is called, "the Indian white doctor," when he writes, "I scarcely knew at the time, but gradually learned afterward, that the Sioux had many grievances and causes for profound discontent, which lay back of and were more or less closely related to the ghost dance craze and the prevailing restlessness and excitement." Eastman speaks the Sioux language, has power vested in him by the U.S. government, and yet does not completely understand the Sioux point of view.

Eastman's powerful narrative conveys details about the day-to-day workings of the Pine Ridge Agency. Explicate with students the apparent role of the agency in the lives of Native Americans and the power the agency could exercise; explore the significance of such "games" as the buffalo hunt on "issue day"; consider the role of the Indian police force at Pine Ridge Agency. Consider as well the meaning of the placement of the doctor's offices: "the assembly room of the Indian police, used also as a council room, opened out of my dispensary."

For the larger narrative of the story of the Ghost Dance religion and the Wounded Knee massacre, Eastman's narrative offers a powerful eyewitness account of impending conflict and of the aftermath and consequences of the massacre. Trace references to the "new religion" that has been proclaimed at about the same time as Eastman's arrival at Pine Ridge. Reread the anthologized versions of Wovoka's "Messiah letters" and compare them with Eastman's careful paraphrase of Wovoka's teachings in Chapter VI (Captain Sword's account of the Ghost Dance religion). Examine Eastman's narrative for evidence that might explain the resistance of white settlers to the Ghost Dance religion.

Then examine carefully Eastman's account of the "Ghost Dance War" itself, including U.S. government's use of black soldiers against the Sioux. While not an eyewitness, Eastman is an "ear-witness," for he hears the sound of the Hotchkiss guns. Yet what he sees of the wounded and dead when he visits the battlefield, although it tests his assimilationism, does not ultimately change his course of action: "All this was a severe ordeal for one who had so lately put all his faith in the Christian love and lofty ideals of the white man," he writes—and sets his day of marriage to a white woman for the following June. Recall here, once again, the words of William Apess's *An Indian's Looking-Glass*; in Eastman, we see at least one Sioux who manages to avail himself of the possibilities of cross-racial marriage. The times—and the terms of the discourse—are different for Eastman than for Apess sixty years earlier.

HAMLIN GARLAND

Garland's *Under the Lion's Paw* usefully contrasts with both Jewett's *The Foreigner* and Freeman's *The Revolt of "Mother."* Although Stephen Council initially helps Haskins get a good start, Garland focuses on the futility of Haskins's labor, and the concluding scene creates a tableau similar in effect to the end of *The Outcasts of Poker Flat.* Haskins is "under the lion's paw," and Butler (and Garland) leave him "seated dumbly on the sunny pile of sheaves, his head sunk into his hands." The reader views Haskins—like Mother Shipton, Piney Woods, and ultimately Oakhurst as well—from the outside. Contrast this with the perspective Jewett offers in *The Foreigner,* in which she depicts the growth of sympathy between characters and in which Mrs. Todd explores and tries to repair the social exclusion of Mrs. Tolland; Haskins ends as an object of exclusion, viewed from outside the story, whereas Jewett's characters expand their circle of community. Or contrast the poverty of the homeless characters in *Under the Lion's Paw* with the inadequately housed Sarah and Nanny Penn in Freeman's *The Revolt of "Mother."* Garland bases the power of his story on its portrait of the bleakness of poverty; Freeman bases hers on her protagonists' awareness of their own strengths.

CHARLOTTE PERKINS GILMAN

Like *The Awakening, The Yellow Wallpaper* shows a woman trying to find some alternative context for self-expression. The speaker in the story looks in vain for any referential reflector of her own reality—until she is incarcerated by her husband in a room with yellow wallpaper and, over the course of the story, comes to identify with or project herself onto the figure of a woman who stoops down and creeps about behind the pattern on the wallpaper. Gilman presents her narrator's "double consciousness" as the tension the woman artist must live with in a context that refuses (with absolute denial of her husband) to mirror her self-concept. Like Edna's suicide at the end of *The Awakening,* Gilman's narrator's madness becomes understandable as her only means of self-expression. Ask students to contrast the story with Poe's *The Fall of the House of Usher* and James's *The Beast in the Jungle* or *The Turn of the Screw.* Consider the narrator as a type of the artist and apply to her Howells's dictum that the imagination "can work only with the stuff of experience." Does the narrator "compose" elements from real life, and if so, are both her madness and her work of art—the story itself—realistic? What happens to a writer when she wants to write referentially about experience that the world refuses to recognize? What does the story tell us about the prevailing medical attitudes toward women in the late nineteenth century? Reading *Why I Wrote "The Yellow Wallpaper"* in conjunction with the story makes it clear to students that Gilman was self-conscious about the possibilities for fiction to intervene in the medical treatment of women as well as in women's understanding of the relationship between their own madness and their lack of social autonomy and intellectual choice.

JANE ADDAMS

In reading the excerpts from *Twenty Years at Hull-House,* students have the opportunity to examine the dialectic between writing and social action. Although Addams challenges the usefulness of literature, she herself also wrote—about her decision to open Hull-House—and she explores the divergent paths open to educated, middle-class women at the end of the nineteenth century. Ask students to take on Addams's challenge. Read her description of her impressions of the poverty of East London in Chapter IV and her "disgust" that to respond to the scene before her she recalls an image from De Quincey that intervenes or mediates between what she sees and how she perceives it. She wishes to act other than "through a literary suggestion," and she states that literature "only served to cloud the really vital situation spread before our eyes." Ask students to comment on this scene and Addams's reactions; if there is truth to Addams's challenge, what, then, is the purpose and use of literature? Some may argue that Addams herself uses writing to pose her challenge and may see in other turn-of-the-century writers (Chopin, Washington, Du Bois, Norris, Crane, and Dreiser) a kindred attempt to use writing to change social conditions. Is Addams rejecting all writing or only that which does not engage social problems? Would she also challenge the importance of literary naturalism? The excerpts from *Twenty Years at Hull-House* become an implicit commentary on Addams's contemporary literary figures. Ask students in particular to examine her statements about women's education and her sense that "the first generation of college women . . . had developed too exclusively the power of acquiring knowledge and of merely receiving impressions," and to comment on James's *Daisy Miller*, in light of Addams's critique. Addams's solution to the disengagement of women's education is to found the settlement house movement in this country, "in which young women who had been given over too exclusively to study, might restore a balance of activity along traditional lines and learn of life from life itself." In doing so, she appears to define social welfare as emerging from a crisis between culture and conduct, especially for middle-class women. Does her version of social work become applied literary studies, despite her apparent rejection of literature and culture as more than "preparation" or foundation education? Critics often move outside the discipline of literary study and find in other fields—psychology, sociology, philosophy, anthropology, history—a perspective by which they read and interpret a particular text. Might we view Jane Addams's choice to open a settlement house and, in effect, to found the field of social welfare as itself a "reading" or "interpretation" of American literature? If so, then *Twenty Years at Hull-House* is, in part, a new form of literary criticism, and in the dialectic between literature and social action, literature provides the basis for knowledge in social welfare, while social work itself becomes a form of literary criticism.

EDITH WHARTON

In the "Introduction" to *Ethan Frome*, Wharton describes her characters in the novel as her "*granite outcroppings*; but half-emerged from the soil, and scarcely more articulate." It is the "outcropping granite" that she states has been overlooked in the New England of fiction, and implicitly, then, *Ethan Frome* is Wharton's challenge to the regionalists Jewett and Freeman who were her contemporaries. Edith Wharton joins the group of late-nineteenth-century writers who concern themselves with point of view, she shares with James a sense of the world's increasing complexity, and she contributes her own version of how to "read" or see the world in light of the decline of omniscience that characterizes the transition to modernism.

You may begin your discussion of the novel by asking students to characterize Wharton's narrator and the stance that narrator takes toward his material. In the "Introduction" she characterizes her narrator as a sophisticated "looker-on" and contrasts him with the "simple" people of her story, and she writes that while each chronicler contributes "*just so much as he or she is capable of understanding*," only the narrator "has scope enough to see it all." How does Wharton's attitude toward her characters contrast with that of Jewett and Freeman? In the opening chapters of the novel, the narrator hopes to get Frome to "at least unseal his lips," establishing the theme of silence as one of Wharton's concerns. And in writing the novel, the narrator claims to present "this vision of [Frome's] story." Instead of drawing Frome out to hear his own story in his own words, the narrator tells it for him; ask students how this contrasts with the regionalists' attempt to listen to rural characters speak in their own voices. In further contrast, discuss Wharton's use of the Starkfield landscape in the novel. What relationship to landscape do her characters have? Part of what distinguishes the regionalist writers from the local color writers is their attitude toward women, acceptance of women's vision, and attempt to give women their own voice. Ask students to comment on Wharton's treatment of Zeena and Mattie. The two seem like split images of woman throughout most of the novel. Zeena is the bad mother figure, "already an old woman," and she turns "queer" on Ethan, an example of what the narrator calls "pathological instances" in Starkfield; Mattie elicits Ethan's "passion of rebellion," and in her request that they die together in the sleigh ride, expresses both sexuality and submission. Zeena is the cold, repressive mother; Mattie, the warm, sexual daughter. Or are both only projections of Ethan's (and the narrator's) imagination? *Ethan Frome* focuses not on the female characters, but on Ethan himself, and just as "all the intercourse" between Ethan and Mattie is made up of "inarticulate flashes," so is the narrator's acquaintance with Ethan. Together, character and narrator paint a portrait of humbled manhood, male suffering (the narrator tells us that, in this story, Ethan himself has suffered the most), and a reprise of themes from early-nineteenth-century fiction: flight from domesticity, the idea that the best American woman is a dead one (Ethan tells Mattie, "'I'd a'most rather have you dead than [married]!'"), and the American hero as male. By the end of the novel, at the point in the story's chronology when the narrator meets the principals, Mattie Silver has become interchangeable with Zeena, proven herself unable to take care of herself and, like Zeena, has lapsed into silence. However, as Ruth Varnum Hale implies to the narrator in the novel's final sentence, the last indignity for Ethan Frome is that the women at his farm aren't able to "hold their tongues" with each other. Ethan's final "punishment" at the hands of his womenfolk is that for all his suffering he is doomed to hear their voices; he has not managed to "silence" them, even though the novel itself succeeds in doing so.

MARY AUSTIN

Austin's writing combines attention to natural detail with the themes and forms of literary regionalism. *The Walking Woman* possesses some of the mystical and visionary qualities of Jewett's Mrs. Todd in *The Foreigner*, and like that story, Austin's portrays a narrator who learns from the character who is her subject and perhaps sees this character as a model for her own life. In the Jewett story, the narrator describes Mrs.

Todd telling her own story about the Frenchwoman; and thus in both Jewett and Austin, regionalism becomes an exercise in listening, reading, and storytelling across lines of difference. One of the features of late-nineteenth-century American life was the increasing independence of American women. James portrays his own version in *Daisy Miller,* where Daisy violates social conventions in an Italian sense but in other ways conforms to American conventions for a middle-class, white, heterosexual woman. In some of the portraits of independent women included in NAAL—Jewett's Sylvy and Mrs. Todd, Chopin's Mlle. Reisz, Freeman's Louisa Ellis, Austin's Walking Woman, and the autobiographical persona of Gertrude Bonnin—regionalist writers present rural, working-class, or poor women; the story line either conflicts with or occurs after any heterosexual interest; and in the case of Bonnin (Zitkala Śa), the narrative presents the experience of a Native American. Students may find that Austin's Walking Woman has so "walked off all sense of society-made values" that she herself has moved into a different "race" of women, and class issues have become irrelevant to her vision; indeed, the narrator writes that "the word she brought about trails and water-holes was as reliable as an Indian's." Living in the desert has given her "both wisdom and information" that are not characteristic of white and non-desert societies. And she certainly tells some truths about the place of (hetero)sexuality in her life and her ultimate independence from men that place her in a liminal category of turn-of-the-century women. The Walking Woman, like the fiction in which she exists, possesses an intimate relation to the desert landscape that promotes the "fullest understanding" between her and her narrator. Help students contrast Austin's narrator's approach to the Walking Woman's difference and to Western life with Bret Harte's local color approach in *The Outcasts of Poker Flat.* Some students may insist that this difference is gendered in some way and that regionalism approaches "different" characters with more empathy and respect than the writings of the local color writers represented in NAAL—Harte, Hamlin Garland, even Samuel Clemens.

W. E. B. DU BOIS

In the anthologized selection from *The Souls of Black Folk,* Du Bois summarizes the history of black leadership in the nineteenth century and proposes nothing less than full suffrage, civic equality, and education as the means to achieve progress. How does this conflict with the position Booker T. Washington articulates in his "Atlanta Compromise"? Du Bois writes about the curious "double movement" within the leadership of social groups in which "real progress may be negative and actual advance be relative retrogression," and he describes Washington "as essentially the leader not of one race but of two,—a compromiser between the South, the North and the Negro." Instructors can point to these statements as an extension of Du Bois's most provocative idea, one he expresses in "Our Spiritual Strivings" (Chapter I of *The Souls of Black Folk*—not anthologized, but it can be placed on reserve), in which he describes the "double consciousness" of the American Negro. As my colleague R. Baxter Miller explains this concept, Du Bois sees black consciousness as existing in some midpoint between two conflicting perspectives. Black consciousness is independent both of a self-contained culture and of mainstream culture and, therefore exists, in a state of constant tension between "black" and "white" worlds. Du Bois moves well beyond Frederick Douglass's ideal of "ultimate assimilation *through* self-assertion, and on no other terms"; Du Bois asks, On whose terms do we define assimilation? Miller explains that, unlike Douglass, for whom slavery was a physical reality, Du Bois can envision slavery in other than physical terms, and therefore, he is really asking for pluralism in *The Souls of Black Folk*, not assimilation—and not compromise. Like the regionalists, Du Bois has also shifted the center of his perception to a pan-ethnic or pan-African view of culture rather than seeing consciousness as centered in Western thought.

The necessary two-ness of Washington and the "double consciousness" that Du Bois expresses are just one of several points in the anthologized selections where students can begin to see the emergence of real stress points in the concept of a referential, universal, or reliable reality. While it would not be accurate to say that the "double consciousness" of American blacks and of American women, beginning with Elizabeth Cady Stanton's address to the Seneca Falls Women's Rights Convention and the *Declaration of Sentiments* in 1848, led directly to ways of thinking that would produce modernism, it was certainly one of the real aspects of the social environment that made and continue to make central concepts of modernism seem directly relevant to American experience. So Du Bois, then, while neither a naturalist nor a modernist, still can be interpreted as a transition thinker—someone who observed social forces at work; who wrote and spoke in the tradition of Benjamin Franklin to move common people; and who located his vision within the increasing sense that reality might not be inherited, but rather, like myth, invented.

FRANK NORRIS

Like realists Howells and James, Norris tried to describe his "art of fiction," in essays such as the anthologized *Weekly Letter*. Discuss with students what Norris means by making his distinction between "accuracy" and "the impression of Truth." Comment on his implication that the purpose or place of fiction is to express those "feelings under stress" that he states people are generally unable to express in "real life." Then, in discussing the excerpt from *Vandover and the Brute,* test out Norris's definition of naturalism as lying "midway between the Realists and Romanticists, taking the best from each." Ask students to identify elements of realism and Romanticism from the excerpted chapter. How do the terms *accuracy* and *truth* characterize the distinction between realism and Romanticism in Norris? Perhaps what Vandover sees, feels, and experiences, narrated from his third-person-limited point of view, expresses the realism of *Vandover,* and the way Norris generalizes Vandover's perception as a depiction of human experience expresses its Romanticism. Vandover becomes both an individual and a type. The prevalence of animal imagery in *Vandover* underscores Norris's naturalism, as he suggests that in moments of crisis, "it was the animal in them all that had come to the surface in an instant." Norris also portrays human beings caught in a hostile environment over which they have no control. In Vandover's struggle, the ship, which becomes the "brute," is also an emblem for the larger environment. Ask students to think about the various forces Vandover must combat and how he changes his behavior in response to these forces. Does his behavioral change signify the capacity for deeper changes in character? In surveying the four major narrative fictional genres—regionalism, realism, local color writing, and naturalism—ask students to consider the extent to which each genre frees or constricts the development of character. In Norris, the narrative acts on Vandover in the same way that the environment does; Norris brings into the act of fictional creation basic assumptions about the limitations of human character, and therefore, he has no interest in the growth of Vandover's perception or his attempts to speak in his own voice. For better or for worse, Norris's characters reflect his own view of human nature; how "realistic" do students find that view?

STEPHEN CRANE

For Crane, even our most intimate self-concepts are contingent on our social context and on the forces of natural environment. The selections in NAAL allow students to see the variety of forces against which the protagonist in the Crane universe must fight. *An Experiment in Misery* demonstrates the forces of poverty for its characters who have been derailed from the pursuit of economic prosperity. Crane uses many of the same devices in this story that he uses in *Red Badge of Courage:* his protagonist wanders the city as if in a dream; the characters are referred to by their prominent characteristics—"a youth," "the seedy man," "the assassin"; and the misery is personified as a malicious force—"a nation forcing its regal head into the clouds, throwing no downward glances; in the sublimity of its aspirations ignoring the wretches who may flounder at its feet." Students can see some of the differences between realism and naturalism if you ask them to compare Huck Finn with the youth in *An Experiment in Misery*. Who is more "real"?

The Open Boat presents the forces of nature as the elements against which the characters are pitted, and *The Blue Hotel* reveals the rage and ultimate lack of control that govern human behavior; *An Episode of War*, read with *An Experiment in Misery* can give students an even fuller experience of Crane's interests in *Red Badge*. *The Bride Comes to Yellow Sky* is anomalous in the collection. Where does the story get its humor? What are the local color elements in the story? Crane suggests that marriage itself is a force; how does the story suggest that each character is controlled by that force?

THEODORE DREISER

Dreiser's fiction conveys his sense of forces ranged against the individual, and in most of his work, these forces act directly. In *Old Rogaum and His Theresa,* students see a more subtle text, for the forces Theresa and her father must battle are revealed to them indirectly. Unlike other women in Dreiser's fiction, such as Carrie Meeber of *Sister Carrie,* Theresa is not "ruined" during her night out but is given a glimpse of how she might be. And Old Rogaum does not lose "his Theresa," but the blond girl who shows up groaning on his doorstep gives him a glimpse of how the night might have turned out. Dreiser reveals the forces within the family as well. Old Rogaum himself is both a force, for his daughter, and is taken over by forces of rage and powerlessness beyond his control. His wife is no force at all; compare her with the bride in Crane's *The Bride Comes to Yellow Sky.*

JOHN M. OSKISON

The Problem of Old Harjo may be discussed both as a Native American text and as regionalist fiction, and the two readings complement each other.

In the context of other Native American works anthologized in the 1865–1914 section of NAAL, begin by comparing Miss Evans with Charles Eastman's wife-to-be, Elaine Goodale, for Miss Evans is the prototype of the young, white, well-meaning, and often female Christian missionary to the Indians. Unlike the more experienced and less idealistic Mrs. Rowell, who expresses racism in her attitude toward "the old and bigamous" among the Creek Indian population (stating that "the country guarantees [Harjo's] idle existence" even though the truth is that he is materially solvent on his farm), Miss Evans is capable of seeing Harjo's situation as he sees it himself and withholding moral judgment. Harjo mutely questions her; she questions Mrs. Rowell, then her old pastor in New York, even implicitly church doctrine when she is tempted to say to him, " 'Stop worrying about your soul; you'll get to Heaven as surely as any of us.' " Yet the "problem of old Harjo" becomes Miss Evans's problem—and although the story seems unresolved at the end, since the problem remains insoluble, her "solution" (if not "solvent") is to recognize that circumstances have somehow tied her to this particular mission station, to this particular "impossible convert." Tied to Harjo "until death . . . came to one of them," does Miss Evans become in effect yet another "wife" to the bigamist? Even if not, Oskison is nevertheless suggesting that the real agenda of the Christian missionaries is to suppress Creek culture in the young until the old men die off. What is this agenda but a continuation of the Ghost Dance War in another form?

Readers familiar with Native American literature may recognize Harjo as a figure of the trickster, a transformative character (in this story) who poses the dilemma of change—change for the old Creek but also change necessarily in the Christians, if anyone is to achieve genuine salvation. The story's apparent lack of resolution—"And meanwhile, what?"—conveys the disruptive effect of the trickster figure but also the process of highlighting trouble in the prevailing moral order. Old Harjo brings into relief the basic contradiction inherent in the encounter between the Christian missionaries and some Native Americans—which perhaps might be summed up in Mrs. Rowell's (long) wait for the "old bigamists" to die out. Yet as the story's ending attests, Harjo's powers include tenacity—and he engages Miss Evans in a temporal "problem" for which the only solution would be genuine change in the moral order of things. She becomes his "wife" to the extent that the trickster figure who appears in some Native American legends may represent sexuality and desire, and her wish to assure him of salvation is humorous within a Native American tradition, for the trickster (as students may recall from the Pima Story of Creation) is already Coyote, the divinely powerful child born when the moon became a mother. So Coyote is another version of the Messiah of the Ghost Dance religion in the sense that, in a "trickster" mode, Coyote—or here, Harjo—becomes incarnate to point up moral failings in the creation.

Read from the perspective of regionalism, the story's portrait of the relationship between Harjo and Miss Evans becomes an exercise in empathic exchange. Miss Evans is capable of moving into Harjo's moral and affectional universe because she is able to look with, not at, the "problem" Harjo presents. At the same time, her sympathy for him works implicitly to challenge the moral, political, and religious control Mrs. Rowell represents. Although Oskison's story may not on initial reading appear to be as sophisticated as Charles Chesnutt's *The Goophered Grapevine*, both involve powerless and disenfranchised persons (old Harjo and Uncle Julius) creating a situation that will force whites to reveal their own moral limitations. In both stories, it is the cunning of the powerless which sets up the "looking-glass" to white society; in posing his "problem" week after week in the church, Harjo is indeed expressing his cunning, for has Miss Evans converted him or has he converted her? As fictional representation of William Apess's critique, *The Problem of Old Harjo* has much in common with the work of Chesnutt and other nineteenth-century regionalists. Or, to put it another way, regionalist writers invented the white characters (like Miss Evans) capable of responding to figures like Harjo—whether we view him as a Native American trickster or as a "realistic" problem occasioned by the encounter of cultures, in this story represented by the conflict between the Christian missionary and the "old and bigamous" Creek.

NATIVE AMERICAN CHANTS AND SONGS

Although teaching the chants and songs may not take the central position in your presentation of Native American literature, they are significant because they give the instructor a way to illustrate the truth that there was an American literature on this continent before there was English here. With this brief set of examples of chants and songs, students can learn that there was also literary form on the North American continent before there was formal literature, indeed, that there was drama, in the ceremonial performance of the nine-day Navajo *Night Chant*; there was dance as a form of language, as the Comanche and Sioux drawings of the Ghost Dance recall; and there was music, particularly represented by drum beats and tonalities. Chants and songs gave poetry breath, considered by some Native American groups to link human life with the hole from which the earliest people emerged (as in the Pima Stories of the Beginning of the World, anthologized in Volume 1).

Given the generally one-dimensional nature of the literature classroom (the printed word is linear, not spatial, and it is difficult, except in moments of textual analysis, to "share" the reading experience persons in the room have separately engaged in before coming to class), teaching the Native American chants and songs invites some transformation from the linear to some other mode—whether it be spatial (asking a group of students to enact at least part of the staging directions for the Navajo *Night Chant*, perhaps without sand!), or aural (asking others to prepare one or two of the songs for presentation). My own preference is to sit at the piano at home and make a very brief tape of the music to accompany the Chippewa song *My Love Has Departed* and the two Ghost Dance songs of the Arapaho: *[Father, have pity on me]* and *[When I met him approaching]*. As an alternative, if you have a student talented enough (or courageous enough) on the recorder or flute, you might ask him or her to perform these songs in class. These songs must be heard to be appreciated for the way they alternate time signatures. *My Love Has Departed* moves back and forth between 2/4 and 3/4 time, which probably complicated performance for dancers as well as drummers, but which calls attention to patterns of breath and duration, the mysteries of life itself and life processes. In the Ghost Dance songs of the Arapaho in particular, there seems to be some correlation between elongated time signatures and the address to the gods. In *[Father, have pity on me]*, the singer takes longer measures to address the "Father," and the singer does the same thing in *[When I met him approaching]* when recreating the moment of trance vision. According to Andrew Wiget (*Native American Literature*, 1985), the songs or prayers in ritual Native American poetry seek "to recreate a state rather than an event" and "achieves substantiality and duration in time and space by repeating many different short songs in sequence." Perhaps the alternation of time signatures or rhythmic meters within these short songs also contribute to achieving this "substantiality and duration in time and space."

Students may feel on most familiar ground in reading the English translations themselves, and certainly the Ghost Dance songs will be evocative if you have discussed the Ghost Dance religion and the Wounded Knee massacre with them previously. These songs convey the losses of the native peoples and their hopes for revelation and salvation. The two excerpts from the Navajo *Night Chant* may produce the most extensive formal analysis of the (translated) language of the chants and songs.

The Navajo Night Chant

The headnote points out that the chant is a healing ceremony, focused on an individual rather than society as a whole—but clearly understood to be inclusive and relevant to the audience-participants. The patient of the first chant comes onto the "trail of song"; prays to ("walks with") the gods; and follows the rainbow (their promise of salvation, associated with rain) progressively to, then into, then within the "fore part of my house with the dawn," where he meets the gods that symbolize generative and regenerative powers. Upon sitting with these gods, the patient experiences restoration of his own powers ("Beautifully my fire to me is restored") and walks a new trail at the end of the prayer, one marked by the pollen, grasshoppers, and dew that represent generativity (and the dawn).

The second chant, according to the notes, represents the prayer for salvation as the prayer for rain. The progression in this chant moves from the repetitions of invocations to the "male divinity" to bring the rain, to the chanter's association of rain with individual healing, to a joyful acknowledgment that healing has taken place ("Happily for me *the spell* is taken off. / Happily may I walk."), to a section of the chant leading up to the benediction and conclusion of the ceremony that widens the circle to include others ("Happily may fair white corn, to the ends of the earth, come with you") and ends with the patient's inhalation of "the breath of dawn," signifying the patient's emergence into health. This chant focuses both on an individual's healing, and on transforming the social order. The patient's healing symbolizes the well-being of all those who live the Navajo "way" or "walk with" their gods.

GERTRUDE SIMMONS BONNIN (ZITKALA ŚA)

Bonnin's three autobiographical essays invite comparison with other autobiographies by women writers. Students may find it interesting to read Mary Rowlandson's *Narrative* (NAAL, Volume 1), in which Rowlandson describes her capture by the Wampanoag Indians, or Elizabeth Ashbridge's *Some Account*, in which she describes her own indenturing and "enslavement" in marriage (NAAL, Volume 1), against Bonnin's narrative of "capture" by the "palefaces." Suggest that Bonnin's account of her removal from the reservation and attempted assimilation into white culture provides an ironic twist on the Indian captivity narrative of the colonial period. It's also interesting to think about Bonnin as a Native American Daisy Miller, particularly in light of what Jane Addams says college education does to women in the first generation (see the excerpt from *Twenty Years at Hull-House*). Like Addams, Bonnin invested most of her energy in social action to improve the lot of Native Americans. Ask students to locate hints, in Bonnin's essays, of the same disenchantment with education that Addams writes about. Although Bonnin's work does not, strictly speaking, belong to the genre of regionalism—it is autobiography, not fiction—nevertheless, there are elements of fictional form, especially in *Impressions of an Indian Childhood.* She uses images—learning the "art of beadwork" or the cropped and "shingled hair"—that characterize both her own life and the larger plight of other Native Americans as well. *Impressions of an Indian Childhood* also possesses an aesthetic distance that students might associate with fiction. At the end of the third selection, *An Indian Teacher among Indians,* Bonnin herself acknowledges that "as I look back upon the recent past, I see it from a distance, as a whole." Perhaps the reason for this distance is that, at least in *Impressions of an Indian Childhood,* she writes about a developing child whose path of development as a Sioux becomes so pinched off that the older child and adult narrator cannot even repair the discontinuity. She also writes in English about events that took place when "I knew but one language, and that was my mother's native tongue." The act of rendering her Sioux childhood into English creates its own fiction, for she writes about herself at a time in her life before speaking and writing in English was even imaginable. Like the regionalists, Bonnin depicts a female-centered universe and her own refusal to be silenced, and she triumphs on behalf of the disenfranchised "squaw" when she writes of winning the oratory contest; but unlike Jewett's world of *The Foreigner*, in which Mrs. Todd can ease her separation anxiety from her mother by telling a comforting story, Bonnin's estrangement from her own mother only deepens as she proceeds with her autobiography. She loses her connection with the world of nature, becoming a "cold bare pole . . . planted in a strange earth."

HENRY ADAMS

Whether or not Henry Adams ever read or heard W. E. B. Du Bois, for pedagogical purposes we can see the excerpts from *The Education* as thematic variations on the Du Boisean theme of "double consciousness." Like Du Bois, who summarizes nineteenth-century black thinking in 1903, Henry Adams writes as one born in 1838, yet wanting "to play the game of the twentieth" century. *The Education* is another book in the tradition of Franklin's *Autobiography* but interesting because of the new directions Adams takes. "As it happened, he never got to the point of playing the game at all; he lost himself in the study of it, watching the errors of the players; but this is the only interest in the story, which otherwise has no moral and little incident. A story of education—seventy years of it—the practical value remains to the end in doubt." The development of self-reliance in the American writer and thinker leads Adams to write that "every one must bear his own universe." Unlike Franklin, Adams does not become a politician but rather finds literary symbols that, as the introduction to Adams in NAAL asserts, make *The Education*, to many readers, "the one indispensable text for students seeking to understand the period between the Civil War and World War I." Students can see this clearly in Chapter I, where Adams writes, anticipating modernism, that the twentieth century is a world without design: "Often in old age he puzzled over the question whether, on the doctrine of chances, he was at liberty to accept himself or his world as an accident. No such accident had ever happened before in human experience. For him, alone, the old universe was thrown into the ash-heap and a new one created." And Adams traces his perception to early events (railroad and telegraph) that presented his six-year-old eyes with a "new world." Even as a boy, he developed "a double nature. Life was a double thing. . . . From earliest childhood the boy was accustomed to feel that, for him, life was double."

Chapter XXV, "The Dynamo and the Virgin," crystallizes the doubleness he feels, presaging modern life, in the symbols that express the split between technology and spirituality. Adams writes clearly, and I ask students to prepare a summary of the argument of this chapter. In class, we continue to focus on Adams's early modernist ideas—what happens to human energies, symbolized by the force and power of the Virgin and of ancient fertility goddesses, in an age and in a country that replaces human with technological power; and whether it is possible to state, "with the least possible comment, such facts as seemed sure," and to "fix for a familiar moment a necessary sequence of human movement."

1914–1945

The realists' inability to determine whether or not there exists a certain reality that can be "fixed" limited the applicability of Howellsian realism to turn-of-the-century life. But the regionalists' interest in shifting the center of perception (producing an early form of Du Boisean "double consciousness" that the local color fiction of the period did not possess), James's use of point of view to create the unfolding of the central consciousness in his fictional characters, and the perceptions of the naturalists and turn-of-the-century polemical writers would all influence the twentieth-century debate over the existence of reality. However I make my choices for any given course from the selections available in the 1914–1945 period, I try to convey three different aspects of modern literature over the course of studying individual writers: (1) how and why modern writers see the world differently from writers from earlier periods and centuries—what we might call a thematic approach to understanding modernism; (2) how and why they choose their images and their narrative and poetic forms—an approach that focuses on modernism as technique; (3) how their gender, ethnic, or class background influences their writing—how pluralism, both within American culture and as it derives from international influence (particularly by Joyce, Woolf, and Yeats), emerges as a determining factor and a consequence of modern literature. In light of recent awareness of the effects of colonialism on colonized peoples, I also ask students to locate evidence of these postcolonial effects and the relationship between modernist poetry and evidence of postcolonialism. Selections from Native American and African-American writers allow students to explore this question, and we look in particular for evidence of continuing colonial attitudes (in both white and minority writers) that manifest themselves in racial segregation and discrimination.

BLACK ELK

In opening discussion on the anthologized excerpts from this work, begin by asking students questions that will help them explore the very interesting narrative form. To the question, Who is speaking?, they will answer, Black Elk. But who is narrating? Black Elk or John Neihardt? I underscore for them points of information from the NAAL headnote, namely that Black Elk could neither read nor write and spoke little

English when he told John Neihardt the story of his great vision. We talk about the context within which *Black Elk Speaks* was created: Black Elk telling his story to his son, Ben Black Elk, who then translated it into English for Black Elk's "adopted" son, John Neihardt, while Neihardt's daughter, Enid, wrote it all down and other Sioux elders contributed their memories of events. Then, later, Neihardt worked from his daughter's transcriptions to produce *Black Elk Speaks*. How do the circumstances of composition affect students' perception of authorship of the work? We discuss differences between Neihardt's work and the work of early-twentieth-century social scientists who often paid Native American informants to tell their stories. Neihardt was himself a poet; in agreeing to tell his story to Neihardt, holy man Black Elk was recognizing a kindred spirit.

"Heyoka Ceremony" provides the text within which to explore the concept of tribal identity for Black Elk and the extent to which his personal life story is also deeply connected to the history of his people, even though, as the NAAL headnote points out, by the time of Black Elk's birth, forced removal of southeastern Indian groups to the plains west of the Mississippi had already dissipated tribal identity. Although performing the dog vision (enacting the entrance of truth "with two faces" into the world, so that the ceremony becomes a kind of Sioux drama) records an essential rite in the development of Black Elk's own power, Black Elk focuses his account of the ceremony on making it possible for the power to come to the people. His participation in the ceremony reflects his commitment to his own religious vision, and he performs and describes each step in the ceremony with great care and seriousness, but his own role is integrally connected with the participation of the people and the power of the ceremony "to make them happier and stronger." "Heyoka Ceremony" thus records the interrelation between Black Elk's vision, his enactment of the ceremony, and the needs of his tribal group.

"The First Cure" expresses the meaning of the Sioux's relation to the universe and Black Elk's own ability to tap into the powers of the universe to become both a holy man and a healer. It also begins to record the decline of Sioux powers in face of the progressive loss of Sioux land to the "Wasichus" (Euro-Americans) in the 1870s and 1880s. For Black Elk's people are forced to live in square houses instead of tepees, which begins to cut them off from the Power of the World that works in circles. In his description of his first cure, Black Elk reveals his role as a medium—"I could feel the power coming through me"—and as an empathic reflector of the sick boy's pain—"I could feel something queer all through my body, something that made me want to cry for all unhappy things." His position as healer allows him to mediate between the clouded vision of his people, expressed in their pain, and the inner knowledge of the spirit world that is located in the "living center" of the sacred hoop, or of all other round things, including the shape of the tepee, the circle around which Black Elk passes the sacred pipe, and the human life cycle that "is a circle from childhood to childhood." The pipe itself acts as a symbolic conduit to the inner center of the powers of the universe. And in discussing the power of Sioux religious beliefs, it becomes possible to make a literary leap to the power of Black Elk's and Neihardt's collaborative text. Neihardt's attempt in *Black Elk Speaks* is to create a character who is as "round" as his vision; in so doing, Neihardt will be capable of contacting and revealing the Power of the World that works in circles.

Black Elk Speaks records only the first twenty-seven years of Black Elk's life, ending with the battle of Wounded Knee. "The Butchering at Wounded Knee" portrays even more strikingly than the two earlier chapters how much Black Elk's identity is intimately connected with Sioux history. Students will be extremely moved by his description of the "butchering" of Sioux women, children, and warriors and by Black Elk's ability to feel in his own body the danger, the terror, and the pain of his own people as well as his own powerlessness to "cure" the ultimate disease—the "dirty work" of the white soldiers. Neihardt ends *Black Elk Speaks* with an image of drifted snow in "one long grave" at Wounded Knee. Although Black Elk himself lived another fifty-nine years, Neihardt ends his text with what some readers have described as Black Elk's spiritual death, as well as the end of tribal independence, for as Black Elk himself states in "The First Cure," after the end of Sioux freedom, he and his people become simply "prisoners of war while we are waiting here."

Black Elk Speaks, therefore, shapes the form of Black Elk's story as Neihardt works to create the full effect of Sioux tragedy "in" his white readers, just as Black Elk himself was capable of feeling "in" himself the pain of the people. The act of the bicultural collaborator creates empathy in the modern reader. Furthermore, the act of teaching *Black Elk Speaks* places the instructor also in the position of bicultural translator, using the classroom and discussion of the text as a way to complete the circle between the American undergraduate student and the text that "writes" Black Elk's name in our canon of collective attempts to define the American identity.

WILLA CATHER

Unlike most of Cather's narrators, who are male, the narrator of the novella *My Mortal Enemy* is Nellie Birdseye. The story portrays a series of changes in perception. Ask students to locate some of these: the narrator's "first glimpse of the real Myra Henshawe" and her first glimpse of the Henshawes' marriage, in which "everything was in ruins." How surprising it may seem to some readers, as it does to the narrator, that when she meets Myra again, in her "temporary eclipse" "she looked much less changed than Oswald." What are some of the objects, images, or motifs that provide continuity for Myra, and for the narrator's view of her? How in particular does the amethyst necklace serve to frame the story? The central love relationship appears to be that between Myra and Oswald; the narrator has her own passion for Myra Henshawe. How does the story reveal it? How does Cather suggest that passion, perception, and self-revelation are interconnected emotions or faculties? The priest says of Myra, " 'She's not at all modern in her make-up, is she?' " What does he mean by this? What does Cather mean?

Rosicky of *Neighbour Rosicky* represents pastoral values in a losing battle with an increasingly urbanized, mechanized world. As a young man living in New York, Rosicky "found out what was the matter with him," and decided to join the Czech community in Nebraska. In the face of his own declining health and the "cruelty" of the cities, Rosicky tries to keep his son Rudolph on the land. How does Cather condemn the materialism, rapaciousness, and cruelty that Rosicky associates with urban life? How does his gift of loving people (his "gypsy hand") offer a corrective? The story ends on a note of tragedy. How long will Rudolph be able to hold out against the forces of nature? How long before he will join the exodus from the farms to the cities?

In both of these stories Cather portrays women's lives as complex and various, rich in love, but contingent on other things—worldly position, friendship, self-esteem, family, the ability to adapt to circumstances. Compare her portraits of women (Myra, and Mary and Polly from *Neighbour Rosicky*) with the women in Jewett and Freeman. What are the regionalist elements of Cather's stories—even of *My Mortal Enemy*, in which the setting moves from urban to rural, East Coast to West Coast? Like the narrator of *My Mortal Enemy*, Doctor Ed of *Neighbour Rosicky* seems to love Rosicky, but the second story creates more aesthetic distance than the first (and is actually more representative of Cather's other work). Does the change affect the dramatic power of the story?

GERTRUDE STEIN

The Good Anna

The Good Anna provides students with an excellent introduction both to Gertrude Stein and to modernism itself. While Stein experiments with prose style in this early novel, her experimentation does not make the work inaccessible to students. Ask them to describe their impressions of *The Good Anna*. Such an open-ended request may elicit from them the significant words for a study of Stein: repetition, stream of consciousness, slow emergence of identification with Anna, empathy, transformations, erotic encoding, self-reflexivity. These become themes to develop in an ensuing discussion of the novel and to prepare students to read the more experimental excerpt from *The Making of Americans.* For example, consider the numerous "repetitions" of "large and careless" women in Anna's life and of the even more numerous animals and people Anna comes to take care of. Ask students how we come to know Anna in the narrative; focus on the present-time aspect of Stein's characterization. What does character development mean with respect to Anna? How do we know how she thinks and feels? Examine the differences between persons and actions that seem to be repeated experiences for Anna. To what extent do the others, especially women, in Anna's life reflect back to her some of her own personality traits, including some she finds hard to accept in herself? Suggest that Anna herself exists as a continuum on which we may locate the other women in her life, and consider the interplay of Anna's projections and introjections of aspects of these women.

Miss Mathilda and Mrs. Lehntman may particularly intrigue students. Examine Stein's portrait of Miss Mathilda as her own self-portrait (she, too, was "large and careless," collected art, and had a "careless way of wearing always her old clothes") and raise questions about the self-reflexivity of the text. In writing about Anna, Stein is also writing about aspects of herself; she is also writing about the way to write a story. Locating images of Stein in the various characters in *The Good Anna* alerts students to looking at the relationship between the modernist writer and her text. Of particular interest here is the passage at the end of "Part I," in which Stein writes about the "troubles" Miss Mathilda has with Anna. Miss Mathilda wants both to have her mind read and have everything done for her and to rebel against the rules she accepts when she allows herself to depend on Anna. The conflict between spontaneity and reliability characterizes the relationship between the two characters in the fiction, between Stein and her own text, and between the reader and what modernist art will, and will not, satisfy. There is no perfect attunement in any of these dyadic conflicts; character, writer, and reader all suffer jarring discontinuities, just as Anna herself does when she tells Miss Mathilda, "I don't see how people can go on and do things so" when she has lived her life with the "old world sense of what was the right way for a girl to do."

Mrs. Lehntman's presence in the novel, and Stein's reiteration that this woman has served as Anna's "romance," may lead some students to pursue Baym's headnote comment that the eroticism in Stein's lesbian love poems (not anthologized) remains "obscure" and "needs to be decoded." Despite the novel's title and the narrator's presentation of Anna as "good," "Part I" opens with Anna's equation of "bad" with sexuality. What other evidence exists to suggest that Anna has an erotic life, or at least is capable of an erotic awareness? In studying the pre-Freudian writers of the previous century, twentieth-century readers may speculate on erotic and homoerotic undertones in American literature, but Gertrude Stein is the first American writer both to live outwardly as a lesbian and to write fiction with lesbian erotic content. Do students find homoerotic passion in Anna's feelings for Mrs. Lehntman or do they prefer to characterize the relationship as friendship? Whether or not Stein is asking her readers to "decode" this relationship, she at least has the courage to write about strong feelings between women, unlike Cather, who appears to have encoded her own erotic life with women into relationships between male and female characters in her fiction or onto her own passion for the Nebraska or Southwest landscape. To what extent did Stein's choice to live as a permanent expatriate in Paris and as an experimentalist in art, as well as in life, make it possible for her to write about love—of whatever kind—between women?

The Making of Americans

The excerpt from *The Making of Americans* becomes readily accessible to students after reading and discussing *The Good Anna.* The anthologized [Introduction] serves as a description of Stein's technique in the novel, a way of using Stein's own language to talk about what she attempts in *The Good Anna.* At the same time, reading the novel gives students a feeling for Stein's "love of repetition," so that they may carry with them into the more experimental work the sense of already having experienced the truth of Stein's statements in the excerpt that "always from the beginning there was to me all living as repeating," and "sometimes every one becomes a whole one to me." The footnotes in NAAL help students gloss Stein's self-reflexivity. Ask them to do some work with her use of language. In the NAAL headnote on Marianne Moore, Baym notes that Stein worked with the word as the unit of composition. Ask students to trace the linguistic transformations of similar sentences in *The Making of Americans,* to note single word changes, and to comment on alterations in meaning. Look also for the development of ideas. Does Stein's insistence on continuing to begin prevent her from developing a concept? Watch in particular for the ways Stein very slowly begins to expand the vocabulary she uses. One word that startles me when I read it is *earth,* which makes a sudden appearance as an adjective for *feeling,* then quickly modulates into *earthy,* and then becomes available for use in the essay's lexicon. What words startle your students? Can they describe their reader response to Stein's use of repetition?

AMY LOWELL

Following chronologically from poets Edgar Lee Masters and Edwin Arlington Robinson, Lowell will continue to beguile students into believing that the poetry in the 1914–1945 period is accessible. Explore both the accessibility and the inaccessibility of imagism by reading Lowell in conjunction with H. D. and Pound. Examine *In the Stadium, Meeting-House Hill, Summer Night Piece,* and *New Heavens for Old* as imagist poems. Lowell's inclusion in NAAL 4 does not fully resolve the question about which critics remain divided: Is Lowell's poetry any good? Is it too sentimental to be good poetry? And in using the word *sentimental* against her are we mistakenly accepting devaluation of the very concept of the sentimental and its legitimate role in poetry?

Whatever the verdict among your students, including Lowell's voice in your syllabus will make room for early discussions of female mythological characters that will inform much poetry by women and men in the twentieth century (in *The Captured Goddess* and *Venus Transiens*), and will introduce what Baym calls "appreciations of female beauty" in poems by women. Indeed, several of the poems included here may be considered love poems to specific women or to women in general: *Venus Transiens, Madonna of the Evening Flowers,* and *Penumbra.* Discuss sexual imagery in *The Weather-Cock Points South.*

Robert Frost

Like Cather, Frost retains elements of realism, and like them, he portrays moments in which his speaker's perception changes as central to his poetry. In my classroom, I spend several class periods on individual poems and read representative poems by other twentieth-century poets through the fulcrum of our analysis of Frost. I prepare for a discussion of *The Oven Bird* by reading *Nothing Gold Can Stay,* with its allusion to Eden and human mortality. I give *The Oven Bird* an important place in our discussion because Frost's other poems, his essay *The Figure a Poem Makes,* many other works of literature by modern writers, and even the concept of modernism itself seem contained and articulated in the poem's last two lines: "The question that he asks in all but words / Is what to make of a diminished thing." The bird and the poet ask questions that express the central modernist theme: How do we confront a world in which reality is subject to agreement or lacks referentiality altogether? How do we express the experience of fragmentation in personal and political life? How do we live with the increasing awareness of our own mortality—whether we face the prospect of human death, as the speaker does in *Home Burial; After Apple-Picking;* or *"Out, Out—"*; the death or absence of God, as Frost considers that possibility in *Desert Places* and *Design;* or mere disappointment at our own powerlessness, as in *An Old Man's Winter Night* or *Stopping by Woods on a Snowy Evening?* In *The Oven Bird* I ask students to hear contrasting ways of intoning the last two lines. I read the lines, first, with emphasis on the phrase "diminished thing"—and the pessimism in Frost and in his conception of modern life receives most of our attention. I read it again, emphasizing the infinitive "to make," and the poem seems to reverse its own despair, to create the possibility that creative activity can ease the face of the lessening, the "diminishing," of modern perception.

Other works offer this positive response to the bird's question. In *The Figure a Poem Makes,* Frost defines the act of writing poetry as "not necessarily a great clarification," but at least "a momentary stay against confusion." Students who have studied the Volume 1 material may see Frost's solution to his own metaphysical problem as one more variable in Edward Taylor's attempt to sustain a metaphor through the length of one of his *Preparatory Meditations* to arrive at the language of salvation. Frost emphasizes, though, that he wants to be just as surprised by the poem as the reader. And his description of the thought process that a poem records applies to our own endeavors in the classroom as well—whenever we try to engage students first, and then teach them how to order their engaged perception. When Frost contrasts scholars, who get their knowledge "with conscientious thoroughness along projected lines of logic," with poets, who get theirs "cavalierly and as it happens in and out of books," most students prefer to identify with the poets. And Frost might, indeed, be describing an American epistemology, as it works best with students: "They stick to nothing deliberately, but let what will stick to them like burrs where they walk in the fields."

No study of Frost, at any class level, is complete without close analysis of the great poems *Birches* and *Directive.* Depending on our time and the students I have in the course, I choose one or the other for a full class period. *Birches* works better with sophomores; even so, students at any level profit from line-by-line discussion of *Directive,* particularly in contrast with the earlier poem *After Apple-Picking.* In this poem, the speaker's troubled sleep results from his realization of the imperfection of human power to "save" fallen apples (or fallen worlds) or to fully complete any task as someone with godlike power (or any "heroic" human being before the modernist era) might have been able to do. *Directive* transcends those limitations, offers a specific path to take ("if you'll let a guide direct you / Who only has at heart your getting lost"), and arrives at a vision of spiritual regeneration unparalleled in any of Frost's other poems: "Here are your waters and your watering place. / Drink and be whole again beyond confusion." How does Frost contain *both* American dream and American nightmare? How does his poetry, as he writes in "Two Tramps in Mud Time," allow him to "unite / My avocation and my vocation / As my two eyes make one in sight"? How do Frost's images suggest that, long after the apparent decline of transcendentalism, the analogical thinking of Emerson and Thoreau would become a permanent part of the American imagination?

SHERWOOD ANDERSON

Looking at the egg on the table—as Anderson's narrator does at the end of *The Egg*—characterizes Anderson's own contribution to developing American fiction in the early twentieth century. He wants to know where it all begins, to focus on a particular house in a particular street, and to try to figure out, by examining origins, who he is and who we are. Anderson's life before he declared himself a writer illustrates a classic theme in nineteeth-century fiction by white male writers; ask your students to recall Irving's *Rip Van Winkle*, Hawthorne's *Wakefield*, or Clemens's *Huckleberry Finn*. Like the characters in that earlier fiction, Anderson also seems to have suffered a form of amnesia, sudden disappearance, or inexplicable departure, one day, from his life with his wife and his job at the paint firm. In leaving his life in Ohio so abruptly, Anderson expressed the incompatibility of living conventionally and also writing an American book. How does this define the role of the writer, for Anderson? *Winesburg, Ohio,* though fiction, emerges from an autobiographical impulse, and the reporter in that work, George Willard, experiences the young writer's conflict. Later in life, Anderson would write a memoir titled *A Storyteller's Story; Winesburg, Ohio,* which tells the story of Anderson himself still within the eggshell, before his "hatching" as a storyteller.

Several related themes characterize the anthologized stories from *Winesburg.* Anderson portrays conflict between inner emotions and outward behavior; Alice Hindman and Elmer Cowley share this conflict although they express it differently. Sexual repression and displaced aggression enter American fiction in *Winesburg,* and each of the anthologized stories shares this theme. In Elizabeth Willard, sexual repression and repressed identity become interconnected, and in *Adventure,* Anderson hints at "the growing modern idea of a woman's owning herself and giving and taking for her own ends in life," although his own fiction explores the stunting of women's lives, not their "modern" alternatives. Writing itself becomes the American passion for George Willard; the "queerness" that interests Anderson in some of his characters (Elmer Cowley and Mook in "*Queer*") suggests an American illness caused by inarticulate inner lives that the fiction writer might be able to "cure." At the end of *Rip Van Winkle,* Rip takes his place as the "chronicler" or storyteller of the village and thus moves from margin to center in his position in the town. Anderson's portrait of the American storyteller—in his character George Willard and in the events of his own life—addresses the marginality of the white male writer. Anderson's marginality is central to his vision; despite his portrait of the way American life has twisted and thwarted individual development, he chooses to portray it from without, not envision recreating it from within. Like Huckleberry Finn, George

Willard escapes Winesburg and, in the process, becomes capable of telling a story.

WALLACE STEVENS

Poems such as Frost's *The Oven Bird* and *Desert Places* allow students to experience modernist feeling; Stevens translates the central thematic concern of modern writers into an intellectual framework. We begin by reading *Of Modern Poetry* line by line and make connections between the idea of "finding what will suffice" and making something "of a diminished thing." This poem links modernist thought to World War I, breaks with the realists' "script," and ends with actions that appear referential ("a man skating, a woman dancing, a woman / Combing") but can be understood only as manifestations of what is spoken "In the delicatest ear of the mind," not as semantic symbols. Students' greatest difficulty in reading Stevens is to move beyond the apparently referential quality of his language and to learn to read it as dynamic forms of abstract ideas. *Anecdote of the Jar* works well to analyze closely. This poem forces them to push beyond the referential features of the language, for its meaning resides not in the jar but in its placement and in the larger design the poem creates and imposes. But that larger design is an arbitrary creation of the poet, not the manifestation of divine presence in the universe, and we work through other Stevens poems that illustrate the poet's power to make his world's design. *Thirteen Ways of Looking at a Blackbird* can help students see the problem of perception in a modern world in which there is no shared reality; in *The Idea of Order at Key West*, the woman makes order out of the diminished thing by singing, thereby becoming "the self / That was her song, for she was the maker"; and *The Emperor of Ice-Cream* proposes as the modernist's reality a world that lets "the lamp affix its beam" to show, as *The Snow Man* states, "Nothing that is not there and the nothing that is." Ask students how the idea that nothing is there—except what the imagination invents—becomes a manifestation of American self-reliance. For Stevens, all forms of order are created by human perception; nature itself reflects human values only as we project our image onto the natural world.

Stevens responds to the oven bird's question directly in the first line of *A High-Toned Old Christian Woman*: "Poetry is the supreme fiction." In discussing this concept, I put together some of the ideas from the Stevens headnote in NAAL. The editor, Nina Baym, directs the reader's attention to two repeated activities in Stevens's poems: (1) looking at things and (2) playing musical instruments or singing. I ask students to identify poems in which these activities appear (for the first, see in particular *The Snow Man, The Emperor of Ice-Cream, Thirteen Ways of Looking at a Blackbird, Study of Two Pears*, excerpts from *An Ordinary*

Evening in New Haven, and *The Plain Sense of Things*; for the second, see in particular *A High-toned Old Christian Woman*, *Peter Quince at the Clavier*, *The Idea of Order at Key West*, *Of Modern Poetry*, and *Asides on the Oboe*), and we identify as parallel concepts making music or singing and writing poetry, and perceiving or observing and giving existence to reality. These parallel activities replace the Christian god, create new gods or mythological forms (see *An Ordinary Evening in New Haven*), and allow us to devise our own supreme fiction. The new mythology or fiction, for whom the poet is both creator and secular priest, explains the presence of so much continually unexpected imagery in Stevens. Furthermore, Stevens's own poetry provides an answer to the woman's musings in *Sunday Morning*.

In *Sunday Morning*, Stevens creates a dialogue between a woman and a narrator, or a dialogue of one that shows the woman thinking within her own mind, and he alters the meaning of Christianity. The poem transforms the religious connotations of Sunday into those of a human-centered "day of the sun," in which, since we live in an "island solitude, unsponsored, free," we invent, as our supreme fiction, our god or our explanation for the way the universe works, the very mortality that is the only "imperishable bliss" we know. Stevens proposes making ritual of the diminished thing, creating fellowship "of men that perish and of summer morn," and seeing "casual flocks of pigeons" not as "homeward bound" but rather as nature's "ambiguous undulations." Nature has no message for us; but in the act of writing (and reading) poetry, we can create our own order, one that becomes more beautiful because it is the projection of "man's rage for order" and, therefore, as fragile as human life. "Death is the mother of beauty" for Stevens because it intensifies the act of "arranging, deepening, enchanting night" (in *The Idea of Order at Key West*), or of taking momentary "dominion" (in *Anecdote of the Jar*), or in the "old chaos of the sun." Poetry serves Stevens (from his book of collected lectures *The Necessary Angel*) as a "means of redemption." What should we make of a world in which there is not external order? Project onto it human mortality and make art out of the moment of sinking "Downward to darkness, on extended wings"; create a "jovial hullabaloo among the spheres."

The images of the sun that form the focus for the woman's meditations in *Sunday Morning* also provide Stevens's central image in other poems. Build class discussion around a group of these poems (*Gubbinal*, *A Postcard from the Volcano*, *The Sense of the Sleight-of-hand Man*, *An Ordinary Evening in New Haven*), and examine the way Stevens builds his real image of what the supreme fiction might look like on the sun itself. In *Sleight-of-hand Man*, he writes, "The fire eye in the clouds survives the gods" and in *New Haven*, calls "imagining of reality, / Much like a new resemblance of the sun." The supreme fiction takes the form of human flesh in *Peter Quince at the Clavier.* Give students time to work through the experience of Stevens's concept of the supreme fiction. For many, reading Stevens will seem like heresy, a fundamental challenge to their own religious practice. Allow them to compare notes on their various perceptions of Stevens's work. Use class discussion as an exemplum of modernist thought; a class of any size may approach "Thirteen Ways of Looking at Stevens," or "a visibility of thought, / In which hundreds of eyes, in one mind, see at once."

ANGELINA WELD GRIMKÉ

Although as editor Nina Baym observes, Grimké's poems about race are few, NAAL has anthologized several of these, along with some of Grimké's love poems to women and poems about nature. One image crosses among these poetic subjects for Grimké—the image of the finger or fingers. Ask students to track the changing meaning of this image, from *The Black Finger* to *Grass Fingers* to *Greenness* and *Tenebris.* Explore the historical difficulties Grimké faced in writing about race, and compare *The Black Finger, Tenebris,* and *Trees* with poems by her contemporaries Sterling Brown and Langston Hughes. *El Beso, The Eyes of My Regret, To Clarissa Scott Delaney,* and *A Mona Lisa* all expand students' awareness of the flexibility of the poetic voice for women. Grimké is not bound by heterosexual conventions in writing love poetry. She may have been more influenced by late-nineteenth-century acceptance of strong feelings between women than by early-twentieth-century Freudian ideas that transformed such acceptance into deviance, and as a result, her poetry about loving women may seem less self-consciously political then her poetry about race; nevertheless, it stands as powerful evidence to students that women—from African-American as well as Euro-American origins—have loved other women and expressed it in poetry despite the cultural suppression of such love.

ANZIA YEZIERSKA

With the inclusion of Yezierska in NAAL, the 1914–1945 section becomes much stronger in terms of its attention to class issues, for Yezierska writes powerfully about the contrast between immigrant expectations and immigrant reality, and between the rhetoric of democracy and its broken promise for the immigrant poor. *The Lost "Beautifulness"* raises these issues painfully and clearly and promotes extensive discussion in the classroom. Ask students to derive two sets of assumptions from the story. The first set includes assumptions about class that Hannah Hayyeh makes, for example, (1) that poverty doesn't mean a person can't also have beauty in life; (2) that even though someone is poor doesn't mean she can't have a rich friend, that friendship can cross class lines; and (3) that "making money ain't everything in life." Explore how Hannah comes to hold these assumptions, what happens to disillusion her with respect to each one, and whether students share any of them. The second set includes assumptions about America and the meaning of democracy, for example, (1) "democracy means that everybody in America is going to be with everybody alike"; (2) it's possible to assimilate into American values—as Hannah tells her husband, "so long my Aby is with America, I want to make myself for an American"; (3) merit is recognized, as in "such a tenant the landlord ought to give out a medal or let down the rent free"; and (4) even a "hungry-eyed ghetto woman" can be an "artist laundress"—the American dream takes many forms, but even a ghetto laundress can have her dreams. The second set will be harder for students to dislodge, in terms of their own dreams and their assumptions about their own future. However, in the 1990s, even middle-class students are more realistic about the hollow ring of some of these assumptions and will observe the validity of the landlord's corrective truth: "in American everybody looks out for himself." Compare the ending with the narrator's behavior in Charlotte Perkins Gilman's *The Yellow Wallpaper*, and ask students to comment on the effectiveness of the course of action Hannah chooses to follow. Examine the final scene as a moment of imagistic prose, in which the insignia of the Statue of Liberty, the gold service stripes, and the "assurance of the United States Army" that Aby Safransky possesses contrast with the image of broken Hannah in her eviction—from her apartment, from her dreams of beauty, and from all things she believed were American.

WILLIAM CARLOS WILLIAMS

How does Williams answer the question, what to make of a diminished thing? We begin with *A Sort of a Song*, which directs its reader to write a poem about the thing. Make nothing of it but the thing itself. Because there may not be meaning, don't insist on it. And we talk about characteristics of Williams's poems, trying to elicit, in discussion, some of the central features of imagism: exactness, precision, compression, common speech, free verse. *The Red Wheelbarrow, The Widow's Lament in Springtime, The Term,* and *Portrait of a Lady* work well for this discussion. We analyze *Spring and All* closely, suggesting that the process Williams describes becomes, in part, analogous to the creation of a poetic image. Some students have difficulty understanding the concept of the image, and in teaching Williams, I often take time out to talk about the eidetic faculty—what happens in the mind when we read a visual description. *Portrait of a Lady*, read aloud with appropriate emphasis ("Agh!"), can help them "hear" another kind of image. We talk about some themes in Williams—love and death—and how the poems strip those themes of sentimentality. What happens to Williams's view of human life in poems such as *Death, The Dead Baby,* and *Landscape with the Fall of Icarus?* Compare Williams and Frost; students may suggest that, despite his objectivity, Williams lacks the pessimism of some of Frost's poems. How does Williams's use of poetic technique develop his themes? Critics often compare Williams with Whitman. Ask students to discuss this connection. Several modern poets try to write longer poems, perhaps with the epic form in mind.

EZRA POUND

We read a few Pound poems to see how he uses the image: *In a Station of the Metro* and *The River-Merchant's Wife: A Letter* work well, although students sometimes have difficulty actually seeing Pound's image in the first poem. Does the poem's second line only work if one sees a contrast between the faces and the black bough? Does Pound assume light-skinned faces? *To Whistler, American, A Pact,* and *The Rest* are easily accessible to students, but what response do they have to *Hugh Selwyn Mauberley (Life and Contacts)* or *The Cantos?* How do students without a classical education understand Pound's dictum, "make it new"?

H. D. (HILDA DOOLITTLE)

There are several strategies for reading H. D. that may enlist student interest. With editor Baym's comments about imagism as a guide, trace H. D.'s formal uses of the image in her poetry, and compare her work with that of Amy Lowell, Williams, and Pound. Alternatively, move ahead to other women poets whose work reflects H. D.'s influence. For example, Susan Gubar (in "The Echoing Spell in H. D.'s *Trilogy,*" in *Shakespeare's Sisters,* edited by Sandra Gilbert and Susan Gubar, 1979) suggests comparing H. D.'s use of the seashell image to Marianne Moore's *To a Snail.* (See also Moore's poem *The Paper Nautilus.*) The last stanzas of *The Walls Do Not Fall* are clearly echoed later in Adrienne Rich's poem *Diving into the Wreck.* Even further, Gubar suggests that really to understand H. D., we need to move beyond discussions of imagism and modernism (and psychoanalysis) to exploring "H. D.'s sense of herself as a woman writing about female confinement, specifically the woman writer's entrapment within male literary conventions, as well as her search for images of female divinity and prophecy." Reading H. D. as a feminist modernist and a poet who is trying to express her discomfort with male-defined representations of women and of history may give students another approach to her poetry. Because H. D. has only been fully appreciated by recent feminist critics who write about modernism, you or your students may find useful Susan Stanford Friedman's critical biography, *Psyche Reborn: The Emergence of H. D.* (1981), in which she traces

H. D.'s development as a feminist modernist and in particular H. D.'s interest in a woman-centered myth making. From *Leda* to *Helen* to the goddesses Isis, Aset, and Astarte in *The Walls Do Not Fall,* students will at least find the female figures to counterbalance the presence of the all-father and Osiris. H. D.'s closing lines of that long poem ("we are voyagers, discoverers / of the not-known, / the unrecorded") have particular resonance for women in a modernist world.

ROBINSON JEFFERS

Jeffers's poetry contrasts sharply with that of both Frost and Stevens; ask students to discuss his ways of transforming poems about nature into philosophical meditations. Jeffers appears to have disdained modernism; is his poetry traditional? Compare Jeffers's use of free verse with Williams's poetic line. How is Jeffers's poetry unique? Discuss his use of the physical landscape of the central California coast. Is Jeffers a regional poet? Identify the source of his cynicism and compare it with Frost's pessimistic poems. Jeffers seems to suggest that "what to make of a diminished thing" is to diminish it still further: "We must unhumanize our views a little." Consider what he means by this. In my own classroom I discuss *Shine, Perishing Republic* line by line—or alternatively assign it to students to explicate in an essay. The poem stands out in contrast to many of the modernist works we read, both in what it lacks (any sense that classical mythology holds the key to understanding our present) and for what it offers (as a view of twentieth-century American life and values). This poem and others (*November Surf* and *Carmel Point*) seem to some students to comment on our own contemporary life. How does *Shine, Perishing Republic* suggest what it means to be an American in the twentieth century?

MARIANNE MOORE

In *Naked and Fiery Forms: Modern American Poetry by Women* (1976), Suzanne Juhasz describes Marianne Moore as "the leading American woman poet" of her generation, but not the "leading American poet," and comments on the contrast between Pound, who "does not have to deny his masculine experience, because it is all of mankind," and Moore, who makes "a neat division between 'woman' and 'poet,' with art and artistry belonging to the domain of the latter." Juhasz's framework is useful for reading modern American women poets; she suggests that the second generation (in which she includes Muriel Rukeyser, Elizabeth Bishop, Louise Bogan, and Gwendolyn Brooks, all anthologized in NAAL) continued to separate "woman" and "poet" but that writers at mid-century (Denise Levertov, Sylvia Plath, and Anne Sexton) begin to function as "woman" and "poet" at the same time. In teaching Marianne

Moore, following Juhasz's framework will help contextualize both Moore's avoidance of women's experience in her poetry and the increasing attention to women's experience by poets later in the century. Indeed, students will find it difficult if not impossible to locate any gendered experience in Moore. She writes either with a gender-neutral first person (in *Poetry, In Distrust of Merits, "Keeping Their World Large,"* and *To Be a Dragon*) or about generic "man" (as in *A Grave* and *What Are Years?*). Only nature is feminized (as in *Bird-Witted* and *The Paper Nautilus*).

Editor Nina Baym comments in her headnote that, in Moore, "the reader almost never finds the conventional poetic allusions that invoke a great tradition and assert the present poet's place in it." In Juhasz's framework, this is because women of Moore's generation could not find or present themselves as part of a great tradition. What Moore does do, like many of her contemporaries, is to reinvent poetry for herself or to find a new form for what she thought poetry should be. Locate and discuss Moore's statements on the act and art of poetry. Analyze, in such a discussion, *To a Snail.* What happens to poetic language when there is an "absence of feet"? Also analyze closely the frequently anthologized *Poetry.* Often students have difficulty understanding why a poet such as Moore would write with such passion about the nature of poetry itself. Build on previous discussions of the image to help them find the contrast, in the poem's middle stanzas, between the discursive statements Moore makes ("we / do not admire what / we cannot understand" and "all these phenomena are important") and her use of images drawn from precise observation of the animal world, such as in the poem *The Paper Nautilus.* What does she mean in trying to create "imaginary gardens with real toads in them"? Analyze *Bird-Witted* and *Nevertheless* to see what Moore does with form in poetry. Comment on the kind of stanza she creates in *Nevertheless* and ask students to locate rhyme in *Bird-Witted* and *The Mind Is an Enchanting Thing.* Most will not have discovered rhyme (as students, in reading Frost, do not immediately perceive rhyme in *After Apple-Picking*). What is the effect of the use of rhyme? Compare *Bird-Witted* with Frost's poem. Is *Bird-Witted* a poem about birds or about poetry? What is Moore's "uneasy new problem"? Does one possibility cancel out the other for her? Which poems illustrate Moore's response to the modern way of seeing the world? Compare *In Distrust of Merits* with Jeffers's earlier *Shine, Perishing Republic.* Which poem seems to be more referential? Discuss Moore's views of war as an "inward" struggle in *In Distrust of Merits.* How does her image of the world as an "orphans' home" comment on the modernist themes of her contemporaries? Ask students to extend Moore's discussions—of enslaver and enslaved and our being "not competent to make our vows" about not hating—to our own contemporary social and global conflicts, to the resurgence of nationalism in the world, and to the significance of "I inwardly did nothing" in the context of bias incidents and hate speech on college campuses and in U.S. society.

T. S. ELIOT

The Love Song of J. Alfred Prufrock works well to read closely with students. Find images in the poem that serve as Eliot's "objective correlative" for Prufrock's particular emotions and for the state of feeling in the modern world (as Eliot saw it). In my own classroom, we read *The Waste Land,* but I recommend that students take an upper-division course in modern poetry if they want to study it in detail. The poem raises a problem students have with modernism generally—that so many twentieth-century poets make extensive use of classical allusions or interweave references to Renaissance painters, or quote writers in languages other than English. Berating students for not having a classical education doesn't help them much. Discuss the poem in context with *Tradition and the Individual Talent,* Eliot defends his own method and describes the good poet as the one who is able to "develop or procure the consciousness of the past." Although Eliot presents a "waste land" as his variation on the "diminished thing" that symbolizes human personality and culture in the modern world, his answer to the oven bird's question is not to make something (entirely) new or to show Stevens's snow man confronting "the nothing that is not there" and inventing a "supreme fiction," but rather to surrender the individual personality of the poet. The poem becomes a medium that expresses the essential history of the culture. Eliot writes in his essay, "Impressions and experiences which are important for the man may take no place in the poetry, and those which become important in the poetry may play quite a negligible part in the man, the personality." How does Eliot depersonalize the poet in *The Waste Land?* He combines traditions from mythology and legend, anthropology (with references to vegetation myths and fertility rites), classical literature and culture (including Shakespeare and Wagner), the Tarot, and comparative religious cultures, and he juxtaposes these traditions with images of isolation, fragmentation, uncertainty, and waste, hoping to use "these fragments" to "shore against" the ruins that are Eliot's variation on Frost's "diminished thing."

EUGENE O'NEILL

Long Day's Journey into Night demonstrates that one of the strong features of twentieth-century American literature is the continuation of what O'Neill's Edmund calls late in the play "faithful realism." But O'Neill's realism differs from that of the late-nineteenth-century writers, even as it seems to extend some of their concerns. In fact, O'Neill's play sometimes seems a compendium or a spectrum of American ideas that long precede the late nineteenth century, for he presents the Tyrones both as deeply conditioned by their past and as characters who face in their daily life (in this classically one-day's play) the fragmentation that is one symptom or consequence of modernist sensibility. In discussing the play, I focus on Mary and Edmund as central figures, and we talk about the different historical influences on each of their characters.

Mary's descent into the madness of morphine addiction becomes the play's emblem, and although O'Neill is writing, in part, about his own mother here, he is also sensitive to Mary's position as woman in the American family and in American history. As the play unfolds the history of Mary's medical treatment and of her husband's attitudes toward her condition, students will make connections between Mary Tyrone and both Edna Pontellier and the narrator of *The Yellow Wallpaper.* O'Neill suggests that modern life is more difficult for women than for men: Mary might have played the piano, but married instead, thereby depriving herself of the coherence of vocation; in marriage, and especially in marriage to the peripatetic James Tyrone (rootlessness itself becomes a modern condition), she cuts herself off from having woman friends with whom she might ease her loneliness (O'Neill adds early scandal to the fact of marriage as a way of doubly cutting Mary off from other women); and in choosing to ease her loneliness by following Tyrone on his tours, she is forced to reject even the traditional solace of making a home for her children, so that the series of choices becomes irreversible, and her need for something to ease her emotional pain and to dull her perception of her own meaninglessness increases.

Within the family structure, Mary also suffers the anachronism (in the twentieth century) of not being able to move beyond the scrutiny of external forces that seem to control her. When she tells her husband, "You really must not watch me all the time, James. I mean, it makes me self-conscious," she is experiencing the radical emotion that led the deist Founding Fathers to revolution in the 1770s. But, unlike the deists, who experienced a fundamental shift in worldview when they accepted the idea that God might not be watching them all the time and fought for self-determination from the system of divinely ordained British monarchy, Mary Tyrone is only made "self-conscious" by Tyrone's scrutiny. She suffers self-consciousness and is not inspired by it. She is not self-conscious in a way that leads other modernists to insight; she is only increasingly made aware of her own worthlessness. O'Neill underscores that worthlessness by presenting the role of wife as one based on constant humiliation and defined by Tyrone's need to feel he has made "good bargains" in life—he makes others pay the price he won't pay.

Throughout the play, O'Neill presents Mary as someone living in a dream (especially as she becomes more and more detached by the effects of taking morphine) that might have made sense for Rip Van Winkle but, protracted into the twentieth century, simply increases her sense of disorientation and alienation. She says at one point, early in the play, "None of us can help the things life has done to us. They're done before you realize it, and once they're done they make you do other things until at last everything comes between you and what you'd like to be, and you've lost your true self forever." For students who have studied Irving, the language Mary uses here will seem reminiscent of Rip's "identity crisis" when he returns to the village after his twenty-year sleep. Later in the play, thinking aloud to the hired woman, Cathleen, Mary ties that disorientation to the death of what students might see as her own American dream. She says, about the fog, "It hides you from the world and the world from you. You feel that everything has changed, and nothing is what it seemed to be. No one can find or touch you any more." Her language clearly echoes Irving's here, but it also conveys the isolation of American self-reliance carried to its historical extreme and ironically epitomized in the role of twentieth-century American wife and mother—Mary must be self-reliant in order to survive and must do so in a world devoid of human context other than her own family. She asks the play's central question: "What is it I'm looking for? I know it's something I lost."

Her son Edmund, the autobiographical voice for O'Neill himself, is the only character who understands his mother's drug addiction as the play progresses, and who suffers the consequences of trying to articulate the kind of pain she feels. In Edmund's statements, students who have read twentieth-century European literature will hear connections to Camus and Beckett. Edmund also feels the absence of home, and referring to his nebulous, nameless lack of power to control his life, he says, "They never come back! Everything is in the bag! It's all a frame-up! We're all fall guys and suckers and we can't beat the game!" Later he calls himself "a stranger who never lives at home." Like Mary, he would like to "be alone with myself in another world where truth is untrue and life can hide from itself," but he chooses poetry rather than morphine to ease his own pain, and then must confront his own failure as a poet. In a scene with his father, Edmund says, "I just stammered. That's the best I'll ever do. I mean, if I live. Well, it will be faithful realism, at least. Stammering is the native eloquence of us fog people!" In depicting Edmund's "stammering," O'Neill underscores both the need to express modern consciousness and the difficulty in finding the words for it. Other twentieth-century writers will take some comfort in making the attempt; Edmund's "faithful realism" prevents him from idealizing his "stammering." In brother Jamie's cynicism ("The truth is there is no cure") and father James's despair ("A waste!, a drunken hulk, done with and finished!"), O'Neill completes his portrait of the disintegration of the American psyche and

American family life and, yet, presents that portrait within the conventions of literary realism.

KATHERINE ANNE PORTER

Miranda, like Mary Tyrone in *Long Day's Journey into Night,* learns in *Old Mortality* to characterize her problem as homelessness. The story is about life not fulfilling its dreamy promise for women like Miranda's Aunt Amy, and about Miranda's own series of disappointments. The ending of the story echoes the language of *Rip Van Winkle* and Mary Tyrone, when Miranda asks, "It is I who have no place. . . . Where are my own people and my own time?" and in posing her final question, she expresses her own version of the oven bird's: "Oh, what is life . . . and what shall I do with it? It is something of my own. . . . What shall I make of it?"

ZORA NEALE HURSTON

Hurston worked as an anthropologist as well as a writer, and wrote *The Eatonville Anthology* after graduating from Barnard College and returning to her birthplace in Eatonville, Florida, to collect and transcribe the folktales and folkways she remembered from childhood. Like her later *Mules and Men* (1935), both the *Anthology* and the essay *How It Feels to Be Colored Me* explore origins of consciousness—both collective and individual—that Hurston transforms into mythology, her attempt to explain the creation of the universe, to understand why the world is the way it is. By writing down the folktales she remembered from the black community in which she grew up, she created a bridge between the "primitive" authority of folk life and the literary power of written texts. (See my introduction to *Conjuring: Black Women, Fiction, and Literary Tradition,* edited by Marjorie Pryse and Hortense Spillers, 1985, for a fuller discussion of Hurston and literary authority.) Mythology does not overpower Hurston's fiction; rather, it empowers her use of folk history. Ask students to locate suggestions of mythology in *The Eatonville Anthology;* see, in particular, the opening of section XIV, "Once 'way back yonder before the stars fell all the animals used to talk just like people." Compare and contrast Hurston's depiction of life against a backdrop of talking animals with the earlier Joel Chandler Harris tales. Hurston writes out from folklore as a source of literary power.

Their Eyes Were Watching God

This excerpt illustrates Hurston's reliance on folklore as a source of literary authority and creates a black woman, Janie, as a powerful speaking voice. Ask students to describe the narrative context in Chapter 2. Who is telling the story, and to whom? Although Pheoby does not emerge as a clear character in this excerpt, she does become the "hungry" listener who helps Janie tell her story. By implication, the presence of a sympathetic ear makes it possible for Janie to discover her own literary authority; and Hurston also suggests, in using the word *hungry*, that Janie's story serves an essential need of Pheoby's. The relationship between narrator and listener—which replicates the relationship between Hurston and her own reader—is one of intimate friendship, self-disclosure, and mutual need. Women turn to each other's stories for understanding and consolation.

Chapter 2 also depicts the generational roots of women's fiction. Before Janie can begin her own story, she must first tell her mother's and grandmother's stories. Discuss the statement: "She thought awhile and decided that her conscious life had commenced at Nanny's gate." Hurston is one of the first American writers to write fiction out of the need to portray the origins of African-American women's consciousness. Here I note again connections between mythology and fiction for Hurston. We discuss the many elements that create Janie's "conscious life," her attempt to locate herself in a universe that has "a personal answer for all other creations." Hurston weaves together in Chapter 2 the source of Janie's burgeoning sexuality; her connection with the natural world as a way of knowing; her recognition of Nanny as a "foundation of ancient power"; the history of black women's oppression during slavery by white men and women; the burden of sexual as well as racial oppression for Janie's mother; the impulse (in Nanny) to accommodate to a world in which "'de nigger woman is de mule" by finding "protection" in a responsible man; the imperative (in Janie) to strike out on one's own in a world in which "the familiar people and things" have failed.

We discuss the novel as Hurston's "sermon"—Nanny had envisioned herself as a preacher—and the act of writing fiction as akin to making a sacred text. After Leafy runs away, Nanny thinks to herself about Janie, " 'Ah said Ah'd save de text for you.' " Janie finds herself in telling Pheoby the story of her life; "saving the text" is precisely what Janie learns to do for her friend, and what Hurston does for the black and white women writers who would come after her. Hurston focuses on a black woman's need to write stories that mirror her own image—unlike the first photograph Janie sees in which she cannot find herself—and in this way she expresses a black woman's modernist concern. What happens to a black woman—or to a woman of any color—when the "familiar people and things" fail? Hurston offers one answer to the question in the rest of her novel; and she suggests Janie as a prototype for the modern female child. As long as Janie has not discovered for herself that what her grandmother wants her to believe is a lie—that in marrying Logan Killicks she will come to love him—she is willing to go along with another's script or formula for her life. But when she walks out to the gate a second time, in

Chapter 3, she has a more realistic view of the road. Hurston suggests that it is only by rejecting the conventional scripts that Janie "became a woman." And for Hurston, *woman* is synonymous with "independent person." In *Their Eyes Were Watching God,* Hurston creates a modernist myth of origins; the process of becoming a woman, for Janie, involves making her own dream, her own story.

DOROTHY PARKER

Discuss Parker's place in the tradition of American humorist writing. Analyze how Parker achieves her linguistic effects, both in her short poems and in *The Waltz.* Does her humor rely on mockery, exclusion, or the "putdown"? Is she writing to entertain? Comment on Baym's suggestion that her poems' "wit and elegance costume moods of emptiness and despair." Compare Parker's *The Waltz* with Charlotte Perkins Gilman's *The Yellow Wallpaper.* What strategies does each narrator choose to deal with her situation?

E. E. CUMMINGS

Consider what it would mean to ask whether Cummings is a "serious" poet. Describe the ways in which he experiments with language in poems such as *anyone lived in a pretty how town* or *my father moved through dooms of love,* and consider their effects. Ask students to read *Buffalo Bill's* or "*next to of course god america i* out loud, and discuss what happens to poetry that is meant to be read, not spoken. Locate modern themes in Cummings; place him in context with Frost (compare *pity this busy monster, manunkind* with Frost's *Departmental*), Jeffers (*i sing of Olaf glad and big* with *Shine, Perishing Republic*), or Moore (*Poem, or Beauty Hurts Mr. Vinal* with *Poetry*).

JEAN TOOMER

Discuss "Georgia Dusk" as a variation on Emerson's call for an American poet a century earlier. What, for Toomer, will be the characteristics of that "genius of the South"? And what will be the literary tradition for that "singer"? Locate Toomer in the context of other black writers or writers about black experience in NAAL—Joel Chandler Harris and Charles W. Chesnutt. What does it mean, in Toomer, to make "folksongs from soul sounds"? Analyze "Fern," first from the narrator's point of view and then focusing on Fern herself. What is happening within the speaker as he imaginatively recreates Fern? What is the literary analogue in Toomer for Du Bois's "double consciousness"? How does Toomer evoke "the souls of black folk" in this excerpt from Cane? Place Fern herself in the context of other works by American male writers, such as Poe's

Ligeia or Anderson's *Mother.* Toomer gives Fern a moment of speech when she asks, "Doesn't it make you mad?" and then his narrator interprets what she means. Does he give her voice? Consider the last sentence in "Fern": "Her name, against the chance that you might happen down that way, is Fernie May Rosen." What, in this sentence, gives the reader more clues to Fern's identity than Toomer's earlier idealization of her? Is there any "real" Fern beneath Toomer's portrait of her as his narrator's muse? Note Toomer's reference to the black woman who "once saw the mother of Christ and drew her in charcoal on the courthouse wall." The allusion is one piece of evidence to suggest that black women, as well as men, have tried to record their visions; they have been artists as well as inspirations for art.

GENEVIEVE TAGGARD

If you have brought Juhasz's framework into your presentation of women poets (see discussion of Marianne Moore), Genevieve Taggard's poetry will seem quite in advance of her generation, because much of her poetry derives from women's experiences (as in *With Child, Mill Town,* and *To My Mother*), and particularly women from poor and working-class origins. Indeed, Taggard's poetry poses a challenge to the conception of aesthetic modernism. In response to Frost's question in *The Oven Bird,* "What to make of a diminished thing?" Taggard would answer: sing! strike! move! In Taggard, poetry and politics become intertwined and women participate in both (as in *At Last the Women Are Moving* and *Mill Town*). Even more startling in Taggard is the presence of class politics. More than any other poet in the 1914–1945 period (with the exception of black poets Sterling Brown and Langston Hughes), Taggard's poetry addresses class issues; indeed, her poetry gives voice to working-class women and men, and like Brown and Hughes, she privileges "everyday" experience (as in *Everyday Alchemy*). To demonstrate the contrast between a white male poet's apolitical approach and Taggard's interweaving of one woman's experience with the experience of class and with politics, read *A Middle-aged, Middle-class Woman at Midnight* against Frost's *An Old Man's Winter Night.* In Taggard's poem, age, cold, and anxiety about the state of the world allow her "middle-class woman" speaker to cross class boundaries and align her own struggle to sleep ("A woman took veronal in vain") with the "stink of poverty": "I hope the people win."

As part of your discussion of Taggard, ask students to think about the relationship between poetry and politics. In Latin America, poetry has long served political ends and has a vital life among people outside the college classroom. In the United States, many people believe that poetry (and all art) should have nothing to do with politics. Taggard is herself aware of her departure from convention in this regard; read *To Mr.*

Maunder Maunder, Professional Poet and focus on the intensity of the last lines: "The English Language is no whore— / What are you making rhyme-schemes for?" For Taggard, poetry must move people, and must move them collectively. Read her poem about poetry, *Definition of Song*, against other modernist poems about poetry, such as Stevens's *Of Modern Poetry* or Moore's *Poetry*. *Definition of Song* not only challenges the primacy of the lyric voice in poetry ("of all forms of song surely the least / Is solo" and "This is the life of song: that it mean, and move, / And state the massive power of our love") but also critiques, like Yezierska's fiction, the individualism that replaces aborted dreams of democracy ("Deepest of all, essential to the song / Is common good.")

F. SCOTT FITZGERALD

Disappointment abounds in modernist fiction, and Fitzgerald's narrator characterizes Dexter Green's story in *Winter Dreams* as a story of life's "mysterious denials and prohibitions." What does life "deny" Dexter? Some students may say that it denies him Judy Jones and the "satiety" Dexter believed she aroused in him. Others may pity this protagonist; despite the welcomed "liberation from webs of tangled emotion" that he feels when he goes off to the war, he ends by regretting his inability to cry or care. Has he, therefore, lost his ability to feel? Explore student interpretations of Fitzgerald's title, *Winter Dreams*. Does he lose Judy Jones herself or the ability to project onto her his own dreams? Consider the various portraits or interpretations of Judy Jones in the story. How do we know her? Which Judy is real, the woman who is Dexter's ideal or the woman who seems to have "faded" in Devlin's anecdote at the end of the story? Does Dexter's achievement of the American dream (he makes a lot of money) ironically cause him to lose his ability to engage in dreaming?

WILLIAM FAULKNER

As I Lay Dying

As students begin to read *As I Lay Dying* they experience fragmentation and dislocation. After assigning only the first five or ten monologues, I spend much of the first class period allowing them to discuss the expectations they bring to a novel as readers, and how *As I Lay Dying* disrupts those expectations. The initial confusion they feel as a result of Faulkner's disparate narrative sections and points of view can help them understand modernism as a challenge to their ways of seeing the world. If allowed to express their own disorientation, they begin to use Faulkner's novel as an exploration of ways of knowing (epistemology) as well as of ways of being (ontology) in a disordered universe.

We begin with a preliminary discussion of the book's title in light of earlier thematic discussions of modernism. What does the reader expect, given this title? And how does the novel, from its opening sections, thwart those expectations? Who *is* the "I" of the title? Just Addie Bundren? What or who else does that first person point of view include? And how does the past tense of the title create a preliminary absurdity before the reader begins the novel? In eliciting students' initial confusion about opening sections, I try to give them the experience of posing Faulkner's own questions as he lets his characters speak. What do they know as they read, and how do they know it? We close read Darl's opening section. Where does Faulkner "locate" the reader? Part of what "lies dying" for readers new to Faulkner is any reliance on the author as someone who will facilitate knowing. Faulkner shows readers only what his characters know, not what readers may feel the need to know.

As students proceed through the novel (over the span of an additional two or three class periods), we spend class time describing what Faulkner is doing. We consider novelistic conventions—character development, plot, use of a narrator, chronology, narrative form—and assess the extent to which Faulkner adheres to or deviates from traditional elements of the novel. In the collective act of description, students make numerous statements about *As I Lay Dying:* they note the number of narrators (fifteen by the novel's end) and sections (fifty-nine separate monologues); they distinguish among the narrative voices by making descriptive observations: Darl has, by far, the most sections; some central characters—Jewel and Addie—have only one monologue; monologues by Darl, Jewel, Dewey Dell, Anse, Vardaman, Cash, and Addie create a nexus of family dynamics; other characters—Cora, Tull, Peabody, Samson, Whitfield, Armstid, MacGowan, Moseley—express a wide range of possible social responses to the Bundrens. These descriptive statements may make some students feel that they have "figured out" the novel, and I may observe that their attempts to "solve" the novel may be premature and may actually be covering over their uneasiness as readers, lest they become lost in a work without omniscient authority.

They also establish collective understandings about the characters in the novel that become shared "facts" and that serve as a prelude to interpretation. The attempt to bury Addie becomes the family members' ostensible reason for the journey to Jefferson, which provides Faulkner with his novel's narrative structure, but most of the Bundrens also have other reasons for the trip. Cash wants the free ride back to Tull's, where he is supposed to work on his barn, and he dreams of a "talking machine." Vardaman remembers something in a store window (the toy train) that Santa wouldn't have sold to town boys. Anse wants to get some new teeth. Dewey Dell hopes to buy a drug-induced abortion. Darl twice narrates events at which he could not have been present, and in other sections appears to "know" things that others have not told him (he knows

Dewey Dell is pregnant and that Anse is not Jewel's father). Among all of Addie's survivors, Jewel seems best able to feel the depths of his connection to his mother, to mourn her death, and to achieve emotional resolution. (At the end of Cora's section just preceding Addie's monologue, Addie tells Cora that Jewel "is my cross and he will be my salvation. He will save me from the water and from the fire," and indeed, Jewel first saves Addie's coffin in the ford, and later from the fire Darl has set to Gillespie's barn.) The group effort to "figure out" what can be known in reading the novel becomes a pedagogical analogue to the Bundrens' own journey. The parallel tensions of burying Addie (for the Bundrens) and figuring out what is happening in the novel (for the members of the class) comment on the act of modernist reading: without the storyteller/guide of traditional narrative, the task of arriving at an understanding of Faulkner's text (analogous to bringing the coffin to Jefferson) places much of the burden of creation on the act of reading itself.

As a result of description, students move toward interpretation. The elements of form they observe lead to their perceptions of character. For example, they note the repetition in the form of the images Jewel and Vardaman create as a way of grieving for Addie: "Jewel's mother is a horse" and "My mother is a fish." Then they can ask, Which image works best to help the character resolve grief? In responding to the question, they explore the relationship between image and feeling, between word and meaning, between the novel as a form and the attempt to order the fragments of human consciousness.

Central to exploring Faulkner's search for theme, meaning, and order is Addie's single monologue, placed off-center in the novel in the second half, long after Addie has died and the Bundrens have begun their journey to Jefferson. To what extent does Addie exist in the novel? Although she gives the other characters their ostensible reason for action, she herself does not act. Neither does she speak, except to acknowledge Cash as he builds her coffin. Her monologue in the novel may appear to give her a voice, but her death has already silenced her and prevents her from making her genuine presence known. She exists for other as their own projected need. Interestingly, what occupies her thinking in her monologue is the uselessness of words. Discuss Addie's various statements about words: "words dont ever fit even what they are trying to say at"; a word is "just a shape to fill a lack"; a name is a "word as a shape, a vessel . . . a significant shape profoundly without life like an empty door frame"; words are "just sounds" that people have "for what they never had and cannot have until they forget the words." In the narrative structure of Faulkner's novel, Addie is herself "just a shape to fill a lack."

The visual image of the coffin that appears in Tull's third monologue typographically disrupts, once again, the reader's expectations—for, although Faulkner has violated readers' expectations of linearity and wholeness in narrating *As I Lay Dying*, he at least uses words. With the visual image of the coffin, followed later by Addie's description of words, Faulkner creates a series of concentric visual images or shapes that serve both to contain his novel's meaning and to express the limits of narrative form. In Faulkner's thinking, each of the following is associatively synonymous: the visual figure of the coffin, the name *Addie*, the narrative form he has chosen for the book (it is spatial, a world laid out by compass and rule), and the book itself. *As I Lay Dying* effectively becomes Addie's coffin, a fiction in which she is silenced by the title, and like her family in Jefferson cemetery, she might be listening to the other fifty-eight monologues, but she'll "be hard to talk to."

As I Lay Dying has a profound effect on students who are themselves struggling to emerge from silence and to begin to explore the world's order and form, to discover whether it has any or whether they must join the human collective task of making form and meaning. Students may empathize with Addie's silence and may find it reflected in Vardaman's obsession with his mother as a fish, or with Cash's inability to speak except to focus on the coffin's construction or need for balance. *As I Lay Dying* demonstrates the novelist's own struggle to emerge from silence, and students may believe that it is only partly successful, or that Faulkner is saying that it is possible to achieve only partial success.

In evaluating the relationship between the construction of form—as a coffin or a novel—and of meaning, ask students to think about Darl. Is he crazy? If so, what makes him crazy? Interestingly, Darl has by far the least difficulty with silence; he can speak for others as well as himself. Is he a mere scapegoat at the novel's end? Do the other members of his family believe he "knows too much"? Or has he failed in some basic way to create a form for what he knows? Darl is the only character who cannot make a connection between himself and some concrete object. He has no coffin, horse, fish, abortion, or reason to go to town. Students may find it difficult to believe that Darl "goes crazy" at the end of the novel, in part because, in many of his monologues, he closely resembles a traditional omniscient narrator, one whose own identity does not intrude. Who, then, is Darl? If he cannot express his connection in terms of an image, a form—coffin, novel—his knowledge and creativity become destructive. Darl simply cannot "be contained" in a form; therefore, as Cash realizes at novel's end, "this world is not his world; this life his life." In Darl's failure to achieve a form for human consciousness, Faulkner implies his own struggle for meaning. What to make of a diminished thing?—make something of it, find a word to fill the lack, write a novel that will reconcile human need for form with the formlessness of human consciousness. Cash's briefest monologue locates *As I Lay Dying* in the progression of Faulkner's career as a novelist: "It wasn't on a balance. I told them that if they wanted it to tote and ride on a balance, they would have to." *As I Lay*

Dying rides precariously, a book about silent knowing necessarily told in words. Expecting to be told, students emerge from *As I Lay Dying* with the uneasy knowledge that words no longer—for the modernist—carry ultimate authority. As Addie expresses it, "the high dead words in time seemed to lose even the significance of their dead sound." Perhaps literary authority itself is at least a part of what "lies dying" in Faulkner's modern fictional universe.

STERLING A. BROWN

Sterling Brown's poetry, as the headnote comments, has as its purpose "to expose and criticize racial injustice." He chooses the principle of contrast between white man and black man as his subject in *Mister Samuel and Sam* and *Master and Man.* In these poems, the difference between white and black are settled by the common denominators of death and harvest time, and yet as the poems appear to resolve differences, they also end by highlighting the inequalities within those common denominators (both Samuel and Sam may die, but the harvest is more bounteous for the Master than for the Man). Other poems (such as *He Was a Man*) also derive their form from the principle of contrast, but the holding back of detail in early stanzas typical of a ballad about the life of a man yields to more detail and the ballad's "story" turns out to be the progress by which this "man" is reduced to not a man in the eyes of white people. The promise of unfolding in the ballad form is negated (and demonstrated by the poem's consistent use of negatives—"It wasn't about," "Didn't catch him," "It didn't come off") by the poem's ultimate irony, that it's impossible to write a story of a man's life when he isn't viewed as a man. Thus the title's assertion (*He Was a Man*) becomes the poem's primary message. *Break of Day* continues the ballad/blues form and a variation on the same theme: "Man in full" becomes "Long past due" by the poem's end.

LANGSTON HUGHES

Before the Harlem Renaissance writers of the 1920s (Angelina Weld Grimké, Zora Neale Hurston, Jean Toomer, Sterling Brown, Langston Hughes, and Countee Cullen are all associated with this period), most black writing either took the form of the slave narrative of the mid-nineteenth century or of "racial uplift" literature or polemical writing characteristic of the turn of the century (and represented in NAAL by Booker T. Washington and W. E. B. Du Bois). While most African-American writers wrote for white audiences (even though they might have written ironically for this audience, as in Charles Chesnutt), Langston Hughes may be the first African-American writer to view his white reader's interest, and his role as speaking voice, as a form of encounter, not unlike those early encounters between Europeans and native peoples during the period of exploration and colonization. Thus I begin teaching Langston Hughes with *Visitors to the Black Belt,* and a discussion of the two-sided perspective this poem gives about Harlem. More than an exercise in language ("Across the tracks" versus "here on this side of the tracks"), the poem ends with a simple question and answer that resonates with the problem of postcolonialism. "Who're you, outsider? / Ask me who am I." In these lines, the poet teaches the reader, by means of the expected question, how to ask the speaker who he or she is rather than to assume he or she already knows. If the outsider learns to know his or her place as outside, then the person on the inside ("To me it's *here* / In Harlem") has room to define himself. So Hughes is pleading with his white audience not to draw conclusions about black life without asking him, without allowing him to define its reality and meaning, and—in other poems (such as *I, Too; Refugee in America; Madam's Calling Cards;* and *Democracy*)—what it means to be an American. The other side of the experience of encounter involves the responsibility it places on the poet. Echoing Whitman in *I, Too* and self-conscious about both calling for a black American poet and responding to that quasi-Emersonian call in *Note on Commercial Theatre,* Hughes responds very simply: "I reckon it'll be / Me myself! / Yes, it'll be me." From the perspective of literature of encounter, if Hughes can imagine a white readership "encountering" black experience and black art with genuine interest (perhaps for the first time on a large scale during the Harlem Renaissance), then he has the responsibility to make certain that experience and that art doesn't become "colonized," commercialized ("You've taken my blues and gone—"). The person who recognizes that colonization is taking place must struggle against it, especially by resisting being appropriated in a white someone else's image. Thus Hughes moves beyond Brown, whose poetry stresses contrast and counterpoint, to include contradiction and the two-way experience of encounter.

Students will also find in Hughes's work an appreciation for black women's struggles and an attempt to give women's experiences representation in his poetry. In one of his greatest poems, *Mother to Son,* he also connects his own answer for the modernist question to a woman's voice and a woman's experience. I read this poem closely with students, focusing on the contrast between the mother's description of the stairway itself and the image she arrives at ("Life for me ain't been no crystal stair") as a controlling metaphor for her vision. The poem shows the mother arriving at modernist order in the chaos of "sometimes goin' in the dark" by making this particular image. I ask students to consider the numerous connotations of the image of the "crystal stair" as well as the way Hughes is experimenting with levels of diction, in effect raising the level of diction in this phrase. Raising the level of diction and "racial uplift" become ground notes in his work; see, for example, *Genius Child,* in which

Hughes moves beyond protest to a transcendent belief in the "genius" of black life ("*Kill him*—and let his soul run wild!"). And in the Alberta K. Johnson poems (here represented by *Madam and Her Madam* and *Madam's Calling Cards*), Hughes demonstrates the complexity of the relationship between black woman and white woman. When Alberta responds to her Madam's profession of love by saying "I'll be dogged / If I love you," Hughes is making a simple statement of fact: if relationship with the Madam means that Alberta Johnson has to work even harder, she will indeed be "dogged," for it will kill her; and indeed, Alberta must stop short of "loving" the woman she works for if she is to love herself at all. And that she does love herself is clear in *Madam's Calling Cards*: "I hankered to see / My name in print." Both like and unlike Yezierska's characters, Alberta Johnson wants to be an American, but doesn't consider herself an immigrant: "There's nothing foreign / To my pedigree."

RICHARD WRIGHT

Discuss what "being a man" means to Dave Saunders. Why does the gun represent manhood to him? Does a black boy in the 1930s South automatically get "to be a man like any body else," or does he have to make that happen? Why does he want the power to "kill anybody, black or white"? How does Dave Saunders move beyond Booker T. Washington's views of black identity in *Up from Slavery?* Is Dave another heroic fugitive, like Frederick Douglass? Does he have a destination at the end of the story?

MURIEL RUKEYSER

Unlike other poets who write about political themes, as the headnote points out, Rukeyser "denied that there was any conflict between poetry written at a high level of technical and textual sophistication and poetry that was politically motivated and dedicated." Ask students to evaluate their response to her poetry, compared with their response to Taggard or Hughes. Does it work (do they believe) to write political poetry at a "high level"? Does Rukeyser reach the audience she might want to reach (and can we tell who that might be)? *Who in One Lifetime* is emblematic of Rukeyser's work, the one poem in the anthologized sequence that can integrate her various styles and concerns. She has seen "all causes lost" and yet has tried to make poetry out of those defeats (in yet another answer to Frost's modernist question, "What to make of a diminished thing"), to explore the contradictions both biographically and poetically in her self-portrait as "a childless goddess of fertility." Read her images of coming to voice (in *Suicide Blues* and "*Long Enough*"), of coming to sight (*The Poem as Mask*), of healing fragmentation (*Who in One Lifetime*). Poems, for Rukeyser, seem to be one way of making sense of all of the wars she has lived through; see *Poem,* with its transformation from historical moment ("I lived in the first century of world wars") to contemporary dilemma ("I lived in the first century of *these* wars," emphasis added). And notice, with students, the extensive range of her historical and political interest, from the poems of the 1930s to the feminist poems of the 1970s (*Myth* and *Painters*). In these poems, Rukeyser seems to have discovered the war she won't live long enough to lose, and the tone of both *Myth* and *Painters* predicts new knowledges (in her suggestion that Oedipus has much to learn) and new connections (in the image of women being among the earliest cave painters). It's only at the end of our discussion of Rukeyser that I return to her earliest poem included in NAAL, *Effort at Speech Between Two People.* This poem moves back into her childhood and, by the end of our discussion, forward into the process by which wars are won and fragmentation healed: "Take my hand. Speak to me."

American Prose since 1945

In the contemporary period, as William Pritchard observes in his general introduction, "even applying exclusive standards, one can easily name fifty or so American novelists and storywriters who are artists of real distinction." As teachers, our decisions to choose certain authors or stories over others in this period likely reflect our own personal reading taste or previous experience that certain authors and works are more successful than others in introducing students to the pleasure and power of contemporary American literature. In making my own selections, I am guided more by my sense of what will please and move students than by current critical evaluations that might grant certain writers more importance than others, since above all I want to leave students with a desire to read more contemporary literature. I am also aware of including as diverse a list as possible from the offerings in the "American Prose since 1945" section.

Introducing Students to Contemporary American Drama

An introductory course in American literature, especially in twentieth-century or contemporary literature, offers students a unique opening into the experience and meaning of drama as an American literary form. American writers have certainly produced great plays before the contemporary period, and drama served a vital function for Americans as early as Royall Tyler's *The Contrast* (included in NAAL, Volume 1), when delighted audiences flocked to view Jonathan's comic rendition of what an "American" in 1787 might look like. I suspect that very few of your students, however, will have thought much about the uses of drama in their own lives.

One way of beginning is simply to ask students to talk about drama in general. What do they associate with drama? Some may reply, "Shakespeare." Almost all of them will have read Shakespeare in high school; they may have learned, as a result, that drama belongs to an elitist category of literary forms. Are any students willing to challenge that impression? Others may recall acting in high school plays of mostly less seriousness—situation comedies, Hollywood musicals, plays written especially for high school acting. A few may have written and/or acted in original plays as children or may have parents who participated in community theater groups. Others may associate a family trip to New York City to view a Broadway play as some initiation rite into adult life and culture. Some may associate drama with television situation comedies. Even with this limited range of responses to the experience of drama in their lives, you can begin to explore the variety of functions drama serves. What are some of the differences between literature that one reads, often alone in a room and a play that may be "taking place" before the viewer's eyes, as that viewer sits in a group with others? Is a play "shown" or "told" when the performers stage it? What kinds of effects does the stage play make possible? And what does it mean to dramatize?

Contemporary drama may elicit students' ability to engage in the reading process more readily than contemporary American poetry, which often seems deliberately to distance the reader with its private meanings, idiosyncratic uses of language and imagery, and sense of barriers between speaking voice and reader of the text. Drama, however, seems to require a viewer; a play creates audience in the process of making character, situation, scene, and dramatic effect; the student, in the act of reading, becomes a collaborator in creating a visual image of the scene.

The plays included in NAAL, Volume 2, by their very choice of subject matter and realistic treatment, may particularly elicit the student's capacity to become engaged, to become created or recreated as audience. When Eugene O'Neill explored American family life in *Long Day's Journey into Night*, he did not exhaust our increasing fascination for the function and fate of the American family. Perhaps the crisis in family life for late-twentieth-century Americans has brought on the crisis of consciousness that, earlier in the century, we associate with World War I and the question of the death or absence of God or design in the modern world. Family life continues to provide a central focus for Tennessee Williams, Arthur Miller, and August Wilson. If the American family is dead or absent, who or what "mirrors" an American identity that continues to evolve?

EUDORA WELTY

Analyze the relationship between Leota and Mrs. Fletcher. Does Mrs. Pike exist? What function does Leota's fantasy life serve? Discuss the undercurrent of violence in *Petrified Man.* How does Leota's story show her attempt to gain control over her life? Is she successful? Who is Billy Boy, why is she taking care of him, and where does he get his own power at the end of the story?

TENNESSEE WILLIAMS

The loss of "'Belle Reve" seems to establish the tarnished American dream as one of Williams's central themes in *A Streetcar Named Desire.* Some students may see Blanche DuBois as a conventional symbol for the loss of that dream—as an unmarried, well-over-thirty southern belle, she worries about her clothes, her appearance, her ability to attract men, and finding alcohol to ease her loneliness. But is the loss of desirability, or desire itself, the play's subject? Does Blanche want to find an object for her desire, or to be a desired object?

Williams might have made desire itself a symbol; instead, throughout the play, he focuses our attention on explicit sexuality. What particular scenes define desire as sexual in the play? Ask students to discuss in particular the relationship between Stanley and Stella. Their attraction for each other is explicitly sexual, and most students will equate sexuality with heterosexuality—and, as it is presented in this play, with a hierarchy of physical dominance (the men in the play, especially Stanley, use physical abuse as part of sexual power; see Stanley's comment to Blanche, " 'Oh! So you want some roughhouse!' ").

But this play revolves around that moment in Blanche's past when she married a "young boy" who tried to find "help" in Blanche for his homosexuality. When she discovers him with "an older man who had been his friend for years," and that day tells him how much he disgusts her, he blows his head off. For most students, presuming that heterosexuality is "normal" and homosexuality "deviant," this moment will establish Blanche's tragedy as a conventional one—she has loved young and lost—and the moment in which homosexuality enters the play will quickly recede. Raise the possibility that from this moment on, Blanche's psychological core gender identity becomes ambiguous—despite the fact that Williams has made her a woman in the play—and suggest also that although Stanley and Stella both seem secure in their gender identities, their very insistence on continuing to reaffirm their sexual relationship by means of violence—thereby asserting Stanley's "manhood" and Stella's "womanliness"—begins to raise the question of the origins of gender determination as well.

What would it mean to say that Blanche's sexual identity becomes ambiguous in the play? Near the end she tells Mitch, " 'I don't want realism, I want magic! . . . I don't tell truth, I tell what *ought* to be truth.' " What are Blanche's props for her "magic"? Ask someone to study her array of furs, costumes, jewelry, and perfume in the play—she wears all of the trappings of gendered femininity, like the lengendary Mae West (ironically, the statuette Mitch wins for Blanche at the amusement park). But her success in establishing her appearance depends on her avoiding the sun and even electric light. Without the costumes, who would Blanche be? What would it mean to call her a "woman"? And who are her consistent objects of desire? Recall, with students, that she has been fired from her teaching job for having a relationship with a young boy, and she tells the paper boy, " 'You make my mouth water.' " Whatever her sexual biology, Williams is not telling truth but "what *ought* to be truth." The play explores what women and homosexual men have in common; it does that (in my view) by focusing on gender construction in Blanche, not on biological sexual identity. Except for the fact that Williams makes her a woman, she might be a drag queen (she shares the queen's fascination with Mae West as a model to be imitated), and in exploring the psychology of the queen (Stanley asks Blanche, " 'What queen do you think you are?' "), Williams is exploring the way female identity is made, not born.

Ask students to think about Stanley's response to Blanche. What motivates Stanley to rape her? What does she represent that makes him want to humiliate her? Blanche sees Stanley—with his phallic "genius"—as subhuman; Stanley sees Blanche as undermining his control over Stella (" 'You remember the way that it was? Them nights we had together? God, honey, it's gonna be sweet when we can make noise in the night the way that we used to and get the colored lights going with nobody's sister behind the curtains to hear us!' "). But Stanley is also acting out of a variation on homophobia—or is homophobia a variation on misogyny? In the homosexual world, it takes courage for a man to become a drag queen, because in wearing women's clothes, the man sets himself up for the full violence of some men's hatred of women. Stanley hates Blanche because she insists on wearing women's costumes and yet refuses to define herself as degenerate or to excuse her sister for her submission to Stanley. In raping Blanche, he is raping the wearing of women's costumes, the flaunting of sexuality by women (or by men who refuse to be "phallic"). No wonder that Stella tells Eunice, " 'I couldn't believe her story and go on living with Stanley.' " The sexual "stories" Blanche and Stanley tell totally contradict each other. Blanche exhibits desire without violence; Stanley achieves his through violence and humiliation. Ask students to talk about Stella's grief at the end of the play: " 'What have I done to my sister?' " How has she betrayed Blanche? Has she also betrayed herself? In what version of sexual desire does the "truth" lie? The play ends with Stanley and Stella, having eliminated Blanche from their world, returning to their hierarchical heterosexual roles: Stella weeps in luxurious abandon, Stanley unbuttons her blouse. Is this desire? Or a more destructive lie than Blanche's "magic"?

BERNARD MALAMUD

The Magic Barrel works well to teach with *A Streetcar Named Desire*, because there are similarities between the works that help students formulate their questions. In *The Magic Barrel*, Malamud creates Salzman the marriage broker as an Old Testament God figure who tries to keep love (and sex) out of the world. As a "commercial cupid," however, he is also someone others hire to refashion Paradise (clearly a "diminished thing" in the world Malamud's characters live in—like "Belle Reve"?). His idea of Paradise is to find a good woman for Leo, the rabbinical student, and to keep Leo away from his own daughter, Stella, a "fallen woman." (Is Williams's Stella also "fallen"?) When Leo falls in love with Stella's picture and arranges to meet her at the end of the story, Malamud depicts their meeting in "fallen" terms: Stella is dressed like a streetwalker, Leo runs forward phallically "with flowers outthrust" (or as if he and Salzman have exchanged places, and Leo is now a cupid or the FTD florist's winged messenger, bearing flowers), and Salzman, convinced that there is no good man, chants prayers for the dead. But Leo pictures, in Stella, "his own redemption," and Malamud suggests that although Leo becomes less than a rabbi by the end of the story, he becomes consequently more of a man, more of a human being. Simply loving, in this story, does recreate Paradise because it makes it possible, once again, for Leo to love God—and even to create God in a human image. In Malamud's terms, Leo's love for the fallen Stella makes him a good man, and although Salzman mourns, the story has a happy ending. Less is more, for Leo. As he becomes the "diminished thing" in Salzman's eyes, he is more capable of human love.

RALPH ELLISON

Compare Ellison's protagonist with David Saunders in Wright's *The Man Who Was Almost a Man.* The two might seem incomparable in educational background and social possibilities; yet, how are they up against similar barriers? In the "Prologue" to *Invisible Man* the older protagonist writes, in retrospect, "responsibility rests upon recognition, and recognition is a form of agreement." How is this observation relevant to his experiences as a young man in Chapter I? How is Blanche's statement in *A Streetcar Named Desire* (" 'I don't tell truth, I tell what *ought* to be truth' ") applicable to Ellison's use of symbolic action in *Invisible Man?* Each of the major events of Chapter I—the fight with Tatlock, the electrified rug, the presence of the white woman, the boy's attempt to talk with blood in his mouth, his reference to "social equality," and the scholarship to the black college he receives at the end—can be read as symbolic. And how does the boy's attempt to deliver the speech he himself has written comment on the literary tradition of American black writers? What are the symbolic and real obstacles he must overcome in trying to find his voice and to express his point of view? What might it take for the white men at the smoker to "recognize" and "accept" the invisible man? Is the white woman in a better position than the black boy? Does either have power in the world of the back room?

ARTHUR MILLER

Madness, confusion, desire, identity: these are the themes O'Neill, Williams, Miller, and Wilson explore in their plays, and the family in each play becomes the place within which characters act out their roles. The family is also the place where we each develop a sense of individual identity and learn the social, emotional, and sexual roles we then choose to revolt against or to play out in our own lives. *Death of a Salesman* gives American family life itself the power to create character—almost as if the play is about the inability of any playwright to invent roles he or she has not already played or watched in the tragedy of family life. The family is both the play and the playwright. And in this play the family prescribes certain roles for each of the four main characters that they continue to reenact in the process of discovering what they are. Students, following Linda's cue, will focus on Willy Loman himself: " 'Attention must be finally paid to such a person.' " Why doesn't Loman accomplish anything? Why does he have such trouble really talking to his sons? Neither of his sons is able to "catch on." How do they all get derailed? Unlike Mary Tyrone or Blanche DuBois, Linda Loman has no identity of her own. Is *Death of a Salesman* realistic in its portrait of Linda? What was her role in Loman's decline? Miller implies that Linda has kept her husband back from going to Alaska and "conquering the world"; is she to blame, or has she seen inadequacies in her husband that he was unable to recognize in himself? Does she never criticize Loman or want to defend Biff against his father? Who raised these children, anyway? Is the role of American father as provider a myth without basis in fact? Who *does* "provide" in this play? And what is Miller indicting?—capitalism? family life in general? American fatherhood?

FLANNERY O'CONNOR

In *Good Country People* Mrs. Hopewell says, " 'Everybody is different. . . . It takes all kinds to make the world,' " but she doesn't really mean it. She would prefer that all the world, and especially her daughter, be "good country people" like herself. What would it mean for Hulga to take her mother as her model? Contrast the two sets of mothers and daughters depicted in the story. What are Hulga's "crimes"? What makes her unforgivably "different" to her mother? What is Hulga looking for in Manley Pointer? What does she find? Look at the mother-child imagery of Pointer's "seduction." What do Manley and Mrs. Hopewell have in common? As unlikely as it might have seemed, Hulga has chosen as a love object a person who both infantilizes her and tries to idealize her—someone whose psychological connection with her resembles her mother's own. And what is the story's final betrayal? Is it possible for Hulga to escape being her mother's daughter?

N. SCOTT MOMADAY

In the selections from *The Way to Rainy Mountain,* Momaday interweaves a Kiowa past to which he is connected by his bicultural memory, family, and tradition and a Native American literary future (or "renaissance," in the terms of critics) that recreates in words a culture that exists only "tenuously," in memory. Ironically, it proves to be Stanford-educated Momaday's thorough acculturation in what his nineteenth-century predecessors would have called "white" or "government" education as well as his command of the English language that makes both possible at once: the preservation of the past and a vision of a future for Native Americans. Unlike most of the Native American texts included in NAAL, Momaday's is not transcribed from a non-English language or from an oral performance—although he collects Kiowa tales and myths, with his father as translator—and he is writing simultaneously to native peoples and Euro-Americans. He is also writing for himself, and for others like himself who want to hold onto a Native American heritage. This can include students, even white students, in the American literature classroom.

In some ways, *The Way to Rainy Mountain* becomes a "final exam" of the new Native American materials in NAAL, a way of testing students' knowledge and integration of their earlier readings. For understanding the form of the poem requires at least some acquaintance with American Indian myths and history. The poem begins with Momaday's contemporary rendition of the Kiowa myth of creation—an emergence myth, like that of the Pima Story of Creation included in Volume 1; he traces the migration of the Kiowas and the legends they make, such as the legend of Tai-me, and their relation to other gods in the sky; he gives his grandmother, Aho, a position of reverence and a godlike voice from Kiowa history; he relates the development and loss of the Sun Dance ritual, what his grandmother remembers as "deicide"; he works through (with his father's help in translation) a series of Kiowa myths, counterpointed (or as if in "encounter" with) other voices—a voice of family and cultural history, and a third personal voice of reflections on his place in the schemes of history and myth; and he ends with a poem, "Rainy Mountain Cemetery," which conveys his own vision. The Native American poet in the late 1960s has been to the mountain, an Indian Moses, and has brought back his vision of "the early sun," on the mountain that "burns and shines," in an image of a new dawn approaching "upon the shadow that your name defines"—an unmarked dark stone that must serve as the marker for the beautiful woman buried in an unmarked grave near his grandmother's house, for all of the unmarked dead Kiowas, for the end of Kiowa culture itself. It is as if, for Momaday, the end of the Sun Dance ritual—like the end of the Ghost Dance religion (both of which occurred in 1890)—required a new vision a century later, and the Native American poet writes a version of the "Messiah letter," one that combines myth, song, and rituals of ceremonial prayer.

ROBERT STONE

If drama externalizes feelings and relationships, then Robert Stone's story *Helping* creates its effect, in part, because it presents internalized violence and a tension that remain unresolved by the story's end, even if Elliot's missed shot at the pheasant provides Elliot himself with momentary relief. Many elements in the story contribute to building a sense that something violent is about to happen: Elliot's interaction with Blankenship, the content of Blankenship's dream and the memories of Vietnam it evokes in Elliot, Grace's description of the Vopotik family and Vopotik's threats, Elliot's fantasy of cutting the necks of the Anderson family with barbed wire, and Elliot's shotgun and his encounter with Professor Anderson on the ski trail. Some violence does occur: Elliot's rage at the psychiatrist, the sugar bowl Grace throws across the room, Elliot's shot at the pheasant. Does "enough" violence actually happen in the story to relieve the weight of suspense the reader carries by the end? Or has Stone managed to provide the antithesis of a cathartic experience for the reader? Are we left with an increasingly internalized sense of foreboding?

One line from *Helping* suggests that, for the contemporary reader, there will be no "help" at all. Elliot thinks, "The gods and I went mad together and made things as they are." If you have talked about modernism with your students in teaching material from the 1914–1945 section of NAAL, ask them how Elliot's thought takes modernism in a new direction. For my own students, I might suggest that, for the modernists, the emotional/psychological/metaphysical "solution" to the recognition of the death or absence of design in the universe was to find consolation in the writer's or poet's vision; it became the writer's job to order those "fragments I have shored against my ruins," as that earlier (T. S.) Eliot concludes at the end of *The Waste Land.* For Robert Stone, post-Vietnam, human beings cannot repair his sense of lost order; in fact, human beings seem to have collaborated with the gods to make things as they are. In the language of self-help programs, Stone seems to be suggesting that the human victims of the loss of order or design have themselves served as codependents; we resemble the Grace of *Helping* who tells Elliot, " 'In my family we stay until the fella dies. That's the tradition. We stay and pour it for them and they die.' " Nothing "helps," especially not the professional helpers, in Stone's world; Elliot ends the story by expressing his need for, if not the helping hand, at least a "show" of hand, which might ease the postmodernist's despair with the modernist's consolation (might he then be free to interpret the hand as helping, much as the viewer in Wallace Stevens's world is free to interpret what the eye sees?). It seems more likely, as *Helping* ends without or before the show of hand, that Elliot will continue to look down the length of the gun and at some point "find himself down the sight."

Compare and contrast the ending of *Helping* with the ending of Malamud's *The Magic Barrel.* How do the different protagonists differently interpret possibly divine signs?

JOYCE CAROL OATES

The "golden gloves" of Oates's story serve to protect the protagonist's hands, but as the reader suspects at the end of *Helping,* the power to make the world safe lies beyond the control of human hands for some contemporary writers. Ask students to compare *Golden Gloves* with *Helping.* Has some external force undermined Stone's Elliot or does his fear, anger, and sense of broken promise result from his own individual character or experience? Oates makes it clear that forces beyond her protagonist's control have altered the course of his life, beginning with his birth defect. She writes, "The blow you can't see coming is the blow that knocks you out—the blow out of nowhere. How can you protect yourself against a blow out of nowhere?" Ask students to differentiate between a benign but absent creator and a malignant external force. Does Oates's protagonist have any control over his life? What is the prognosis for the protagonist's relationship with his, as yet, unborn child? Several of the short stories included in the post-1945 section explore adult relationships between men and women. And for several of these relationships, Oates's description of what happens to her own protagonist may also apply: "It was his own death that had crashed into him—yet no more than he deserved. He was hit as one is hit only once in a lifetime. He was hit and time stopped." Comparing the protagonist's feelings about his wife at the end of *Golden Gloves* with the male protagonist's feelings in John Updike's *Separating* and Robert Stone's *Helping,* assess the sense of arrested development that each of these authors conveys as time stops in some way for their characters. Has Oates managed accurately to convey the determinism of contemporary American life, or has she distorted what we have become? And is the protagonist's wife his new sparring partner, his double, his projected shadow self?

BOBBIE ANN MASON

The NAAL headnote gives Mason credit for resisting the temptation to present her characters "as caricatures to be ridiculed or pitied by a presumably more sensitive author and reader." Resisting this temptation marks a writer *of* rather than *about* region and, if the statement about Mason is accurate, suggests a new integration of *New Yorker* style with regionalist perception. In introducing Bobbie Ann Mason, I ask students to contrast her with Peter Taylor's *What You Hear from 'Em?*, an earlier (1954) story by another author associated with *The New Yorker* who writes from Mason's neighbor state of Tennessee. Does the critical comment from Mason's headnote (above) also apply to Taylor's story, or does Taylor fall into caricature in his presentation of Aunt Munsie? I also ask students to read Mason in the context of recent Native American and Latina writers (Silko, Erdrich, and Chávez, included in NAAL, all of whom explore lost family connections and the need to test out the power of storytelling to re-form or reclaim some sense of family, ethnic, or "antique" heritage. How does Mason's Carolyn retain her sense of possibility in human connection, even in family life, despite the images of failed connection and fractured family that pervade *Drawing Names?*

Ask students to consider the joke about the silent monks that Carolyn's father tells at Christmas dinner and to analyze her mother's response: "Can you imagine anybody not a-talking all year long?" Mason presents a family in which there is much talk and very little real conversation. Then look closely at the ending of the story. How do students interpret the gift left under the tree? One "gift" that remains "unopened" for Carolyn is conversation; she finds hope, as she imagines Jim and Laura Jean alone, in the "certainty that they would not be economical with words." One of the features readers have come to expect from *New Yorker* fiction is linguistic economy. Mason seems to be pushing the limits of economy at the end of this story, drawing out the visual image of the "old-fashioned scene," adding the (perhaps to some) unnecessary "Cheers" to Carolyn's vision of possibility in family as well as fictional forms. Is Mason arguing that in an era of lost family connections, it is time for writers to become more "wasteful" in their use of words?

ALICE WALKER

Walker's depiction of her mother-daughter bond differs considerably from O'Connor's. Where Mrs. Hopewell defines herself and her daughter by listening to the voices of conventional "good country people," the mother who narrates *Everyday Use* listens to her own inner voice and creates her own values. How are Dee and Maggie different? What explains Dee's decision to rename herself Wangero? How do the quilt's values change for her, and what do they mean to Maggie and the narrator? What does Walker mean by valuing "everyday use"—even though the quilts may be, as Dee claims, "priceless"?

AUGUST WILSON

The headnote for *Fences* compares the play to Arthur Miller's *Death of a Salesman*, and students might usefully compare the two, either in class discussion or in a paper assignment. If Wilson's artistic mission has been to write a collective history of black American experience, students may be interested in asking whether there is any difference between white fatherhood and black fatherhood, as Miller and Wilson portray them.

In *Fences*, Troy focuses on responsibility, not love, in his treatment of son Cory, but can fatherhood include one without the other, given the way Troy cuts off Cory's chances in life? And he professes fidelity and love in his relationship with Rose until he discovers "a different understanding about myself" with the younger Alberta. Students may find Rose an improvement over Arthur Miller's Linda Loman, but does the fact that she can stand up for herself against Troy change Wilson's characterization of woman-as-mother?

The trope of fences allows students to make some thematic statements about the play: Troy has been unable to play in the majors, "fenced out" by racism; the heritage he received from his own father's raising becomes the barrier to communication with his son; men and women live as if behind invisible but firm fences; and the line between the "whites driving and the colored lifting" requires union intervention on a case-by-case basis.

Despite its critique of American racism, *Fences* is fundamentally a play about men, fathers, and their foibles. Women students of any color may find this limited "family" perspective a topic for analysis and discussion.

ANN BEATTIE

Beattie's *Weekend* alludes to the film of the same name by Jean Luc Godard, and what violence takes place in this *New Yorker* story takes place only in the language and as disjunction. Houseplants play a significant role in this story (the contemporary writer's concession to the loss of the external green world?) and Lenore projects and simultaneously contains her own violent fantasies when Beattie writes about her that she "will not offer to hack shoots off her plant for these girls." Otherwise, "nothing happens" in this story; Lenore, the "simple" character, asks Beattie's quintessential contemporary question, "Why do I let *what* go on?" Ask students how they interpret Lenore's statement that she is "simple." What does it mean to be simple in contemporary life? "It is true; she likes simple things." Yet Lenore's life and Beattie's *Weekend* are more complex than that; does the word *simple* for Lenore allow her to defend against noticing the full extent of the lack of communication between her and George? *Weekend* presents a simple world of women, in which women are out of place; all of George's guests are "girls," and living with George without being married offers Lenore only the illusion of choice.

George joins a large list of contemporary characters who drink their way through their fictions, and as George drinks, Beattie shifts to passive voice: "another bottle has been opened." The point of the sentence seems to be that no one knows who has opened the bottle; agency unknown reflects the postmodern dysfunction.

How do students respond to Lenore's last action in the story, as she moves next to George on the couch? Beattie writes that Lenore leans her head on George's shoulder "as if he could protect her from the awful things he has wished into being." Lenore ends by giving George credit for "wishing" the existence of "awful things" in the world. Is this what Beattie means by simple? Does Lenore stay with George because she can attribute to him the agony of not being in touch? Because she can listen to him teach that "there can be too much communication between people" and, therefore, not have to look too closely at herself? Does simple mean attributing the state of the contemporary world to some other, human, agency, rather than focusing more clearly on the unknown agency of passive voice?

DAVID MAMET

If you ask students to describe their experience with drama, some may talk about movies as the form of drama with which they are most familiar, and they may have seen either *House of Games* or Mamet's *Glengarry Glen Ross*, both of which have appeared in local theaters. Because *House of Games* is a screenplay intended for performance, I encourage you to show your students the film. The film itself is clearly a play and not a "movie"; seeing it will lead to a discussion of the differences between drama and cinema, even when drama is scripted for film.

House of Games is a tightly constructed drama that focuses on the emerging self-recognition of psychiatrist Margaret Ford and plays on the multiple contexts in which this screenplay and implicitly American life become a series of confidence games. The psychiatrist who has written the book on compulsion and obsession discovers that she herself is "driven"; she becomes one of the con artists in the play, in the guise of helping others, she discovers that she herself has their problems. Margaret Ford begins to reveal her obsession when she breaks the frame of her profession and tries to "help" Billy Hahn by confronting Mike about Billy's gambling debt, but until she finally learns that she has been "taken," she becomes the mark for ever-expanding victimization. She has what Mike refers to as the "tell," a quality that reveals her obsession to others but not, until the end of the play, to herself. And numerous lines play on the similarities between psychiatry and the con game; for example, Mike equates lessons in the con game with "a short course in psychology."

Without offering any alternatives, *House of Games* also reveals the con game that gender roles construct. One of the biggest con games of all turns out to be the "gender con," wherein women and men play their socialized roles as part of a larger scheme to bilk the "other" and, ultimately, each other. Indeed, gender roles may be the ultimate game in which most of us are socialized as obsessive-compulsives. As Margaret Ford writes about Billy, "Compulsive succeeds in establishing a situation where he is out of control"; yet in taking on the ("female") roles of helper for Billy, then later "whore" when she allows herself to be drawn into the con man's world and into sex with Mike, she manages to establish a situation where she too is out of control, but which looks like the usual Hollywood seduction scene, with the con better known as the sexual come-on. Yet in her own terms, if such a situation is the mark of the compulsive, then the screenplay defines sexual games as con games and their players as socially constructed obsessives.

In the closing scenes, this point becomes particularly clear. By the end of the screenplay, Margaret Ford has learned that she has been taken. In the scene in which she listens to the con men talking about the way they have victimized her, one of them says, "Took her money, and screwed her too." The ultimate con is taking the vulnerable woman. In the closing scene with Mike, having discovered herself doubly vulnerable, Margaret Ford doubles back to con Mike by playing the vulnerable woman once again: "Don't leave me . . . how can I do it without you." Cagey as he is, Mike believes in some essential vulnerability in Margaret; when she plays this role it is Mike this time who is taken in. She has already entrusted him with so much of her money, why not believe she wants to give it all away? Mike is as driven (read: socialized) to victimize as he believes Margaret is driven to be a victim.

While the ending of the screenplay does show Margaret knowing herself, in the vulgar language of the con men, as both "bitch" and "booster," some students may wonder what such cynicism does to resolve the problem: If heterosexual relations are themselves revealed to be a con, or at best the behavior of obsessive-compulsives, then where do Mike and Margaret find respite from those larger confidence games that look respectable (like psychiatry, or like writing best-selling books) but have begun, in the play's language, to "crack out of turn"?

Ultimately, it is the screenplay itself, and its con game, that interests Mamet. Ironically, it is the tell that becomes the unwitting mark of the victim; by implication, any story that becomes self-disclosing sets the "teller" up to be conned. Yet Mamet uses the tell as a form for his own expression. When readers (or viewers) of *House of Games* fall into the trap of believing Mike when he asks Margaret to "protect" him from the Vegas gambler, we reveal ourselves to be compulsives. By making ourselves Mamet's audience, we give him our "confidence." His screenplay is an exercise in proving to us that we, too, can be "conned." This, more than any genuine gender analysis, explains the ending of *House of Games*. Mamet knows that we too will fall into the trap of "believing" in Margaret's vulnerability. When we watch her forgive herself for killing Mike, then "boosting" the gold lighter, Mamet does more than create a surprise ending, or reverse gender roles: he cons his own readers and viewers. And, like any other compulsive, it probably will not stop us from running to see his next film—and paying top prices for the experience.

LESLIE MARMON SILKO

At that point early in *Lullaby* at which Ayah does not want to think about her dead son, she thinks instead "about the weaving and the way her mother had done it." Craft defends against sorrow, for Ayah, and for Silko, who weaves the loss of Pueblo culture into Ayah's lullaby at the end of the story. Yet the promise passed down from generation to generation of Pueblo children from their mothers has been broken: "We are together always / There never was a time / when this was not so." Ask students to explore thematic similarities between Silko's story and others in the post-1945 section. Like Stone, Mason, Walker, and Beattie, Silko also portrays the family in dissolution; however, Ayah has lost her children to the Bureau of Indian Affairs and to cultural assimilation with white people. It is not possible for her to reclaim them or to restore her sense of family. The loss of the possibility of family affects the relationship between Ayah and Chato, as it does the relationship between Elliot and Grace in Stone's *Helping*, and like Elliot, Chato and many other Native American men in *Lullaby* turn to alcohol to numb their despair. Ayah does not drink; her experience makes the men afraid of her and to look at her "like she was a spider crawling slowly across the room." Ask students to compare Ayah with the mother in Gertrude Simmons Bonnin's *Impressions of an Indian Childhood* and to compare Bonnin's portrait of the removal of Sioux children from their reservations with Silko's, almost a hundred years later. Ask students to examine the problems in the mother-daughter relationship that Alice Walker portrays in *Everyday Use* when Dee also "emigrates" to another culture.

DENISE CHÁVEZ

Like her contemporaries included here, Chávez also writes about loss, but unlike most others, she sees in loss some potential for growth, choice, and humor. Although references to Mexican and Chicano culture pervade *The Last of the Menu Girls*—the "half lost melodies" of "Cielito Lindo," the illegal alien Juan Maria the Nose—Rocio Esquibel seems to see her own life as a menu, herself on the verge of making "that awesome leap into myself." When she does begin school and a new life, then has an accident that makes her a patient at Altavista Memorial, she experiences firsthand how rapidly things change: "No one took my menu order. I guess that system had finally died out" Despite the humor of *The Last of the Menu Girls,* Chávez also hints at some serious questions. Will it be Rocio's and Chávez's goal to expand the choices on the Chicana "menu"? Do "wetbacks and healthy college students" represent the two extremes of possibility for young Mexican-Americans, or are there other models? If Rocio refuses to nurse the dying, will she find a living Chicano culture to nourish? When she returns to Altavista as a patient, Rocio's sister thinks she has lost part of her nose in the accident. What does link Rocio with Juan Maria the wetback? If Rocio emigrates beyond the world of Altavista Memorial, will she return to her childhood culture only as an alien? Is the Chicana writer who chooses to write in English, and thus becomes accessible in the American literature classroom (and thus, teachable by English departments instead of Spanish departments), a kind of literary "wetback"? Or is she creating a model, a menu, of assimilation into biculturalism?

LOUISE ERDRICH

The two Lamartine brothers in *Lulu's Boys,* and indeed Lulu's boys themselves, become interconnected, their identities complementary and even interchangeable. Beverly Lamartine becomes a hero of contemporary Chippewa culture in *Lulu's Boys,* for he leaves behind Minneapolis, where "there were great relocation opportunities for Indians with a certain amount of natural stick-to-it-iveness and pride," to return "westward," as Erdrich describes his trip, "over the state line and on across to the casual and lonely fields, the rich, dry violet hills of the reservation." For Beverly, the reservation represents home because Lulu's Henry Junior is a boy he considers his son. Is Erdrich suggesting here that contemporary urban Native Americans ironically associate hopeful new beginnings with life on the reservation? Or is she writing a parable of lost paternity?

Certainly, parenthood is a problem for a decimated culture; recall Silko's *Lullaby* with your students. Bev's attempt to find a boy to father, however, expresses a hope of redemption for the American family that few characters in contemporary fiction share. Specifically compare the moments of Ayah's reunion with Ella, in *Lullaby*, with Bev's reunion with Henry Junior. Bev encounters "a moment of confusion at the utter indifference in the boy's eyes," but unlike Ayah, Bev has a chance to make reparation for all the absent fathers, especially for the drunk Henry who commits suicide on the train tracks.

Ask students to look at Erdrich's implicit use of Chippewa imagery in her portraits of Bev and Henry. Specifically, Lulu remembers each brother by their tattoos, contemporary equivalents of Indian names: for example, might Bev, given his act of heroism in choosing to risk the return to domesticity and intimacy in Lulu's arms, in Chippewa culture have earned some kind of bird's name? Might he have been called Lone Swallow or Soaring Eagle? Despite Lulu's presence in the story's title, Erdrich's story tells Bev's tale, and it is a tale of flight. Even Bev's working-class urban Indian customers, who buy his workbook sets, envision their children as "fledglings before they learn how to glide."

Compare and contrast Erdrich's Beverly Lamartine with Flannery O'Connor's Bible salesman, Manly Pointer, in *Good Country People*. Recall Hawthorne's *Wakefield*, for students who have read that story. Erdrich tells a different tale in *Lulu's Boys*. Or does she? Consider the portrait of Lulu as a woman who "seemed to fill pots with food by pointing at them and take things from the oven that she'd never put in." Has Erdrich given us the portrait of Bev's heroic return to domesticity, only to sacrifice the freedom of Lulu herself, or at least her realism? Lulu, like Ann Beattie's Lenore in *Weekend*, inhabits "the sacred domain of her feminity." Is that the price Lulu must pay for easing the fragmented family?

American Poetry since 1945

You may find the general introduction to the "American Poetry since 1945" section extremely useful for your own preparation in the classroom. After building the introduction on the work of three generations of postwar, 1960s and 1970s era, and 1980s and contemporary poets, the editors comment on "the distinctive work of individual writers" who produce dazzling poems apart from major trends. They write, "the living world of contemporary poetry changes: new poets emerge, and existing poets, previously inaccessible or neglected, make themselves heard." In the interweaving of individual poems and groups of poets who wrote in the context of each other's work, of poetic influence that crosses generations and ethnic boundaries, and of shapes and sizes of poems, the introduction recalls for me the experience of wandering down the spiral ramp inside the Boston Aquarium, or watching the vertical tanks in the Monterey Bay Aquarium.

The anthology section becomes such an aquarium, poems and poets selected because they represent their kind, show how large and small can cohabit, resemble others and swim in schools, emerge remarkably to follow their own pursuits, and, above all, alter the viewer's perception of the depths, shapes, movement, and ecological balance of the microcosm of marine life. We associate some poets with "schools"—Vanderbilt, Black Mountain, Iowa; others, such as Niedecker, wrote without participating in any literary community. Some poets resemble their mentors; others deny their influence after incorporating the techniques of their predecessors. The possibilities of extending the metaphor may seem endless, but the point is somehow to provide a larger view for students that will give them a point of entry. No single class or course can teach undergraduate students all there is to know about "American Poetry since 1945," but with the help of the general introduction to the period, the anthologized selections, and your own personal preferences, you may at least facilitate for your students the experience of knowing certain poets are in the "tank" and watching some of them swim by.

Coincidentally, I like to introduce contemporary American poetry with Robert Lowell's *For the Union Dead,* which opens with an image of the speaker pressing his nose against the glass of the old South Boston Aquarium. This poem first appeared in *Life Studies,* one of the collections that the editors credit with administering a "transforming shock" to postwar American poetry. The poem explores Lowell's autobiographical relationship to massive upheavals in American life and challenges readers not to be cowed, compliant, or servile. Other significant poems also reflect marine imagery: Lorine Niedecker's *Paean to Place,* Elizabeth Bishop's *The Fish,* James Wright's *With the Shell of a Hermit Crab,* Anne Sexton's *Lobster,* and Adrienne Rich's *Diving into the Wreck.* Together with *For the Union Dead,* Rich's *Diving into the Wreck* can serve as a frame for your discussion of the material.

As the editors observe, "Many American poets do not want to think of their work as the fragments of modern literature." The general introduction to the period pulls the fragments together. In my own observations about the poetry, I have considered the general introduction as itself a "course guide," and in making the notes that follow, I hope merely to augment its usefulness as a way to organize your own classroom preparations or course outline. The editors describe their generalizations as provisional; the classroom can become, in part, a testing ground for what we can say about a body of literature that continues to change shape almost as we read it.

The individual headnotes will also help you manage your task of introducing students to the works. When in doubt about your own familiarity with a poet, work directly from the headnote, asking students to place the editors' statements against individual poems to see whether they make sense. In writing exam questions and essay topics for this section (see Chapter 8), I have worked from specific statements in the headnotes, and you may find these questions useful to organize classroom discussion.

As the period introduction observes, many of these writers learned their craft while majoring in English or studying with professors of English in colleges and universities. Contemporary poets have created their own industry and their own markets for their products by giving readings, teaching in writers' workshops, staffing creative writing programs, and working by means of writing book reviews and media commentary to promote the readership for their work. Both as students and consumers, then, we are all likely to encounter living poets; indeed, we may argue that our poets are made and not born and that, for reasons we may not yet understand, our poets serve a socially and culturally useful function. Ask students to consider whether, as consumers and present or future taxpayers (who fund some of the grants that keep poets alive), they are getting anything that is useful to them. What are, or ought to be, the "uses" of poetry in contemporary American life? If you have read *Rip Van Winkle* with students a semester ago, ask them to consider whether the role of the American writer has changed since Washington Irving's time (see discussion of *Rip Van Winkle* in this Guide). Do we still need poet-chroniclers to tell us where we have been, where we are going? How much farther down the path—than we—are our poets? Do they truly see new directions we should follow? Can we trust them? What might we want our poets to do for us that they seem not to be doing at present?

In beginning to teach individual poets or poems, I choose the works I know and the writers I love. I also ask students to survey the table of contents for the "American Poetry since 1945" section and to identify those poets and poems they recognize. Those works can become useful starting points for the rest of us, and I ask students to identify the points of contact they may have with the large body of texts included here. I may then work from their responses to the question concerning the "uses" of poetry to help match them up with unfamiliar poets or poems. If someone believes, for example, that poetry should make us aware of the fragility of our environment, I send them off to read Gary Snyder or Galway Kinnell. If students want to hear a strong woman's voice, I assign Adrienne Rich or Audre Lorde. Much as contemporary poets from all ethnic and regional backgrounds may be said to write for all of us, it can seem helpful to students interested in finding common ground to know what regions or ethnic groups individual poets represent.

Or they may identify with biographical details. Does it interest students to know that Robert Duncan never met his mother because she died at his birth, that Richard Hugo's mother abandoned him, or that Elizabeth Bishop lost both parents by the time she was five and was raised by relatives? that Berryman, Plath, and Sexton committed suicide? that Levertov was born British? that Lowell and Roethke suffered nervous breakdowns? that Niedecker wrote "on the margins" of literary culture? that Robert Hayden was raised by foster parents? that Rich, Lorde, Duncan, Ginsberg, and Merrill made lesbian and gay choices in their personal lives? that Baraka changed his name from LeRoi Jones? Assign students the task of choosing to read one new poet based on purely biographical, ethical, or regional information; then ask them to write briefly, even in class, about their reading experience. To what extent does familiarity or strangeness motivate their choice? To what extent does their choice become self-disclosing for them?

Consider also your own training and predilections. What "works" for you? Having early been taught to close read individual poems, I pass the method along to students, balancing the need for coverage with luxurious class time on single poems. What kind of training did you have, and what would you like your students to have? Do you want them to be able to move beyond close reading to see larger intersections between poems and poets, between poetry and prose, between poetry and contemporary culture, between poetry and politics? Are any students willing to challenge your own approach with their own? Do any wish to read their own poems to the class?

CHAPTER 8

Exam Questions and Essay Topics

The teaching notes in Chapter 7 contain many questions that you may easily adapt as topics for writing. In offering the following additional exam questions and essay topics, I have tried to suggest further directions for student thinking and research that may or may not emerge directly from class discussion. Similarly, the exam questions and essay topics are also easily adaptable to questions for discussion, either for the class as a whole, or for small groups.

The first and most extensive set lists questions that address literary, historical, and genre connections between authors, followed in each period by questions related to the interpretation of some individual authors and texts. The second set includes problems and topics that emerge from examining authors within their own literary traditions or that focus on comparing authors across traditions.

Here, as throughout this Guide, I've been somewhat idiosyncratic in my choices of which authors to include. Just as each of us makes choices for a course outline that reflect at some level personal interest and knowledge, my own inclusions and omissions resemble that process. To the extent that you choose to focus on authors or works for which I have not provided exam questions and essay topics, I hope you will be able to adapt general models for questions in the period to your specific needs.

Part I

Volume 1

Literature to 1620

HISTORICAL QUESTIONS

1. Wayne Franklin calls this period a "many-sided process of influence and exchange." He also writes that "much of what was new . . . came about through struggle rather than cooperation." Choose either statement and write a short essay in which you comment on its accuracy by citing references to specific writers and narratives included in the period.

2. The "Introduction" to the period identifies three purposes of European colonization. Recall at least two of these and cite texts that specifically reflect European purpose.

3. Much of the literature of encounter and discovery rests on inventories of one kind or another. The lists stand in verbally for the accumulation of wealth and riches. Choose inventories from three of the writers we have read. From the perspective of a postcolonial world, identify their rhetorical purpose for the writer, what they reveal about the author's assumptions about the New World and its inhabitants, and how the language in each inventory serves to enhance the inventory's rhetorical effect.

4. Many European reporters from the Americas rely on lists or inventories to convince their readers of the value of the land. Discuss the idea that inventories become a textual form of mapping. Making specific references to texts, comment on the relationship between landscape or geography and human beings or their artifacts.

5. From a Eurocentric perspective, historians once discussed the "Age of Discovery" but now instead refer to the era of "encounter." The narratives in the "Literature to 1620" section may accurately be viewed as narratives of encounter. Choose several significant moments of encounter from different narratives included in this section and identify the different positions from which the Europeans and native peoples view each moment.

6. Research the myths of Dona Marina and Pocahontas and report on their cultural survival in Mexico and North America.

7. Based on several specific accounts or passages in the "Literature to 1620" section, reconstruct and interpret several specific moments of encounters between arriving Europeans and indigenous peoples. Viewing the encounters as moments of communication, interpret how each side views the other and what messages they convey in their own behavior. Ground at least part of your reconstruction on a reading of the Stories of the Beginning of the World.

Questions on Individual Authors and Works

Christopher Columbus

1. Discuss how Columbus's expectations, "thinking that I should not fail to find great cities and towns," reflect the contrast between European ideas of greatness and a more indigenous perspective on "great" civilizations in the New World. Be specific.

Bartolomé de las Casas

1. Cite evidence from Casas to support the observations that resistance to exploitation and violence against native peoples and critique of the purposes of colonization appear in the discourse about colonial exploration as early as the sixteenth century.

Hernán Cortés

1. Throughout the narratives of Cortés, he conveys the sense that the Spaniards believed they could create their own laws. Recall some specific moments that reflect this belief.

2. Find an account of the Conquest of Mexico by a twentieth-century historian and compare that account with Cortés's own version of events.

Bernal Díaz del Castillo

1. The headnote suggests that *The True History of the Conquest of New Spain* amounts to "an ironic commentary on the Christian culture of Europe." With specific references to *The True History* and to at least two additional narratives of encounter, explore the accuracy of this statement.

2. More than other narratives of encounter, Díaz del Castillo's becomes a narrative of witness. Locate and discuss several moments in the narrative where he demonstrates his self-consciousness and responsibility about his role as witness.

Álvar Núñez Cabeza de Vaca

1. Focusing on the texts of Cabeza de Vaca and Díaz del Castillo, write an essay that brings into focus the lives of native women in North America.

Stories of the Beginning of the World

1. Locate and read another Native American creation story and discuss it in light of the Iroquois and Pima stories included in NAAL.

Arthur Barlowe and Thomas Harriot

1. Demonstrate the contrast between Barlowe's and Harriot's description of the native peoples each comes in contact with. Locate moments in Harriot where propaganda seems to obscure his ability to provide a more accurate report of the encounter between the English and Native Americans.

Samuel de Champlain

1. Read Champlain with particular attention to his descriptions of American Indian agricultural life. Making specific references to passages you find most significant, reconstruct in brief form the portrait of native life (food, customs, housing, activities, manners, relationships between men and women, domestic arrangements) that Champlain offers.

2. Evaluate the narrative voice in which Champlain describes the Native Americans he encounters. Can we trust his account? What evidence might you offer to support your position?

John Smith

1. The headnote states that the "First Charter" in Virginia, which John Smith's *General History* recounts, "marked a more corporate approach to colonization that was to become standard practice over the next hundred years." Locate evidence in Smith's narratives that demonstrates this "corporate approach." Pay particular attention to how the approach becomes manifest in Smith's attitudes toward native peoples.

2. Research a multinational corporation's recent expansion into a new market. Test the headnote's statement (from previous question) and add to it several hundred years. Or apply the following statement from Smith himself, near the beginning of the excerpt from "The Third Book," in which he writes: "Such actions have ever since the world's beginning been subject to such accidents, and everything of worth is found full of difficulties, but nothing [is] so difficult as to establish a commonwealth so far remote from men and means and where men's minds are so untoward as neither do well themselves nor suffer others."

3. At the end of the excerpt from "The Third Book," Smith writes, "Thus you may see what difficulties still crossed any good endeavor; and the good success of the business being thus oft brought to the very period of destruction." Locate other passages throughout Smith's writing where he expresses his concern for the reputation of the "business" endeavor in which he is engaged or where he uses metaphors from the world of work or business to describe his activities.

1620–1820

HISTORICAL QUESTIONS

1. Define some of the basic concepts of Puritan ideology and illustrate their significance in specific works. Choose from among the following: (a) "new world" consciousness, (b) covenant theology, (c) typology, (d) innate depravity, and (e) irresistible grace. A few of the writers who address each of these concepts, and whom you will need to discuss, include (a) Bradford and Bradstreet; (b) Bradford, Wigglesworth, and Edwards; (c) Bradstreet (in *Here Follows Some Verses upon the Burning of Our House*), Taylor, Winthrop, and Wigglesworth; (d) Taylor, Wigglesworth, and Edwards; and (e) Winthrop and Edwards.

2. Trace the connection between the Puritans' reliance on written covenant in Bradford's [The Mayflower Compact] and their emphasis on didactic to the exclusion of dramatic or personal vision in their literature.

3. Octavio Paz, among others, has called Puritan society a culture based on the principle of exclusion. Discuss, with particular references to literary works, the evidence of this principle in Puritan life and culture.

4. Consider secular consequences of Puritan theology: the Puritans' attitudes toward Native Americans, ordinary life, witches, house servants, slavery, and infant damnation. Choose two of these topics and explore their treatment in literary works from the period.

5. Identify and discuss literary texts that reveal stresses on Puritanism or that illustrate schisms within Puritan and colonial consciousness.

6. Explore the contrast between personal and didactic voice in Puritan and early colonial literature.

7. Identify the literary forms available to colonial American writers. What limited their choice? How did they invent within these forms? What forms would survive for later writers to work within?

8. Cite several fundamental differences between Puritan thinking and deist thinking. Analyze specific literary works that illustrate these differences.

9. Describe the way the concepts of the self and of self-reliance develop and find expression in colonial and early American literature. Identify those specific figures or works that you see as significant and explain their contributions.

10. Trace the power of the written convenant in colonial and early American literature, beginning with [The Mayflower Compact].

11. Discuss the ways in which Benjamin Franklin and Thomas Jefferson alter the content of Puritan thinking without changing its form. How do their writings reflect earlier forms?

12. Slavery is an issue of conscience for some colonial and early American writers; for others it is fraught with ambivalence. Discuss the issue with references to several specific texts.

QUESTIONS ON INDIVIDUAL AUTHORS AND WORKS

Anne Bradstreet

1. Write a close analysis of a single lyric poem. Depending on how much analysis you have already done in class, choose from among the following: *The Prologue, The Flesh and the Spirit, The Author to Her Book, Here Follows Some Verses upon the Burning of Our House*, and *As Weary Pilgrim*.

2. Analyze a related series of stanzas from *Contemplations*, and then discuss the relationship between these particular stanzas and the entire poem.

3. Compare and contrast the imagery of *To My Dear and Loving Husband* with Taylor's *Huswifery*. How does the imagery characterize each poet's work?

4. Discuss the extent to which Bradstreet's poetry reflects Puritan thinking. Analyze in particular the way Bradstreet reflects her own spiritual and metaphysical fears in the process of describing an actual event in *Here Follows Some Verses upon the Burning of Our House*.

5. Analyze the contrast between form and feeling in Bradstreet's work. In what ways does she use self-disclosure as a challenge to Puritan theology?

6. Trace imagery of nurturance and provision in Bradstreet's lyrics. Reread with particular attention to maternal and paternal imagery and references.

Edward Taylor

1. Write a close analysis of any of the poems from *Preparatory Meditations*. Identify the central metaphor or series of related metaphors and describe the process by which Taylor converts the terms of each metaphor into an assurance of his own salvation.

2. Discuss the title of Taylor's group of poems *Preparatory Meditations*. How does the title reflect his sense of the purpose of poetry?

3. Trace Taylor's use of objects from the natural world or of secular experience in *Upon Wedlock, and Death of Children*; *Upon a Wasp Chilled with Cold*; or *A Fig for Thee, Oh! Death* and examine the relationship in the poem between earthly life and spiritual salvation.

4. Discuss the extent to which Taylor's poetry reflects specific concepts of Puritan theology.

William Byrd

1. Write an essay in which you compare and contrast Byrd's *The Secret Diary* with a work by any of his New England contemporaries. Does Byrd reveal a colonial consciousness that transcends a specifically Puritan ideology?

Jonathan Edwards

1. Analyze the form and significance of *A Divine and Supernatural Light*. (This topic works well if you have already analyzed *Sinners in the Hands of an Angry God* closely in class.)

2. Discuss Edwards's manipulation of biblical language in *Sinners in the Hands of an Angry God*. What specific transformations does he perform? And how does his use of language in the "Application" section of the sermon differ from and comment on the earlier doctrinal section?

3. Discuss the fact that Jonathan Edwards and Benjamin Franklin were contemporaries. Explain, with specific references to their works and more general

comments on their ideas, why this fact seems startling. (I expect students to consider scientific influences on Edwards and a Puritan heritage on Franklin.)

4. Write a brief comparative analysis of form and function in Edward Taylor's poems and Jonathan Edwards's sermons. (Students need to see the way each of these Puritans tried to demonstrate or even "prove," in Edwards's case, spiritual salvation, and the way each associates being saved with the authority of being able to find the right language.)

5. Discuss the following statement, from *The Nature of True Virtue*, in light of colonial American history: "Things are in natural regularity . . . when he whose heart opposes the general system, should have the hearts of that system, or the heart of the ruler of the system, against him." Include in your discussion both the decision of the Puritans to settle in the New World and the later struggle of the colonists for independence.

Benjamin Franklin

1. Explain why the eighteenth century was called the Age of Experiment and consider the relevance of this term as a description of Franklin's writing.

2. Analyze the numerous metaphors Franklin uses in Poor Richard's maxims in *The Way to Wealth.* Count and categorize the metaphors; summarize your findings. What are their origins, and how does he use them?

3. What is the "religion" Franklin "preaches" to his readers in Father Abraham's speech? How do you explain Franklin's use of religious metaphors in his writing?

4. Discuss several permanent contributions Franklin made to American life, ranging from the practical to the ideological.

5. Choose any single section or aspect of *The Autobiography* as the basis for analysis. *Or* contrast Franklin's choice of focus in its four parts; consider the significance of his choice to address the book to his son; read closely the letters that begin "Part Two" and comment on their significance to *The Autobiography* as a whole; discuss Franklin's various practical attempts to alter his moral character.

6. Following notes from class discussion, explain the various ways in which Franklin's *Autobiography* may be seen as "self-invention."

Elizabeth Ashbridge

1. Trace Ashbridge's search for voice in *Some Account of the Fore-Part of the Life.* Incorporate in your discussion her response to the voices of others, especially spiritual voices.

2. Compare Ashbridge with Anne Bradstreet. How do their attitudes toward writing, motherhood, and God illuminate their similarities and their differences? How do their attitudes illuminate differences between Puritans and Quakers?

3. Trace Ashbridge's thought process in *Some Account of the Fore-Part of the Life*. By what logical arguments does she reject what she terms "priestcraft" and come to accept herself as a Quaker? To what extent does Ashbridge rely on contextual experience in making decisions?

John Woolman

1. Compare the specific imagery of *The Journal* with that of Jonathan Edwards's *Personal Narrative*, with the goal of demonstrating differences between Woolman's religious beliefs and worldview and those of the Puritans.

2. Compare and contrast Woolman's *Journal* with Ashbridge's *Some Account*. What can we infer about Quaker life in the colonies from these two writers? To what extent are differences in their narratives attributable to gender?

Samson Occom

1. Compare and contrast the rhetorical devices in Occom's *Sermon Preached at the Execution of Moses Paul* with Jonathan Edwards's *Sinners in the Hands of an Angry God*.

2. Trace and analyze Occom's references to American Indians. How does he represent them? How does he suggest whites have represented native peoples? Find subtle evidence to support the interpretation that Occom believes Euro-Americans have misrepresented American Indians.

J. Hector St. Jean de Crèvecoeur

1. For eighteenth-century writer Crèvecoeur, witnessing slavery firsthand leads him to lament the "strange order of things" in Letter IX from *Letters from an American Farmer*. Analyze the difficulty he has reconciling the existence of slavery and the great contrast between lives of plantation owners and slaves in Charles-Town with his own belief in a "sublime hand which guides the planets round the sun."

2. Evaluate Woolman's (in "Some Considerations on the Keeping of Negroes") and Crèvecoeur's (in Letter III) different uses of the phrase *self-interest*. How does the phrase become central to two very different arguments about who Americans are and what they should be?

3. Compare and contrast Woolman's and Crèvecoeur's understanding of "strangers" and their place in "American" society.

John Adams and Abigail Adams

1. Compare and contrast one of Abigail Adams's letters to John with one of Anne Bradstreet's poems that serve as letters to her husband, "absent upon public employment." How does Bradstreet's use of eighteenth-century poetic forms constrain feeling? How does feeling alter the potential for form in Adams's letters?

2. The letters that pass between John and Abigail Adams during July 1776 locate *The Declaration of Independence* within a context of private meaning. Examine the hopes these writers have for independence and identify those that are not explicit within the document itself.

3. Debate the plausibility of the following statement: "The frequent intrusions of personal feeling into the letters of John and Abigail Adams reflect more than the intersection of personal and public life; they also suggest a change in values that would inspire other political and cultural revolutions at the turn of the nineteenth century."

Thomas Jefferson

1. Analyze specific ways in which *The Declaration of Independence* demonstrates the influence of eighteenth-century thought.

2. Based on class discussion, recapitulate the ways *The Declaration of Independence* uses literary devices to achieve its power.

3. Describe the evidence of Franklin's interests in "self-invention" in *The Autobiography,* and suggest ways in which Jefferson, with the assistance of Franklin, carries these interests into the political sphere of *The Declaration of Independence.*

4. Write a linguistic analysis of the antislavery grievance from *The Declaration of Independence* that the Continental Congress eliminated from its final version.

5. Edwin Gittelman has called *The Declaration of Independence* a slave narrative. In the colonial period, the only indigenous precedent for such a form was the Indian captivity narrative, represented in NAAL by Mary Rowlandson's *Narrative of the Captivity and Restoration.* Compare and contrast the form of Rowlandson's narrative with Jefferson's text, and explore the extent to which *The Declaration of Independence* may be considered a variant on the genre of Indian captivity narrative.

Olaudah Equiano

1. Examine those points of resemblance between Elizabeth Ashbridge's *Some Account* and Olaudah Equiano's *Narrative.* What does Ashbridge confirm about the horrors of servitude? What does Equiano tell us about the role the Quakers played in the struggle for human freedom?

2. Reread the early chapters of Bradford's *Of Plymouth Plantation* and contrast the portrait of life aboard the *Mayflower* with Equiano's account of life aboard the slave ship. Consider the various meanings different colonial authors attribute to the word *removal.*

Philip Freneau

1. Although Freneau's *To Sir Toby* is ostensibly about a sugar planter on the island of Jamaica, examine the poem for evidence that Freneau is also writing about southern slavery. Locate references to slavery in his other anthologized

poems and summarize the way slavery, for Freneau, contradicts eighteenth-century principles of reason and human rights.

2. Evaluate the language of Freneau's historical poems against specific passages in Paine or Jefferson, and discuss the relative effectiveness of political and poetic voices within the context of American revolution.

Phillis Wheatley

1. Locate and discuss imagery in Wheatley's poems that directly or indirectly comments on her experience as a freed slave.

Royall Tyler

1. Explicate *The Contrast*'s "Prologue" as Tyler's commentary on his own play.

2. Analyze references to style and fashion in *The Contrast.* Discuss ways in which Tyler uses these to convey the beginnings of American cultural identity.

1820–1865

HISTORICAL QUESTIONS

1. Discuss the following statement with reference and relevance to specific literary works: the Puritans were typological, the eighteenth-century writers were logical, but the early-nineteenth-century writers were analogical in their way of knowing and expressing what it means to be an American.

2. Discuss changes in the concept of the American self in the early nineteenth century. Locate your discussion within specific works by Emerson, Thoreau, and Hawthorne.

3. Cite several fundamental differences between early-nineteenth-century writers and their deist predecessors. Focus on the concept of self-invention and, in specific literary works, discuss the early-nineteenth-century evolution of this concept.

4. Research and explain the theory of romantic organicism in Bryant and Poe, at the same time exploring differences between these two poets.

5. Consider literary portraits of women engaged in heroic struggle or of escaping slaves portrayed as heroic fugitives. Compare and contrast portraits by Stowe, Fuller, Jacobs, and Douglass with Hester Prynne in *The Scarlet Letter* or Thoreau's autobiographical narrator in *Walden.*

6. Read some of Elizabeth Cady Stanton's lectures, addresses, and letters (not anthologized). Then compare and contrast *The Declaration of Sentiments* (1848, see Appendix) with its model, *The Declaration of Independence.* Analyze the nineteenth-century document with respect to style, imagery, concepts of nature and authority, and relative political effect.

7. Whether or not the earliest American realists wrote in a distinctive and innovative form, they make different choices of language and genre than their contemporaries. Choose to analyze a text by any of the following writers and explore elements of realism in the work: Longstreet, Stowe, Thorpe, Stoddard, and Davis.

QUESTIONS ON INDIVIDUAL AUTHORS AND WORKS

Washington Irving

1. Compare and contrast Freneau's and Irving's uses of the historical situation as the subject of imaginative literature. What makes Irving more successful, and why is he more successful?

2. Discuss several different ways in which *Rip Van Winkle* addresses versions of the American dream.

3. Compare Rip Van Winkle with Franklin's Father Abraham in *The Way to Wealth.* What do the two have in common?

4. *Rip Van Winkle* is an early work that casts the American woman as the cultural villain. Analyze the character of Dame Van Winkle in the story and discuss the significance Irving attributes to her death.

5. Although Irving's *Rip Van Winkle* and *The Legend of Sleepy Hollow* may make it appear that Irving wrote primarily fiction, a reading of the longer *Sketch-Book,* in which these stories first appeared, makes it clear that for Irving himself writing the literary sketch both preceded and made it possible for him to write works we now consider stories. For an out-of-class essay, read *The Sketch-Book* and write an essay in which you describe the various literary genres that Irving uses in the book. Then focus on either *Rip Van Winkle* or *The Legend of Sleepy Hollow* and explore both what the story's form shares with the other works in *The Sketch-Book* and how it deviates from them. Speculate on what, in either story, makes it possible for Irving to cross over into fiction.

The Cherokee Memorials

1. Based primarily on direct references or inferences you can draw from the Cherokee Memorials, write an essay in which you describe the Cherokees' particular economic, cultural, and political situation in Georgia at the time of the writing of these Memorials. If you consult any historical source(s) to verify your inferences, provide appropriate citations.

2. Summarize the argument or arguments that the Memorials urge on members of the Senate and House.

Augustus Baldwin Longstreet and the Old Southwest Humorists

1. Create a composite type of the Old Southwest humorist storyteller by analyzing the narrators in one tale by each of Longstreet, Thorpe, and Harris.

2. Critics have noted the influence of Washington Irving's *The Legend of Sleepy Hollow* on the development of Southwest humor. Analyze Irving's charac-

ter Brom Bones as a precursor of Sut Lovingood or another "ring-tailed roarer" from the humorist group.

3. Contrast the portrait of women in Longstreet's *A Sage Conversation* and Harris's *Mrs. Yardley's Quilting* with Stowe's portrait of Huldy in *The Minister's Housekeeper*. Generalize, to comment on the divergence between "Southwest humor" and early regionalism.

4. Read Samuel Clemens's short essay *How to Tell a Story* (NAAL, Volume 2). Choose one of the tales by the Old Southwest humorists and evaluate the humor and the effectiveness of the narrator by Clemens's standards.

William Cullen Bryant

1. In his essays, Emerson repeatedly called for the emergence of an American poet. Focusing on Bryant's *The Prairies*, argue that Bryant satisfied, in part, Emerson's demand. In what ways does Bryant move away from imitating British poetry? In what ways does the poem address American themes?

William Apess

1. Write an essay in which you explore *An Indian's Looking-Glass for the White Man* as an American work. To what extent does it address American themes? To what extent does the emergence of a Native American literature in the English language coincide with and contribute to the emergence of an indigenous (here, as distinguished from imitative) American tradition?

2. Compare and contrast Apess's *Indian's Looking-Glass* with Frederick Douglass's *The Meaning of July Fourth for the Negro*.

3. William Cullen Bryant wrote his poem *The Prairies* within a year of Apess's *Indian's Looking-Glass*. Read *The Prairies* with Apess's perspective and comment on Bryant's portrait of "the red man" in light of Apess's text.

Ralph Waldo Emerson

1. Discuss one of the following statements from *Nature:* (a) "The use of natural history is to give us aid in supernatural history. The use of the outer creation, to give us language for the beings and changes of the inward creation"; (b) "A man is a god in ruins. When men are innocent, life shall be longer, and shall pass into the immortal as gently as we awake from dreams."

2. Trace Emerson's thinking, image patterns, and particular forms of expression in one of the poems.

3. Explain why the poet is so important for Emerson, summarizing his argument in *The Poet*.

4. Discuss the usefulness of analogy for Emerson. Choose several analogies he creates in *Nature* and explain their significance.

5. Explore any one of the following central concepts in Emerson's work in the context of your reading: the spiritual vision of unity with nature, the significance of language in achieving spiritual vision, basic differences between thinking and writing by means of analogy and by means of discursive logic, the theme of self-reliance, and the significance of self-expression.

6. Explain how Emerson's philosophy, as he expresses it in *Nature*, represents the culmination of what it means to be an American in his time and place.

7. Explore what Emerson says, explicitly or implicitly, about race, class, or gender in American culture, and analyze Emerson's position in light of subsequent American history and political thought. If you choose to interpret Emerson from within an ideological position, define the terms of that position and analyze the way it distorts at the same time that it illuminates Emerson's work.

Nathaniel Hawthorne

1. Explicate character, theme, language patterns, style, use of point of view, setting, or design in any particular short story or in *The Scarlet Letter*. (The problem with assigning one of these topics, of course, is that you then have to deal with the standard interpretations students are likely to find if they go straight to the library. If I use a version of this question, I use it in in-class writing where the only book they may use is NAAL.)

2. View the video adaptation (if you have one in your library) of *Young Goodman Brown*. After examining the way the video interprets Brown's dream, argue that the adaptation is or is not a useful "reading" of the story.

3. Explain what Melville means by Hawthorne's "blackness" in his essay *Hawthorne and His Mosses* and discuss it with specific references to any two of the stories in the text (or any three, or with reference to specific characters in *The Scarlet Letter*).

4. Explore the moral ambiguity in any given Hawthorne character or work. What does reading *Rappaccini's Daughter* (or *The Minister's Black Veil* or *Young Goodman Brown*) do to the reader's ability to discern "good" and "evil" characters?

5. Consider Hawthorne's presentation of women in his fiction. What attitudes inform his portraits of Beatrice Rappaccini, or of Hester Prynne?

6. Consider the relationship between "The Custom-House" and *The Scarlet Letter*. Where does the narrator stand in each work? In what ways might we consider "The Custom-House" an integral part of the longer fiction? Consider the particular use of "The Custom-House" as a way of "explaining" or delaying the fiction: might "The Custom-House" serve as Hawthorne's "black veil" in facing his readers?

7. Given the autobiographical references in "The Custom-House," consider the possibility that each of the major characters in *The Scarlet Letter* might also be aspects of the narrator's own persona. Discuss ways in which Hester Prynne,

Arthur Dimmesdale, Roger Chillingworth, and Pearl complement each other thematically.

8. Given your earlier study of Puritan literature, trace elements of Puritanism in Hawthorne's stories or *The Scarlet Letter* and discuss the extent to which Hawthorne himself embraces or critiques Puritan ideology. (Compare actual Puritans you have studied with Hawthorne's fictional characters: Anne Bradstreet with Hester Prynne; Edward Taylor with Arthur Dimmesdale; Jonathan Edwards with various ministers in Hawthorne, or with the narrator himself.)

9. Locate references to childhood in *The Scarlet Letter* and, focusing on Pearl, discuss Hawthorne's portrait of what it might have been like to be a Puritan child.

Edgar Allan Poe

1. Summarize Poe's theory of aesthetics as he expresses it in *The Philosophy of Composition* and discuss his application of that philosophy in *The Raven.*

2. Explicate a short lyric (*The Lake, Preface,* or *To Helen*) and discuss Poe's creation of the persona of the poet.

3. Discuss *The Sleeper, The Raven, Annabel Lee,* and *Ligeia* in light of Poe's statement, in *The Philosophy of Composition,* that "the death, then, of a beautiful woman is, unquestionably, the most poetical topic in the world—and equally is it beyond doubt that the lips best suited for such topic are those of a bereaved lover."

4. Explain what Poe means by his attempt to achieve "unity of effect," and trace the particular ways he manages this in *Fall of the House of Usher, The Man of the Crowd,* or *The Black Cat.*

Margaret Fuller

1. Read the excerpt from Margaret Fuller's *The Great Lawsuit,* published the year before Emerson published *The Poet.* Focusing on comparison with Emerson, discuss Fuller's critique of the masculine assumptions of her generation of intellectuals.

2. At the end of the anthologized excerpt from *The Great Lawsuit,* Fuller writes: "And will not she soon appear? The woman who shall vindicate their birthright for all women; who shall teach them what to claim, and how to use what they obtain?" Going beyond the boundaries of NAAL, investigate the appearance of women speakers and political writers during the 1840s, when Fuller published her work. Research the work of Elizabeth Cady Stanton, in particular (see Appendix A to this Guide for the text of *The Declaration of Sentiments*), and argue that, just as Whitman fulfilled Emerson's prophecy at the end of *The Poet,* Stanton "soon appeared" to provide the context of continuity for the developing voices of American women in the new republic.

Harriet Beecher Stowe

1. From its origins in Harriet Beecher Stowe, regionalism as a genre took women characters and women's values seriously. Analyze Stowe's portraits of Eliza in the excerpt from *Uncle Tom's Cabin* and Huldy in *The Minister's Housekeeper*, and discuss the values explicit in Stowe's work.

2. Stowe's regional sketch *The Minister's Housekeeper* ends in comedy, with Huldy's marriage to the minister. Argue that the sketch does or does not belong to the literary tradition of early-nineteenth-century American humor.

Harriet Jacobs

1. Compare and contrast Linda Brent with Hester Prynne in *The Scarlet Letter*. See especially the following quotation from *Incidents* that equates unwed motherhood with stigma: "My unconscious babe was the ever-present witness of my shame."

2. Write a paper comparing Jacobs and Douglass and based on the following central quotations from each narrative: "Slavery is terrible for men; but it is far more terrible for women" (Jacobs) and "You have seen how a man was made a slave; you shall see how a slave was made a man" (Douglass).

3. Explore the particular obstacles Linda Brent faces and their significance for women at the end of the twentieth century: sexual harassment, poor mothers' legal rights, and difficulties for advancement when faced with responsibilities and care for children.

4. Jacobs ends her narrative "with freedom, not in the usual way, with marriage." Comment on the implication here that freedom matters more to Linda Brent than marriage. To what extent does *Incidents* suggest that the "life story" is different for enslaved women than for free (white) women?

5. Identify the contradictions implied in Dr. Flint's promise to Linda that if she moves into the house he has built for her, he will "make her a lady."

Henry David Thoreau

1. Discuss one of the following statements from *Walden:* (a) "Every morning . . . I got up early and bathed in the pond; that was a religious exercise, and one of the best things which I did"; (b) "I fear chiefly lest my expression may not be *extra-vagant* enough, may not wander far enough beyond the narrow limits of my daily experience, so as to be adequate to the truth of which I have been convinced."

2. Cite several points of connection and divergence between Emerson's *Nature* and Thoreau's *Walden.*

3. Discuss in detail one point of significant comparison between Franklin's *Autobiography* and Thoreau's *Walden* and one point of significant contrast.

4. Explain specific ways in which Thoreau's *Walden* may be considered "practice" to Emerson's theory.

5. Emerson, whose philosophy influenced Thoreau, wrote that "words are also actions, and actions are a kind of words." Write an essay on *Walden* in which you demonstrate Thoreau's insistence on the truth of this statement or apply the same quotation from Emerson to *Resistance to Civil Government*, paying particular attention to the relationship between self-expression and personal conscience.

6. Explore any of the following central concepts in Thoreau: the spiritual vision of unity with nature, the significance of language in achieving such a vision, the theme of self-reliance, the use of analogy as meditation (perhaps contrasting Thoreau with Edward Taylor), and the significance of self-expression.

Frederick Douglass

1. Discuss the extent to which Douglass may be considered a transcendentalist.

2. Compare and contrast the way Douglass sets himself up as a model with the way Benjamin Franklin does it in *The Autobiography*.

3. Douglass writes his slave narrative as a series of incidents or adventures. Discuss the picaresque elements of the *Narrative of the Life*.

4. Compare Harriet Jacobs, *Incidents in the Life of a Slave Girl*, with Douglass's *Narrative*. Was the model of "heroic fugitive" possible for female slaves? Jacobs's *Incidents* depicts the network of relationships within the slave community and between black and white communities. Look for evidence of such a network in Douglass's *Narrative*. What explains Douglass's lack of attention to emotional connections?

5. In his prefatory letter to the *Narrative*, abolitionist Wendell Phillips compares Douglass with the signers of *The Declaration of Independence*: "You, too, publish your declaration of freedom with danger compassing you around." Does the *Narrative* share formal similarities with *The Declaration of Independence* as well as rhetorical ones? Compare Jefferson's characterization of the British king and his itemizing of grievances with the design and structure of Douglass's *Narrative*.

6. Compare and contrast A *Narrative of the Captivity and Restoration of Mrs. Mary Rowlandson* with *Narrative of the Life of Frederick Douglass, an American Slave*. What formal, thematic, and historical continuities exist between these indigenous genres?

7. In *The Meaning of July Fourth for the Negro*, Douglass writes that the reformer's heart "may well beat lighter at the thought that America is young," and that "were the nation older," its "great streams" may dry up, leaving "the sad tale of departed glory." Explain why Douglass takes hope from America's youth, and contrast this expression with the twentieth-century poet Robinson Jeffers's sentiments in *Shine, Perishing Republic*.

8. Trace Douglass's views concerning the role of reform and dissent in the American republic in *The Meaning of July Fourth for the Negro.*

Walt Whitman

1. Write an essay in which you analyze A *Noiseless Patient Spider* (or *I Sit and Look Out,* or any other short lyric poem) within the context of *Song of Myself.*

2. Focusing on the following two quotations—from *Nature:* "I become a transparent eyeball. I am nothing. I see all" and from *Preface to "Leaves of Grass":* "[the greatest poet] is a seer . . . is individual . . . he is complete in himself. . . . What the eyesight does to the rest he does to the rest"—discuss thematic, philosophical, and technical connections between Emerson and Whitman.

3. Compare Emerson's *The Poet* with *Preface to "Leaves of Grass."* In what ways does Whitman claim to embody Emerson's idea of the American poet?

4. Choose one of the following quotations from *Song of Myself* and discuss it by suggesting several ways in which it describes what Whitman is attempting in the poem: (a) "I know I am solid and sound, / To me the converging objects of the universe perpetually flow, / All are written to me, and I must get what the writing means"; (b) "I am an acme of things accomplish'd, and I am an encloser of things to be"; (c) "I know I have the best of time and space, and was never measured and never will be measured."

5. Discuss Whitman's poetry as a culmination point in the development of American identity. How does Whitman contribute to the ongoing evolution of self-reliance? of human freedom? of concepts of democracy?

6. Analyze the form of *The Sleepers.* How does the speaker characterize himself? Is the poem a variation on an American dream?

7. Trace Whitman's various responses to the Civil War throughout the poems anthologized from *Drum-Taps.* Compare and contrast Whitman's war poems with the anthologized lyrics from Melville's *Battle-Pieces.*

8. Do a study of Whitman's use of the catalog as a poetic device. Then illustrate, by means of close analysis, the effects Whitman achieves in a particular catalog from *Song of Myself* or in the poems *There Was a Child Went Forth* and *The Sleepers.*

9. Alternatively, study and illustrate Whitman's use of parallel construction as a poetic device in the same poems.

10. Analyze Whitman's extensive use of ecstatic language in *Passage to India.* How does it differ from the language of *Song of Myself*? How does *Passage to India* refine Whitman's vision?

11. Read *Live Oak, With Moss* in conjunction with Douglass's question, "What to the slave is the fourth of July?" Trace the contradictions and inconsistencies Whitman expresses in this sequence of poems and compare and contrast it to the contradictions and inconsistencies Douglass expresses in his speech.

Herman Melville

1. Argue that in describing Hawthorne's "power of blackness" in his review of *Mosses,* Melville was actually characterizing his own work. Focus on *Benito Cereno* in your analysis and consider whether or not Melville focuses on black slaves as human beings.

2. Newton Arvin has written about *Benito Cereno* that "the story is an artistic miscarriage, with moments of undeniable power." Evaluate the fairness of this statement given your own reading of the story.

3. Imagine a retelling of *Benito Cereno* in which Babo becomes the hero. What particular inconsistencies within the story as it stands would the narrator have to resolve?

4. In Chapter 54 of *Moby-Dick,* Ishmael, the narrator, relates a tale of mutiny he once narrated—long before "telling" *Moby-Dick* itself—to a group of Spanish friends "smoking upon the thick-gilt tiled piazza of the Golden Inn." The story may appear to be as much a rehearsal for Melville's later stories as it was for *Moby-Dick* itself. Focusing either on *Benito Cereno* or on *Billy Budd, Sailor* in light of "The Town-Ho's Story," examine Melville's later explorations of mutiny or feared mutiny and the characters who develop or refine attributes Melville embodies in Steelkilt and Radney.

5. *The Encantadas* may appear to demonstrate Melville's powers of observation, and yet in these sketches, as in his other work, the narrator locates his fascination as much in the symbolic significance he attributes to nature as in the scene itself. Explore the particular symbolism of *The Encantadas* and link it to the symbolism of any other Melville work you have read in the course.

6. In *The Tartarus of Maids,* Melville appears to identify with the maids; in *Billy Budd, Sailor,* he gives Billy feminine characteristics. Reconstruct, from these two works and from "Sketch Eighth" of *The Encantadas,* Melville's portrait of the feminine.

7. Part of what fascinates the reader (and possibly Melville himself) about Bartleby is his inscrutability. Describe the various "walls" Bartleby finds himself trapped behind and explore the ways in which the story's structure or design reinforces the reader's inability to penetrate the inscrutability of those walls.

8. Choose any one of the following moments of dialogue in Melville and use it as a prism through which to "read" the work in which it appears: (a) " 'Ah, Bartleby! Ah, humanity!' " (b) " 'Follow your leader.' " (c) " 'God bless Captain Vere!' "

9. Explore the two kinds of justice Melville sets in opposition in *Billy Budd, Sailor* and discuss the moral and thematic consequences of Billy's death.

Emily Dickinson

In considering possible exam questions and essay topics for Dickinson, please refer back to my discussion of her poetry in Chapter 7. I suggest several "exercises" there and groupings of her poems—including some not anthologized in NAAL—that lend themselves readily to questions and topics.

1. Compare and contrast Whitman's *A Noiseless Patient Spider* with Dickinson's 1138 ("A Spider sewed at Night")

Study a group of poems with related themes. Then write an interpretation of one of the poems that includes your expanded understanding of the way Dickinson uses the theme in other poems in the group. Choose from among the following: (a) poems of loss and defeat: 49, 67, 305; (b) poems about ecstasy or vision: 185, 214, 249, 322, 465, 501, 632; (c) poems about solitude: 280, 303, 441, 664; (d) poems about death: 49, 67, 241, 258, 280, 341, 449, 510, 712, 1078, 1732; (e) poems about madness and suffering: 315, 348, 435, 536; (f) poems about entrapment: 187, 528, 754, 1099; and (g) poems about craft: 441, 448, 505, 1129.

3. Poems 130, 328, 348, and 824 all contain images of birds. Trace and analyze the image from poem to poem. Or study one of the following groups of poems and trace the related image pattern: (a) a bee or bees in 130, 214, 216, 348, 1405; (b) a fly or flies in 187 and 465; (c) butterflies in 214, 341, and 1099; and (d) church imagery or biblical references in 130, 216, 258, 322, 1545.

4. Closely analyze the central image in one of the following poems: 754 ("My Life had stood—a Loaded Gun—"), 1099 ("My Cocoon tightens—Colors teaze—"), or 1575 ("The Bat is dun, with wrinkled Wings—").

5. Locate images of size, particularly of smallness, in Dickinson's poetry. Working out from 185 ("'Faith' is a fine invention"), trace evidence that Dickinson perceived a relationship between size and literary authority. Alternatively, locate images of authority in the world (king, emperor, gentlemen) and contrast these with images Dickinson uses to create her own persona as poet.

6. Many Dickinson poems illustrate change in the consciousness of the poet or speaker. Choose a poem in which this happens and trace the process by which the poem reflects and creates the change.

Rebecca Harding Davis

1. Compare the relationships between Hester and Dimmesdale in *The Scarlet Letter* and between Hugh Wolfe and Deborah in *Life in the Iron-Mills*.

2. Recall what Thoreau has to say in *Walden* about the "lives of quiet desperation" most men lead. Might Hugh Wolfe, like Thoreau, have chosen to simplify his life and retreat to a pond outside of town? Compare and contrast the conditions under which Wolfe makes his art with those Thoreau describes.

3. Study all of Davis's references to Deborah, who is generally depicted as being a "thwarted woman" who leads a "colorless life." Contrast her with the korl woman. Discuss the distance Davis creates between the real and the ideal woman in Wolfe's life.

Volume 2

1865–1914

HISTORICAL QUESTIONS

1. Compare and contrast uses of humor in Clemens's *The Notorious Jumping Frog of Calaveras County*, Harte's *The Outcasts of Poker Flat*, and Freeman's *The Revolt of "Mother."*

2. Writers following the Civil War introduced a new strain of pessimism and despair into American literature. Compare and contrast evidence of this mood in Bierce's *Chickamauga* and Stephen Crane's *An Episode of War*.

3. Although frequently grouped together as local color writers, Bret Harte and Hamlin Garland reflect quite different concerns in their work than do Sarah Orne Jewett and Mary Wilkins Freeman. Examine the use of point of view in a male and a female writer from this group. Does the narrator look at or with the characters? What characters are excluded from sharing the point of view? What effect does this have on the fiction?

4. Choosing specific characters on which to base your analysis, discuss differences in the portrayal of women characters and women's experience in local color writers Harte and Garland and regionalist writers Freeman, Jewett, Chopin, and Austin.

5. In each of the following stories, the female character behaves in an unconventional way: Freeman's *A New England Nun*, James's *Daisy Miller*, and Dreiser's *Old Rogaum and His Theresa*. Analyze the female characters in such a way as to explain some of the similarities and differences between regionalism, realism, and naturalism.

6. Unlike many of their early nineteenth-century predecessors, writers following the Civil War depicted people and places that might have been real by means of referential language. Others continued to use dream imagery in their work. Analyze Bierce's *Chickamauga*, Jewett's *A White Heron*, Gilman's *The Yellow Wallpaper*, and even Wovoka's vision of the Messiah, focusing on how the use of dream, vision, or altered perception affects the realism of the fiction.

7. Many late-nineteenth-century writers wrote in response to social conditions. Present a composite picture of their concerns by discussing the following group of texts: Clemens's "Letter IV," Charlot's *[He has filled graves with our bones]*, Garland's *Under the Lion's Paw*, and Washington's "The Atlanta Exposition Address."

8. Discuss one of the following groups of works, with the goal of explaining differences between regionalist, realist, and naturalist writers: (a) Freeman's *A New England Nun*, James's *Daisy Miller*, and Dreiser's *Old Rogaum and His Theresa;* (b) Jewett's *The Foreigner*, Wharton's *Ethan Frome*, and Crane's *The Blue Hotel;* and (c) Austin's *The Walking Woman*, Howell's *Editha*, and Crane's *The Bride Comes to Yellow Sky.*

9. Reexamine the poems of Whitman or Dickinson in light of the focus on fiction by most post-1865 writers. Choose any single lyric poem and consider its patterns of language or symbolism in light of similar patterns in fiction by local color, regionalist, or realist writers.

10. Research literary history of the post-1865 period and find other poets besides Whitman, Dickinson, and Crane. Write an essay analyzing individual poems and describing the larger context of work by a white woman such as Lydia Huntley Sigourney or a black woman such as Frances E. W. Harper.

11. Examine political writing by Cochise, Charlot, Washington, and Du Bois in the context of political writing in earlier periods of American literature. Does it share the same form? Does it innovate within the form? Does it combine forms? To what extent does it comment, implicitly or explicitly, on other literary genres of the late nineteenth or early twentieth centuries?

12. Read literary historians (Fred Lewis Pattee, V. L. Parrington, Robert Spillers) for their discussions of local color and regional writing. Analyze any story in the text by Jewett, Chopin, Freeman, Austin, Chesnutt, Harte, Garland, or Oskison in light of the historical commentary.

13. Research a regional writer from your home state or region. Write an essay analyzing one of the sketches or stories by this writer.

14. Reread Howells's *Novel-Writing and Novel-Reading* and James's *The Art of Fiction* and construct the theory of realism that is possible using only these two texts.

15. Turn-of-the-century critics used the phrase *new realists* to describe the work of naturalists Crane, Dreiser, Norris, and London. Choose a work of fiction by any of these writers and consider the accuracy of the phrase. Based on your analysis, would you identify naturalism as a new genre or a derivative one (a "new" realism)? (Students interested in French literature may do a comparative essay on a novel by Zola and any of the American realist or naturalist texts, or might research some of Zola's own literary statements and evaluate those in light of statements and prefaces by Howells and James. Or read a novel by Flaubert and focus on connections between Flaubert and James.)

16. Whether in anticipation of or in the general climate of Freud's *The Interpretation of Dreams* (1900), sexuality concerns several writers of the 1865–1914 period. Analyze sexual imagery or attitudes toward sexuality in several of the following works: Howells's *Editha;* James's *The Turn of the Screw;* Jewett's *A White Heron;* Chopin's *The Awakening, At the 'Cadian Ball,* or *The Storm;* Freeman's *A New England Nun;* and Wharton's *Ethan Frome.*

17. Locate and read Mary Austin's introduction to George Cronyn's 1918 *The Path on the Rainbow*. Then analyze the imagery of the Native American texts included in the 1865–1914 section, with particular emphasis on the imagery in the songs, as a test of Austin's critical theory.

QUESTIONS ON INDIVIDUAL AUTHORS AND WORKS

Samuel Clemens

1. Many readers of *Adventures of Huckleberry Finn* consider the ending flawed—Hemingway, for example, said that Twain "cheated"—while others have praised it. Write an essay in which you either defend or criticize the novel's ending, focusing on Huck's treatment of Jim.

2. The theme of pretending is one that unifies *Adventures of Huckleberry Finn*, although the word *pretending* takes on several different meanings and levels of significance as the novel unfolds. Describe three of these, and illustrate each by analyzing a specific character, scene, or incident from the novel.

3. If one were constructing a list of "classic" American books, *Adventures of Huckleberry Finn* would almost certainly appear on the list. Explore in detail why this is the case. In what ways does Clemens take American experience as his subject? What are the elements of Clemens's language and form that readers might consider particularly "American"?

4. Explore the relationship between the symbolism of the river and Clemens's narrative design or structure in the novel.

5. Analyze Clemens's portrait of Jim in light of your reading of Frederick Douglass. Is *Adventures of Huckleberry Finn* a slave narrative, or does Clemens use the discussion of slavery as a pretext to write about some other issue?

6. Consider Huckleberry Finn as an abused child. Explore the novel as a reflection of late-nineteenth-century attitudes toward child rearing.

7. Analyze Clemens's use of humor, focusing on *The Notorious Jumping Frog of Calaveras County* or "Letter IV" and one incident from *Adventures of Huckleberry Finn*.

8. Analyze Huck Finn's language in the opening passages of *Adventures of Huckleberry Finn*. Identify specific features of his syntax and discuss how Clemens uses Huck's style as a way to construct his character.

9. Analyze evidence of dialect in Huck Finn's speech and compare it with dialects spoken by several other characters in the novel. Compare Clemens's depiction of dialect in general with that of Bret Harte, Joel Chandler Harris, or Sarah Orne Jewett.

10. Identify and discuss features of the picaresque novel that Clemens uses in *Adventures of Huckleberry Finn*.

11. Analyze Clemens's portrait of Tom Sawyer. Is he model, rival, alter ego, or mirror for Huck? Does he develop in the novel?

12. Analyze Clemens's portrait of Jim. Does he have an independent existence in the novel or does he merely reflect the way others see him? Compare his portrait with portraits of black characters in the Joel Chandler Harris tales or in Charles Chesnutt's *The Goophered Grapevine.*

13. Study the female characters in the novel. What stereotypes does Clemens use? Do any of his female characters transcend stereotype?

14. Death is a frequent motif in the novel. Comment on its various thematic and symbolic uses, and analyze in particular Huck's symbolic death in Chapter VI.

15. Write an essay on elements of theater in Clemens's work (as anthologized in NAAL), commenting on the relationship between the art and act of oral storytelling and the narrative form Clemens devises for written stories.

W. D. Howells

1. Analyze Howells's *Editha* in terms of his assertions in *Novel-Writing and Novel-Reading* that "the truth which is the only beauty, is truth to human experience," and that "the imagination . . . can absolutely create nothing; it can only compose."

2. Study *Novel-Writing and Novel-Reading* for what it tells us about Howells's attitudes toward gender and class. Consider whether the character Editha reflects those attitudes or the referential experience of late-nineteenth-century women. Contrast Editha with Freeman's character Louisa Ellis in *A New England Nun.*

Native American Oratory

1. Compare and contrast Charlot's critique of Euro-Americans with William Apess's *An Indian's Looking-Glass for the White Man."*

2. Compare Charlot's rhetorical construction of "the white man" with rhetorical constructions of "King George" in *The Declaration of Independence* and "man" in *The Declaration of Sentiments* (in the Appendix to this Guide).

3. Explore and comment on the Christian base of Wovoka's vision and the Ghost Dance religion.

Henry James

1. Examine Howells's *Novel-Writing and Novel-Reading* and James's *The Art of Fiction* and discuss points of convergence and divergence.

2. In *The Art of Fiction,* James writes, "A novel is in its broadest definition a personal, a direct impression of life." With this quotation as your point of refer-

ence, analyze the particular "impression" James is trying to create in *Daisy Miller, The Real Thing,* or *The Beast in the Jungle.*

3. James has often been called a psychological realist, more interested in the development of consciousness than in portraying character types and social reality. Discuss the extent to which this observation holds true in *Daisy Miller* or *The Beast in the Jungle.*

4. Analyze *The Real Thing* as a story in which James explicitly chooses to define the word *real,* and show how James's characterization of the Monarchs evolves a theory of fiction.

5. Although *Daisy Miller* appears to focus on the portrait of Daisy herself, a reader might argue that James's real interest is in Winterbourne. Rethink the events of the story as Daisy herself might have viewed them and suggest ways in which the author of *A White Heron* or of *A New England Nun* might have differently handled both the story and the portrait of Daisy.

6. Bring together evidence of James's interest in convention and social forms from all four anthologized stories and analyze a particular scene from one of them that illustrates James's analysis of social reality.

7. James perfected the use of point of view as a narrative device. Choose one incident from *The Beast in the Jungle* and analyze his use of point of view in that story. What does it reveal? What does it conceal? How does it achieve its effectiveness? What is its significance in terms of the story's themes?

8. In Chapter XXII of *The Turn of the Screw,* the governess writes: "I could only get on at all by taking 'nature' into my confidence and my account, by treating my monstrous ordeal as a push in a direction unusual, of course, and unpleasant, but demanding, after all, for a fair front, only another turn of the screw of ordinary human virtue." Explore James's use of the term *nature* for the governess and evaluate how it motivates her "turn of the screw of ordinary human virtue."

9. Choose an interpretation of *The Turn of the Screw* that you find particularly compelling and defend it with a close reading of the text.

Sarah Orne Jewett

1. Compare and contrast Jewett's Sylvy in *A White Heron* with May Bartram of James's *The Beast in the Jungle.*

2. The tree, the hunter, the cow, and the heron all seem to possess mythical significance in *A White Heron.* Choose to discuss one of them in relationship to Sylvy, and explore the way Jewett combines elements of folk or fairy tale and literary realism.

3. Compare and contrast the relationship between James's governess/narrator and Mrs. Grose in *The Turn of the Screw* with the relationship between the narrator and Mrs. Todd in Jewett's *The Foreigner.*

4. Read T. B. Thorpe's *The Big Bear of Arkansas* (NAAL, Volume 1). Viewing the Southwest humorists as precursors of the late-nineteenth-century local color writers, contrast Thorpe's attitude toward the bear hunt with Jewett's attitude toward Sylvy's search for the bird in *A White Heron*. Or imagine *A White Heron* told from the point of view of the young ornithologist, and explain why this other story might have been accepted for publication in the sporting magazine of the Southwest humorists, *The Spirit of the Times*.

5. Unlike Clemens, Howells, and James, Jewett did not write essays about writing or reading. Fill in the gap in literary history, using the two anthologized stories as a foundation, and write the essay that wasn't: "How to Tell a Story," by Sarah Orne Jewett. You may also choose to title the essay, "Fiction-Writing and Fiction-Reading" or "The Art of Fiction."

6. In an attempt to differentiate between regionalism and realism, compare and contrast Jewett's *The Foreigner* and James's *The Turn of the Screw* as ghost stories.

7. Research other writers in the regionalist tradition and write about work by Alice Cary, Rose Terry Cooke, Harriet Beecher Stowe *(The Pearl of Orr's Island)*, or Mary Austin, all of which are available in paperback texts.

Kate Chopin

1. Kate Chopin writes in *The Awakening*, "The children appeared before her like antagonists who had overcome her; who had over-powered and sought to drag her into the soul's slavery for the rest of her days." Using this quotation as a springboard, discuss it with respect to Aunt Sally from *Adventures of Huckleberry Finn*.

2. Consider alternative titles for Clemens's and Chopin's novels: "The Awakening of Huckleberry Finn" and "The Adventures of Edna Pontellier." Comment on the incongruity of each of these alternative titles in terms of the novels' designs, themes, and development of the central character.

3. Analyze the character of Mlle. Reisz in *The Awakening* and compare her with Louisa Ellis in Freeman's *A New England Nun*. How does Chopin limit Mlle. Reisz's possibilities and influence on Edna in her novel?

4. Edna Pontellier is caught in the contradictions between the way others see her and the way she sees herself. Identify several moments in which this becomes apparent, and show Edna's growing awareness of the contradiction.

5. Count, characterize, and analyze the numerous women of color in *The Awakening*. What does their presence and their treatment in the novel suggest about Edna's (and Chopin's) attitudes toward human development for nonwhite and poor women?

6. Find and read Elizabeth Cady Stanton's essay *The Solitude of Self* (1896) and analyze the character of Edna Pontellier in light of the essay by Chopin's feminist contemporary.

7. Some readers have described Edna's death in *The Awakening* as suicide; others view it as her attempt at self-realization. Argue the relative truth of both interpretations.

8. *The Awakening* contains elements of regionalism, realism, and naturalism. Identify these by choosing exemplary characters or scenes from the novel and basing your distinctions on close analysis.

9. Compare the relationship between Edna Pontellier and Mlle. Reisz in *The Awakening* with the relationship between the narrator and Mrs. Todd in Jewett's *The Foreigner*.

10. In *At the 'Cadian Ball*, Chopin explores the dimensions of sexual power and desire conferred by racial and class status and marked by dialect. Identify the numerous relationships among characters that can be understood in terms of power dynamics and explicate those dynamics.

11. *The Storm* serves as a sequel or companion story to *At the 'Cadian Ball*. Describe the ways Chopin differently constructs Cajun ('Cadian) masculinity in Bobinot with Creole masculinity in Laballiere and the way she differently constructs sexuality in Cajun Calixta and Creole Clarisse.

Mary E. Wilkins Freeman

1. Identify the common theme (or themes) that link *A New England Nun* and Chopin's *The Awakening* and briefly discuss the way each work develops its theme.

2. One central theme in nineteenth-century American literature portrays the individual in conflict with the community. Discuss the specific ways in which Louisa Ellis enacts this conflict.

3. Both *The Revolt of "Mother"* and *A New England Nun* portray women who triumph over the material conditions of their existence. Describe the nature of that triumph and the process by which they achieve it.

4. Examine the use of the window and the barn doors as framing devices in the two anthologized stories. As an option, read other stories in which Freeman uses framing devices (see *An Honest Soul*, *A Mistaken Charity*, *A Village Singer*, or *A Church Mouse* from *Selected Stories of Mary E. Wilkins Freeman*, edited by Marjorie Pryse). Compare form in Freeman's fiction with form in Howells, James, or Jewett.

5. Compare and contrast Oakhurst in Harte's *The Outcasts of Poker Flat* and Freeman's Adoniram Penn. Do they triumph or are they defeated men?

Charles W. Chesnutt

1. Explore the way in which Chesnutt manipulates point of view in *The Goophered Grapevine* and the effect this has on the story's ending.

2. Read the anthologized "Uncle Remus" stories by Joel Chandler Harris. Compare and contrast Chesnutt's use of the folk tale and the folk narrator with that of Harris.

3. Compare and contrast Irving's use of folk materials early in the nineteenth century with Chesnutt's use of folk materials in *The Goophered Grapevine.*

4. While almost all of the writers in the genre of regionalism were women, Charles Chesnutt uses elements of regionalism in *The Goophered Grapevine.* With references to anthologized works by Stowe (NAAL, Volume 1), Jewett, Freeman, Chopin, Austin, Oskison, and Bonnin, analyze Chesnutt as a regionalist writer.

Charles Alexander Eastman (Ohiyesa)

1. Research Elaine Goodale (perhaps by reading *Sister to the Sioux: The Memoirs of Elaine Goodale Eastman,* edited by Kay Graber, 1978) and construct a portrait of the young white women who became missionaries to the American Indians in the West.

2. Calling the adherents of the Ghost Dance religion "prophets of the 'Red Christ,' " Eastman writes about what he calls this religious "craze": "It meant that the last hope of race entity had departed, and my people were groping blindly after spiritual relief in their bewilderment and misery." Set this comment against Captain Sword's account of the Ghost Dance religion and evaluate it in terms of the confusion that becomes evident among "hostiles" and "friendlies" during the Ghost Dance War.

Hamlin Garland

1. Compare and contrast Garland's portrait of the women in *Under the Lion's Paw* with Freeman's in *The Revolt of "Mother."* How does each author present women's ability to confront poverty?

2. Garland's narrator views his characters from the outside. Analyze specific scenes in the story to show how this outsider's view predetermines the reader's understanding of the characters' actions.

3. Are the characters in *Under the Lion's Paw* individuals or types? Compare the story with Howells's *Editha.* Does the use of types or stereotypes limit the effect of realism?

Charlotte Perkins Gilman

1. How does Gilman's realism differ from the realism of W. D. Howells? Does the narrator of *The Yellow Wallpaper* recognize any correspondence between her own perception and external reality? In what ways does Gilman violate Howells's proscriptions in *Novel-Writing and Novel-Reading?*

2. Consider *The Yellow Wallpaper* as Gilman's portrait of the American woman as writer. What does the story suggest about the literary authority of the woman writer? What obstacles stand in the way of her creation? What is her ultimate work of art?

3. Compare and contrast Gilman's narrator of *The Yellow Wallpaper* with James's governess in *The Turn of the Screw*. Are both women mad? If you argue that they are, evaluate James's and Gilman's differing perspectives on women's madness.

Jane Addams

1. Explain what Addams means by her chapter's title, "The Snare of Preparation," from *Twenty Years at Hull-House.*

2. Consider James's *Daisy Miller* from the perspective Addams presents in the excerpts from *Twenty Years at Hull-House.* To what extent is James's novella a critique of women's education? To what extent is Addams's portrait of the "sheltered, educated girl" an explanation of Daisy Miller's vulnerability?

Edith Wharton

1. Compare and contrast James's Daisy Miller with Wharton's Mattie Silver in such a way as to illustrate differences between Wharton's realism and that of Henry James.

2. Consider the relationship to landscape that Jewett's Mrs. Todd in *The Foreigner* or Freeman's Louisa Ellis in *A New England Nun* appear to have. How does Wharton's use of landscape contrast with that of Jewett and Freeman?

3. Compare Ethan Frome with Irving's Rip Van Winkle, Melville's Bartleby, or Hawthorne's Wakefield. Argue that, for all her interest in the narrative technique of the late nineteenth century, Wharton's thematic interests more closely resemble her male predecessors and those of romantic American fiction.

4. In her critical biography of Edith Wharton, *A Feast of Words,* Cynthia Griffin Wolff identifies the motif of the threshold in *Ethan Frome* and associates it with the novel's central theme. Examine references to thresholds throughout the novel, consider their thematic significance, and write an essay based on the implications for character and theme.

5. Compare and contrast the marital relationship between Wharton's Zeena and Ethan Frome in *Ethan Frome,* and Freeman's Sarah and Adoniram Penn in *The Revolt of "Mother."*

Mary Austin

1. A number of fictions by writers in the late nineteenth century are "studies" of women. Compare Austin's *Walking Woman* with other "studies," such as Howells's *Editha* or James's *Daisy Miller.*

2. Austin writes Western literature from the perspective of the insider. Compare and contrast her portrait of the West with that of Bret Harte in *The Outcasts of Poker Flat,* Gertrude Simmons Bonnin in *Impressions of an Indian Childhood,* or Stephen Crane in *The Bride Comes to Yellow Sky.*

3. Interpret the narrator's final perception of the Walking Woman at the end of Austin's story. What does she believe she learns from her moments of contact with this woman? How does the Walking Woman confound the stereotypes others hold of a woman's life?

4. Read Mary Austin's introduction to George Cronyn's collection of Indian poetry, *The Path on the Rainbow* (1918). Summarize her perspective on Native American poetry and apply it to the images in the songs and chants included in NAAL.

5. Read Mary Austin's fiction that focuses on Native American protagonists, either "The Basket Maker," from *The Land of Little Rain* (1903), or her play *The Basket Woman* (1904). Analyze her representation of Native American characters in light of the anthologized texts in NAAL.

W. E. B. Du Bois

1. Explore the points of conflict between Du Bois and Booker T. Washington, as illustrated in the anthologized selections from both writers. What reality do African-American people face, according to Du Bois? Do they inherit it? Can they change it? And in what way is their identity contingent on that reality?

Frank Norris

1. Locate Norris's allusions to animals and animal-like behavior in the excerpt from *Vandover and the Brute.* Analyze what he is trying to say about human motivation and character.

2. Compare and contrast the correspondent from Stephen Crane's *The Open Boat* with Norris's Vandover. Analyze the prose style, thematic content, use of narrative point of view, and portrait of human nature that these works convey.

Stephen Crane

1. Analyze the natural "forces" that the characters struggle against in *The Open Boat.* How do they deal with their lack of control over those forces?

2. *An Experiment in Misery* suggests that society is made up of forces beyond an individual's control. Trace the protagonist's encounter with these forces, and

analyze the language by which Crane personifies the malicious intent of the city's misery.

3. Despite the apparent irrationality of its characters, *The Blue Hotel* moves logically and inexorably toward its conclusion. Study the evidence of irrationality in the story's portraits of human behavior; then describe the linear progression by which the Swede's initial comment—" 'I suppose there have been a good many men killed in this room' "—comes to control events.

4. In *The Bride Comes to Yellow Sky,* Jack Potter's marriage appears to alter forever Scratchy Wilson's perception of reality. Argue that, for Crane, marriage itself becomes an external force. Does the story's humor mitigate the oppressiveness of this force?

5. Explore the relationship between Crane's poems and his fiction. Does Crane's choice of the lyric poem allow him to develop aspects of his major themes that his fiction does not fully explore?

Theodore Dreiser

1. Examine the portrait of family life Dreiser presents in *Old Rogaum and His Theresa.* What forces make it, like the city in Crane's story, such "an experiment in misery"?

John M. Oskison

1. Write a research paper in which you locate *The Problem of Old Harjo* in the history of Christian intervention in the lives of Native Americans in the nineteenth century. Cite evidence from other anthologized texts, including William Apess's *An Indian's Looking-Glass,* Charles Alexander Eastman's *From the Deep Woods to Civilization,* Wovoka's vision, and Gertrude Simmons Bonnin's *Impressions of an Indian Childhood.*

2. Explore William Apess's figure of speech, the "Indian's looking-glass," as it applies to *The Problem of Old Harjo.* To what extent does Harjo possess the cunning of the powerless? To what extent is Harjo the powerless character in the story?

Henry Adams

1. Henry Adams writes in his *Education* that "From earliest childhood the boy was accustomed to feel that, for him, life was double." Explain the significance of Adams's particular kind of "double vision." Compare it with the internal contradiction Edna Pontellier feels in *The Awakening* and the "double consciousness" of Du Boisean black identity.

2. What happens to Adams's perception of design and order in the universe over the course of his *Education?* How does it happen that "he found himself lying in the Gallery of Machines at the Great Exposition of 1900, his historical neck broken by the sudden irruption of forces totally new"?

3. Explain and comment on the following statement from the *Education:* "Adams began to ponder, asking himself whether he knew of any American artist who had ever insisted on the power of sex, as every classic had always done; but he could think only of Walt Whitman; Bret Harte, as far as the magazines would let him venture; and one or two painters, for the flesh-tones. . . . American art, like the American language and American education, was as far as possible sexless."

4. The anthologized chapters from *The Education* contain much evidence that Adams viewed himself as a transitional figure. Identify several points at which he "broke his life in halves again," and trace his progress from his early sense that the eighteenth century was his companion to his entrance into the twentieth century at the close of Chapter XXV.

5. Compare William Bradford's *Of Plymouth Plantation* and *The Education of Henry Adams.* Do the two works belong to the same genre?

1914–1945

HISTORICAL QUESTIONS

1. At the end of Frost's poem *The Oven Bird,* we find the following lines: "The question that he frames in all but words / Is what to make of a diminished thing." Making specific references to several works by other poets and prose writers, explain how this statement expresses a common theme in twentieth-century American writing.

2. Choosing several different works, discuss changes in American writers' attitudes toward God or religion in the twentieth century.

3. Compare an early-nineteenth-century poem (such as Bryant's *Thanatopsis,* NAAL, Volume 1) with an early-twentieth-century poem (Frost's *Directive*). Discuss the way both poems reflect dramatic radical shifts in paradigm or perspective in their time.

4. Choose any three twentieth-century works and show how they respond to the following quotation from Wallace Stevens's *Of Modern Poetry:* The poem of the mind in the act of finding / What will suffice. It has not always had / To find: the scene was set; it repeated what / Was in the script.

5. Explain the parallel concerns in the following statements: (a) "The poem is a momentary stay against confusion" (Frost, *The Figure a Poem Makes*); (b) "These fragments I have shored against my ruins" (Eliot, *The Waste Land*); (c) "Poetry is the supreme fiction, madame" (Stevens, *A High-Toned Old Christian Woman*).

6. Examine traditional twentieth-century lyric poems by Robinson and Millay. How does each of these poets turn traditional form to the service of twentieth-century themes?

7. Read a short story by a British modernist writer, such as Lawrence, Woolf, or Joyce. Compare and contrast it with a story by an American modernist.

8. Many modernist lyric poems are about poetic form itself. Analyze one of the following poems (or any other poems by Frost, Stevens, or Williams) with particular attention to the poet's awareness of form: *The Wood-Pile, A Quiet Normal Life,* or *To Elsie.*

9. Analyze the use of poetic forms by modernist poets. Examine the following: Frost's sonnets, *Mowing, The Oven Bird, Once by the Pacific, Design,* or *The Gift Outright* (or find and read all of Frost's sonnets in his complete poems and write about his use of the form); Stevens's use of the ballad stanza in *Anecdote of the Jar* or his use of tercet stanza form in *The Snow Man* and *A Quiet Normal Life;* Williams's near-sonnet *The Dance;* Pound's sonnet, *A Virginal,* or the poem he calls a villanelle although it is not, *Villanelle: The Psychological Hour;* or Bishop's nearly perfect villanelle, *One Art.*

10. Examine modernist poets' use of traditional metric forms. Analyze what Frost does to and with iambic pentameter in *Desert Places* or how Stevens uses it in *The Idea of Order at Key West.*

11. In the introduction to Marianne Moore in NAAL, Nina Baym writes, "Pound worked with the clause, Williams with the line, H. D. with the image, and Stevens and Stein with the word; Moore, unlike these modernist contemporaries, used the entire stanza as the unit of her poetry." In an out-of-class essay, choose poems by each of these writers that will allow you to further explain the distinctions Baym creates in this statement.

12. In British poetry, Robert Browning developed and perfected the dramatic monologue. Find and discuss dramatic monologues by several American modernists. Evaluate their uses of, or variations on, Browning's form.

13. Although American poets have not yet—according to critical consensus—produced an epic poem, several twentieth-century poets have made the attempt. Research features of classical epic poetry and identify epic characteristics in Pound's *The Cantos,* H. D.'s *The Walls Do Not Fall,* Eliot's *Four Quartets,* and Crane's *The Bridge.*

14. Locate and read one of the following modernist poetic statements, and then analyze one of the author's anthologized poems in light of what he has written about craft: Frost, *The Figure a Poem Makes* (included in NAAL); Stevens, from *The Necessary Angel;* Williams, *Edgar Allan Poe;* Pound, *A Treatise on Metre* or another essay from *The ABC of Reading;* and Crane, *General Aims and Theories.*

15. Compare and contrast the realism of a twentieth-century story with the realism of Clemens, Howells, James, or Wharton. Analyze Sherwood Anderson's *The Egg,* William Faulkner's *Barn Burning,* or Ernest Hemingway's *The Snows of Kilimanjaro,* paying particular attention to the twentieth-century writer's innovations in point of view or use of symbolism.

16. In Suzanne Juhasz's framework for twentieth-century women poets (see discussion in the Marianne Moore section of Chapter 7 in this Guide), she suggests a progression from Moore to Muriel Rukeyser to Sylvia Plath and Anne

Sexton to Adrienne Rich in terms of the particular writer's willingness to write about women's experience in poetry. Choosing specific poems for your focus, trace this progression and comment on its usefulness as a framework.

17. Although traditionally the period 1914–1945 has focused on modernism, numerous writers during the period wrote political poetry that may have been influenced by modernism but reflects other artistic intent. Analyze representative poems by Genevieve Taggard, Muriel Rukeyser, Sterling Brown, and Langston Hughes for evidence of political intent in poetry, and comment on the relationship between this poetry and what we call modernism.

18. Although the modernist poets do not explicitly concern themselves with gender, race, or class issues, there are exceptions to this statement. Discuss the relationship between modernism and gender in H. D., race in Langston Hughes, and class in Muriel Rukeyser.

19. While writers like Pound and Eliot were concerned with tracing the origins of modernist consciousness in classical mythology, other writers were more interested in becoming assimilated into American society. Identify and discuss the issues of concern to writers, fictional characters, or lyric voices who concern themselves with issues of immigration and assimilation.

QUESTIONS ON INDIVIDUAL AUTHORS AND WORKS

Black Elk

1. Why does Black Elk seem to think it important that his story be told? Why does John Neihardt think it is important? Do they both have the same reasons? Analyze "Heyoka Ceremony" as Black Elk's attempt at making a connection with an audience, and comment on how the chapter offers a working definition of the very process of "raising consciousness."

2. Arnold Krupat (in "The Indian Autobiography: Origins, Type, and Function," *American Literature,* 1981) has written that "to see the Indian autobiography as a ground on which two cultures meet is to see it as the textual equivalent of the 'frontier.' " Write an essay in which you comment on this statement and its significance for understanding *Black Elk Speaks.*

3. In the second (1961) edition of *Black Elk Speaks,* John Neihardt changed the title page of the text from "as told to John Neihardt" to "as told through John Neihardt." Explain the significance of this change, and interpret the relationship it suggests between Neihardt and Black Elk, and between Neihardt and *Black Elk Speaks.*

4. Compare and contrast *Black Elk Speaks* with two other American texts, Benjamin Franklin's *The Autobiography,* and *Narrative of the Life of Frederick Douglass, an American Slave* (both in NAAL, Volume 1). Focus on the relationship between central narrator and autobiographical text. How does each text reflect different choices by the speaker in terms of self-presentation, connection to history, choice of significant events, and literary form?

5. Compare and contrast Gertrude Simmons Bonnin's autobiographical writing *(Impressions of an Indian Childhood, The School Days of an Indian Girl, An Indian Teacher among Indians)* and narrative voice with that of Black Elk in the excerpts from *Black Elk Speaks.* Both writers were Sioux; evaluate their respective roles as "holy man" and "teacher," comment on their different experiences with biculturalism, and compare the points at which they break off their autobiographical accounts.

7. Read Mary Austin's "Shoshone Land" and "The Basket Maker" from *The Land of Little Rain* (available in Mary Austin, *Stories from the Country of Lost Borders,* edited by Marjorie Pryse, 1987) and evaluate Austin's biculturalism in light of Neihardt's description of collaborating with Black Elk.

Willa Cather

1. Cather writes as an early-twentieth-century regionalist in *Neighbour Rosicky.* How does this story reflect the themes and point of view of earlier regionalist writers Jewett and Freeman?

2. Like Garland's *Under the Lion's Paw, Neighbour Rosicky* is set in the West. Compare and contrast the influence of place in these stories. What mitigating vision does Cather offer and how does it contrast with Garland's forces of economic despair?

Gertrude Stein

1. In characterizing her "description of the loving of repetition" in *The Making of Americans,* Stein writes, "Then there will be realised the complete history of every one, the fundamental character of every one, the bottom nature in them, the mixtures in them, the strength and weakness of everything they have inside them, the flavor of them, the meaning in them, the being in them, and then you have a whole history then of each one. Everything then they do in living is clear to the completed understanding, their living, loving, eating, pleasing, smoking, thinking, scolding, drinking, working, dancing, walking, talking, laughing, sleeping, everything in them." Apply the statement specifically as a description of what she attempts in *The Good Anna.*

2. Some twentieth-century critics have identified Walt Whitman as a modernist poet. Reread *Song of Myself* (NAAL, Volume 1) and examine the uses of the expansive first-person narrator in Whitman and in the excerpt from Stein's *The Making of Americans.* Based on what you find in Stein's experimental prose, argue that Whitman also experiments in modernist writing.

3. Analyze the linguistic transformations Stein performs on individual sentences in the excerpt from *The Making of Americans.* Locate similar sentences, identify points of transition in the prose, and compile a lexicon, and note the appearance of new and startling words.

4. *The Good Anna* depicts a series of hierarchical relationships between women. Explore the theme of power and influence in friendship, as Stein explic-

itly writes about it in Part II of the novel, and comment on Stein's view of women in general, as it emerges from the text. In contemporary terms, to what extent does Anna identify with traditionally male attitudes toward women?

5. Sarah Orne Jewett, like Gertrude Stein, lived for many years with a woman (Annie Adams Fields, the widow of Hawthorne's publisher James T. Fields) and wrote much about relationships between women in her fiction. Reread Jewett's *The Foreigner* and compare and contrast Jewett and Stein in terms of their treatment of relationships between women, their respective conception of mothers, and the extent to which their work expresses differences between regionalism and modernism.

6. Analyze closely the relationship Stein's Anna has with Jane and Edgar Wadsmith in *The Good Anna.* Compare and contrast Anna and Stein's portrait of Anna with the governess and her narrative portrait in James's *The Turn of the Screw.* Comment on the relationship between realism and modernism that the two works express. What happens if you imagine interchanging the characters in the two works?

7. Examine Stein's use of humor in *The Good Anna.* Reread Stowe's *The Minister's Housekeeper* (NAAL, Volume 1), analyze Anna's relationship with Doctor Shonjen, and consider differences between Stowe and Stein as humorists.

Amy Lowell

1. Pound termed Lowell's poetry "Amygism," perhaps as a way of minimizing its value, perhaps to distinguish it from "imagism." Locate early essays by the imagists in *Poetry* magazine (F. S. Flint, "Imagism," and Ezra Pound, "A Few Don'ts by an Imagist," both in the March 1913 issue), Lowell's own anthologies (referred to in the Lowell headnote), or any other references you can find that clarify the terms *imagism* and *Amygism.* Then compare and contrast Lowell's uses of the image with that of Pound's and Williams's, and evaluate the extent to which Lowell has been stigmatized both for writing as a "woman poet" and for writing about women's beauty.

Robert Frost

1. Analyze the narrator's attitude toward death in *After Apple-Picking* and in *An Old Man's Winter Night.* How does each poem serve as a buffer against mortality and meaninglessness?

2. Analyze one of the following poems to show how Frost's poetic technique itself serves as his own "momentary stay against confusion": *Once by the Pacific, Desert Places,* or *Design.*

3. Illustrate how Frost applies the following statement from *The Figure a Poem Makes* to his use of iambic pentameter in *Home Burial:* "The possibilities for tune from the dramatic tones of meaning struck across the rigidity of a limited meter are endless."

4. Analyze Frost's use of the sonnet form in the following poems: *Mowing, The Oven Bird, Once by the Pacific,* and *Design.*

5. One of the most striking characteristics of Frost's poetry is his creation of a speaking voice. Examine the following poems and analyze the relationship between speaker and hearer: *The Pasture, The Tuft of Flowers,* and *A Servant to Servants.*

6. Examine the image of loss of Paradise, or the Fall, in *Fire and Ice, The Oven Bird,* and *After Apple-Picking.*

7. Analyze *"Out, Out—"* in light of the last two lines of *The Oven Bird.*

8. Choose one of the following poems not anthologized in NAAL for further close analysis: *A Minor Bird, The Investment, The Hill Wife,* or *The Cow in Apple-Time.*

9. In *The Gift Outright,* Frost has written a small history of American literature. In the poem, he personifies the American land as female. Trace the imagery of sexual conquest in the poem and explore what it reveals about Frost's conception of the American poet.

10. *Directive* advises its readers to get lost to find themselves. How does this poem reflect Frost's twentieth-century worldview? What are the relative values of disorientation and reorientation? How does *Directive* offer a modern version of the American dream?

Sherwood Anderson

1. At the end of *The Egg,* Anderson's narrator writes, "I wondered why eggs had to be and why from the egg came the hen who again laid the egg." Analyze the multiple symbolism of the egg, what it comes to represent by the end of the story, and how Anderson uses it to unify his narrative.

2. Paraphrase the above quotation from *The Egg* as follows: "I wondered why stories had to be and why from the story came the storyteller who again produced the story." Each of the anthologized stories from *Winesburg, Ohio* bears some relation to George Willard. Discuss the significance of this relation, using the paraphrased quotation, if helpful.

3. Anderson and Cather were contemporaries and each chose to write about regional life. Compare and contrast the narrators of *The Egg* and *My Mortal Enemy.* What significance does the story each narrator tells have for the narrator's own developing consciousness? What role does region play in that developing consciousness?

Wallace Stevens

1. Apply Stevens's statement, "Poetry is the supreme fiction, madame," from *A High-Toned Old Christian Woman,* in close analysis of *A Quiet Normal Life.* What does Stevens mean by the concept of a "supreme fiction," and how does the man in *A Quiet Normal Life* live by it?

2. One of the most famous lines from Stevens, and one of the most enigmatic, appears in *Sunday Morning:* "Death is the mother of beauty." Summarize the major points in the argument by which the speaker in this poem transforms Sunday morning from a day of religious observance for the dead into a celebratory day of the sun.

3. Closely analyze the sun imagery in stanza VII of *Sunday Morning.* Then write an interpretation of *Gubbinal* that builds on what you have observed.

4. Both *Anecdote of the Jar* and *Study of Two Pears* take as their central focus some inanimate object. Analyze the meaning these two poems share and the syntactic and semantic techniques Stevens uses to create that meaning.

5. Discuss the particular kind of technical experiment Stevens uses in *Thirteen Ways of Looking at a Blackbird.* How does this poem convey meaning?

6. *The Idea of Order at Key West* contains two poems or singers: the woman who sings and the poem's speaker. Analyze the relationship that exists between the two of them.

7. Compare and contrast the poems of Robert Frost and Wallace Stevens, focusing on one of the following pairs: Frost's *An Old Man's Winter Night* and Stevens's *A Quiet Normal Life;* Frost's *Desert Places* and Stevens's *The Snow Man;* Frost's *Directive* and Stevens's *A Postcard from the Volcano.* In what ways do Frost and Stevens each contribute to the modernist's ways of knowing the world? (Alternatively, assign Richard Poirier's book on the two poets, *The Way of Knowing,* and ask students to critique his argument with reference to specific anthologized poems.)

8. Examine the poems in which repeated activities of (1) looking at things or (2) playing musical instruments or singing appear (see discussion of Stevens in Chapter 7 for the groups of these poems), and explore the significance of the activity for the writing of poetry in Stevens.

9. Explicate, with references to other poems by Wallace Stevens, Professor Eucalyptus's statement in *An Ordinary Evening in New Haven:* " 'The search / For reality is as momentous as / The search for god.' "

Angelina Weld Grimké

1. Amy Lowell and Angelina Weld Grimké have in common that they have been neglected by critics, that they both write love poems about women, and that they both use techniques of imagism in their poetry. Study their anthologized (and other) poems and locate finer points of comparison and contrast in their work.

2. As Baym writes, Grimké is associated with the Harlem Renaissance movement even though she was not a resident of Harlem. Compare her poetry with the work of Sterling Brown, Countee Cullen, and Langston Hughes, and explore possible differences in Grimké's treatment of racial themes.

Anzia Yezierska

1. Read another story from Yezierska's collection *Hungry Hearts*, and explore her themes of class difference and disillusionment with American promise (as she expresses them in *The Lost "Beautifulness"*).

2. Compare *The Lost "Beautifulness"* with Genevieve Taggard's poems about poor and working-class women. Evaluate their respective concerns, choice of literary genre, and effectiveness as spokepersons for their class.

3. Write an essay based on Hannah Hayyeh's statement "Democracy means that everybody in America is going to be with everybody alike." Choose other works from American literature that either explore or critique this statement.

4. Compare and contrast Hannah Hayyeh with the narrator in Charlotte Perkins Gilman's story *The Yellow Wallpaper.*

William Carlos Williams

1. At the end of *To Elsie* Williams writes, "No one / to witness / and adjust, no one to drive the car." Analyze the poem to show how he arrives at this image; then comment on how this image addresses Frost's concerns in *The Oven Bird* or *Desert Places* and Stevens's in *A High-Toned Old Christian Woman* or *Of Modern Poetry.*

2. In *A Sort of a Song*, Williams writes, "No ideas / but in things." Analyze the anthologized poems that appear to be about things rather than ideas: *The Red Wheelbarrow, Death, Classic Scene.*

3. Some of William's poems directly or indirectly address the writing of poetry. Discuss what the following poems tell us about his poetic theory: *Portrait of a Lady, Spring and All, The Wind Increases, The Term.*

4. Analyze the specific features of Williams's use of language in *To Elsie.*

5. Describe the form Williams invents in *The Ivy Crown.* Discuss the effects this form has on the reader. How does the form contribute to a reader's understanding of the poem?

6. Compare the two Williams poems that derive from paintings by Brueghel: *The Dance* and *Landscape with the Fall of Icarus.* Locate and study these paintings in the library. What relationship does Williams achieve between the visual and the verbal experience? Is it necessary to see the paintings to "see" the poems?

Robinson Jeffers

1. Compare and contrast Jeffers's use of nature in his poems with Frost's. Choose one of the following pairs: *Once by the Pacific* and *Shine, Perishing Republic*; *Birches* and *Hurt Hawks.*

2. In several poems Jeffers takes birds as his central symbol. Closely analyze *Vulture* in the context of his other bird poems, *Hurt Hawks* and *Birds and Fishes.*

3. Unlike most of his contemporaries, Jeffers locates his poems in an actual place—the central California coastline. Study his references to Point Lobos, Carmel, and Monterey. Then, closely analyze *Carmel Point*, paying particular attention to the significance of a place.

Marianne Moore

1. Moore's work resembles that of Wallace Stevens in its interest in ideas. Choose one of the following pairs of poems, focusing on your analysis of Moore, and discuss the resemblance: *The Idea of Order at Key West* and *A Grave; Of Modern Poetry* and *Poetry.*

2. Moore experiments with form and line lengths in *The Mind Is an Enchanting Thing.* Analyze this poem, paying close attention to the relationship between form and meaning. How does *O to Be a Dragon* serve as a postscript to such a discussion?

3. Like Jeffers, Moore also writes poems about birds. Compare and contrast *Bird-Witted* with *Hurt Hawks.*

4. Study Moore's work for explicit statements about what poetry is and does. Analyze these statements in light of class discussion, and construct a prose version of her poetic theory.

5. Analyze one of the following poems by Marianne Moore with the aim of describing the poem's form and demonstrating the relationship between form and meaning in the poem: *To a Snail, Poetry, The Paper Nautilus,* and *Nevertheless.*

T. S. Eliot

1. Eliot writes, in *Tradition and the Individual Talent,* that the individual personality and emotions of the poet recede in importance and his meaning emerges from his place in cultural tradition. He writes that "no poet . . . has his complete meaning alone." Examine his use of classical allusions in *Sweeney among the Nightingales.* What does a modern reader need to know to understand the allusions and how does that understanding enhance our meaning of the poem?

2. Describe the progression of images and themes in *The Waste Land,* locating the central image in each of the five sections of the poem.

3. Eliot himself considered *The Waste Land* to be "a poem in fragments." Explain why this is an appropriate description of the poem, how it addresses Eliot's twentieth-century worldview, and how he attempts to resolve the fragmentation at the end of the poem.

4. Analyze the persona of the speaker in *The Love Song of J. Alfred Prufrock* by examining the way he sees the world.

5. Like Williams, Eliot tried to achieve exactness and compression in creating his visual image. Find *Preludes* in the library and analyze Eliot's use of the image in that poem.

6. Eliot dedicates *The Waste Land* to Ezra Pound, who offered suggestions for revision. Read Pound's *Hugh Selwyn Mauberley*, published just before *The Waste Land*, and locate similarities between the two poems.

Eugene O'Neill

1. Discuss what O'Neill's character Edmund calls "faithful realism" in *Long Day's Journey into Night*. Is this play a work of realism in the Howellsian or Jamesian sense? In what way does it extend the concerns of the earlier realists to include twentieth-century concerns?

2. O'Neill suggests that modern life is more difficult for women than for men—if morphine addiction becomes a more extreme response to the modern condition than the alcoholism of Mary Tyrone's husband James. Discuss continuities between Edna Pontellier in Chopin's *The Awakening* and Mary Tyrone in *Long Day's Journey into Night*.

3. If you have studied early-nineteenth-century American literature, locate *Long Day's Journey into Night* as the culmination of themes and concerns that have set a direction in American fiction from *Rip Van Winkle* on. What does the play have to say about versions of the American dream, about individual identity, about self-reliance, about social exclusion, and about the development of consciousness?

Katherine Anne Porter

1. Trace the evolution of Miranda's expanding consciousness in *Old Mortality*. Analyze how Porter uses time to dramatize that evolution.

2. Amy makes the following statement about family: " 'The whole hideous institution should be wiped from the face of the earth. It is the root of all human wrongs.' " Discuss homelessness as a condition for the twentieth-century writer. Include in your discussion Anderson, from *Winesburg, Ohio*, and O'Neill, *Long Day's Journey into Night*.

3. Consider Porter's characterization of Miranda in the context of other portraits of American women: Chopin's Edna Pontellier and O'Neill's Mary Tyrone.

Zora Neale Hurston

1. Compare and contrast Hurston's Janie with Jean Toomer's Fern. Consider especially the development of "conscious life" for each character.

2. Finish reading *Their Eyes Were Watching God*. Analyze Janie's development as an independent person in light of class discussion of Chapter 2. Comment further on the relationship between Janie and her listening friend, Pheoby. Or trace Hurston's use of folklore through the novel and comment on its significance.

3. One of the commonplaces about American slavery is that slaveholders often separated members of slave families from each other. Analyze the excerpt from *Their Eyes Were Watching God* as Hurston's attempt to heal the lingering impact of separation imposed by slavery and sexism.

Genevieve Taggard

1. Write an analysis of Taggard's understanding of the form and function of poetry in *Definition of Song*. How does her understanding contrast with the view of her contemporary Marianne Moore, in *Poetry?*

2. Locate other poems from the 1930s in the anthology, read Taggard's poems from the 1930s, and explore to what extent this period of national economic depression provided a context for the themes and forms of its poetry.

3. Taggard, unlike Marianne Moore and even Muriel Rukeyser, seems to have no difficulty writing about women's experience. Write an essay about her representations of women's experience.

4. Compare and contrast Taggard's poem A *Middle-aged, Middle-class Woman at Midnight* with Frost's *An Old Man's Winter Night*.

F. Scott Fitzgerald

1. In Hemingway's *The Snows of Kilimanjaro*, the narrator/protagonist recalls his friend Julian, a pseudonym for Fitzgerald, and his friend's fascination with the rich. Hemingway writes, "He thought they were a special glamorous race and when he found they weren't it wrecked him just as much as any other thing that wrecked him." Consider Hemingway's description of Fitzgerald as an interpretation of what happens to Dexter Green in *Winter Dreams*. What gets "wrecked" for Dexter?

2. Many protagonists in modern American fiction strive to achieve individual goals that express their lives' meaning. Explore the diversity among these goals and meanings by analyzing what motivates the following fictional characters and comparing them with the "winter dreams" of Dexter Green: Gertrude Stein's Anna of *The Good Anna*, Zora Neale Hurston's Janie from *Their Eyes Were Watching God*, and Hemingway's Harry from *The Snows of Kilimanjaro*.

3. Analyze Dexter Green as a paradigmatic twentieth-century "modern." Discuss him in context with Anderson's Elmer Cowley in "*Queer*," Pound's Hugh Selwyn Mauberley, Eliot's J. Alfred Prufrock, or O'Neill's Edmund.

William Faulkner

1. Keep a journal of your thoughts, frustrations, and insights as you read *As I Lay Dying*. In particular, note your use of visual reading skills. Does the novel allow you to develop visualization as a reading technique, and if so, how? Pay close attention to Faulkner's effects on your actual reading process, and comment.

2. Often the use of the journey as a plot device in a novel implies character development. Which character(s) develop in *As I Lay Dying?* Analyze the evidence of character development or lack of it, and discuss how Faulkner's use of character affects interpretation in *As I Lay Dying*.

3. Faulkner once stated that he wrote *As I Lay Dying* from start to finish in six weeks, and that he didn't change a word. While Faulkner was known to exaggerate, he conveys an essential fact about this novel, that he wrote it easily, quickly, and as if it were the product of a single action. Explore the ironies inherent in such a description of the novel's creation. Compare Faulkner's description of how he wrote *As I Lay Dying* with Addie's statement, "I would think how words go straight up in a thin line, quick and harmless, and how terribly doing goes along the earth, clinging to it, so that after a while the two lines are too far apart for the same person to straddle from one to the other."

4. Throughout *As I Lay Dying,* Faulkner's characters use measurement and geometry as a way to depict the world, and Faulkner himself created a map of Jefferson County that "located" the Bundrens' journey within the larger world of his fiction. Find the map on the flyleaf of an edition of *Absalom, Absalom!* Consider Faulkner's use of spatial form and spatial relations as a unifying element in *As I Lay Dying.*

5. In class we have discussed *As I Lay Dying* as epistemology, a set of ways of knowing the world. Explore the idea of the novelist as a carpenter and *As I Lay Dying* as one of the tools—rather than one of the products—of Faulkner's trade.

6. Critics have often commented on Faulkner's use of comedy in *As I Lay Dying.* Think about the various meanings of comedy, and evaluate the extent to which *As I Lay Dying* may be considered a comic novel.

7. Examine *As I Lay Dying* from the point of view of family dynamics or social process. Is "Bundren" an identity these family members all share? What is the ontology, the way of being a Bundren? To what extent is Faulkner commenting on the American, especially the southern, family? Evaluate the perspectives with which the outsiders in the novel view the Bundrens. Which is reality? How does Faulkner demonstrate his characters constructing it?

8. Critics often associate Faulkner's portrait of the Snopeses with his perception that the "New South" following Reconstruction had lost its agrarian values. Analyze the particular "Snopesism" in *Barn Burning.*

Langston Hughes

1. Discuss what Hughes's poetry tells a reader about his theory of poetry.

2. Place Hughes's work in the context of black musical forms invented in Harlem in the early twentieth century. Is black poetry the way Hughes writes it, like jazz, a new genre? If so, is it invented or derivative? What are its characteristics? If "black poetry" is a genre, does Countee Cullen write in it?

3. Hughes's poetry makes room for the experiences of women. Analyze *Mother to Son, Madam and Her Madam,* and *Madam's Calling Card,* and explore the way he turns women's experiences into emblems of African-American experience.

4. Traditional critics have not called Hughes's poetry modernist, and yet his poetry reflects modernism both in his themes, his use of the image, and in terms

of style. Locate specific points where you can see Hughes's modernism and demonstrate it in an essay.

Richard Wright

1. Although Wright's work appeared later than the poets of the Harlem Renaissance, he reflects some of their concerns. Trace the theme of manhood in poems by Sterling Brown and Wright's *The Man Who Was Almost a Man.* What do these writers tell us about manhood as an American experience?

2. Compare and contrast Richard Wright's story with Zora Neale Hurston's prose. Are these writers exploring race or gender, or both?

AMERICAN PROSE SINCE 1945

The teaching notes on this period in Chapter 7 include questions that will work either to stimulate discussion or as exam questions or essay topics. In addition, in assigning writing on contemporary literature, I often ask students to place a story, play, or poem within the context of literary tradition, genre, or theme (see the lists in Chapter 6). Occasionally, I ask students to write an interpretation of a short story or a line-by-line analysis of the dialogue in a scene or a lyric poem in an out-of-class essay. On examinations I try to ask questions that will lead them to look at works in new ways.

1. In the opening passages of *Life-Story,* John Barth's narrator writes, "He being by vocation an author of novels and stories it was perhaps inevitable that one afternoon the possibility would occur to the writer of these lines that his own life might be a fiction, in which he was the leading or an accessory character." Explore the variety of themes and techniques by which late-twentieth-century writers depict their life stories. Include the following works in your discussion: Edmund Wilson, *The Old Stone House;* Ralph Ellison, *Invisible Man;* Norman Mailer, *The Armies of the Night;* James Baldwin, *The Fire Next Time;* Barth, *Life-Story;* and N. Scott Momaday, *The Way to Rainy Mountain.*

2. Is heroism possible in contemporary society as it is portrayed by our fiction writers? Discuss the possibilities for heroism in the following heroes or antiheroes: Vladimir Nabokov's Pnin; Saul Bellow's Tommy Wilhelm; Arthur Miller's Willy Loman; Norman Mailer's "Mailer"; Philip Roth's Sheldon Grossbart; Robert Stone's Chas Elliot; and August Wilson's Troy.

3. In their efforts to record and understand the mystery of life, many contemporary writers reflect a fascination with the grotesque, the inexplicable, or the fantastic. Compare and contrast evidence of this fascination in the following works: Eudora Welty's *Petrified Man,* Bernard Malamud's *The Magic Barrel,* Flannery O'Connor's *The Life You Save May Be Your Own* or *Good Country People,* and Thomas Pynchon's *The Crying of Lot 49.*

4. White middle-class suburban life and marriage become a central subject for several contemporary writers. Discuss the different treatment of this subject in the following works: John Cheever's *The Country Husband,* John Barth's *Life-Story,* John Updike's *The Happiest I've Been* and *Separating,* and Robert Stone's *Helping.*

5. While contemporary writers no longer take on themselves the responsibility for "defining" what it means to be an American, many continue to reflect on what Norman Mailer describes as "the forces now mounting in America" and "the intensely peculiar American aspect" of contemporary life. Discuss current criticisms or assessments of American life in the following works: Edmund Wilson's *Upstate,* Ralph Ellison's *Invisible Man,* Arthur Miller's *Death of a Salesman,* Norman Mailer's *The Armies of the Night,* James Baldwin's *The Fire Next Time,* and Thomas Pynchon's *The Crying of Lot 49.*

6. Betrayal by mothers—or by sisters—is one variation of the exploration of the influence of family on contemporary life. Stella, at the end of *A Streetcar Named Desire,* cries, " 'Oh God, what have I done to my sister?' " Explore relationships between women in Eudora Welty's *Petrified Man,* Williams's *Streetcar,* Flannery O'Connor's *The Life You Save May Be Your Own* and *Good Country People,* Bobbie Ann Mason's *Drawing Names,* and Alice Walker's *Everyday Use.*

7. Examine as a group the anthologized stories by twentieth-century southern writers Porter, Welty, and O'Connor. Do these writers alter the nineteenth-century concept of regionalism, and if so, how? if not, how do they extend the genre? Are twentieth-century regional writers also modernist writers?

8. Read Thomas Wolfe's *The Lost Boy,* and the anthologized fiction by William Faulkner, focusing in particular on their use of southern material. Do they present that material differently from the southern women writers Porter, Welty, Mason, Walker, and O'Connor or from playwright Tennessee Williams?

9. Only dramatists, among contemporary writers, appear to perceive the possibility for genuine tragedy in American character and American life. The antiheroes of fiction disappear in Tennessee Williams, Arthur Miller, and August Wilson. Despite the pathos of their lives, Blanche Dubois, Willy Loman, and Troy Maxson are tragic. Analyze one of these characters as a tragic hero, paying particular attention to the way the dramatic form precludes the experimentation of Mailer, Barth, or Pynchon. Alternatively, compare and contrast Blanche DuBois, Willy Loman, or Troy Maxson with Saul Bellow's Tommy Wilhelm in *Seize the Day.*

10. Comment on the way the American plays included in NAAL use formal divisions: O'Neill's acts in *Long Day's Journey into Night,* Williams's series of scenes in *A Streetcar Named Desire,* Miller's free movements from scene to scene in *Death of a Salesman,* and the use of scene divisions by David Mamet.

11. Compare and contrast the way Williams constructs Blanche DuBois's southern speech with the way Faulkner, Welty, or O'Connor do for their southern characters in the anthologized stories.

12. Read a play by Lillian Hellman *(Little Foxes, The Children's Hour)*, Lorraine Hansberry *(A Raisin in the Sun)*, Ntozake Shange *(For Colored Girls Who Have Considered Suicide)*, Marsha Norman *('Night, Mother)*, or Wendy Wasserstein *(The Heidi Chronicles)* and compare it with one of the plays in NAAL.

13. Locate and read one of O'Neill's earlier "expressionistic" plays written during the 1920s and compare it with *Long Day's Journey into Night.*

14. Note that three of the major plays included in NAAL were written and produced during the 1940s. Read an essay on theater history in that period and try to find out what made that decade such a productive one for drama.

15. Find a play, verse drama, or adaptation by a twentieth-century poet or fiction writer and compare it with one of the plays included in NAAL and with the poet's or novelist's other work.

16. Read anthologized selections by John Cheever, John Updike, Robert Stone, Bobbie Ann Mason, and Ann Beattie. Based on these stories, identify formal and thematic features of *The New Yorker* story. Then read a short story published in *The New Yorker* during the past year and evaluate it as an example of the "genre" of *New Yorker* fiction you have described.

17. Choose one of the following statements from contemporary American fiction or drama and argue that it articulates a central theme for postmodernist or contemporary writers. Use references to several additional writers or works in supporting your argument. (a) "The gods and I went mad together and made things as they are" (Robert Stone, *Helping*); (b) "The blow you can't see coming is the blow that knocks you out—the blow out of nowhere. How can you protect yourself against a blow out of nowhere?" (Joyce Carol Oates, *Golden Gloves*); (c) " 'You don't do *nothing,* maan, it's all a con game, you do nothing' " (David Mamet, *House of Games*); (d) " 'Everybody gets something out of every transaction' " (David Mamet, *House of Games*); (e) "There can be too much communication between people" (Ann Beattie, *Weekend*); and (f) "We are together always / There never was a time / when this / was not so" (Leslie Marmon Silko, *Lullaby*).

18. One of the central questions for readers of *Black Elk Speaks* involves understanding the meaning of biculturalism. Explore the concept of biculturalism for contemporary Native American writers N. Scott Momaday, Leslie Marmon Silko, and Louise Erdrich. Alternatively, consider the meaning of cultural assimilation for members of minority groups in America and examine the following works and their treatment of assimilation: Ralph Ellison's *Invisible Man,* Alice Walker's *Everyday Use,* Leslie Marmon Silko's *Lullaby,* and Denise Chávez's *The Last of the Menu Girls.*

19. American playwrights have often used siblings within a family to stand for divisions within the self or for two opposing forces. Consider the relationships between James Jr. and Edmund in *Long Day's Journey into Night;* Blanche and Stella in *A Streetcar Named Desire;* Biff and Happy in *Death of a Salesman;* and Troy and Gabriel in *Fences.*

20. At the end of his headnote on Louise Erdrich, William Pritchard writes: "She is a strongly regional and ethnic writer, yet in reading her one feels those qualities not as limitations but as rooted solidities out of which ranging, even universal, values and situations may be experienced." Implicit in Pritchard's statement is the assertion that the terms *regional* and *universal* are opposites and that regional and ethnic fiction may have limitations. In exploring the validity of this assertion, choose two works of short fiction included in the post-1945 section, one which you consider "regional" and one "universal" in theme or appeal. Compare and contrast the two works, in an attempt to explore the meaning of these two apparently contradictory terms.

AMERICAN POETRY SINCE 1945

1. Test the accuracy of the following statements from the poets' headnotes by evaluating them in the context of your own reading of the poet's work.

(a) Lorine Niedecker: "Like other experimental American poets, she uses the space of the page to suggest the movement of the eye and mind across a field of experience."

(b) Robert Penn Warren: " 'What poetry most significantly celebrates is the capacity of man to face the deep, dark inwardness of his nature and fate.' "

(c) George Oppen: "Oppen's distinctive measure, with its hesitancies and silences, becomes itself a measure of language's capacity to say with clarity what is real."

(d) Randall Jarrell: "He is master of the heartbreak of everyday and identifies with ordinary forms of loneliness."

(e) Richard Wilbur: " 'The most adequate and convincing poetry is that which accommodates mixed feelings, clashing ideas, and incongruous images.' "

(f) A. R. Ammons: "Ammons has often conducted experiments with poetic forms in his effort to make his verse responsive to the engaging but evasive particularity of natural process. This formal inventiveness is part of the appeal of this work."

(g) Denise Levertov: "Her overtly political poems are not often among her best, however; their very explicitness restricts her distinctive strengths as a poet, which include a feeling for the inexplicable, a language lyrical enough to express wish and desire, and a capacity for playfulness."

(h) Adrienne Rich: "Our culture, she believes, is 'split at the root.' . . ; art is separated from politics and the poet's identity as a woman is separated from her art. Rich's work seeks a language that will expose and integrate these divisions in the self and in the world."

(i) " 'I try to hold both history and wildness in my mind, that my poems may approach the true measure of things and stand against the unbalance and ignorance of our time,'" Gary Snyder has said. Throughout his life Snyder has sought alternatives to this imbalance.

(j) Sylvia Plath: "Seizing a mythic power, the Plath of the poems transmutes the domestic and the ordinary into the hallucinatory, the utterly strange."

(k) Michael Harper: "Harper writes poems to remember and to witness, but at times the urgency of the content overpowers his form and his language cannot sustain the urgency the poem asserts."

(l) Simon J. Ortiz: "His sense of contemporary life, especially its absurdities, is acute. But the America he travels conceals within it an older landscape, one animated by spirit."

(m) Rita Dove: "The experience of displacement, of what she has called living in 'two different worlds, seeing things with double vision,' consistently compels this poet's imagination."

2. Lorine Niedecker and Richard Hugo both wrote poetry about significant landscapes. Compare and contrast the technical or formal features of their attempts to create a spirit of place in their work.

3. Research Charles Olson's theory of poetics; read his manifesto, *Projective Verse,* from *Human Universe.* Extend your reading of Olson's poetry beyond the anthologized selections, then test the accuracy of the following statement from the Olson headnote: "Like certain techniques of meditation and yoga, Olson's theory seems an effort to bring mental activity (here, writing) in touch with its instinctive physical origins."

4. Many of Elizabeth Bishop's poems concern themselves with loss and exile. Examine the relationship between biography and specific poems in which these themes dominate. Then test the following statement from the Bishop headnote: "her remarkable formal gifts allowed her to create ordered and lucid structures that hold strong feelings in place."

5. Robert Hayden, Gwendolyn Brooks, and Rita Dove all wrote sequences of poems based on life in African-American communities. Compare and contrast Hayden's sequence *Elegies for Paradise Valley,* Brooks's anthologized poems from *A Street in Bronzeville,* and Dove's poems from *Thomas and Beulah.* How do all three poets make use of the technique of collage? What are their technical and thematic differences?

6. Write an essay about contemporary American poetry based on Randall Jarrell's observation, "the gods who had taken away the poet's audience had given him students."

7. The Robert Lowell headnote describes Lowell's poetry as moving between poles: of repetition and revision, of the random event and history, of New England and "elsewhere." Choose one of the anthologized poems and explore the presence of poles or tensions.

8. Almost as if they are poetic "siblings," Denise Levertov, Robert Duncan, and Robert Creeley trace their formative influences to W. C. Williams and H. D. Choosing representative poems by each of these three, related by their choice of literary models, explore "family" influence. You may choose to trace the influence of Williams or H. D., or you may focus instead on the "sibling" qualities of Levertov, Duncan, and Creeley.

9. Working out from the headnote's comment on Robert Creeley that "he may be the most self-conscious passionate poet we have," focus on several specific poems and explore the tensions in Creeley between "the self-conscious mind and the instincts of the body."

10. Allen Ginsberg's use of long lines was a deliberate experiment for him, the "long clanky statement" that permits "not the way you would *say* it, a thought, but the way you would think it—i.e., we think rapidly in visual images as well as words, and if each successive thought were transcribed in its confusion . . . you get a slightly different prosody than if you were talking slowly." Read *Howl* and other anthologized poems, paying particular attention to Ginsberg's use of the long line.

11. Frank O'Hara has written about his work, "The poem is at last between two persons instead of two pages." Explore your own sense of audience and connection with O'Hara's poems, then consider whether his statement also applies to other contemporary American poets.

12. Galway Kinnell and Philip Levine have written of Walt Whitman's influence on their work as well as their influence on each other. Choosing specific poems as the basis for your commentary, examine thematic and formal connections between Kinnell, Levine, and Whitman.

13. The John Ashbery headnote identifies Ashbery with a group of Language poets, Charles Bernstein, Lyn Hejinian, and Michael Palmer. Locate the work of one of these poets and read representative poems, in light of Ashbery's own work. Or trace the claims the headnote makes for Ashbery, that "his poems show an awareness of the various linguistic codes (including clichés and conventional public speech) in which we live and through which we define ourselves."

14. The headnote on James Wright identifies one of this poet's strengths as "a reliance on the power of a poetic image to evoke association deep within the unconscious." Yet, in many of Wright's poems, he also depicts a real, external landscape. Close-read one of Wright's poems and examine the relationship between internal and external "landscape" in his work.

15. In one of the poetry seminars that Robert Lowell taught at Boston University, both Sylvia Plath and Anne Sexton were students in the class. Imagine that they went out for coffee one night after class, and reconstruct a discussion they might have had. What might they have had to say to each other about their work?

16. More than any other contemporary American poet, Adrienne Rich has located and explicated women's lives and their relationships to each other, to their

communities, to history. Her poems also reflect her "understanding of change as the expression of will and desire." Write an essay in which you trace the continuum of women's relationships to each other that appear in Rich's poetry and in which you also locate the poems along the timeline of composition dates that Rich provides, examining evidence of what she has termed, in an essay by the same title, *When We Dead Awaken: Writing as Re-Vision.*

17. Consider the appropriateness of Audre Lorde's own phrase to describe her poetry: "a war against the tyrannies of silence."

18. Locate Simon Ortiz within the Native American tradition of literature as represented in NAAL. What themes, forms, and images link his work with earlier Native American writers, or with contemporaries Leslie Marmon Silko or Louise Erdrich?

19. Explore the themes of Simon Ortiz's poetry: traveling a journey, the power of storytelling, dislocations of American Indian identity, exploitation of the American land.

20. Explore the connections Rita Dove draws between individual moments of her personal history and larger historical forces. Compare and contrast her use of black history with that of other anthologized black women poets: Angelina Weld Grimké, Gwendolyn Brooks, and Audre Lorde.

22. All three Latino writers included in NAAL intermix Spanish phrases and lines in their work. Choose one or more of the three (Alberto Ríos, Lorna Dee Cervantes, and Denise Chávez), and analyze the effects and effectiveness of the inclusion of Spanish in the work.

23. Like other contemporary American women poets—Adrienne Rich and Rita Dove—Cathy Song writes about family ties and ancestors. Explore the power of family in Song' work.

24. Find examples of the use of traditional poetic or metric forms by post-1945 poets and analyze the relationship between form and meaning. Choose, for example, among the following sonnets or near-sonnets: Jarrell's *Well Water,* Brooks's *kitchenette building,* or any of Rich's *Twenty-One Love Poems.*

25. The following poems all reflect the autobiography of the poet: Elizabeth Bishop's *In the Waiting Room,* Robert Lowell's *My Last Afternoon with Uncle Devereux Winslow,* Allen Ginsberg's *To Aunt Rose,* James Merrill's *The Broken Home,* Frank O'Hara's *In Memory of My Feelings,* and Sylvia Plath's *Lady Lazarus.* Choose one of these poems for close analysis, locating it in the context of autobiographical poems by other writers.

26. Poems that are addressed to or are about family members tell us a great deal about differences between contemporary poets as well as family relationships in the twentieth century. Explore one of the following groups of poems: (a) mothers: Gwendolyn Brooks's *the mother* and Adrienne Rich's *Snapshots of a Daughter-in-Law;* (b) fathers: Theodore Roethke's *My Papa's Waltz,* John Berryman's *Dream Song #384,* James Merrill's *The Broken Home,* James Wright's *Autumn*

Begins in Martins Ferry, Ohio, Sylvia Plath's *Daddy,* and Li-Young Lee's *The Gift* and *Persimmons;* and (c) sisters: Denise Levertov's *Olga Poems* and Cathy Song's *Lost Sister;* and brothers: W. S. Merwin's *To My Brother Hanson.*

27. Poems addressed to other contemporary poets, living or dead, tell us a great deal about the poet writing the poem and the poet honored by the dedication. Choose any of the following poems for close analysis, working within the context of the anthologized work by the poet to whom the poem is dedicated or addressed: (a) Elizabeth Bishop's *The Armadillo,* for Robert Lowell; (b) Robert Lowell's *Skunk Hour,* for Elizabeth Bishop; and (c) Anne Sexton's *Sylvia's Death,* for Sylvia Plath.

28. Contemporary poets have written about nature in many different ways. Explore some of the variations: does nature become the object of perception and the reason for precision in language? does it serve as the symbolic projection of human emotions and fears? does it provide an alternative world within which the poet can locate a coherent vision? Choose several poems from the following list: Elizabeth Bishop, *The Moose;* James Dickey, *The Heaven of Animals;* Richard Hugo, *The Lady in Kicking Horse Reservoir;* A. R. Ammons, *Corsons Inlet;* James Wright, *A Blessing;* and Sylvia Plath, *Blackberrying.*

29. Locate and read statements on poetry by post-1945 poets; then analyze particular poems in light of the poets' statements. Choose, for example, Levertov, "Some Notes on Organic Form," from *Poet in the World;* Baraka, "Expressive Language" and other excerpts from *Home: Social Essays;* Snyder, "Poetry and the Primitive," from *Earth House Hold;* Rich, "When We Dead Awaken," from *On Lies, Secrets, and Silence.*

30. Poets often first publish their poems in small books or collections. Find and read one of the following titles, study the order of poems in the collection, and then analyze the poem included in the NAAL within the context of the other poems with which it was originally published. The titles of the anthologized poems appear in parentheses.

(a) Elizabeth Bishop, *Geography III* ("In the Waiting Room," "The Moose," or "One Art")

(b) Robert Lowell, *Life Studies* ("Memories of West Street and Lepke")

(c) Gwendolyn Brooks, *A Street in Bronzeville* ("kitchenette building" or "a song in the front yard")

(d) James Wright, *The Branch Will Not Break* ("A Blessing")

(e) Adrienne Rich, *The Dream of a Common Language* ("Twenty-One Love Poems")

31. Read the anthologized poems from one of the following connected poem sequences and describe the intertextual connections within the sequences: Gwendolyn Brooks, *A Street in Bronzeville;* John Berryman, *Dream Songs;* Adrienne Rich, *Twenty-One Love Poems;* or Rita Dove, *Thomas and Beulah.* Or ex-

tend your reading to include all of the poems in the Brooks, Rich, or Dove sequences and consider them as a single connected work.

32. What do contemporary poets have to say about some of the traditional themes of poetry: love, death, loss, or the passing of time? Choose to analyze two or three poems from one of the following groups:

(a) Love: Lorine Niedecker, [*Well, spring overflows the land*]; Robert Lowell, *Skunk Hour;* Robert Creeley, *For Love;* Adrienne Rich, *Twenty-One Love Poems;* Gary Snyder, *Beneath My Hand and Eye the Distant Hills. Your Body*

(b) Death: Randall Jarrell, *The Death of the Ball Turret Gunner;* John Berryman, No. 384 ("The marker slants, flowerless, day's almost done"); Frank O'Hara, *The Day Lady Died;* W. S. Merwin, *For the Anniversary of My Death;* Anne Sexton, *The Truth the Dead Know* or *Sylvia's Death;* Michael Harper, *Deathwatch*

(c) Loss: Theodore Roethke, *The Lost Son;* Elizabeth Bishop, *One Art;* Randall Jarrell, *Thinking of the Lost World;* James Merrill, *Lost in Translation;* W. S. Merwin, *Losing a Language;* Philip Levine, *Animals Are Passing from Our Lives;* Audre Lorde, *Separation;* and Cathy Song, *Lost Sister*

(d) The passing of time: Lorine Niedecker, *[He lived—childhood summers];* Elizabeth Bishop, *In the Waiting Room;* Robert Hayden, *Middle Passage;* Robert Lowell, *Memories of West Street and Lepke*

Part II

Questions and Topics That Emerge from Examining Literary Traditions: Some Representative Models

1. In *Of Plymouth Plantation,* William Bradford writes, "But here I cannot but stay and make a pause, and stand half amazed at this poor people's present condition; and so I think will the reader, too, when he well considers the same." With this quotation in mind, examine *Narrative of the Life of Frederick Douglass.* Look for patterns in the two prose texts: How does each construct an audience? On what terms does each writer convey a sense of beginning, of "new world," both in historical and literary terms? What specific material and ideological circumstances oppress the writers of these texts? In what way does each text establish questions that later writers will address? How do the texts differently deal with the problem of literary authority? What are the didactic purposes of the narratives?

2. Bradstreet and Wheatley were the first white and black American women to publish poetry. Examine Wheatley's poems in light of Bradstreet's *The Prologue.* Can you find any evidence of conscious encoding in Wheatley's poems? Is she aware, as Bradstreet was, that as a woman or an African-American her poems might be "obnoxious" to "each carping tongue"? Compare in particular the formal elements of Wheatley's poems with some of Bradstreet's, especially stanzas from *Contemplations, The Flesh and the Spirit,* and As *Weary Pilgrim.*

3. Consider the extent of Bradstreet's and Wheatley's acceptance of received theology by examining one of the following pairs of poems: *Contemplations* and *Thoughts on the Works of Providence; The Flesh and the Spirit* and *To the University of Cambridge, in New England;* and *As Weary Pilgrim* and *On the Death of the Rev. Mr. George Whitefield, 1770.*

4. Polemical writers in each literary tradition use rhetorical language to move their audiences. Choose works from the following writers as the basis for cross-traditional analysis: Edwards, Occom, Jefferson, Apess, Fuller, Stanton (*Declaration of Sentiments,* in Appendix A to this Guide), Charlot, Washington, and Du Bois. In particular, examine Stanton's *The Declaration of Sentiments* in the context of Jefferson's *The Declaration of Independence* and Charlot's *[He has filled graves with our bones];* consider ideological similarities between Jonathan Edwards's "great revival" thinking in *Sinners in the Hands of an Angry God,* Apess's looking-glass in *An Indian's Looking-Glass for the White Man,* and the "Atlanta Compromise" of Booker T. Washington's "The Atlanta Exposition Address"; or discuss the radicalism (for their contemporaries) of Jefferson, Fuller or Stanton, and Du Bois.

5. Show how the lyric poem develops across historical periods in the works of each of the following groups of writers: Edward Taylor, Emerson, and Whitman; Wheatley, Grimké, Brooks, and Lorde.

6. Demonstrate how concepts of black identity determine prose forms in works by the following writers: Douglass, Jacobs, Chesnutt, Hurston, Toomer, Ellison, and Walker.

7. The genre of autobiography reveals many differences between writers from separate literary traditions. Examine segments of some of the following autobiographical narratives, choosing figures from each tradition, and outline contrasts in social position and economic class, educational background, audience, or didactic purpose: Jonathan Edwards's *Personal Narrative,* Franklin's *The Autobiography,* or Hawthorne's "The Custom-House"; Jacobs's *Incidents in the Life of a Slave Girl* or Hurston's *How It Feels to Be Colored Me;* Equiano's *The Interesting Narrative,* Douglass's *Narrative,* or Baldwin's *The Fire Next Time;* Eastman's *From the Deep Woods to Civilization,* Black Elk's *Black Elk Speaks,* or Momaday's *The Way to Rainy Mountain.*

8. Some writers, while not choosing the genre of autobiography, still include enough autobiographical allusions in their poetry or fiction to tantalize the reader or critic. Consider the use of autobiographical material in literature outside the genre of autobiography from several traditions, perhaps choosing from among the following lists: Edward Taylor, Thoreau, Whitman, Melville, or Robert Lowell; Bradstreet, Dickinson, Gilman, Porter, Levertov, or Rich; Wheatley, Grimké, or Brooks; Brown, Hughes, Ellison, or Harper.

9. In an out-of-class essay, consider points of connection, useful contrasts, or central themes in each of several works that may be considered focal points for their respective literary traditions: Douglass's *Narrative,* Clemens's *Adventures of*

Huckleberry Finn, Chopin's *The Awakening*, and Momaday's *The Way to Rainy Mountain*.

10. Examine a play by Susan Glaspell (such as *Trifles*), Baraka (such as *Dutchman*), or Lorraine Hansberry (such as *A Raisin in the Sun*) in the context of class discussion of O'Neill's *Long Day's Journey into Night*.

11. Choose a pivotal writer in a tradition other than white male. Write an essay in which you compare the perspective a reader achieves in examining a particular text within the context of the writer's literary tradition with the perspective he or she might have in placing the text within the context of the writer's white male contemporaries. Useful writers for this assignment include: Jewett, Cather, Austin, or Welty; Hurston, Brooks, or Walker; Chesnutt, Brown, Hughes, or Richard Wright; or Eastman, Bonnin, Momaday, and Erdrich.

12. Analyse the following lyric poems from different literary traditions: Frost, *The Gift Outright;* Brooks, *kitchenette building;* Rich, *Twenty-One Love Poems;* Ortiz, *Poems from the Veterans Hospital;* Ríos, *Madre Sofía;* Cervantes, *Visions of Mexico;* Song, *Chinatown;* and Lee, *Persimmons.* Focus on the disparate voices and perspectives the poems reveal.

13. Examine characters who have been created by writers of the opposite gender. Choose to compare a male protagonist created by a woman writer, such as Rosicky in Cather's *Neighbour Rosicky* or Mr. Shiftlet in O'Connor's *The Life You Save May Be Your Own,* with a female protagonist in a male writer's fiction, such as Hawthorne's Beatrice Rappaccini, James's Daisy Miller, or O'Neill's Mary Tyrone.

14. Compare black characters created by white writers with black characters created by black writers, in pairings such as Melville's Babo and the autobiographical persona in Douglass's *Narrative;* Stowe's Eliza and Linda Brent in Jacob's *Incidents in the Life of a Slave Girl;* Clemens's Jim and Chesnutt's Uncle Julius.

15. Compare women characters created by male writers, such as Irving's Dame Van Winkle, Hawthorne's Hester Prynne, James's Daisy Miller or May Bartram, O'Neill's Mary Tyrone, Toomer's Fern, Faulkner's Addie Bundren or Dewey Dell, or Williams's Blanche DuBois, with women characters created by female writers, such as Stowe's Eliza, Jewett's Sylvy *(A White Heron),* the narrator of Gilman's *The Yellow Wallpaper,* Edna Pontellier in Chopin's *The Awakening,* Porter's Miranda, or Walker's Mama *(Everyday Use).*

16. Read works by writers outside the list of major authors in the literary traditions approach that illuminate questions of cross-gender or cross-racial interest or that increase our understanding of the development of literary traditions and explain how and why they are significant. Choose from the following list: Mary Rowlandson, *A Narrative of the Captivity and Restoration* (to examine a Euro-American woman's view of Native American men); Edgar Allan Poe, poems and stories about women; Rebecca Harding Davis, *Life in the Iron-Mills* (to raise is-

sues of class and working conditions in pre–Civil War industrialism); W. D. Howells, *Editha* (to examine another realist's portrait of a woman character); Joel Chandler Harris (for a white man's transcription of black folk life); Henry Adams, "The Dynamo and the Virgin" from *The Education* (for a white male writer's sense of woman as a source of symbolism); Sherwood Anderson, "Mother" from *Winesburg, Ohio* (to compare a woman character by a writer who deeply influenced Faulkner with one of Faulkner's own female characters); William Carlos Williams, *Portrait of a Lady* (a poem that raises questions of literary convention); H. D., *Leda* or *Helen* (a woman poet's sense of woman as a source of mythology); Dorothy Parker, sketches (for an example of humor in the white women's tradition); Thomas Wolfe, *The Lost Boy* (another example of a writer using autobiographical material in a genre other than autobiography); Hart Crane, *At Melville's Tomb;* John Berryman, *Homage to Mistress Bradstreet;* Allen Ginsberg, *On Burroughs' Work;* and Anne Sexton, *Sylvia's Death* (for questions of literary influence).

17. Examine the southern tradition as represented in NAAL. Focus in particular on those writers who do not figure as major authors in any literary tradition, such as John Smith, Byrd, Longstreet, Thorpe, George Harris, Wolfe, Warren, or Dickey. What generic or thematic concerns link some of these writers? Can you describe the development of southern literature in a chronological reading of the representative figures in NAAL? In examining writers from the literary traditions, to what extent are their works informed by southern history or identity? Consider minority writers in the context of their chronological contemporaries. Are Douglass, Hurston, or Richard Wright anomalous in their respective literary periods when we consider them as southern, rather than as black or women writers? Consider writers in different genres, such as Byrd and Jefferson; Poe and Douglass; Faulkner or Wolfe; Dickey or Warren; and Welty or Walker. Are these writers so diverse in form and theme that their southern ties become negligible, or does that southern heritage link them significantly, in spite of their differences?

18. Define a literary tradition on your own according to genre or theme. Defend your list of writers and works, and choose for class analysis a particular work that both represents your larger list and illustrates its central concerns. (Some possibilities include the writers interested in protest, populist, or activist themes—Gilman, Ginsberg, and possibly Mailer; or women who wrote works with feminist themes or characters, such as Bradstreet, Fuller, Stowe, Stoddard, Dickinson, Davis, Jewett, Chopin, Freeman, Gilman, Wharton, Cather, Stein, H. D., Porter, Parker, Hurston, Welty, Walker, Sexton, Rich, and Plath—you may break down this list into feminist writers by century or by genre or by region; writers interested in animals; lesbian and gay writers or writers interested in lesbian or gay themes.)

19. Study the Jewish writers represented in NAAL—Yezierska, Rukeyser, Malamud, Miller, Bellow, Roth, and Ginsberg. Choose a representative text for close analysis and view it either within the context of other works in the tradition, with works by the writer's contemporaries from a variety of traditions, or paired with a significant work from another tradition.

20. Study the relationship between marginality and vision or social stigma and literary authority in works by white male writers: (a) The colonial period appears to be unique in American literature, in that it did not produce white male writers who considered themselves marginal (with the exception of Roger Williams and John Woolman, who were not part of the Puritan community). Speculate concerning some of the reasons why this is the case. Might the absence of men who wrote against the established ideology have somehow made it easier for Anne Bradstreet to write at all? (None of her contemporaries chose to establish themselves as marginal, perhaps leaving the possibility open to a woman; and in Puritan culture, where marginality might lead a man to predict his own damnation, a woman—a flawed version of an already flawed creation—might have less to lose by embracing marginality.) (b) Many white male writers in the early nineteenth century wrote as if they were marginal. Choose representative texts (by Irving, Hawthorne, Thoreau, Whitman, or Melville) and consider what the marginal characters in these fictions have to say about the relationship between white male authors and marginality. (c) Examine Clemens's Huck Finn or James's John Marcher *(The Beast in the Jungle)* as representative of lonely, isolated, and marginalized characters. (d) Twentieth-century white male authors frequently explore the theme of social difference. Some created their most powerful fictions based on this theme. Examine the theme in Anderson, Jeffers, O'Neill, Faulkner, Bellow, or Williams and speculate on the white male writer's fascination with marginality.

APPENDIX: *THE DECLARATION OF SENTIMENTS*

Seneca Falls Woman's Rights Convention, July 19–20, 1848

In July 1848, Elizabeth Cady Stanton and Lucretia Mott gathered together a group of women to plan the first women's rights convention to be held in Seneca Falls, New York. They modeled their agenda on antislavery and temperance conventions, and Stanton modeled her draft of *The Declaration of Sentiments* on the 1776 *The Declaration of Independence.* After discussion and amendments, the document received a hundred signatures from both women and men. Following the convention, the proceedings were ridiculed by clergy and in the press, and many of the women who had signed the declaration subsequently removed their names and their influence. In her autobiography, *Eighty Years and More* (1898), Stanton wrote, "If I had had the slightest premonition of all that was to follow that convention, I fear I should not have had the courage to risk it." *The Declaration of Sentiments* initiated Stanton's writing career on behalf of women's lives and women's rights, a career that would extend until her death in 1902.

—M. P.

Declaration of Sentiments

When, in the course of human events, it becomes necessary for one portion of the family of man to assume among the people of the earth a position different from that which they have hitherto occupied, but one to which the laws of nature and of nature's God entitle them, a decent respect to the opinions of mankind requires that they should declare the causes that impel them to such a course.

We hold these truths to be self-evident: that all men and women are created equal; that they are endowed by their Creator with certain inalienable rights; that among these are life, liberty, and the pursuit of happiness; that to secure these rights governments are instituted, deriving their just powers from the consent of the governed. Whenever any form of government becomes destructive of these ends, it is the right of those who suffer from it to refuse allegiance to it, and to insist upon the institution of a new government, laying its foundation on such principles, and organizing its powers in such form, as to them shall seem most likely to effect their safety and happiness. Prudence, indeed, will dictate that governments long established should not be changed for light and transient causes; and accordingly all experience hath shown that mankind are more disposed to suffer, while evils are sufferable, than to right themselves by abolishing the forms to which they were accustomed. But when a long train of abuses and usurpations, pursuing invariably the same object, evinces a design to reduce them under absolute despotism, it is their duty to throw off such government, and to provide new guards for their future security. Such has been the patient sufferance of the women under this government, and such is now the necessity which constrains them to demand the equal station to which they are entitled.

The history of mankind is a history of repeated injuries and usurpations on the part of man toward woman, having in direct object the establishment of an absolute tyranny over her. To prove this, let facts be submitted to a candid world.

He has never permitted her to exercise her inalienable right to the elective franchise.

He has compelled her to submit to laws, in the formation of which she had no voice.

He has withheld from her rights which are given to the most ignorant and degraded men—both natives and foreigners.

Having deprived her of this first right of a citizen, the elective franchise, thereby leaving her without representation in the halls of legislation, he has oppressed her on all sides.

He has made her, if married, in the eye of the law, civilly dead.

He has taken from her all right in property, even to the wages she earns.

He has made her, morally, an irresponsible being, as she can commit many crimes with impunity, provided they be done in the presence of her husband. In the covenant of marriage, she is compelled to promise obedience to her husband, he becoming, to all intents and purposes, her master—the law giving him power to deprive her of her liberty, and to administer chastisement.

He has so framed the laws of divorce, as to what shall be the proper causes, and in case of separation, to whom the guardianship of the children shall be given, as to be wholly regardless of the happiness of women—the law, in all cases, going upon the false supposition of the supremacy of man, and giving all power into his hands.

After depriving her of all rights as a married woman, if single, and the owner of property, he has taxed her to support a government which recognizes her only when her property can be made profitable to it.

He has monopolized nearly all the profitable employments and from those she is permitted to follow, she receives but a scanty remuneration. He closes against her all the avenues to wealth and distinction which he considers most honorable to himself. As a teacher of theology, medicine, or law, she is not known.

He has denied her the facilities for obtaining a thorough education, all colleges being closed against her.

He allows her in Church, as well as State, but a subordinate position, claiming Apostolic authority for her exclusion from the ministry, and, with some exceptions, from any public participation in the affairs of the Church.

He has created a false public sentiment by giving to the world a different code of morals for men and women, by which moral delinquencies which exclude women from society, are not only tolerated, but deemed of little account in man.

He has usurped the prerogative of Jehovah himself, claiming it as his right to assign for her a sphere of action, when that belongs to her conscience and to her God.

He has endeavored, in every way that he could, to destroy her confidence in her own powers, to lessen her self-respect, and to make her willing to lead a dependent and abject life.

Now, in view of this entire disfranchisement of one-half the people of this country, their social and religious degradation—in view of the unjust laws above mentioned, and because women do feel themselves aggrieved, oppressed, and fraudulently deprived of their most sacred rights, we insist that they have immediate admission to all the rights and privileges which belong to them as citizens of the United States.

In entering upon the great work before us, we anticipate no small amount of misconception, misrepresentation, and ridicule; but we shall use every instrumentality within our power to effect our object. We shall employ agents, circulate tracts, petition the State and National legislatures, and endeavor to enlist the pulpit and the press in our behalf. We hope this Convention will be followed by a series of Conventions embracing every part of the country.

Resolutions: Whereas, The great precept of nature is conceded to be, that "man shall pursue his own true and substantial happiness." Blackstone in his Commentaries remarks, that this law of Nature being coeval with mankind, and dictated by God himself, is of course superior in obligation to any other. It is binding over all the globe, in all countries and at all times; no human laws are of any validity if contrary to this, and such of them as are valid, derive all their force, and all their validity, and all their authority, mediately and immediately, from this original; therefore,

Resolved, That such laws as conflict, in any way, with the true and substantial happiness of woman, are contrary to the great precept of nature and of no validity, for this is "superior in obligation to any other."

Resolved, That all laws which prevent woman from occupying such a state in society as her conscience shall dictate, or which place her in a position inferior to that of man, are contrary to the great precept of nature, and therefore of no force or authority.

Resolved, That woman is man's equal—was intended to be so by the Creator, and the highest good of the race demands that she should be recognized as such.

Resolved, That the women of this country ought to be enlightened in regard to the laws under which they live, that they may no longer publish their degradation by declaring themselves satisfied with their present position, nor their ignorance, by asserting that they have all the rights they want.

Resolved, That inasmuch as man, while claiming for himself intellectual superiority, does accord to woman moral superiority, it is pre-eminently his duty to encourage her to speak and teach, as she has an opportunity, in all religious assemblies.

Resolved, That the same amount of virtue, delicacy, and refinement of behavior that is required of woman in the social state, should also be required of man, and the same transgressions should be visited with equal severity on both man and woman.

Resolved, That the objection of indelicacy and impropriety, which is so often brought against woman when she addresses a public audience, comes with a very ill-grace from those who encourage, by their attendance, her appearance on the stage, in the concert, or in feats of the circus.

Resolved, That woman has too long rested satisfied in the circumscribed limits which corrupt customs and a perverted application of the Scriptures have marked out for her, and that it is time she should move in the enlarged sphere which her great Creator has assigned her.

Resolved, That it is the duty of the women of this country to secure to themselves their sacred right to the elective franchise.

Resolved, That the equality of human rights results necessarily from the fact of the identity of the race in capabilities and responsibilities.

Resolved, therefore, That, being invested by the Creator with the same capabilities, and the same consciousness of responsibility for their exercise, it is demonstrably the right and duty of woman, equally with man, to promote every righteous cause by every righteous means; and especially in regard to the great subjects of morals and religion, it is self-evidently her right to participate with her brother in teaching them, both in private and in public, by writing and by speaking, by any instrumentalities proper to be used, and in any assemblies proper to be held; and this being a self-evident truth growing out of the divinely implanted principles of human nature, any custom or authority adverse to it, whether modern or wearing the hoary sanction of antiquity, is to be regarded as a self-evident falsehood, and at war with mankind.

Resolved, That the speedy success of our cause depends upon the zealous and untiring efforts of both men and women, for the overthrow of the monopoly of the pulpit, and for the securing to woman an equal participation with men in the various trades, professions, and commerce.

Index

Page numbers in **bold face** indicate main discussions of works and authors.